VARIEGATED
Trees & Shrubs

VARIEGATED Trees & Shrubs

THE ILLUSTRATED ENCYCLOPEDIA

Ronald Houtman

TIMBER PRESS
Portland • Cambridge

In association with the Royal Boskoop Horticultural Society

Frontispiece: *Quercus cerris* 'Argenteovariegata' RONALD HOUTMAN
Page 21: *Elaeagnus ×ebbingei* 'Limelight' RONALD HOUTMAN
Page 301: *Acer palmatum* 'Orido-no-nishiki' RONALD HOUTMAN

Published in 2004 by

Timber Press, Inc.
The Haseltine Building
133 S.W. Second Avenue, Suite 450
Portland, Oregon 97204-3527, U.S.A.

Timber Press
2 Station Road
Swavesey
Cambridge CB4 5QJ, U.K.

www.timberpress.com

Designed by Susan Applegate
Printed through Colorcraft Ltd., Hong Kong

Library of Congress Cataloging-in-Publication Data

Houtman, Ronald.
Variegated trees and shrubs: the illustrated encyclopedia / Ronald Houtman for the Royal Boskoop Horticultural Society.
p. cm.
Includes bibliographical references (p.).
ISBN 0-88192-649-3 (hardback)
1. Ornamental trees—Encyclopedias. 2. Ornamental shrubs—Encyclopedias. 3. Variegated plants—Encyclopedias. 4. Ornamental trees—Pictorial works. 5. Ornamental shrubs—Pictorial works. 6. Variegated plants—Pictorial works. I. Royal Boskoop Horticultural Society. II. Title.
SB435.H825 2004
635.9′75′03—dc22 2003026330

A catalog record for this book is also available from the British Library.

CONTENTS

FOREWORD

Barry Yinger

Nurseryman and Plant Hunter
York Haven, Pennsylvania

IN JAPAN IT IS SAID that a man has succumbed beyond all reasoning to the lust for collecting plants when he starts to collect ferns or variegated plants. He will then have made a full transition from a love of the conventional and superficial beauty of flowers to the appreciation of subtle differences in form, color, and texture of foliage. This shift in perception is akin to what an art lover experiences when he makes the shift to nonrepresentational art from a life adorned by paintings of waterfalls, windmills, and golden retrievers.

We are fortunate to live in an age in which one can be unequivocally devoted to plants with colored or variegated foliage and not be lonely. Such times are rare in what we know of history. The Japanese have had the longest run of it, with a more or less unbroken history of interest in colored and variegated foliage going back at least 300 years. Interest in the West extends back at least 150 years in England, continuing to the present throughout Europe, and more recently, most of the rest of the gardening world. Although many kinds of plants were collected obsessively throughout the history of the Chinese and Ottoman empires, there is little evidence of any interest in variegated plants there. Despite the lack of any historical record, it is likely that various cultures in Southeast Asia have appreciated plants with colored foliage for a very long time. The enduring popularity of plants such as *Pisonia grandis* (moonlight tree), *Erythrina variegata*, *Codiaeum*, and *Cordyline terminalis* in their many splendid forms suggests a long history of appreciation of the nongreen.

It was not too long ago that most plant lovers in much of the West turned up their noses at variegated plants. When I started my career in horticulture thirty years ago, there was little market for variegated plants in the United States. There was a widespread view that such plants must be infected by virus or otherwise diseased. Such opinions are seldom heard these days, but I doubt if many gardeners really appreciate just how important colored-leaved plants are to the world of horticulture. The large wholesale nursery that employs me grows about 9000 kinds of plants, and more than half of these do not have green foliage. I doubt if any gardener would guess that such a large proportion of popular ornamental plants are not green. This nursery alone sells nearly 400 million dollars worth of plants per year—the commercial value of plants with colorful foliage is enormous.

Considering the long history of interest in variegated plants and their very considerable commercial value, it is remarkable how few books have been solely devoted to such plants. Throughout the entire history of variegated plant cultivation there have been only a few encyclopedic efforts, nearly all in Japan. Two works from the late 1800s, *So Moku Kin Yo Shu* and *So Moku Ki Hin Kagami*, are among the most magnificent horticultural publications of all time. At about the same time Lowe's much less comprehensive, but very splendid, *Beautiful Leaved Plants* was published in England in several editions. After that we must wait until the end of the twentieth century for the works of Hirose and Yokoi to see comprehensive illustrated works in Japan. These, along with the reprints of *So Moku Kin Yo Shu* and *So Moku Ki Hin Kagami*, have all appeared within the past thirty years.

Mr. Houtman's book is thus quite an event for those of us who collect and appreciate plants with variegated and colored foliage. His efforts to identify the origins of the plants, his interest in correct nomenclature, and his careful descriptions make his work an essential historical record. His book is unique in its appreciation for the ornamental value of variegated plants in the garden. When writers in another century review the short list of essential historical works about plants with colored foliage, Mr. Houtman's name will be joined with Lowe, Hirose, Yokoi, and the other pioneers who have chronicled an ever more important horticultural movement.

PREFACE

Willem A. Sanders

Chairman
Royal Boskoop Horticultural Society

The Royal Boskoop Horticultural Society, founded in 1861, has a long publishing tradition. This tradition began in 1868 with *de Nederlandsche Boomgaard* (*The Dutch Orchard*) and it has brought us to this new book on variegated woody plants. Sometimes the initiative to publish a work is taken by members who are also the authors, as was the case with *Conifers: The Illustrated Encyclopedia* (1996) by D. M. van Gelderen and J. R. P. van Hoey Smith. This volume of variegated woody plants has been realized in a different way: Wim van Nierop, one of our members and a well-known collector of variegated plants, felt there was no good book on this subject. Therefore, the board asked Ronald Houtman, Secretary of Royal Boskoop Horticultural Society Trials Committee, to write this book. Many society members were of assistance. The question of why and when a plant is variegated was answered by Ben Zonneveld. Klaas Verboom, Wout Kromhout, and Dirk van Gelderen were helpful in selecting the photographs. The English text was edited by Jan Hooftman, Winnie Zunderdorp, and Wim Snoeijer. The motor behind this project was Wim van der Poel, chairman of our Publications Committee. As chairman of the Royal Boskoop Horticultural Society, I am very pleased and proud that we are able to work with Timber Press to publish this book.

I hope that the audience feels the same pleasure in reading this book as our members did in making it.

ACKNOWLEDGMENTS

I AM VERY GRATEFUL FOR THE HELP of the following people, who shared their vast knowledge of plants. Publications Committee of the Royal Boskoop Horticultural Society: Wim van der Poel (Chairman), Boskoop; Dirk van Gelderen, Boskoop; Dick Ploeger, De Bilt; Wout Kromhout, Ede; Klaas Verboom, Boskoop. Of further help were Jo and Maarten Bömer, Zundert; Mark Bulk, Boskoop; Allen Coombes, The Sir Harold Hillier Arboretum, Ampfield, United Kingdom; Gert Fortgens, Waddinxveen; Jim Gardiner, Wisley, Surrey, United Kingdom; Jan Hooftman, Boskoop; Wiel Linssen, Baexem; Wim van Nierop, Boskoop; André van Nijnatten, Zundert; Wim Snoeijer, Gouda; Aad Vergeer, Boskoop; Piet Vergeldt, Lottum; Winnie Zunderdorp, Boskoop; and other members of the Royal Boskoop Horticultural Society too numerous to mention here. I am especially grateful to Barry R. Yinger of Lewisberry, Pennsylvania, an expert on Japanese plants, who read the manuscript and advised me on cultivar names.

More than 4000 slides were viewed to make a final selection for this book. I took many photographs specifically for this book, but a lot of slides were available from other sources as well. The following people have supplied slides for this book: Maarten van Atten, Boskoop; Jo Bömer, Zundert; Gert Fortgens, Waddinxveen; Cor van Gelderen, Boskoop; Dan Heims, Tigard, Oregon; J. R. P. van Hoey Smith, Rotterdam; Marco Hoffman, Odijk; Henny Kolster, Boskoop; Wout Kromhout, Ede; Arjan Laros, Boskoop; George Otter, IJsselstein; Plant Publicity Holland (collection Harry van de Laar), Boskoop; Chris Sanders, Eccleshall, United Kingdom; Wim Snoeijer, Gouda; Gerard Stolwijk, Boskoop; Pierre Theunissen, Beesel; and Klaas Verboom, Boskoop. Photographers' names are included in the photo captions.

INTRODUCTION

THE IDEA TO COMPILE THIS WORK came from Wim van Nierop, an enthusiastic collector of variegated plants and the former chairman of the Publications Committee of the Royal Boskoop Horticultural Society (RBHS). Late in 1996, a few months after *Conifers: The Illustrated Encyclopedia* was published, he proposed writing a book on variegated plants. As the secretary of the RBHS and of the Trials Committee, I was asked to write the manuscript. I agreed with excitement, not aware of any difficulties or problems ahead.

At first we decided that both woody and herbaceous plants were to be included, resulting in a list of several thousand variegated plants, about two-thirds of them herbaceous. Because I am not a specialist on herbaceous plants, however, and to avoid the risk of copying large parts of text from other works, the RBHS decided to deal with the woody plants only. This left us a list of about 800 variegated trees, shrubs, and conifers. We soon discovered, however, that it is impossible to write a book that covers *all* variegated woody plants. Thus, the aim of this book was to give a clear picture of variegated plants and to include the vast majority of known variegated plants.

Another question that arose within the Publications Committee was defining a variegated plant. In this book, we focus on woody plants with more than one leaf color. Plants can also have variegated bark, variegated flowers, variegated shoots, even variegated roots, but we will have to leave these plants for other books. Readers interested in a technical understanding of the types and causes of variegation are encouraged to consult Dr. Ben Zonneveld's essay in Appendix A. For the purposes of the general reader, however, we offer this brief summary of Dr. Zonneveld's thorough discussion.

Some plants are naturally variegated, and this variegation is passed on to offspring via genetic material in the seeds. It is assumed that this variegation confers some advantage in the plant's wild habitat and is the product of natural selection. An example of a plant with natural variegation is *Actinidia kolomikta*. You can assume that any plant in this book without a cultivar name after its botanical name is a natural variegate.

Plants may also exhibit environmental variegation when they are sick or struggling. The soil's lack of a necessary element, such as iron, can lead to yellowed

Acer pseudoplatanus 'Brilliantissimum', not regarded as variegated in this work RONALD HOUTMAN

Pieris 'Forest Flame', not regarded as variegated in this work RONALD HOUTMAN

leaves. Insect damage, lack of water or sunlight, or high temperatures may all result in yellowing. Such variegation disappears when conditions improve. A particularly dangerous type of environmental variegation is caused by viral agents, usually spread by insects such as aphids. In this case, the plant cannot be saved and must be destroyed. Paradoxically, some viruses can cause quite attractive patterns in flowers and leaves, which tempt the gardener to share the diseased plant.

The seasons also affect variegation in plants. Many plants exhibit red or yellow shoots in spring that later turn green as they mature. Other plants respond to intense heat and sunlight by producing red or other pigments. We have tended to avoid these plants in this work. However, nursery people and breeders sometimes select plants that seem genetically "stuck" in a given stage of seasonal variegation so that unusual coloring may be enjoyed for longer periods.

By far, the majority of plants found in this book are chimeras; that is, they contain genetically different cell layers. These differences are caused by mutation, usually in just a part of otherwise normal plants. Such mutated portions of plants are known as sports or bud variants. These sports are generally first taken from the mother plant as cuttings and propagated asexually. All plants with the same cultivar name are genetically identical. However, chimeral variegation can be somewhat unstable, and any variegated clone can revert unexpectedly to normal leaf color. The gardener must always be on the lookout for any instance of "reverse mutation." Chimeral variegation can be around leaf edges or along veins. Spots may be white, gold, or other colors. Each of these kinds of variations may be given their own names and categories.

Variegation in conifers is a tricky subject. When describing conifers, I sometimes had to deviate from our strict definition. In plants such as *Pinus* a distinct variegation can be seen. But in conifers with scaly foliage, such as *Chamaecyparis* and *Thuja*, we also call a plant variegated when branchlets or small tufts of scales have more than one color. Conifers with entirely yellow or white foliage are excluded from this book.

I have tried to trace the origin of every plant described. This was very difficult in some cases and impossible for many plants. In Japan, people planted ornamentals in their gardens centuries before they did in the rest of the world. Together with the natural botan-

Chamaecyparis lawsoniana 'Hillieri', not regarded as variegated in this work RONALD HOUTMAN

ical richness of the Japanese archipelago this resulted in thousands of cultivars, many of which are—and were—variegated. In Europe, awareness of ornamental plants began about 1750. The oldest European variegated plants derived from wild specimens, such as *Ilex aquifolium* and *Quercus robur*, date back to the seventeenth and eighteenth centuries. Some of these, such as *Ilex aquifolium* 'Ferox Argentea' (1662), are still widely grown. During the nineteenth and twentieth centuries the popularity of ornamental plants grew to an unprecedented level. Today most new cultivars are introduced from the United States and Europe, but over the last fifty years there has been an increase of new plants from Australia and New Zealand.

Cold resistance is an important issue for gardeners. A good tool for measuring cold resistance is the hardiness zone system of the U.S. Department of Agriculture, a worldwide standard (see hardiness zone temperature ranges in Appendix D). When possible, I provide hardiness zone information at the end of each entry in the encyclopedia. Plants strongly respond to the climatological circumstances in the area they are grown. For instance, when a particular plant is grown in a continental climate, such as the Midwest of the United States, it is usually one zone hardier than the same plant grown in a coastal climate, such as northwestern Europe. The reason for this is that a plant growing in a continental climate usually hardens off better in autumn, the cells contain less water when the first frosts arrive, and the soil is usually dryer. In northwestern Europe, however, the autumns are usually quite wet and rainy, resulting in larger, fully saturated cells that will be damaged sooner than less-saturated cells. The U.S. Department of Agriculture hardiness zones were devised for general U.S. climatological circumstances. In Europe most plants will be graded one or half a zone higher.

USING VARIEGATED PLANTS IN A GARDEN

W. M. van Nierop

Collector and Nurseryman
Boskoop, The Netherlands

When designing a garden the first question should be, "What do we expect from our garden?" After drawing the plan and laying the hardscaping, the following stage is the planting of trees, shrubs, and perennials.

Too often the use of variegated plants is overlooked. As a devotee and collector of variegated plants, I think this is a pity. Golden and silver variegated plants offer so much to enjoy, for the devoted amateur in particular. There are many beautiful variegated trees, some not too vigorous in growth. Many colorful shrubs, conifers, and dwarf subjects give a wealth of color, which can cheer up a garden when added to the various green tints.

Until now the use of variegated plants in private and public gardens has often been restricted to *Aucuba*, *Elaeagnus*, and *Cornus*. This book illustrates the vast possibilities of diversifying a garden design by using variegated plants. They can be used easily to create distinct color schemes in shrub borders or flower beds. The bright leaves of variegated plants contrast well with darker green foliage and deeper colored flowers.

In the moderate regions of the Northern Hemisphere there is a rather long season when gardens have few or no flowers, roughly from October until May. People long for something cheerful and colorful in their garden during that period. For example, *Chamaecyparis nootkatensis* 'Aureovariegata' and 'Variegata', golden and silver variegated Nootka cypress, are both very winter hardy. Numerous shrubs also retain their color well in winter; *Elaeagnus pungens* 'Goldrim' is a personal favorite. However, another member of this genus, *Elaeagnus* ×*ebbingei* 'Gilt Edge', only shows its radiant colors from summer until late autumn.

Variegated plants are often chimeras, that is, they contain genetically different cell layers (see Appendix A). Therefore, the plants are somewhat weaker than green plants of the same genera. In particular, in severe winters chimeras can suffer more than their green counterparts. Moreover, there are also variegated plants that will barely survive in the Northern Hemisphere due to harsh climatic conditions. It is often sufficient to give these a protective layer of straw or reed, although sometimes it is advisable to place these tender plants indoors. In many cases it is useful to propagate some of the weaker plants well before winter sets

A garden in the English national collection of variegated plants in Enstone, United Kingdom RONALD HOUTMAN

Part of the garden of Wim van Nierop in Boskoop, The Netherlands RONALD HOUTMAN

Cornus alternifolia 'Argentea' at Beth Chatto Gardens in Elmstead Market, United Kingdom RONALD HOUTMAN

A beautiful combination of *Cornus alba* 'Elegantissima', *Berberis thunbergii* 'Atropurpurea', and *Clematis* 'Rouge Cardinal' RONALD HOUTMAN

in, so that they will be available as young plants the following spring after having overwintered under protection in frames or greenhouses.

Certain variegated plants may scorch when exposed to direct sunlight and these should be planted in a semi-shaded location. This can be done by planting them partly underneath evergreen shrubs or giving temporary shading by means of lattices or rushmats. Such a method can be useful in climates in which hot sunny days occur only now and then.

Long lists of variegated plants that are suitable for private gardens, public parks, and urban green areas can be made easily, but there is always a danger that such lists become compulsory. It is better to be attracted by the beauty of a plant noticed in a garden here or there, which will prompt you to start further investigations into the origin, name, and source of supply of that particular plant. Enquiries made with plant centers or specialist retail nurseries may result in a gem for your garden that will be admired by friends and neighbors.

I wish the readers of this comprehensive work much pleasure, and I hope and expect that they will enjoy reading it as much as I have enjoyed collecting and working with variegated plants for the past forty years.

ENCYCLOPEDIA OF VARIEGATED WOODY PLANTS

Abelia ×*grandiflora* 'Conti' CONFETTI™

James Gwaltney, Flowerwood Nurseries, Mobile, Alabama, United States, 1987

Originating as a sport of *A.* ×*grandiflora* 'Sherwood', this is a compact, bushy shrub with a broad spreading habit that will eventually grow 1.2 m wide and 80 cm high. The foliage is dark green with creamy white margins. During autumn and winter, the leaves show a purplish red pigment, especially when kept relatively dry. The broadly funnel-shaped flowers are pale pink to almost pure white. They appear during late summer and early autumn in leafy terminal racemes. Like other *A.* ×*grandiflora* cultivars, 'Conti' can be regarded as a deciduous shrub in most parts of western Europe and the United States. In milder areas 'Conti', as well as similar cultivars, can be treated as a semi-evergreen. Zone 6

Abelia ×*grandiflora* 'Conti' CONFETTI™ FA. C. ESVELD

Abelia ×*grandiflora* 'Francis Mason'

Mason's Nurseries, New Zealand, about 1950

Fine compact shrub that eventually will reach a height and spread of 1.3 m. Gracefully arching branches carry rich yellow variegated leaves, whereas young shoots are an attractive reddish brown with a distinct bronze-coppery hue. Light pink blossoms appear from late summer into autumn. Flowers are broadly funnel-shaped and about 1.2 cm long. This is one of the older variegated cultivars of *Abelia*. Zone 6

Abelia ×*grandiflora* 'Francis Mason' RONALD HOUTMAN

Abelia ×*grandiflora* 'Gold Spot'

Garden origin, United Kingdom, after 1950

There is quite some confusion about this cultivar. The name is sometimes spelled 'Gold Sport' or 'Goldsport'. Plants known under these names are derived as golden-leaved or variegated sports from *A.* ×*grandiflora* and cultivars and have golden variegated foliage or entirely golden yellow foliage. Like other *Abelia* cultivars, they are quite useful when grown in containers, and perennial borders and will not grow higher than about 1.5 m. 'Gold Strike', 'Aurea', and 'Golden Glow' are also very similar to 'Gold Spot', if not the same. Zone 6

Abelia ×*grandiflora* 'Hopleys'

Hopleys Plants Ltd., Much Hadham, United Kingdom, 1992

This interesting new cultivar originated as a sport of 'Francis Mason'. The foliage is rich dark green with irregular golden yellow margins. The yellow is most intense during spring and early summer. The flowers

Abelia ×*grandiflora* 'Hopleys' RONALD HOUTMAN

Abelia ×grandiflora 'Sunrise' RONALD HOUTMAN

Acer buergerianum 'Goshiki' FA. C. ESVELD

Acer buergerianum 'Hanachiru Sato' RONALD HOUTMAN

have the same shape as other *A. ×grandiflora* cultivars, but are darker pink, especially in autumn. This gives a magnificent effect together with the foliage. Zone 6

Abelia ×grandiflora 'Sunrise'

North Carolina State Arboretum, Raleigh, North Carolina, United States, 1998

Glossy deep green leaves edged with bright gold, turning silvery cream and green on older leaves. The young foliage is attractively reddish in spring. In autumn the leaves are bright orange and red. The flowers are pale pink to almost white flushed with pink. Like 'Hopleys' this plant also originated as a sport of 'Francis Mason'. Although raised at Taylor's Nursery, Raleigh, North Carolina, it was introduced by the NCSA. Zone 6

Acer

This is a very important genus, varying from small shrubs to large trees. Maples are widely spread throughout temperate regions of the Northern Hemisphere: North America, Europe, and Asia. *Acer palmatum*, the Japanese maple, is an important species from which many cultivars are derived. These handsome medium-sized shrubs to small trees have attractive foliage, both in color and in shape. Another good feature of most *A. palmatum* cultivars is the fantastic autumn colors. The majority of the variegated maples have been developed from *A. palmatum* or its cultivars. Many are old Japanese cultivars, but in recent years various good cultivars have been developed elsewhere in the world. Due to their rather difficult propagation and culture, the Japanese maples are more highly valued ornamentals and are always attractive in the garden. Other species with a number of variegated cultivars are *A. platanoides* and *A. pseudoplatanus*.

Acer buergerianum 'Goshiki'

Japan

This old, traditional, Japanese cultivar is usually referred to as 'Goshiki Kaede'. The word *kaede* is the Japanese colloquial name for maple, so it cannot be used in a legitimate cultivar name. *Acer buergerianum* 'Goshiki' is a colorful large shrub to medium-sized tree of Japanese origin. This plant usually grows to 2.5 m high, but it may exceed 3 or 4 m. The leaves are very irregularly variegated and vary from almost entirely green to green with white or pink parts. Some leaves or leaf parts turn cream or almost yellow when maturing. Because this cultivar tends to revert to green, these branches must be removed at an early stage. Although very beautiful, 'Goshiki' is not hardy enough for some parts of the United States and continental Europe. Zone 5

Acer buergerianum 'Hanachiru Sato'

Japan

This interesting cultivar was recently introduced from Japan. It has an upright, broad vase-shaped habit. The young foliage emerges pinkish red, and mature leaves are heavily speckled creamy white. Unfortunately the foliage tends to burn during warm and sunny spells. When planted in a semi-shaded location, however, this should not be a problem. It seems slightly hardier than similar varieties such as 'Wako Nishiki', which is also less vigorous. Zone 6b

Acer campestre 'Carnival' FA. C. ESVELD

Acer campestre 'Carnival'

André van Nijnatten, Zundert, The Netherlands, 1989

Slow-growing and densely branched shrub that grows to 3 m high. It was raised as a seedling and will therefore not often revert to green. The leaves are three-lobed with creamy white edges. Because of its slow-growing habit, 'Carnival' is very suitable for the small garden, both as a shrub or grafted on a stem. 'Carnival' is prone to some sunburn and is best planted in semi-shade. When used in hot climates, it has proven rather weak. Zone 4

Acer campestre 'Carnival' RONALD HOUTMAN

Acer campestre 'Magic Spring'

André van Nijnatten, Zundert, The Netherlands, 1997

Shrub or small tree that originated as a sport in *A. campestre* 'Royal Ruby'. The leaves are identical to 'Royal Ruby' in shape, but the color is quite unique. In spring the exfoliating leaves are dark yellow with orange margins. During summer these colors change to dark green with irregular creamy white blotches, whereas the young shoots are deep orange-red to red. 'Magic Spring' is very susceptible to sunburn during spring and needs to be protected from direct sunlight. Zone 5a

Acer campestre 'Magic Spring' GERT FORTGENS

Acer campestre 'Pulverulentum'

Muskau Arboretum, Muskau, Poland, 1859

Compact and densely branched shrub that grows to 2.5 to 3 m high, only rarely exceeding 4 m. 'Pulveru-

Acer campestre 'Pulverulentum' FA. C. ESVELD

Acer campestre 'Silver Celebration' RONALD HOUTMAN

lentum' usually grows much wider than high. The leaves are heavily speckled with creamy white to white. Some leaves are half green and half speckled. It tends to revert to green, and these branches must be removed at an early stage. This nice shrub is excellent in semi-shade or lightly shaded places. In full sun, it tends to burn slightly. Zone 5a

Acer campestre 'Silver Celebration'

Junker's Nursery, West Hatch, Taunton, United Kingdom, 2001

This interesting new cultivar was found as a sport in *Acer campestre* 'Carnival'. The foliage is less variegated but still colorful enough to attract attention immediately. The leaves are shaped like the species and are grayish green with irregular narrow silvery white margins. Due to the fact that 'Silver Celebration' has more chlorophyll in the leaves, it grows distinctly stronger than 'Carnival' but is slightly less vigorous than the common green-leaved cultivars such as 'Elsrijk'. The foliage is stable and does not scorch in full sun. 'Silver Celebration' is a beautiful and refined cultivar with a great future. Zone 5

Acer crataegifolium 'Veitchii'

United Kingdom, 1881

Small to medium-sized shrub to small tree that grows to 4 m high, although often not higher than 2.5 m. The foliage is attractive pink to white variegated. The leaves, 5 to 7 cm long, are mostly unlobed and conspicuously variegated pink and creamy white. This old cultivar strongly tends to revert to green, so regular removal of these branches is necessary. Because of propagation difficulties 'Veitchii' is a rare shrub, but some-

Acer campestre 'Silver Celebration' RONALD HOUTMAN

Acer crataegifolium 'Veitchii' J. R. P. VAN HOEY SMITH

times available in the trade. Suitable for the smaller garden. Zone 5b

Acer negundo 'Aureomarginatum'

Dieck Baumschulen, Germany, 1885

Old and well-known cultivar forming a large shrub or small tree that grows to 10 m high. The foliage has creamy yellow margins, whereas the centers of the leaves are dark green. Because the flowers are sterile, no seeds develop. 'Aureomarginatum' is an attractive cultivar that is very suitable for large gardens or parks. Zone 4

Acer negundo 'Aureomarginatum' RONALD HOUTMAN

Acer negundo 'Elegans'

Fritz Graf von Schwerin, Zoeschen, Germany, before 1901

An attractive golden-variegated cultivar of *Acer negundo*, forming a small tree or large shrub of about 8 m high. In contrast to 'Aureomarginatum', this cultivar has slightly smaller leaves and the leaflets are more yellow. The leaflets are conspicuously convex. This is a good cultivar that has been neglected for too long. Zone 4

Acer negundo 'Elegans' RONALD HOUTMAN

Acer negundo 'Flamingo'

J. Bastiaanse, Oudenbosch, The Netherlands, 1977

Tall shrub to small tree of about 5 m high that immediately catches attention in spring, when the young

Acer negundo 'Flamingo' FA. C. ESVELD

Acer negundo 'Flamingo' FA. C. ESVELD

foliage is pink to pink edged. Later in summer the pink colors fade to creamy white or white leaf edges. 'Flamingo' differs from the well-known 'Variegatum' in its pink young foliage. The spectacular color is best seen when the shrub is pruned on a regular basis. With such pruning, it is possible to grow 'Flamingo' even in a small garden. This cultivar is available as shrub or grafted on a stem. 'Flamingo' was given an Award of Merit by the Royal Boskoop Horticultural Society in 1977. Zone 4

Acer negundo 'Variegatum' FA. C. ESVELD

Acer negundo 'Variegatum'

F. A. Wiegers, Germany, 1809

'Variegatum' is perhaps the best-known variegated cultivar of *Acer negundo*. It forms a very large shrub or small tree that grows to 12 m high, sometimes even taller. The leaves are dark green with conspicuous creamy white margins. Very good cultivar that is widely distributed and commonly used. Zone 4

Acer palmatum 'Aka Shigi Tatsu Sawa' FA. C. ESVELD

Acer palmatum 'Aka Shigi Tatsu Sawa'

Japan, before 1960

Large shrub to small tree, that grows to 5 m wide and high. The normally seven-lobed leaves are dark reddish green and delicately pink and white variegated. Autumn color is a spectacular orange-red. Sometimes confused with another Japanese cultivar 'Beni Shigi Tatsu Sawa' (both *aka* and *beni* mean "red"), this cultivar differs in its slightly darker leaves. Although not common in cultivation, this excellent shrub is well worth planting. Zone 5

Acer palmatum 'Ao Kanzashi' FA. C. ESVELD

Acer palmatum 'Ao Kanzashi'

Japan

Japanese introduction of recent date that is still an unusual shrub in Western gardens. 'Ao Kanzashi' has a broad, upright, somewhat vase-shaped habit and will grow to 8 m high. The foliage is light green with narrow greenish white margins. The leaves are five- to seven-lobed and the lobes are slightly convex. 'Ao Kanzashi' strongly resembles other Japanese cultivars such as 'Chirimen Nishiki' (very rare in cultivation) and 'Taiyo Nishiki', but the leaves of these cultivars are more pointed and starlike than those of 'Ao Kanzashi'. Zone 5

Acer palmatum 'Asahi Zuru'

Koichiro Wada, Yokohama, Japan, 1938

Beautiful and vigorous upright shrub that grows to 10 m high with a deceptively narrow habit when young. The leaves are variegated white and pink and shaped as the species. The young branches are purplish and striped pink. On young plants the variegation is sometimes absent but will return when plants grow older. 'Asahi Zuru' is a strong cultivar, sometimes seen and sold as 'Versicolor', that can develop into wonderful specimens, especially when planted in poor soil. Closely related to 'Orido-no-nishiki', this cultivar is more fragile. Zone 5

Acer palmatum 'Asahi Zuru' FA. C. ESVELD

Acer palmatum 'Beni Shichi Henge'

Angyo Maple Nursery, Japan, 1967

Rather slow-growing upright shrub, reaching 5 m after many years. Poor and open branched, the branches are thin and fragile. Very conspicuous grayish green foliage with white and orange to orange-brown margins. Quite similar to 'Butterfly' (see below), but this cultivar lacks the orange to orange-brown variegation. 'Beni Shichi Henge' makes a fine shrub but, due to the open habit and poor branching, it needs a few years to establish. Rather difficult to propagate and therefore not very common in the trade. Zone 5

Acer palmatum 'Beni Shichi Henge' FA. C. ESVELD

Acer palmatum 'Butterfly'

Koichiro Wada, Yokohama, Japan, 1938

'Butterfly' is the nearest ally of 'Beni Shichi Henge', but less colorful. It makes a rather upright bush of about 3 m high. 'Butterfly' is a densely branched shrub with thin branches and exquisite variegated foliage. The leaves are variable in shape and grayish green, margins creamy white to cream. Sometimes the leaves revert to green, and these branches must be removed at an early stage. 'Butterfly' is sometimes grown from cuttings, but this is not recommended because these plants are weaker and more fragile than plants propagated by grafting. The stiff upright growth makes 'Butterfly' excellent for the smaller garden.

It was given an Award of Merit by the Royal Boskoop Horticultural Society in 1977. Although 'Butterfly' sounds reasonably modern, Wada first named this plant in 1938. It is uncertain as to whether he renamed an old Japanese cultivar, 'Kocho Nishiki' (1882). Zone 5

Acer palmatum 'Butterfly' RONALD HOUTMAN

Acer palmatum 'Goshiki Shidare' RONALD HOUTMAN

Acer palmatum 'Higasayama' FA. C. ESVELD

Acer palmatum 'Kagiri Nishiki' FA. C. ESVELD

Acer palmatum 'Goshiki Shidare'

Japan

Extraordinary plant with mushroom-shaped habit and arching, nearly pendulous branches. It will attain a height up to 2 m and grows as wide. The foliage is dull green to purplish or grayish green with an irregular creamy white variegation. It is uncertain whether 'Beni Shidare Tricolor', a closely related variegated cultivar, is the same. Due to the thin branches and the fact that it is a rather weak plant, propagation is difficult and 'Goshiki Shidare' is rare in the trade. This should not discourage planting this cultivar, however, because once established in a sheltered location it can make an excellent specimen. Zone 5

Acer palmatum 'Higasayama'

Yokohama Nurseries Co., Yokohama, Japan, 1901

Large shrub to small tree with a narrow, upright, sometimes almost columnar habit that will easily grow to 7 or 8 m high. The usually seven-lobed leaves are very heavily variegated cream to pale yellow, leaving only a narrow green center on each lobe. The leaf tips are often slightly curled, which gives the leaves a crinkly appearance. The major problem with this spectacular cultivar is that it very easily reverts, leaving the owner with an unattractive, "common" *Acer palmatum*. Branches with green leaves must be removed at an early stage, otherwise the whole plant will revert in a short time. To maintain the variegated aspects in the offspring, one needs to have good variegated scions. Zone 5

Acer palmatum 'Kagiri Nishiki'

Japan, before 1710

'Kagiri Nishiki' is one of the better and more widely distributed variegated Japanese maples. It makes a large shrub to small tree that grows to 8 m high or more. The leaves are relatively small, with creamy white to pink margins. Although much older, it was first introduced in Europe in 1865 and given a First Class Certificate by the Royal Horticultural Society in the same year. Sometimes 'Kagiri Nishiki' is offered under its synonym 'Roseomarginatum'. The problem lies in the fact that 'Roseomarginatum' is a name that is used for several, only slightly aberrant, clones. The cultivar name 'Kagiri Nishiki' is strongly recommended for this cultivar. Zone 5

Acer palmatum 'Kara Ori Nishiki' FA. C. ESVELD

Acer palmatum 'Kara Ori Nishiki'

Japan, before 1733

Upright shrub that eventually will reach a height of 4 m. Very similar to *Acer palmatum* 'Butterfly'. In fact, these two cultivars are very difficult to distinguish. The leaves of 'Kara Ori Nishiki' are slightly more pinkish brown and appear pinker in spring. 'Kara Ori Nishiki' is a very good variegated Japanese maple that rarely reverts to green. Therefore, it makes an excellent specimen plant for gardens of any size. Zone 5

Acer palmatum 'Karasugawa' FA. C. ESVELD

Acer palmatum 'Karasugawa'

Angyo Maple Nursery, Japan, 1930

Beautiful but rather fragile, large and narrow, upright shrub to 4.5 m high. The young branches are conspicuously pinkish red, but tend do die back in winter. The leaves are dark green and heavily variegated white, pink, and pinkish red. 'Karasugawa' is an exceptionally beautiful cultivar, but quite weak. It is difficult to establish and not suitable to be grown in full sun. Two similar cultivars, both hardier but less variegated, are 'Asahi Zuru' and 'Orido-no-nishiki'. Zone 5

Acer palmatum 'Kasagiyama' FA. C. ESVELD

Acer palmatum 'Kasagiyama'

Japan

Broad, upright, quite open-branched large shrub that grows to 5 m high (sometimes more). The leaves are

Acer palmatum 'Kiyo Hime' GEORGE OTTER

Acer palmatum 'Matsugae' FA. C. ESVELD

Acer palmatum 'Nishiki Gasane' RONALD HOUTMAN

seven-lobed, brownish red, and attractively reticulate variegated green. It resembles cultivars such as 'Aka Shigi Tatsu Sawa', 'Ariadne', and 'Beni Shigi Tatsu Sawa'. 'Kasagiyama' is a conspicuous cultivar, but difficult to propagate and therefore rare in the trade. Zone 5

Acer palmatum 'Kiyo Hime'

Japan

Small shrub with a dense, globe-shaped habit. Eventually 'Kiyo Hime' will attain a height and spread of about 2 m. The small, five-lobed leaves are dark green with red margins and tips. It makes a good dwarf shrub and can also be used for bonsai. A problem can be that young shoots tend to die back without obvious reason. This rather rare shrub is well worth trying. Zone 5

Acer palmatum 'Matsugae'

Fritz Graf von Schwerin, Zoeschen, Germany, 1893

Another cultivar that is very similar to 'Butterfly', 'Kagiri Nishiki', and 'Kara Ori Nishiki'. It is a rather narrow, upright cultivar, rarely exceeding 4 m in height. The foliage is five-lobed, variegated creamy white to white with dark pink. Like 'Kagiri Nishiki', this cultivar is also offered under the synonym 'Roseomarginatum', an illegitimate cultivar name that should be rejected. Zone 5

Acer palmatum 'Nishiki Gasane'

Yokohama Nurseries Co., Yokohama, Japan, 1896 (listed 1882)

The best golden variegated Japanese maple, but very difficult to establish. The five- to seven-lobed leaves are splashed and striped golden yellow. It is an unstable variegation that mainly appears on slow-growing branches. Sometimes young branches do not show any variegation and must therefore be removed at an early stage. 'Nishiki Gasane' is also very susceptible to sunburn. When planted in a shady location the leaves show less variegation or no variegation at all. Because there are no better golden variegated forms, 'Nishiki Gasane', although rare, is still in cultivation. Zone 5

Acer palmatum 'Okukuji Nishiki'

Japan

Compact and densely branched shrub that can attain a height of 4 to 5 m and will grow as wide. It resembles 'Butterfly' and 'Kara Ori Nishiki' a lot and, although it has a slightly different color ('Okukuji Nishiki' has a more cream-colored aspect), these other two cultivars are recommended because 'Okukuji Nishiki' has no conspicuous autumn colors. Nevertheless, it is an interesting shrub for collectors and connoisseurs and is quite stable in its variegation. 'Okukuji Nishiki' is not widely grown, but slowly becoming more available. Zone 5

Acer palmatum 'Okukuji Nishiki' RONALD HOUTMAN

Acer palmatum 'Orido-no-nishiki'

Yokohama Nurseries Co., Yokohama, Japan, 1896 (listed 1882)

This is probably the best of all variegated Japanese maples. It is an upright shrub that can reach 5 or 6 m in height. Densely branched with rather thin branches that sometimes die back when young, a trait that is not uncommon and appears with several similar cultivars. The foliage is irregularly but strongly pink and white variegated. Sometimes twigs with entirely green leaves appear; these must be removed for they will eventually overgrow the variegated branches. Clones named 'Versicolor' are usually 'Orido-no-nishiki'; the true 'Versicolor' has disappeared. This is not a great pity because 'Orido-no-nishiki' surpasses 'Versicolor' in every aspect. Zone 5

Acer palmatum 'Pevé Multicolor'

Piet Vergeldt, Lottum, The Netherlands, 2001

Relatively densely branched upright shrub with a vase-shaped habit. The leaves are five- to seven-lobed and

Acer palmatum 'Pevé Multicolor' RONALD HOUTMAN

Acer palmatum 'Orido-no-nishiki' RONALD HOUTMAN

Acer palmatum 'Pink Ballerina' RONALD HOUTMAN

Acer palmatum 'Rugose Select' FA. C. ESVELD

Acer palmatum 'Shojo-no-mai' FA. C. ESVELD

bright pink when emerging in spring. Later in the spring they turn light green with numerous small white dots. During summer the leaves become deeper green, still showing the white variegation. The autumn foliage color is yellow, occasionally with a pinkish haze. 'Pevé Multicolor' was raised as a seedling of *A. palmatum*. It was first shown to the public at the show of the Royal Boskoop Horticultural Society during the Floriade 2002. Zone 5

Acer palmatum 'Pink Ballerina'

This new cultivar combines the gorgeous habit of a Dissectum Group Japanese maple with attractive incised and variegated foliage. 'Pink Ballerina' has the typical mushroom-shaped habit. The leaves are a deep reddish brown with clear pink parts. Its closest relative, 'Goshiki Shidare', has foliage that is variegated creamy white. The combination of dark reddish brown and pink in 'Pink Ballerina' is far more attractive than the color combination in 'Goshiki Shidare'. Due to the darker foliage colors, 'Pink Ballerina' is less prone to sunburn as well. Zone 5

Acer palmatum 'Rugose Select'

J. D. Vertrees, Roseburg, Oregon, United States, 1980

Broad, upright shrub reaching about 2.5 m in height. It has an open branched habit. The leaves are seven-lobed and brownish purple. Around the midribs of the irregularly shaped lobes there is a pinkish variegation. The leaf aspect is slightly rugose and has a somewhat dull appearance. These features make 'Rugose Select', together with 'Kasagiyama', quite interesting among variegated Japanese maples. Zone 5

Acer palmatum 'Shojo-no-mai'

Edward Rodd, Raraflora Nursery, Kinterfield, Pennsylvania, United States

This is a fairly upright cultivar that is heavily branched with thin branches, especially on second year's wood. In variegation it resembles 'Beni Shichi Henge', but the orange-brown color of the margins is even more intense, giving 'Shojo-no-mai' a warmer appearance. Nice cultivar that definitely deserves to be more widely grown. Zone 5

Acer palmatum 'Toyama Nishiki'

J. Dickson & Sons, United Kingdom, 1882

One of the few variegated Japanese maples from the Dissectum Group (together with 'Goshiki Shidare' and 'Pink Ballerina'). It is a low, mushroom-shaped shrub that rarely exceeds more than 1 m in height, but becoming much wider. The leaves are seven-lobed and deeply dissected. Their color is dark brownish purple with pink and some white speckles. Because of its darker variegation 'Toyama Nishiki' is preferable to 'Goshiki Shidare'. Both cultivars are not widely available and only grown by specialist nurseries. Zone 5

Acer palmatum 'Toyama Nishiki' FA. C. ESVELD

Acer palmatum 'Tsuma Gaki'

Japan

Medium-sized to large shrub that grows to 3 m high with a broad, spreading habit. This plant has exceptionally good foliage coloring in spring, summer, and autumn. The young leaves are yellowish green, whereas the five to seven lobes have attractive purplish red margins and tips. During summer the purple colors are less strong, but in autumn the foliage turns bright yellow with dark crimson and purple. Although this is an old Japanese cultivar, it is still rare, mainly due to the fact that propagation and cultivation are rather difficult. Zone 5

Acer palmatum 'Tsuma Gaki' FA. C. ESVELD

Acer palmatum 'Uki Gumo'

Japan

This rather curious plant forms a densely branched, medium-sized shrub that grows to 3.5 m high and wide. The leaves are deeply five-lobed and the young foliage is heavily speckled pink. During late spring and summer the speckles turn white, giving the foliage its extraordinary radiation. The very well-chosen Japanese name means "floating clouds." Quite rare in cultivation. Zone 5

Acer pectinatum 'Alice'

Fa. C. Esveld, Boskoop, The Netherlands, 1981

Medium-sized to large shrub that grows to 6 m high with conspicuously variegated foliage. The branches are dark reddish striped pink. The leaves are dark brownish green when young, later in the season they turn white and pink, leaving only the veins green. On older plants the leaves tend to show less variegation, so regular pruning (every three or four years) is rec-

Acer palmatum 'Uki Gumo' FA. C. ESVELD

Acer pectinatum 'Alice' KLAAS VERBOOM

Acer pictum 'Hoshi Yadori' FA. C. ESVELD

Acer pictum 'Usu Gumo' RONALD HOUTMAN

ommended. 'Alice' is in fact a cultivar of *Acer pectinatum* subsp. *forrestii*, which differs from *Acer pectinatum* subsp. *pectinatum* in having broader lobes and sharper tips on the leaves. 'Alice' was given an Award of Merit by the Royal Boskoop Horticultural Society in 1987. Zone 5b

Acer pictum 'Hoshi Yadori'

Kingsville Nursery, Maryland, United States, 1968

Large shrub to small shrubby tree that rarely exceeds 6 m in height. The leaves are five- to seven-lobed and have entire margins. They are very conspicuously speckled and dotted white and cream. The young foliage is tinted pink.

In the past the species was known as *Acer mono*; the name *Acer pictum* was once a synonym for *Kalopanax septemlobus*, a large tree from eastern Asia with prickly stems and branches and large five-lobed leaves, resembling this maple. However, modern views and recent studies resulted in *Acer pictum* as the correct name for this attractive, but relatively unknown species. Zone 4

Acer pictum 'Usu Gumo'

Japan

Dense and compact shrub that seldom exceeds 2 m in height. In spring the unfolding foliage has a conspicuously dull dark yellow color. It has very attractive foliage, which is heavily speckled with small white dots. The shape of the leaves is also extraordinary: seven- to nine-lobed, each lobe is triangular, and the tip is acuminate. The leaves are prone to sunburn, therefore this plant is best planted in semi-shade. Because 'Usu Gumo' is very difficult to propagate, it is a rare plant. Zone 4

Acer platanoides 'Drummondii'

Messrs. Drummond, Stirling, Scotland, United Kingdom, before 1910

Medium-sized to large tree that grows to 12 m high. It has a dense and well-branched crown that is quite broad and sometimes slightly irregularly shaped. The leaves have a splendid variegation. They have light yellow margins when young, later becoming creamy white. 'Drummondii' makes a marvelous specimen tree for gardens and parks, but can also be used as a street tree. Because the foliage tends to revert to green, these shoots must be removed as early as possible. Although the plant was found by Messrs. Drummond of Scotland, the name was first published by Fritz Graf von Schwerin in 1910. Zone 4b

***Acer platanoides* 'Walderseei'**

Späth Nurseries, Berlin, Germany, 1904

Small to medium-sized tree rarely exceeding 10 m in height with an elliptic to ovate crown. The leaves are conspicuously speckled white, which gives the whole tree a silvery look. Like 'Drummondii', this tree also tends to revert and green shoots must be removed at an early stage. It is an old cultivar that was introduced by Späth as an improvement of *Acer platanoides foliis pictis*, a clone that is no longer in cultivation. Zone 4b

***Acer pseudoplatanus* 'Esk Sunset'**

R. Cave, Hamilton, New Zealand, 1985

The young foliage of this cultivar is light yellowish pink at first, later becoming clear pink. When the leaves mature they turn cream, with irregular dark green

Acer platanoides 'Drummondii' FA. C. ESVELD

Acer platanoides 'Walderseei' PPH (COLLECTION OF HARRY VAN DE LAAR)

Acer platanoides 'Drummondii' RONALD HOUTMAN

Acer pseudoplatanus 'Esk Sunset' RONALD HOUTMAN

Acer pseudoplatanus 'Leopoldii' PIERRE THEUNISSEN

blotches. The undersides are deep pinkish purple and impart a pink glow to all the foliage. 'Esk Sunset' is one of the better variegated cultivars of *Acer pseudoplatanus*, from which it was raised as a seedling. Its relatively slow growth makes 'Esk Sunset' suitable for smaller gardens as well. All together it is a lovely variegated maple. Zone 5

Acer pseudoplatanus 'Leopoldii'

Vervaene Nursery, Belgium, 1864

'Leopoldii' is one of the largest of all variegated trees. It can grow up to 20 m high or more with a rather broad pyramidal crown, sometimes quite open. The leaves are irregularly speckled and splashed creamy white, whereas the young foliage is pink. It is a quite a handsome tree for parks and wide avenues, and it is widely grown throughout Europe. Plants sold as 'Variegatum' in the trade often are 'Leopoldii'. When propagating, the scions must be taken from verified trees, so one can be sure it is a true clone. Zone 4b

Acer pseudoplatanus 'Nizetii'

Makoy Nurseries, France, 1887

Medium-sized to large tree, not unlike 'Leopoldii', but it will not grow as high and the leaves are more heavily speckled and mottled. Whereas 'Leopoldii' has white variegated foliage, 'Nizetii' has a more yellowish variegation. A more conspicuous difference is the purple leaf undersides of 'Nizetii', making it a colorful tree. It is not as commonly planted as 'Leopoldii', but deserves to be more widely cultivated. Zone 4b

Acer pseudoplatanus 'Leopoldii' PIERRE THEUNISSEN

Acer pseudoplatanus 'Nizetii' J. R. P. VAN HOEY SMITH

Acer pseudoplatanus 'Purpureum Variegatum' WOUT KROMHOUT

Acer pseudoplatanus 'Purpureum Variegatum'

Bois de Boulogne, Paris, France, 1875

Very rare tree with strongly variegated leaves, colored purple, pink, and whitish pink. It is not commercially available but can be found in old botanic gardens, mainly in Europe. Zone 4b

Acer pseudoplatanus 'Simon-Louis Frères'

F. Deegen, Simon-Louis Frères Nurseries, Metz, France, 1881

Small, slow-growing tree that will not grow more than 10 m high, with a round but irregularly shaped crown. The foliage is pink when unfolding and later dotted white. A good quality of 'Simon-Louis Frères' is that it does not revert much. Only a few green leaves are produced. This slow-growing cultivar is only occasionally available in the trade and deserves to be more widely planted. Zone 4b

Acer pseudoplatanus 'Simon-Louis Frères' FA. C. ESVELD

Acer rubescens 'Silver Cardinal'

Crown Estate Commissioners, Windsor Great Park, Windsor, United Kingdom, 1985

Large, upright shrub to small tree that grows to 5 m high that was said to have arisen as a chance seedling of *Acer pensylvanicum*. The young branches are conspicuously coral red, which gives a stunning effect to the variegated foliage. The leaves are slightly wrinkled and heavily pink and silvery white speckled. The leaves turn more green during summer and eventually turn yellow in autumn. Although 'Silver Cardinal' tends to revert to green, when pruned hard the variegated foliage will appear again.

It was first described as a cultivar of *Acer* ×*conspicuum*

Acer pseudoplatanus 'Simon-Louis Frères' RONALD HOUTMAN

Acer rubescens 'Silver Cardinal' RONALD HOUTMAN

Acer rubescens 'Summer Surprise' FA. C. ESVELD

Acer rubescens 'Silver Cardinal' RONALD HOUTMAN

but recent studies have proven it is a cultivar of *A. rubescens*. Still quite rare in the trade. *Acer rubescens* 'Summer Snow', a Japanese cultivar that was renamed by Fa. C. Esveld of Boskoop, The Netherlands, is a similar variety with heavily white-speckled foliage. Zone 6a

Acer rubescens 'Summer Surprise'

R. Cave, Hamilton, New Zealand, 1987

Showy, large shrub that grows to about 5 m high with a broad spreading habit. The species belongs to the group of so called "snakebark maples," and the branches are red and rather inconspicuously striped pale green. The leaves are heavily speckled pink and white, but tend to become crinkly and are prone to sunburn. When planted on a semi-shaded spot it can develop into a nice specimen shrub, but it is not a very strong plant. *Acer rubescens* itself is an uncommon species, closely related to *Acer caudatifolium*. Zone 8a

Acer rubrum 'Candy Ice'

The first named variegated cultivar of *Acer rubrum*, 'Candy Ice' is a large shrub to small shrubby tree that can reach a height of more than 5 m. The colors are at their best in late spring and early summer. The young shoots are clear pink, turning lighter with age. Eventually the mature foliage is green, sparsely mottled with creamy white. The mature leaves are slightly smaller than in the species. During warm and sunny spells in spring, the young foliage might be burned. Moist soil and some protection from sunlight might help to prevent this. The strong foliage colors of 'Candy Ice' make this cultivar worthwhile in every garden. Zone 5

Acer rubrum 'Candy Ice' RONALD HOUTMAN

Acer rufinerve 'Albolimbatum'

J. D. Hooker, China, 1869

This cultivar was originally described as a botanical variation of *Acer rufinerve* by J. D. Hooker in 1869. It forms a large shrub or small, often multistemmed, tree. The bark is less conspicuously striped than the species. Foliage is attractively variegated, especially at the margins. Some leaves are heavily variegated white, others are almost entirely green with only white margins. Branches with entirely green leaves must be removed. Zone 5a

Acer rufinerve 'Albolimbatum' FA. C. ESVELD

Acer rufinerve 'Sunshine'

K. W. Verboom, Boskoop, The Netherlands, 2003

Discovered as a sport in *A. rufinerve*, this stunning variegated cultivar lives up to its name. The leaves have the same shape as in the species, but are clear yellow with relatively small green centers. During summer the yellow changes to greenish yellow. Due to the heavily variegated foliage its growth is slightly weaker than the species, resulting in a medium-sized shrubby tree. 'Sunshine' is slightly prone to sunburn, but when planted in a semi-shaded location this can largely be avoided. Zone 6

Acer rufinerve 'Sunshine' KLAAS VERBOOM

Acer truncatum 'Aki Kaze Nishiki'

Japan, before 1960

Strong-growing shrub that grows to 6 m high. It forms a multistemmed, often well-branched shrub. Leaves are irregularly variegated, sometimes half a lobe or half

Acer truncatum 'Aki Kaze Nishiki' J. R. P. VAN HOEY SMITH

Actinidia kolomikta FA. C. ESVELD

Actinidia pilosula RONALD HOUTMAN

a leaf is white. The young foliage is remarkably pinkish red. Although 'Aki Kaze Nishiki' tends to revert to green, it makes a nice specimen shrub that should be used more often. Zone 4

Actinidia kolomikta

Eastern Asia

Climbing plant that can grow to 8 m high, but in cultivation it will usually not exceed 4 m. It is a native of eastern Asia, especially Manchuria, Korea, Japan, and western China. Like many other species in this genus, *Actinidia kolomikta* is dioecious. Especially the male plants carry leaves that have a striking white-colored upper half. In many cases the young leaves are flushed pink, which makes the plant even more attractive. The white flowers are fragrant. The fruits (on female plants) are yellowish to pale green and sweet. It is a pity the female plants lack the pronounced and attractive variegation. Zone 4

Actinidia pilosula

China

At first sight, this unusual species looks a bit like *Actinidia kolomikta*. However, the leaves are distinctly narrower with more tapered tips. The upper half of each

Actinidia pilosula WOUT KROMHOUT

leaf is clear white, giving the whole plant the same general appearance as *A. kolomikta*. The biggest surprise this species offers is the pink color of the flowers. They are usually born in small clusters and open from mid-May to early June. It is a vigorous climber, but because of the relatively thin twigs and long internodes, *A. pilosula* has a rather loose and open habit. With its attractive flowers and graceful foliage, this plant deserves to be more widely grown. Zone 6

Aesculus ×*carnea* 'Aureomarginata'

Unusual and rare cultivar of the red horse chestnut. 'Aureomarginata' makes a large shrub to small tree, much lower than the original hybrid or the well-known cultivar 'Briotii' that easily exceeds 10 m. As the name suggests, the foliage of 'Aureomarginata' has yellow margins. However, the variegation is quite unstable and the foliage easily reverts to green. Under intense sunlight, the leaf margins sometimes burn later in the season. The flowers are pale orange-red to salmon-orange. A rare and similar variety is 'Foliis Marginatis'. Very little is known about this cultivar, except that it also reverts to green easily. Zone 5

Aesculus ×*carnea* 'Aureomarginata' RONALD HOUTMAN

Aesculus hippocastanum 'Luteovariegata'

United Kingdom, 1770

A rare cultivar of the horse chestnut. Although very old, it is rarely planted and highly unusual in cultivation. The leaves have yellow dots, which is especially attractive on young plants and in the spring. The flowers are like those of *Aesculus hippocastanum*, white and in erect pyramidal panicles. Variegated cultivars of *Aesculus* are quite uncommon in the trade because they easily revert to green and do not surpass their green allies. Other variegated cultivars of *Aesculus hippocastanum* are 'Albovariegata' (leaves speckled white) and 'Aureovariegata' (leaves dotted yellow). There seems to be little or no difference between 'Aureovariegata' and 'Luteovariegata'. Zone 4

Aesculus hippocastanum 'Variegata' KLAAS VERBOOM

Aesculus hippocastanum 'Variegata'

United Kingdom, before 1629

An old cultivar with dark green leaves that are partly clear white. It forms a small tree with an irregular habit. The foliage easily burns during hot and sunny spells. Therefore 'Variegata' definitely must be protected against direct sunlight. It is a very rare tree and, due to its weak habit and susceptibility to sunburn, not recommended. Zone 5

Ailanthus altissima 'Aucubaefolia'

G. Dieck, Zoeschen Nursery, Zoeschen, Germany, before 1889

Ailanthus is a small genus from the family of Simaroubaceae (the obscure genus *Picrasma* is its closest ally). The tree of heaven, as it is commonly referred to, grows quickly to more than 20 m high. The leaves are pinnately compound and consist of ten to sixteen pairs of leaflets. The foliage gives the tree an attractive appearance. The leaves of 'Aucubaefolia' are speckled yellow throughout the season. A large specimen can be observed in the Budapest Botanic Garden, Hungary. Zone 5

Akebia quinata 'Variegata' KLAAS VERBOOM

Ampelopsis glandulosa 'Elegans' RONALD HOUTMAN

Akebia quinata 'Variegata'

Vigorous climber, similar to the species, except for the variegated foliage. The leaves are attractively divided into five obovate-elliptic leaflets. These are dark green and irregularly speckled white. The flowers, which open in April and May, are monoecious, but male and female flowers are usually carried in the same raceme. The male flowers are about 0.5 cm wide and pale lilac-purple, whereas the female flowers are much larger, about 1.8 cm, and slightly darker. They spread a sweet and pleasant fragrance. 'Variegata' is a curious variegated plant, not widely available. It is only recommended for collectors. Otherwise the species is recommended over 'Variegata'. Zone 6a

Ampelopsis glandulosa 'Elegans'

Garden origin, before 1855

An attractive climbing plant that still is much better known by its old name: *Ampelopsis brevipedunculata* 'Variegata'. In fact, 'Elegans' belongs to *A. glandulosa* var. *brevipedunculata*. This plant was renamed several times, with synonyms including *Ampelopsis heterophylla* var. *elegans*, *Ampelopsis tricolor*, and *Vitis elegans*. It is a luxuriant climbing plant with three-lobed leaves. The leaves are strikingly variegated with white, yellowish white, and pale green. Young leaves and shoots are often pink as well. Although it is a shrub, in colder areas it will die back almost entirely during winter. Zone 4

Aralia

Small genus of about thirty-five species originating in North America and eastern Asia. Some species are shrubby, eventually becoming small trees, whereas other are herbaceous perennials. The attractive leaves are usually large and bipinnate. The branches are very prickly, which give the plant its common name, devil's club. They are especially decorative in winter.

All variegated cultivars of *Aralia* make excellent specimen plants in semi-shaded places where more contrast is wanted. For best results, plant all variegated *Aralia* cultivars in a wind-sheltered location. Unfortunately, the variegated forms of *A. elata* are difficult to propagate and therefore not common. The two older cultivars 'Aureovariegata' and 'Variegata' grow less tall than the newer 'Golden Umbrella' and 'Silver Umbrella'. Zone 4

Aralia elata 'Aureovariegata'

Boskoop, The Netherlands, about 1870

Large shrub that grows to 4 m with an open habit. The leaves, mainly growing at the ends of the branches, are very large. One leaf can be more than 75 cm long. The leaflets are ovate with yellow margins, although yellow-splashed leaves also appear. Later in the season the yellow leaf margins fade to silvery white, comparable with *Aralia elata* 'Variegata'.

Aralia elata 'Golden Umbrella'

A. J. van Niekerk, Boskoop, The Netherlands, 1995

This cultivar originated as a sport (stolon) of *A. elata* 'Aureovariegata' and only differs in minor features. The main characteristic of 'Golden Umbrella' is that the leaves are less variegated, which gives the whole plant a neater appearance than 'Aureovariegata'. The young foliage is green at first, later turning variegated. In contrast to 'Aureovariegata' the leaflets are only

Aralia elata 'Golden Umbrella' RONALD HOUTMAN

Aralia elata 'Aureovariegata' WOUT KROMHOUT

edged yellow and not splashed. During summer the leaves also turn more silvery variegated. This combination of green young leaves and older golden-and-silver variegated leaves occasionally can give the plant a somewhat sloppy appearance. The branches are slightly more prickly than 'Aureovariegata', and 'Golden Umbrella' grows conspicuously better. Especially as a young plant, this cultivar is preferable to 'Aureovariegata'. Zone 4

Aralia elata 'Silver Umbrella'

A. J. van Niekerk, Boskoop, The Netherlands, 1980

Like 'Golden Umbrella', this cultivar originated as a sport (of 'Variegata'). It has the same characteristics as 'Golden Umbrella', but the leaflets have silver edges. During summer the leaf color does not change, which makes 'Silver Umbrella' a healthy and extremely attractive shrub. It supersedes 'Variegata', not only in its more healthy appearance, but also in its much finer texture. Zone 4

Aralia elata 'Variegata'

Boskoop, The Netherlands, about 1885

A well-known and popular variegated form. 'Variegata' has the same aspects as 'Aureovariegata', but the leaflets have silver edges and do not change color during summer. The difficult propagation and slow growth of 'Variegata' make 'Silver Umbrella' a better choice. Zone 4

Aucuba

This small genus has only three species. Historically it was placed in the Cornaceae (the dogwood family), although taxonomists today place it in its own family, Aucubaceae. Of these three species *A. japonica* is the most widely distributed. The variegated cultivars of this species, of which there are more than fifteen, are among the best and most distinctive variegated plants. Many gardeners refer to them as "old-fashioned" and neglect variegated *Aucuba* cultivars, but they can be of outstanding beauty and great value in every garden as

Aralia elata 'Silver Umbrella' FA. C. ESVELD

they are well adapted to shady locations. It is best to use *Aucuba* against north-facing walls or hedges, but they also will do great in combination with bamboo or as a contrast-plant in the semi-shaded perennial border. Female plants bring extra value with their shiny red berries, which contrast well against the variegated foliage. Grow *Aucuba* in a well-drained soil and protect the plants from late frosts in spring. The variegated cultivars sometimes only differ in minor features, and there is a lot of confusion in names and gender of these plants. All *A. japonica* cultivars are hardy to zones 6b/7

Aucuba japonica 'Angelon'

The leaves of this cultivar are heavily spotted and blotched yellow. 'Angelon' is not widely cultivated.

Aucuba japonica 'Crotonifolia'

Evergreen, bushy shrub that grows to 2 m (or slightly higher) with a rounded habit. The heavily variegated leathery foliage is its most characteristic feature. The leaves of 'Crotonifolia' are oval to elliptic with sparsely toothed margins. The plant is glossy dark green with large spots and splashes of yellow throughout the leaf, as well as smaller dots. The typical 'Crotonifolia' is a female plant, but male plants under the same name are also in circulation. It is a first-class variegated plant and one of the most popular in this genus.

Aralia elata 'Variegata' MARCO HOFFMAN

Aucuba japonica 'Crotonifolia' RONALD HOUTMAN

Aucuba japonica 'Angelon' RONALD HOUTMAN

Aucuba japonica 'Gold Dust' RONALD HOUTMAN

Aucuba japonica 'Golden King' RONALD HOUTMAN

Aucuba japonica 'Picturata' RONALD HOUTMAN

Aucuba japonica 'Gold Dust'

Evergreen shrub, similar to 'Crotonifolia' in overall appearance and habit. The leaves, however, are not like 'Crotonifolia' at all. They are narrow, elliptic, and distinctly toothed. The glossy green upper surface is sparsely sprinkled with small golden yellow dots. 'Gold Dust' is a female plant with a well-chosen name.

Aucuba japonica 'Golden King'

A male clone with glossy green leaves that are densely spotted and splashed golden yellow. Some literature sources state this cultivar is a female clone, but this is incorrect.

Aucuba japonica 'Meigetsu'

Asahi Shokobutsu Nursery, Japan, before 1983

'Meigetsu' is a very distinctive cultivar with dark green foliage that is conspicuously toothed. The leaves have only one large, golden yellow central splash and no additional dots or blotches.

This plant was long known as 'Sun Dance', a name first published by Barry R. Yinger in *Arnoldia* (Vol. 43, No. 4, Autumn 1983). It was an English name for a clone that was known as 'Nakafu' in Japan and originated before 1978. Because there were several aberrant clones named 'Nakafu' and the ICNCP (1980) legitimated translation of Japanese names, it seemed the right thing to do to avoid further misunderstandings. (The plant described as 'Nakabu', probably a misspelling of 'Nakafu', in *Dendroflora* [No. 15/16, 1979] is not identical to 'Sun Dance'.) Later, Yinger found that the same cultivar was published in an older Japanese catalogue as 'Meigetsu'. According the rules of the ICNCP, this is the only legitimate cultivar name.

Aucuba japonica 'Picturata'

This widely distributed cultivar is easily distinguished by the large central splash in each leaf. The green parts of the leaves are also dotted yellow. The leaves are narrow, elliptic, and only sparsely toothed. As with 'Crotonifolia', there seems to be confusion over the gender. 'Picturata' is supposed to be a male clone, but female clones under the same name are also offered. A major disadvantage compared to many other cultivars is that 'Picturata' easily reverts. Shoots commonly show only a splashed and dotted variegation, lacking the characteristic central splash. This happens more often on young, strong-growing specimens than on older established plants.

Aucuba japonica 'Sulphurea Marginata'

Japan, before 1865

Very distinctive and recognizable female cultivar. The leaves are glossy green, with pale yellow to yellowish green margins. The leaf surface is not uniformly colored, but layered in various shades of green. When grown in full shade the foliage will show less or no variegation at all. Therefore, this plant is best planted in a light, but not sunny, location.

Aucuba japonica 'Sulphurea Marginata' RONALD HOUTMAN

Aucuba japonica 'Variegata'

Japan, before 1783

The leaves of this well-known female cultivar resemble those of 'Gold Dust', but are more heavily speckled golden yellow. Sometimes this cultivar is called 'Maculata', an illegitimate name belonging to a variegated male clone. The true 'Maculata' is most likely no longer in cultivation.

'Variegata' is the oldest of all variegated cultivars of *A. japonica*. It has been grown in Japan for centuries and was first introduced in Europe by John Graefer of London. Because Japan was closed to foreigners until the mid-nineteenth century, it was 1860 before Europeans saw *A. japonica* (the species) in fruit. Not long after, people were able to enjoy 'Variegata' in all its beauty.

Aucuba japonica 'Variegata' PPH (COLLECTION OF HARRY VAN DE LAAR)

Azara microphylla 'Variegata'

W. E. Gumbleton, Belgrove House, Cobh, Ireland, 1908

Azara is a small genus of evergreen shrubs originating from the southern parts of South America. They are only suitable for the mildest areas in Europe and the United States.

This cultivar was originally called 'Belgroveana', but the name 'Variegata', which was given in 1921, is now widely used. 'Variegata' is a loosely upright evergreen. The leaves are small and rounded, with entire or sparsely toothed margins. They are glossy dark green edged with creamy white to white. In spring, masses of light yellow flowers appear, almost covering the plant. The flowers spread a sweet and pleasant scent. Occasionally plants with more creamy yellow to light yellow variegated leaves are offered. These are called

Azara microphylla 'Variegata' RONALD HOUTMAN

Azara microphylla 'Variegata' RONALD HOUTMAN

Berberis ×*ottawensis* 'Silver Miles' RONALD HOUTMAN

'Variegata' as well. Although 'Variegata' is an old cultivar, it is still quite rare in cultivation, probably due to the limited cold-resistance. Zone 8b

Berberis ×*ottawensis* 'Silver Miles'

Before 1988

Vigorous upright deciduous shrub that grows to 3 m high with spiny twigs and branches. The hybrid *B.* ×*ottawensis* originated in Ottawa, Ontario, Canada and was first described in 1923. It is a hybrid between *Berberis thunbergii* and *B. vulgaris*. The first clone described was the purple-leaved 'Purpurea'. Over the years several cultivars were introduced, of which the most well known are undoubtedly 'Decora' (around 1953) and 'Superba' (1943). 'Silver Miles' is the only variegated cultivar raised from this hybrid. The purple foliage is irregularly veined and striped silvery white. Zone 4

Berberis ×*stenophylla* 'Pink Pearl'

Before 1994

Very curious and rather unusual evergreen that will attain a height of about 1.5 m and will grow as wide. The foliage is dark green and spotted white and pink. Most unusual is the color of the flowers: they can be creamy yellow, orange, or pink. Occasionally flowers of different colors appear on different branches on the same plant. 'Pink Pearl' strongly tends to revert to green. These branches must be removed at an early stage to prohibit further reversion. Zone 6

Berberis ×*stenophylla* 'Pink Pearl' RONALD HOUTMAN

Berberis thunbergii

Quite variable deciduous species from Japan. The leaves are obovate to spathulate or oblong and bright green, turning a striking red in autumn. Under each axillary bud there is one thorn. These prickly twigs and long-persistent foliage make *Berberis thunbergii* a very functional plant for hedging, group, and defensive plantings. Variegated *B. thunbergii* is usually pinkish or purplish variegated, whereas pure white or yellow variegation is much less common. The variegated cultivars of *B. thunbergii* combine excellently with white flowering perennials and yellow or green-leaved foliage plants. Apart from the green-leaved and some yellow-leaved cultivars, the most popular are the purple-leaved plants, especially *B. thunbergii* 'Atropurpurea' and 'Atropurpurea Nana'. Many variegated cultivars originally derived from these purple-leaved forms. All *B. thunbergii* are hardy to zone 4.

Berberis thunbergii 'Coronita' RONALD HOUTMAN

Berberis thunbergii 'Coronita'

Gebr. van Vliet Nurseries, Boskoop, The Netherlands, 1988

Compact shrub with a dense rounded habit that will not grow higher than about 1 m. The leaves are broad elliptic and purplish brown with narrow, light greenish yellow margins. From some distance the variegation is rather inconspicuous, but seen from a closer range it gives 'Coronita' quite a distinctive aspect. On dry soils the foliage can become brilliant red in autumn, keeping the colored margins. 'Coronita' differs from the older cultivar 'Golden Ring' in having a much denser habit and more pronounced foliage colors.

Berberis thunbergii 'Golden Ring' RONALD HOUTMAN

Berberis thunbergii 'Golden Ring'

Royal Nurseries Pierre Lombarts, Zundert, The Netherlands, about 1950

Very similar to 'Coronita', but differs in having a more upright habit. The leaf shape and color is the same, although the margins seem slightly more greenish.

Berberis thunbergii 'Harlequin'

Hanno Hardijzer, Boskoop, The Netherlands, 1969

Dense and compact shrub that grows considerably more delicate and has smaller leaves than the majority of *B. thunbergii* cultivars. Contrary to most other variegated cultivars, the foliage is much more white and cream variegated.

Berberis thunbergii 'Harlequin' RONALD HOUTMAN

Berberis thunbergii 'Kelleriis'

D. T. Poulsen, Kelleriis, Denmark, before 1959

Broad and dense shrub with green leaves that are spotted and blotched white. In autumn the foliage turns pinkish to deep pinkish red, and the variegation is still visible. 'Kelleriis' is quite similar to the older 'Silver Beauty', but differs in having larger leaves.

Berberis thunbergii 'Kelleriis' RONALD HOUTMAN

Berberis thunbergii 'Pink Attraction'

H. Kolster, Boskoop, The Netherlands, 1980

'Pink Attraction' is one of the newer variegated cultivars derived from *B. thunbergii*. It forms a densely branched bushy shrub of only 1 m high with attractively arching branches. The young foliage is bright salmon-pink to pinkish red and later becomes more pink, creamy white, and purple blotched during summer. This cultivar was found as a seedling of *B. thunbergii* 'Atropurpurea', so the basic leaf color is dark purplish brown. 'Pink Attraction' was given an Award of Merit by the Royal Boskoop Horticultural Society in 1992.

Berberis thunbergii 'Pink Queen'

Veerman Bros., Boskoop, The Netherlands, 1965

Elegant shrub with a similar habit to *B. thunbergii* 'Rose Glow', but more dense. The young foliage is almost red, later becoming more brownish purple with pink and gray blotches. In autumn the leaves become a color marvelous crimson-red. Contrary to 'Rose Glow' the leaves are less striped and blotched white and

Berberis thunbergii 'Pink Attraction' PPH (COLLECTION OF HARRY VAN DE LAAR)

therefore give a more pink impression. 'Pink Queen' was found in the 1950s and first introduced as 'Atropurpurea Rosea'. In 1965 it was legitimately published for the first time and renamed 'Pink Queen'.

Berberis thunbergii 'Rose Glow'

Fa. J. Spaargaren & Zonen, Boskoop, The Netherlands, 1957

Compact deciduous shrub that grows to 1.5 m high with an elegant habit. The young foliage is almost entirely red, later becoming purplish red with pink and whitish stripes and spots. 'Rose Glow' will show its young red foliage throughout summer into autumn. It is one of a group of quite similar cultivars with pink, purple, and reddish variegated foliage.

Berberis thunbergii 'Rosetta'

Hanno Hardijzer, Boskoop, The Netherlands, 1971

A sister-seedling of *B. thunbergii* 'Harlequin', but larger in all its features and with the leaves less white variegated. 'Rosetta' is not very common in the trade but is still available.

Berberis thunbergii 'Pink Queen' PPH (COLLECTION OF HARRY VAN DE LAAR)

Berberis thunbergii 'Rosetta' RONALD HOUTMAN

Berberis thunbergii 'Rose Glow' RONALD HOUTMAN

Berberis thunbergii 'Silver Beauty' RONALD HOUTMAN

Berberis thunbergii 'Silver Carpet' RONALD HOUTMAN

Berberis thunbergii 'Silver Bells' KLAAS VERBOOM

Berberis thunbergii 'Silver Beauty'

Van Leeuwen, The Netherlands, about 1911

This old cultivar was first known as 'Argenteomarginata' and can still be found under this illegitimate name. It is a rather weak and slow-growing shrub with green leaves spotted and blotched white. In periods of sunny weather the leaves easily burn. This old cultivar is surpassed by the newer cultivar 'Kelleriis'.

Berberis thunbergii 'Silver Bells'

Another cultivar that is very similar to 'Kelleriis' and 'Silver Beauty'. The young shoots are tinted slightly orange in spring. The light green leaves are irregularly mottled silvery white. In autumn they become a deep orange-red.

Berberis thunbergii 'Silver Carpet'

P. Koster, Maartensdijk, The Netherlands, 1991

Dense and low-growing shrub with a spreading habit that grows to 75 cm high (after many years) and twice as wide. It originated as a sport of *B. thunbergii* 'Green Carpet' and has roughly the same habit, although it remains even lower. The young foliage is pale green to grayish green. During summer the leaves show an inconspicuous pale gray and grayish green variegation, which gives the plant a gray impression. Because of its moderate height and good habit 'Silver Carpet' can be used in both private gardens as well as urban plantings or as an amenity plant. In 2000 this plant was given an Award of Recommendation by the Royal Boskoop Horticultural Society.

Berchemia scandens 'Variegata'

Hillier Gardens & Arboretum, Romsey, United Kingdom, early 1970s

Rare variegated climbing plant belonging to the family Rhamnaceae (buckthorn family). *Berchemia* is a small genus of approximately twelve climbing perennials and deciduous shrubs growing in Southeast Asia, eastern Africa, the southern United States, and Central America.

Berchemia scandens is a vigorous climbing shrub from the United States that grows to 4 m high. The thin green leaves are ovate with a cordate base, giving them a somewhat heart-shaped appearance. The leaves are distinctively veined. In late summer small and rather inconspicuous creamy white flowers appear on terminal and axillary panicles. In warm and sunny summers, flowers can be followed by small glossy berries, first red, later turning black. The foliage of 'Variegata' is heavily variegated creamy white to cream. Both the species and the variegated cultivar are not often seen in the trade; however, they are well worth planting. Zone 7

Buddleja davidii 'Harlequin'

United Kingdom, before 1964

Shrub of moderate size, that grows to 2 m high. It has a loose habit and is not very densely set with leaves, giving it an open appearance. The foliage is dull dark grayish green with a creamy white edge, more yellow on young foliage. The reddish purple flowers are borne in showy terminal panicles. 'Harlequin' arose as a sport of *Buddleja davidii* 'Royal Red'. It was originally launched as an improvement of the old and very unstable cultivar 'Variegata'. Although 'Harlequin' is an improvement, it still tends to revert easily. Zone 5/6

Buddleja davidii 'Notbud' MASQUERADE™

Deciduous shrub that closely resembles *B. davidii* 'Harlequin' but seems more stable in its variegation. The foliage also has cream edges, but the flowers appear more reddish. It also grows slightly taller, up to 2.5 m high. Zone 6b

Buddleja davidii 'Santana'

Rod Dranesfield, Yorkshire, United Kingdom, about 1994

Medium-sized, broad, upright shrub that grows to about 3 m high. The relatively large ovate leaves are

Buddleja davidii 'Harlequin' GERT FORTGENS

Buddleja davidii 'Variegata' RONALD HOUTMAN

Buddleja davidii 'Notbud' MASQUERADE™ PPH (COLLECTION OF HARRY VAN DE LAAR)

Buddleja davidii 'Santana' RONALD HOUTMAN

Buxus microphylla 'Golden Triumph' RONALD HOUTMAN

Buxus microphylla 'Kinsha' GEORGE OTTER

dark grayish green with broad, clear yellow margins. Later during summer these become more creamy yellow. Like all *B. davidii* cultivars, the flowers of 'Santana' are carried in dense terminal panicles. 'Santana' was discovered as a sport of 'Royal Red', and the flowers are also dark purple, adding much to the variegation of the foliage. Zone 6b

Buxus

Throughout gardening history many variegated clones of the well-known boxwood were raised and introduced. Although many are derived from *Buxus sempervirens*, there are a few cultivars derived from *B. microphylla*. Most of the variegated boxwood cultivars originated in the nineteenth century and were originally described as botanical varieties of a species. Later, when the ICNCP was introduced, these clones were made into cultivars. As with the green-leaved cultivars, the variegated ones also make great hedging or specimen plants. They are also suitable for group plantings. Unless otherwise stated, all cultivars described here are hardy to zone 6.

Buxus microphylla 'Golden Triumph'

H. Kolster, Boskoop, The Netherlands, 1994

Compact, broad, upright evergreen, eventually with a flattened globular habit. 'Golden Triumph' will reach a height of about 1 m and becomes slightly wider. The small leaves are ovate and dark green, with greenish yellow to creamy yellow margins. The foliage of this plant is not very conspicuously variegated, but it gives the whole plant a rather yellowish appearance. 'Golden Triumph' was discovered as a sport of *B. microphylla* 'Faulkner' and is one of the few golden-variegated boxwoods.

Buxus microphylla 'Kinsha'

Fa. C. Esveld, Boskoop, The Netherlands, 1992

Relatively low-growing evergreen with a flattened, more or less spreading-upright habit. It will grow about 60 cm high, but much wider. The green, broad ovate leaves are heavily mottled light yellow. Usually more than 50 percent of the leaf blade is variegated, and seen from a distance this plant looks entirely yellow. Do not plant 'Kinsha' in full sun because it is prone to burn. However, a semi-shaded location in a (perennial) border can create a dramatic and colorful effect.

Cor van Gelderen of the Esveld Nursery took this plant from Japan as *B. microphylla* var. *japonica* f. *major* 'Variegata' (*B. microphylla* 'Variegata' in practice) in 1989. This name proved to be illegitimate, and the plant was renamed 'Kinsha'. Later the same plant was named 'Hachijo Delight' by Mr. Masato Yokoi in Japan. This cultivar is not yet widely distributed and is still quite rare. Zone 5

***Buxus sempervirens* 'Argentea'**

United Kingdom, before 1844

Broad spreading shrub with grayish green leaves with creamy white margins. This old cultivar tends to revert and is only rarely available in the trade. Because of its slightly unstable habit, it is surpassed by other cultivars, such as 'Elegantissima'.

Buxus sempervirens 'Argentea' RONALD HOUTMAN

***Buxus sempervirens* 'Argenteovariegata'**

United Kingdom, before 1770

Another old cultivar from England with ovate to elliptic-oblong leaves that are white variegated. 'Argenteovariegata' is only rarely available in the trade. Like *B. sempervirens* 'Argentea', this cultivar is also surpassed by other variegated cultivars. The name is sometimes misspelled 'Argentea Variegata'.

Buxus sempervirens 'Argenteovariegata' RONALD HOUTMAN

***Buxus sempervirens* 'Aurea Pendula'**

United Kingdom, 1896

Upright shrub to small tree that grows to about 4 m high with a capricious habit. The branches are attractively weeping and the foliage is elliptic, growing to 2 cm long and half as wide. The leaves are irregularly variegated with creamy yellow to golden yellow splashes and blotches. The elegant habit and striking variegation make 'Aurea Pendula' an interesting evergreen worth planting in every garden. An additional benefit is that it is very stable in its variegation.

Buxus sempervirens 'Aurea Pendula' GERT FORTGENS

***Buxus sempervirens* 'Aureovariegata'**

United Kingdom, before 1844

Large shrub that grows to 3 m high with an open and pyramidal habit. The leaves are ovate and relatively broad. They are splashed and striped yellow to pale yellow. Although there seems to be some misunderstanding about the status of this cultivar, it is definitely different from 'Latifolia Maculata'. The main difference is the habit of these plants, which is open and pyrami-

Buxus sempervirens 'Aureovariegata' RONALD HOUTMAN

Buxus sempervirens 'Elegans' MARCO HOFFMAN

dal in 'Aureovariegata' and dense and rounded in 'Latifolia Maculata'. 'Aureovariegata' is not uncommon in the trade, although it is sometimes sold as 'Aurea'.

Buxus sempervirens 'Elegans'

This dense upright shrub grows to 1.5 m high. The leaves have creamy white to white margins. There seems to be some misunderstanding about the status of this cultivar in relation to 'Elegantissima'; they definitely differ, although in minor details. 'Elegantissima' has a better habit, shows lesser reversion, and has more silvery white variegation. Like *B. sempervirens* 'Argentea' and 'Argenteovariegata', this cultivar is also surpassed by 'Elegantissima'.

Buxus sempervirens 'Elegantissima'

Europe, before 1860

Compact and dense upright shrub with a broad ovate habit. It will reach a height of about 2 m. The leaves are elliptic to ovate-oblong, growing to 2 cm long and half as wide. They have irregular silvery white margins with a green center. 'Elegantissima' is excellent as a specimen plant, but also very useful for hedging. This is undoubtedly one of the best variegated boxwood cultivars and therefore very popular.

Buxus sempervirens 'Karmen'

Herman Geers, Boskoop, The Netherlands, 1995

This broad upright evergreen will eventually have a broad ovate habit and grow to about 1.5 m high. The leaves are narrow elliptic to narrow ovate and dark green. They are irregularly variegated light yellow to

Buxus sempervirens 'Elegantissima' RONALD HOUTMAN

cream. Occasionally shoots with entirely yellow or green leaves are formed. The green-leaved shoots must be removed to maintain the variegated habit of 'Karmen'. The plant was named after Karmen Rosalie van Gelderen, daughter of Cor van Gelderen of the Esveld Nursery. This nursery holds the Dutch National Collection of *Buxus*.

Buxus sempervirens 'Karmen' GEORGE OTTER

Buxus sempervirens 'Latifolia Maculata'

Large shrub that grows to 2.5 m high with a dense and bushy habit. The leaves are ovate and relatively broad. They are very irregularly striped, splashed, and blotched yellow to creamy yellow. The young leaves are entirely yellow, which is a very distinctive feature of 'Latifolia Maculata'. At a young age plants tend to grow deceptively slowly, but once established they can grow quite tall. 'Latifolia Maculata' is very attractive as a specimen plant, less useful for hedging or group plantings. One of the better variegated boxwood cultivars.

Buxus sempervirens 'Latifolia Maculata' FA. C. ESVELD

Buxus sempervirens 'Lawson's Golden'

Upright, bushy shrub with an ovate habit. The relatively small leaves are very dark green, irregularly variegated light yellow to clear yellow. Usually only 30 percent to half of the leaf blade is variegated.

Buxus sempervirens 'Lawson's Golden' GEORGE OTTER

Buxus sempervirens 'Marginata'

France, before 1755

Tall shrub with a dense rounded habit that grows to 2.5 m high and 3 m wide. At a young age it grows rather stiff and upright, later becoming more densely branched. 'Marginata' originated as a sport of 'Hard-

Buxus sempervirens 'Marginata' PIERRE THEUNISSEN

Buxus sempervirens 'Ponteyi Variegata' RONALD HOUTMAN

Buxus sempervirens 'Variegata' GEORGE OTTER

Calocedrus decurrens 'Aureovariegata' RONALD HOUTMAN

wickensis'. The leaves are rounded to broad ovate and distinctively bullate. They are dark green and narrow, with conspicuous yellow margins. 'Marginata', sometimes found under its synonym 'Aureomarginata', is an excellent plant for hedging but will also make a good specimen plant.

Buxus sempervirens 'Ponteyi Variegata'

Upright evergreen with a relatively narrow ovate habit. The leaves are ovate to elliptic. They are dark green with cream margins. At first sight 'Ponteyi Variegata' looks similar to 'Elegantissima', but the leaves of 'Ponteyi Variegata' are coarser and the habit is more upright. 'Ponteyi Variegata' is likely to be an old cultivar, however, little is known about it. The nice growing habit seems one of the advantages over similar varieties. Zone 6a

Buxus sempervirens 'Variegata'

Another cultivar with white-margined leaves. It grows as a broad upright shrub up to 3 m high. 'Variegata' is an old cultivar long surpassed by 'Elegantissima'.

Calocedrus decurrens 'Aureovariegata'

Germany, 1904

Golden variegated cultivar of the California incense cedar, not uncommon in the trade. Like the species, it eventually forms a large broad columnar tree, but will not grow as tall. 'Aureovariegata' will reach a height of about 20 m after many years. The foliage is shiny dark green with conspicuous golden yellow sprays. In some parts of the tree these sprays are small, better called "spots," in other parts they are much larger, sometimes even with entirely golden yellow branches. This cultivar is known to be more heavily variegated when grown in a warm climate. 'Aureovariegata' is a stable variegated cultivar that can be a true eye-catcher in the garden. Zone 7a

Calocedrus decurrens 'Maupin Glow'

A new variegated conifer with attractive foliage colors. It has the same rather narrow, upright habit as the species and will eventually become a medium-sized to large tree. The foliage is clear green with a lively yellow to greenish yellow variegation. 'Maupin Glow' is not widely grown yet, but looks very promising. Zone 7a

Camellia ×*williamsii* 'Golden Spangles'

The Royal Horticultural Society, Wisley, United Kingdom, 1960

Large, broad, upright, evergreen shrub. The leaves are glossy dark green and have a yellow-green central spot. During winter, when 'Golden Spangles' flowers, the variegation is less pronounced than in summer. The single flowers open from mid-February into March. They are clear cherry pink with golden yellow anthers. The winter-flowering habit and conspicuous variegated foliage during summer make 'Golden Spangles' quite unique among variegated plants. Belonging to the hybrid *C.* ×*williamsii*, it is slightly more cold-hardy than *C. japonica* cultivars.

'Golden Spangles' grew in a batch of several cultivars at Wisley Garden, labeled 'Mary Christian'. However, 'Mary Christian' is not a variegated cultivar and, to avoid confusion, the plant was renamed 'Golden Spangles'. Zone 7b

Caragana arborescens 'Anny's Golden Cascade'

André van Nijnatten B.V., Zundert, The Netherlands, 2003

Originating as a sport of *C. arborescens* 'Pendula', this plant has the same weeping habit. The pinnate leaves

Camellia ×*williamsii* 'Golden Spangles' RONALD HOUTMAN

Caragana arborescens 'Anny's Golden Cascade' RONALD HOUTMAN

Calocedrus decurrens 'Maupin Glow' KLAAS VERBOOM

Caragana arborescens 'Anny's Golden Cascade' RONALD HOUTMAN

are dark green and heavily mottled yellow to creamy yellow. Occasionally leaflets are entirely yellow. The effect is quite dramatic. It is best grown as a weeping plant on a stem. When grown as a shrub, 'Anny's Golden Cascade' will take a creeping habit. This is not recommended, however, because the foliage will burn easily during sunny spells. Like all *C. arborescens* cultivars, 'Anny's Golden Cascade' is exceptionally winter hardy. Zone 2

Caryopteris ×*clandonensis* 'Summer Sorbet' RONALD HOUTMAN

Caryopteris ×*clandonensis* 'Moody Blue' RONALD HOUTMAN

Carpinus betulus 'Variegata'

United Kingdom, 1770

An upright tree that grows to 15 m high (sometimes taller). The variegated common hornbeam is similar to the species but less vigorous and with variegated foliage. The leaves are dark green irregularly spotted with yellow to yellowish green. It is quite densely branched, which benefits the variegated aspect of this cultivar. It often reverts with age, eventually becoming entirely green-leaved. This old cultivar seems forgotten and is only rarely available in the trade. Other, perhaps even rarer, variegated cultivars of *C. betulus* are 'Marmorata', with finely white variegated leaves, and 'Punctata', with white variegated leaves. Zone 5a

Caryopteris ×*clandonensis* 'Summer Sorbet'

Peter van Delft, West End Nurseries, Paignton, United Kingdom, 2001

Interesting new cultivar with the same dense globular habit as the hybrid parent *Caryopteris* ×*clandonensis*. This hybrid was originally raised by Arthur Simmonds, sometime before 1933. Simmonds found *C.* ×*clandonensis* as a chance seedling of a *Caryopteris mongholica* that grew close to a *Caryopteris incana*. The grayish green foliage of 'Summer Sorbet' has conspicuous golden yellow margins. In August and September the plant bears deep blue flowers, making an excellent contrast to the variegated foliage. 'Summer Sorbet' was found as a branch sport in *C.* ×*clandonensis* 'Kew Blue'. Another very similar variegated *C.* ×*clandonensis* is 'Moody Blue'. This plant was also raised in the United Kingdom and introduced in 2002. Both cultivars are relatively new on the market and closer examination of hardiness and use is necessary. However, both cultivars look stable and well worth growing. Zone 7

Castanea sativa 'Albomarginata'

France, 1755

Medium-sized to large tree that grows to 25 m high, which is slightly smaller than the species. It has relatively thick branches and very distinctive lanceolate to oblong-lanceolate leaves with sharp serrate margins. The leaves can be up to 20 cm long. They are glossy dark green with irregular pale creamy white to silvery white margins. Contrary to the name, some leaves do not have white margins, but white centers. This is not restricted to separate specimens, but is seen together

Castanea sativa 'Albomarginata' RONALD HOUTMAN

with white-margined leaves on the same branches. Its fruits, the well-known prickly burrs, are also cream-colored.

This cultivar is not uncommon in the trade, but is sometimes sold as 'Argenteomarginata' or 'Argenteo-variegata', which are both illegitimate cultivar names. More often it is wrongly offered as 'Variegata', which is the correct name for the golden variegated cultivar. Surely *C. sativa* 'Albomarginata' belongs to the best of all variegated trees. Its good and contrasting variegation, neat habit, and stable character make it an excellent specimen tree for both smaller and larger gardens. Zone 6a

Castanea sativa 'Aureomaculata'

Germany, 1862

Very rare and probably a completely disappeared cultivar with the same overall features as *C. sativa* 'Albomarginata'. The leaves have the same shape, but their

Castanea sativa 'Aureomaculata' KLAAS VERBOOM

Castanea sativa 'Albomarginata' RONALD HOUTMAN

Castanea sativa 'Aureomaculata' FA. C. ESVELD

Castanea sativa 'Variegata' GERT FORTGENS

Catalpa ×*erubescens* 'Variegata' RONALD HOUTMAN

Catalpa speciosa 'Pulverulenta' GERT FORTGENS

coloring is different. Each leaf is very irregularly spotted and blotched golden yellow to greenish yellow. Both 'Albomarginata' and 'Aureomaculata' were first described by Georg Kirchner of the Muskau Arboretum, at the time in Germany, now belonging to Poland. Zone 6a

Castanea sativa 'Variegata'

France, before 1755

This is the oldest known variegated cultivar of *C. sativa*. Like 'Aureomaculata', it is very rare and only very occasionally available. It has the same characteristics as 'Albomarginata', but the leaves have irregular yellow margins. Zone 6a

Catalpa ×*erubescens* 'Variegata'

Yellow variegated cultivar of unknown origin, but probably raised in the nineteenth century (the hybrid *C.* ×*erubescens* was first described in 1869 by Carrière). Despite its probable long existence, 'Variegata' is only rarely found in gardens and collections. The foliage is broad ovate to cordate and slightly pinkish brown when young, which is a typical characteristic of *C.* ×*erubescens*. The leaves are green with broad greenish yellow margins. Although only little is known about this plant, it seems prone to sunburn during hot summers. It is therefore best to plant it in a light but shady location. This plant is definitely underrated and should be planted more. Zone 6a

Catalpa speciosa 'Pulverulenta'

B. Paul & Son, United Kingdom, 1908

Small to medium-sized tree that grows to more than 15 m high with thick branches. The large cordate-ovate shaped leaves are in whorls of three and are up to 30 cm long. The variegation is quite unusual. The leaf blades are densely covered with many small white dots. Because the variegation has proven quite stable, 'Pulverulenta' makes an excellent contrast-plant in semi-shaded places. It is an odd cultivar, but well worth planting. Zone 6a

Ceanothus griseus 'Diamond Heights'

East Bay Nursery, Diamond Height Village, California, United States, 1995

Relatively new cultivar with a dense spreading habit. The evergreen leaves are about 4 cm long and elliptic to obovate. Not unlike other *Ceanothus* species and cultivars, the veins are distinctly visible as grooves on the upper side of the leaves, giving them a slightly rugose aspect. The leaves are light greenish yellow with a dark green central spot that is usually narrow. 'Diamond Heights' flowers in spring with light blue flowers, carried in dense panicles. It is actually derived from *C. griseus* var. *horizontalis*, hence its spreading habit. A similar cultivar is called 'Bright Eyes', which was discovered in Ireland about 1995. Zones 8/9

Ceanothus griseus 'Diamond Heights' RONALD HOUTMAN

Ceanothus griseus 'Silver Surprise'

A. Brand & Sons, Hatfield, United Kingdom, 1994

Dense, broad, upright, medium-sized to large shrub that will attain a height of about 3 m in cultivation, but often stays much smaller. The leaves are glossy dark green, obovate, and sparsely toothed. They have an irregular white variegation. Basically the leaves have white margins but often half the leaf blade is colored white. The light blue flowers appear in dense panicles in spring. 'Silver Surprise' was discovered as a sport of *C. griseus* 'Yankee Point'. It can be used as a specimen shrub, container plant, or against a wall. In milder areas, it makes an excellent contrast-plant in the perennial border. Otherwise it must be treated as a container plant. Zone 8

Ceanothus griseus 'Silver Surprise' RONALD HOUTMAN

Ceanothus 'Perado' EL DORADO™

Pershore College, Pershore, United Kingdom, 1996

Within the range of variegated *Ceanothus*, 'Perado' represents a new type of plant. Whereas several golden-variegated cultivars have relatively large leaves, those of 'Perado' are much smaller. It is a broad, upright, evergreen shrub with light green twigs. The leaves are green with broad, irregular greenish yellow margins. The bright colors of 'Perado' make it look rather fresh, which is intensified by the fine branching and relatively small leaves. The flowers are light blue and open in spring. Zone 8

Ceanothus 'Perado' EL DORADO™ RONALD HOUTMAN

Ceanothus 'Pershore Zanzibar' ZANZIBAR™

Pershore College, Pershore, United Kingdom, 1993

Rather vigorous hybrid with strongly variegated foliage. The leaves are bright yellow to light greenish yellow, and only a small central spot is colored green. The flowers are light blue and carried in short, dense panicles. Although it is not one of the hardiest cultivars,

Ceanothus 'Pershore Zanzibar' ZANZIBAR™ RONALD HOUTMAN

Cedrus deodara 'First Snow' RONALD HOUTMAN

Cedrus deodara 'Fructu-luteo' RONALD HOUTMAN

the colorful foliage makes it excellent for planting in borders or as a container plant. It was discovered as a sport in C. 'A. T. Johnson'. Zones 8/9

Cedrus

Small conifer genus of only a few species confined to northern Africa, Asia Minor, and the Himalayas. All species grow into large trees, but several cultivars are small and shrubby. Only a few cultivars are truly variegated, for example, they have multicolored foliage. Several other cultivars, especially *C. deodara* 'Albospica', 'Cream Puff', and 'Silver Spring', are sometimes regarded as variegated. Here these cultivars are not regarded as variegated, because only the young shoots have a different color than the older foliage and they change to green during summer.

Cedrus deodara 'First Snow'

Yoshimichi Hirose, Iwakuni, Yamaguchi, Japan, before 1998

Upright tree with a pyramidal habit that can reach a height of more than 20 m. The branches are gracefully arching and slightly weeping. The needles of 'First Snow' are grayish green interspersed with tufts of creamy white needles. Altogether this results in a spectacularly variegated tree. Originating in Japan, it is also grown in Europe, although not on a large scale. This cultivar is probably similar to *C. deodara* 'Bewley's Variegated' from Australia. Zone 7b

Cedrus deodara 'Fructu-luteo'

Upright, medium-sized to large tree that grows to a height of about 15 m. The needles are bluish green with irregularly placed tufts of creamy white needles. It is a curious and probably old cultivar. A similar cultivar, 'Variegata', is most likely no longer in cultivation. Both 'Fructu-luteo' and 'Variegata' are rather unstable and easily revert to green. Zone 7a

Cedrus deodara 'Luteolineata'

This cultivar of unknown origin is very similar to 'First Snow', if not identical. In the nursery it seems 'Luteolineata' is slightly less vigorous; this is a negligible difference, however. Zone 7a

Cercis canadensis 'Silver Cloud'

T. Klein, Kentucky, United States, before 1997

Very attractive tall shrub that grows to 5 m high with a

Cedrus deodara 'Luteolineata' RONALD HOUTMAN

Cercis canadensis 'Silver Cloud' GERT FORTGENS

broad, upright habit. The leaves are cordate with acute tips and are wonderfully variegated, especially when young. Unfolding leaves are heavily variegated to almost completely white. Usually they are tinged pink. During spring an irregular green center becomes visible. Eventually the older leaves will become dark green, while the younger leaves are still variegated. The pinkish red flowers are borne in the spring, just before the foliage appears. 'Silver Cloud' is a spectacular variegated plant that can be used in many places. It will tolerate both sunny and semi-shaded locations and will thrive best in any well-drained soil. Zone 4

Chamaecyparis

This very important genus consists of only a few species growing in the wild, but it has more than 400 cultivars. All species have a juvenile and adult stage. The leaves are needle shaped when the plants are in a juvenile stage, and they turn scale shaped when the plant reaches its adult stage. Members of this genus are monoecious, carrying small, usually yellow male cones, and larger female seed cones. The seed cones usually ripen in the same year they have flowered.

Only four species have variegated cultivars, but in total *Chamaecyparis* has the majority of the variegated conifer cultivars. *Chamaecyparis lawsoniana*, which is native to southern Oregon and northern California, is a very well-known species and widely grown in all temperate regions. This is also the case with *C. nootkatensis* (also native to the Pacific Northwest), *C. obtusa* (Japan), and *C. pisifera* (Japan). All species become large trees in the wild. As to be expected, the majority of the variegated cultivars do not grow as tall. Most of them will eventually become small trees or stay shrubby. Due to the change in fashion and trends, many of the old and the variegated *Chamaecyparis* cultivars have disappeared from the trade or have become very rare.

Chamaecyparis lawsoniana 'Albovariegata'

J. Veitch & Sons, London, United Kingdom, 1881

Dense, shrubby conifer with a broad and conical but eventually an almost rounded habit. It can reach a height of 2 m, but fully grown specimens are rare and in gardens it is usually smaller. The scale-shaped foliage is green and heavily cream to creamy white variegated. This old and very conspicuous cultivar was originally found by James Veitch & Sons in the Coombe Wood Nursery, United Kingdom. Although 'Albovariegata' is a quite stable cultivar, it is very prone to sunburn during hot and sunny spells. Zone 6b

Chamaecyparis lawsoniana 'Argenteovariegata'

Lawson's Nurseries, Edinburgh, Scotland, United Kingdom, 1875

Another old cultivar from the United Kingdom that is very similar to 'Albovariegata'. It has the same dense broad conical to almost rounded habit. The foliage is green to grayish green and very heavily blotched cream to creamy white. In 'Argenteovariegata' the variegated blotches are smaller than in 'Albovariegata',

Chamaecyparis lawsoniana 'Argenteovariegata' J. R. P. VAN HOEY SMITH

Chamaecyparis lawsoniana 'Argenteovariegata Nova' J. R. P. VAN HOEY SMITH

which has fewer but larger variegated parts. Like 'Albovariegata', it is very prone to sunburn. Zone 6b

Chamaecyparis lawsoniana 'Argenteovariegata Nova'

Overeynder Nursery, Boskoop, The Netherlands, 1887

This cultivar is very similar to 'Argenteovariegata' in variegation and color. It will grow broadly conical to broadly upright at first, later becoming more narrowly upright. This plant was originally raised by the Overeynder Nursery as an improvement of 'Argenteovariegata' because it is not prone to sunburn. This cultivar seems to be rare and almost forgotten in cultivation. Zone 6b

Chamaecyparis lawsoniana 'Eclipse'

Andrew Cassells, Markinch, Fife, Scotland, United Kingdom, 1978

Rather narrow, upright conifer with bluish green scale-shaped foliage. The foliage is heavily golden yellow variegated. This interesting cultivar was raised as a seedling of *C. lawsoniana* 'Columnaris' by Andrew Cassells but was introduced by Kenwith Nurseries of Great Torrington, Devon, United Kingdom, in 1987. Zone 6a

Chamaecyparis lawsoniana 'Eclipse' RONALD HOUTMAN

Chamaecyparis lawsoniana 'Ellwood's Splashed'

A new cultivar derived from the famous 'Ellwoodii'. The foliage of this dense, upright conifer is dark bluish green. It is moderately speckled with small tufts of creamy white. Zone 7a

Chamaecyparis lawsoniana 'Ellwood's White'

P. den Ouden, Boskoop, The Netherlands, 1965

Compact, densely branched conifer that grows to about 1 m high but occasionally slightly taller. The foliage is needle shaped, as in *C. lawsoniana* 'Ellwoodii'. The needles are grayish blue-green and heavily speckled and dotted creamy white to white. Unfortunately, the foliage tends to turn brown in winter, which is not appreciated by many people.

It sometimes is sold as 'Ellwoodii Variegata', which is an illegitimate name for this plant. 'Ellwood's White' is one of the many cultivars that derived as a sport from the famous *C. lawsoniana* 'Ellwoodii', which was raised in the 1930s in Swanmore Park, Bishop's Waltham, United Kingdom. Zone 7a

Chamaecyparis lawsoniana 'Erecta Argenteovariegata'

A. Koster, Boskoop, The Netherlands, 1874

Discovered as a sport of *C. lawsoniana* 'Erecta Viridis', this old cultivar has the same columnar habit. The

Chamaecyparis lawsoniana 'Ellwood's Splashed' RONALD HOUTMAN

Chamaecyparis lawsoniana 'Erecta Argenteovariegata' J. R. P. VAN HOEY SMITH

Chamaecyparis lawsoniana 'Ellwood's White' J. R. P. VAN HOEY SMITH

branches grow conspicuously upright, almost fastigiate. The dark green foliage is densely covered with creamy white branchlets. This old cultivar is rare in the trade; however, it is still occasionally grown. Zone 6b

Chamaecyparis lawsoniana 'Fletcher's White' J. R. P. VAN HOEY SMITH

Chamaecyparis lawsoniana 'Fletcher's White'

P. den Ouden, Boskoop, The Netherlands, 1965

Upright conifer with some similarities to 'Ellwoodii' in general habit and texture. It will keep a rather narrow habit and become a conical large shrub, about 3 m high. The dense foliage is grayish green to slightly bluish, and the entire plant is heavily mottled creamy white. Contrary to many other variegated conifers, 'Fletcher's White' is a reasonably good grower and not very prone to sunburn, depending on the moisture of the soil and the location in which it is planted. Zone 7a

Chamaecyparis lawsoniana 'Gold Flake'

L. Konijn, Reeuwijk, The Netherlands, 1968

Although discovered as a sport in *C. lawsoniana* 'Ellwoodii', this cultivar lacks the typical juvenile foliage

Chamaecyparis lawsoniana 'Gold Flake' RONALD HOUTMAN

Chamaecyparis lawsoniana 'Goldregen' J. R. P. VAN HOEY SMITH

of 'Ellwoodii'. 'Gold Flake' is an upright conifer with a broad conical habit. The foliage is bluish green with large spots of creamy yellow. Zone 6b

Chamaecyparis lawsoniana 'Goldregen'

Germany

Rather slender, upright conifer with an open habit, similar to the well-known 'Intertexta'. The dull green foliage is attractively variegated yellow. Due to the very regular variegation, the general appearance of 'Goldregen' is rather more yellow than variegated. Zone 6b

Chamaecyparis lawsoniana 'Handcross Park'

Compact, dome-shaped conifer with a dense habit. The dark green foliage has remarkably uniform yellow variegation. It is not very prone to sunburn and is perfect for planting in smaller gardens. According to literature, this is the correct name for both *C. lawsoniana* 'Nana Aureovariegata', an illegitimate name dating from 1988, and *C. lawsoniana* 'Nymans'.

Chamaecyparis lawsoniana 'Handcross Park' RONALD HOUTMAN

Chamaecyparis lawsoniana 'Konijn's Silver'

L. Konijn, Reeuwijk, The Netherlands

Upright conifer with an irregular conical habit. Young plants are broadly dome shaped, but become more open and irregular as they age. The foliage is dull green to bluish green and heavily variegated white to creamy white. When planted in a location that suits the irregular habit, it can be quite useful. Otherwise the habit leaves much to be desired. Zone 6b

Chamaecyparis lawsoniana 'Konijn's Silver' RONALD HOUTMAN

Chamaecyparis lawsoniana 'Minima Argenteovariegata'

Germany, 1900

Compact and dense bushy conifer with an almost spherical habit, eventually with an obtuse top. The foliage is medium green to slightly bluish green and irregularly splashed creamy white. Although it was originally raised in 1900, over the years several variegated sports, derived from *C. lawsoniana* 'Minima', have been recorded. These are all very similar. All clones that go as 'Minima Argenteovariegata' are highly unstable and easily revert to green. It is very likely that the original named clone is no longer in cultivation. Zone 6b

Chamaecyparis lawsoniana 'President Roosevelt' KLAAS VERBOOM

Chamaecyparis lawsoniana 'Pygmaea Argentea' RONALD HOUTMAN

Chamaecyparis lawsoniana 'President Roosevelt'

J. Hogger, East Grinstead, United Kingdom, 1945

Loosely branched upright conifer with a nice broad columnar habit. The spreading branches have spreading and decumbent tips, which give this plant an attractive structure. The foliage is light green and heavily spotted yellow. 'President Roosevelt' is one of the better variegated cultivars of *C. lawsoniana*. It is still in cultivation, although not widely grown. Zone 6b

Chamaecyparis lawsoniana 'Pygmaea Argentea'

J. Backhouse & Son, York, United Kingdom, 1907

Relatively small conifer with a very dense and broad dome-shaped habit. The young growth is very light cream colored to creamy yellow. During summer this fades to light green, eventually turning bluish green. Although not truly variegated (according to the definition in this book), the general appearance of 'Pyg-

Chamaecyparis lawsoniana 'Schneeball' J. R. P. VAN HOEY SMITH

maea Argentea' is variegated, and for that reason it is mentioned here. This cultivar is also offered under its synonym 'Backhouse Silver'. Zone 6b

Chamaecyparis lawsoniana 'Schneeball'

Barabits Nurseries, Sopron, Hungary, 1982

Densely branched conifer with a flattened globular habit, similar to *C. lawsoniana* 'Barabits Globe' (also known under its illegitimate name 'Mini Globus'). The spreading foliage is green and heavily variegated white. It is best planted in a semi-shaded location. In full sun the light parts of the foliage will easily burn during warm and sunny spells. Zone 6b

Chamaecyparis lawsoniana 'Silver Threads'

K. Lawrence, Tilford, United Kingdom, 1974

Discovered as a sport of *C. lawsoniana* 'Ellwood's Gold', 'Silver Threads' has the same narrow conical habit. In time it will become a small tree about 3 m high. The foliage is bluish green and nicely variegated silvery white. 'Silver Threads' is an attractive variegated conifer that is grown in large quantities to be sold as a container plant. However, large specimens are rare. Zone 6b

Chamaecyparis lawsoniana 'Silver Tip'

J. Konijn & Son, Ederveen, The Netherlands, 1968

Another densely branched conifer with a broad conical habit. Young plants are more globular, but in time they grow more upright. The foliage is bluish green, variegated cream. The name is sometimes misspelled as 'Silver Tips'. Zone 6b

Chamaecyparis lawsoniana 'Silver Threads' RONALD HOUTMAN

Chamaecyparis lawsoniana 'Silver Tip' RONALD HOUTMAN

Chamaecyparis lawsoniana 'Summer Snow' RONALD HOUTMAN

Chamaecyparis lawsoniana 'Treasure' RONALD HOUTMAN

Chamaecyparis lawsoniana 'Versicolor' J. R. P. VAN HOEY SMITH

Chamaecyparis lawsoniana 'Versicolor' J. R. P. VAN HOEY SMITH

Chamaecyparis lawsoniana 'Summer Snow'

Harraway Nurseries, Warminster, United Kingdom, 1965

Loosely branched conifer with an irregular broad spreading to broad, upright habit. Young shoots are creamy white to creamy yellow, later fading to green. Like *C. lawsoniana* 'Pygmaea Argentea', this is not a truly variegated plant, but considering its general appearance it is mentioned here. This cultivar must not be confused with *C. pisifera* 'Snow', sometimes referred to as 'Summersnow', which is totally different from *C. lawsoniana* 'Summer Snow': as it has a dense, broad, columnar, upright habit and the typical foliage of *C. pisifera*. Zone 6b

Chamaecyparis lawsoniana 'Whitewater' RONALD HOUTMAN

Chamaecyparis lawsoniana 'Treasure'

Floravista Gardens, Vancouver, British Columbia, Canada, 1980

Another variegated conifer discovered as a sport in 'Ellwoodii'. 'Treasure' has the same narrow, upright habit and typical juvenile foliage. The needles are bluish yellow-green with tufts of cream. Zone 6b

Chamaecyparis lawsoniana 'Versicolor'

J. Coninck, Tottenham Nurseries, Dedemsvaart, The Netherlands, 1882

Very attractive conifer with a pyramidal habit. The weeping branch tips add considerably to the general appearance of this plant. The foliage is dark green and regularly variegated creamy white. Despite the fact that it was raised more than 100 years ago, it is still not a common plant in nurseries and gardens. However, 'Versicolor' is one of the most beautiful variegated conifers and definitely deserves to be grown more widely. Zone 6b

Chamaecyparis lawsoniana 'Whitewater'

Whitewater Nursery & Plant Centre, Hook, United Kingdom, 2003

Upright plant with a pyramidal habit. Eventually it will grow more than 4 m in height and become narrower. It was raised as a seedling of *C. lawsoniana* 'Albovariegata'. The foliage is green, heavily variegated creamy yellow. On the north-facing side (in the shade) of the plant, the foliage is considerably more white variegated. At Whitewater Nursery, several slightly varying seedlings and descendants were planted. 'Whitewater' was named after it was judged to be the best of this batch. Zone 6b

Chamaecyparis lawsoniana 'Whitewater' RONALD HOUTMAN

Chamaecyparis nootkatensis 'Aureovariegata' KLAAS VERBOOM

Chamaecyparis nootkatensis 'Laura Aurora' KLAAS VERBOOM

Chamaecyparis nootkatensis

After study of a recently discovered Vietnamese conifer (*Xanthocyparis vietnamensis*) it became clear that the plant known as *Chamaecyparis nootkatensis* needs to be reclassified. Researchers doubted the relationship of this species with the other *Chamaecyparis* species for a long time. With the discovery of *Xanthocyparis vietnamensis* it became clear *Chamaecyparis nootkatensis* is closely related to it. Therefore, it is highly likely the name for this well-known conifer will be changed into *Xanthocyparis nootkatensis* (see also under ×*Cupressocyparis*).

Chamaecyparis nootkatensis 'Aureovariegata'

M. Young, Milford, United Kingdom, before 1872

Upright, medium-sized tree with an open, broad conical habit. As a young plant the habit is quite neat, but it needs regular pruning to maintain a good shape. The foliage is clear green with patches of yellow, especially in the young growth. This old cultivar is still in cultivation. Zone 5b

Chamaecyparis nootkatensis 'Laura Aurora'

This cultivar is very similar to 'Aureovariegata' in habit and foliage texture. However, the variegation in the foliage is much more yellow. Although it also tends to get an open habit with age, it stays more dense. 'Laura Aurora' is recommended over 'Aureovariegata' as the foliage colors and the habit are better. Zone 5b

Chamaecyparis nootkatensis 'Variegata'

K. Koch, Germany, 1873

Like the species, this cultivar has a broad conical habit. The foliage is dull green and densely covered with white to creamy white patches. Due to the variegation the texture of the foliage looks more delicate than in the species. 'Variegata' is also known under its synonym 'Argenteovariegata'. Zone 5b

Chamaecyparis obtusa 'Alaska'

K. A. Koemans, Boskoop, The Netherlands, 1992

Relatively low-growing conifer with a capricious habit. The thin filiform branches are dark green, variegated yellow to cream. 'Alaska' is an attractive cultivar that is excellent for the use in small gardens (like many other *C. obtusa* cultivars). It was imported to The Netherlands as 'Mariesii', but proven to be a different culti-

Chamaecyparis obtusa 'Alaska' J. R. P. VAN HOEY SMITH

Chamaecyparis obtusa 'Albovariegata' J. R. P. VAN HOEY SMITH

var. 'Alaska' is stronger and its habit is more irregular. Zone 6b

Chamaecyparis obtusa 'Albovariegata'

Beissner, Germany, 1884

Upright tree with a broad conical habit. The foliage is dark yellowish green and heavily variegated white. Old foliage is much less variegated. This cultivar is very rare or has even completely disappeared from cultivation. Some authorities claim it is a synonym with 'Argentea', a cultivar imported from Japan by Robert Fortune in 1860. 'Argentea' is very similar, but it is more vigorous than 'Albovariegata'. Zone 6b

Chamaecyparis obtusa 'Aureovariegata'

Upright cultivar of unknown origin. It becomes a medium-sized shrub with a relatively open habit, similar to the yellow-leaved 'Crippsii'. The foliage of 'Aureovariegata' is dark green with large pale yellow splashes, irregularly spread over the plant.

Chamaecyparis nootkatensis 'Variegata' RONALD HOUTMAN

The name 'Aureovariegata' is illegitimate. It has never been published properly, and any publications after January 1, 1959, are illegitimate. Also, Latinized cultivar names are no longer permitted. According to some literature 'Aureovariegata' is a synonym of *C. obtusa* 'Opaal'. However, 'Opaal' is not a variegated cultivar. 'Aureovariegata' is similar to *C. obtusa* 'Nana Gracilis' in habit and foliage structure, but the young foliage is yellow and the older foliage is light yellowish green. 'Aureovariegata' is either very rare or has completely disappeared from cultivation. Thus, there is no purpose in renaming the cultivar, except as a matter of taxonomical correctness. Zone 6b

Chamaecyparis obtusa 'Mariesii' RONALD HOUTMAN

Chamaecyparis obtusa 'Mariesii'

Kent, United Kingdom, 1900

Broad, upright conifer with a dense habit. Eventually it will grow into a small tree about 3 m high and wide. The foliage is very heavily variegated creamy white and pale yellow. Its foliage is less filiform than in 'Alaska'. This old cultivar is perhaps the best-known variegated cultivar of *C. obtusa*. It must be protected from full sun because it burns easily. Zone 6b

Chamaecyparis obtusa 'Snowflake'

Drue Wholesale Nursery, Berry, Australia, 1989

Small conifer with a dense, very broad conical habit that consists of juvenile foliage only. It is dull green to slightly bluish green and sparsely covered with small creamy white spots like little snowflakes. 'Snowflake' originated as a sport in *C. obtusa* 'Chabo Yadori'. It is an attractive cultivar, but slightly unstable. Reverted

Chamaecyparis obtusa 'Snowflake' RONALD HOUTMAN

Chamaecyparis obtusa 'Snowkist' J. R. P. VAN HOEY SMITH

Chamaecyparis obtusa 'Tonia' FA. C. ESVELD

branches must be pruned back to keep 'Snowflake' variegated. Zone 6b

Chamaecyparis obtusa 'Snowkist'

Floravista Gardens, Vancouver, British Columbia, Canada, 1981

Discovered as a sport of *C. obtusa* 'Tonia', this cultivar has a dense, almost dwarfish flattened globular habit. The foliage texture is typical for many of the smaller cultivars of *C. obtusa*. Its color is yellowish green and the young growth is variegated yellow. It is not a truly variegated plant, according to the definition followed here, but only partially variegated. Zone 6b

Chamaecyparis obtusa 'Tonia'

Wm. Hage, Boskoop, The Netherlands, 1928

This is the variegated counterpart of 'Nana Gracilis' and was discovered as a sport of this best-known cultivar of *C. obtusa*. 'Tonia' forms an irregular, broad, upright shrub. This dramatic growing habit is one of the main advantages of many *C. obtusa* cultivars over other conifers for the smaller garden. The foliage is lustrous dark green with many yellowish branchlets. 'Tonia' has proven quite stable and can be regarded as one of the best variegated cultivars of *C. obtusa*. Zone 6b

Chamaecyparis pisifera 'Argenteovariegata'

Bagshot, United Kingdom, 1861

Medium-sized tree that grows to about 7 m high. It has an open, conical habit and dark green foliage with white branchlets intermixed throughout the entire plant. 'Argenteovariegata' was imported to the United Kingdom from Japan by Robert Fortune in 1861. Like the majority of the variegated conifers, it is not very common in cultivation. Zone 6a

Chamaecyparis pisifera 'Cloverleaf'

Broad, upright conifer with a pyramidal habit. Discovered as a sport of *C. pisifera* 'Boulevard', 'Cloverleaf' has the same feathery leaf structure. The silvery blue foliage is irregularly splashed creamy yellow to pale yellow. Like 'Boulevard', it is suitable for the use in small arrangements on balconies or terraces. Zone 6a

Chamaecyparis pisifera 'Filifera Aureovariegata'

Germany, 1891

Medium-sized shrub with a broad conical to pyramidal habit that grows to about 3 m high. The filiform

Chamaecyparis pisifera 'Argenteovariegata' J. R. P. VAN HOEY SMITH

Chamaecyparis pisifera 'Cloverleaf' RONALD HOUTMAN

Chamaecyparis pisifera 'Filifera Aureovariegata' RONALD HOUTMAN

Chamaecyparis pisifera 'Gold Dust' RONALD HOUTMAN

Chamaecyparis pisifera 'Nana Aureovariegata' RONALD HOUTMAN

Chamaecyparis pisifera 'Plumosa Albopicta' RONALD HOUTMAN

foliage is one of the main characteristics of this group of cultivars. The thin branchlets of 'Filifera Aureovariegata' are clear green and lively variegated light yellow. It is a handsome conifer that should be more widely grown and used. Zone 6a

Chamaecyparis pisifera 'Gold Dust'

Floravista Gardens, Vancouver, British Columbia, Canada, before 1991

Dwarf conifer with a dense and very compact, flattened globular habit. The fine needles are dull green, and the whole plant is sparsely covered with small yellow spots. It must be planted in semi-shade or full sun to maintain its variegated habit. When planted in a shaded location, the chances of reversion will increase. Some authorities claim 'Gold Dust' is a synonym to *C. pisifera* 'Plumosa Aurea', a cultivar with entirely greenish yellow foliage. However, 'Gold Dust' is a variegated cultivar with green and yellow foliage. Zone 6a

Chamaecyparis pisifera 'Nana Aureovariegata'

Hornibrook, United Kingdom, 1939

Another old cultivar with a dwarfish, flattened globular habit. The green foliage is creamy yellow variegated with a golden sheen on it. Zone 6a

Chamaecyparis pisifera 'Plumosa Albopicta'

Veitch/Nicholson, 1884

This broad, upright conifer with a bushy habit belongs to a distinct group of cultivars with semi-juvenile foliage, being an intermediate between the short, thick, and adpressed adult foliage and the feathery texture of

Chamaecyparis pisifera 'Plumosa Argentea' RONALD HOUTMAN

juvenile foliage. The needles are dark green, variegated white. The variegation is strongest in spring and early summer. 'Plumosa Albopicta' was imported from Japan by Veitch in 1884. Zone 6a

Chamaecyparis pisifera 'Plumosa Argentea'

Sénéclause Nurseries, Bourg Argental, France, 1868

This cultivar is very similar to 'Plumosa Albopicta' in general appearance and foliage texture. 'Plumosa Argentea' is almost indistinguishable from 'Plumosa Albopicta' but is slightly more variegated. It is also reported to be slightly more tender. Zone 6b

Chamaecyparis pisifera 'Silver and Gold'

Before 1984

A nice but unusual variegated cultivar with a broad conical habit. The habit remains bushy and it will not develop into a tree. The juvenile foliage is bronzy yellow with creamy white branchlets. 'Silver and Gold' is best planted in a semi-shaded location, because in full sun it will be prone to sunburn.

This cultivar was discovered as a sport in *C. pisifera* 'Plumosa Aurea'. The late Humphrey Welch (Wansdyke Nurseries, Devizes, United Kingdom) got it from an unknown source and in 1984 introduced it as 'Silver and Gold', an illegitimate name under the ICNCP. It is occasionally offered as 'Plumosa Silver and Gold', which is also an illegitimate name. Zone 6a

Chamaecyparis pisifera 'Silver Lode'

Floravista Gardens, Vancouver, British Columbia, Canada, 1985

Like 'Plumosa Albopicta' and 'Plumosa Argentea', this is a dense and compact conifer with a flattened globular habit. Eventually it will become a broad and flat plant. The foliage is green and variegated creamy white. Zone 6a

Chamaecyparis pisifera 'Squarrosa Argentea'

Japan, before 1847

Upright conifer with a broad conical habit and gracefully arching branches and branchlets. The foliage is green to bluish green, spotted white. Zone 6a

Chamaecyparis pisifera 'Squarrosa Intermedia Variegata'

Broad spreading to somewhat upright conifer with a flattened globular habit. This cultivar has an open

Chamaecyparis pisifera 'Silver Lode' RONALD HOUTMAN

Chamaecyparis pisifera 'Squarrosa Argentea' RONALD HOUTMAN

Chamaecyparis pisifera 'Squarrosa Intermedia Variegata' RONALD HOUTMAN

Chamaecyparis thyoides 'Variegata' RONALD HOUTMAN

Chamaecyparis thyoides 'Variegata' RONALD HOUTMAN

Cistus ×argenteus 'Nepond' GOLDEN TREASURE™ RONALD HOUTMAN

structure and elegant arching branches. The foliage is green and heavily variegated light yellow. The name 'Squarrosa Intermedia Variegata' cannot be traced, and it seems illegitimate. This plant is in cultivation and therefore it needs a proper and legitimate cultivar name. Zone 6a

Chamaecyparis thyoides 'Variegata'

Hodgins' Nursery, Dunganstown, Ireland, 1831

The only known variegated cultivar of *C. thyoides* is perhaps one of the most beautiful of all variegated conifers. With its upright growth it will develop into a large conical shrub with a rather open habit. The foliage is lustrous dark green and speckled clear yellow. This old cultivar is quite common in cultivation and can be used in large gardens as well as smaller gardens. It does not tend to revert and is not prone to sunburn. Zone 6b

Cistus 'Candy Stripe'

Lincolnshire, United Kingdom, about 1991

Compact slow-growing evergreen that will not exceed 1 m in height. The opposite leaves are dull green with striking, slightly irregular pale yellow margins. The flowers are delicately light pink with golden yellow anthers. They appear during late spring and early summer. As with many *Cistus* species and cultivars, the petals are slightly crinkled. 'Candy Stripe' originated as a sport from *Cistus* 'Grayswood Pink', a cultivar that is known for its hardiness and ease of cultivation. Zone 7

Cistus ×argenteus 'Nepond' GOLDEN TREASURE™

United Kingdom, 1994

Compact evergreen that grows to 1 m high or slightly more. The foliage is grayish green with irregular, golden yellow margins. 'Nepond' was found as a sport on *C.* 'Peggy Sammons' and has identical flowers. They are deep purplish pink with golden yellow anthers and contrast well against the variegated foliage. It also inherited the floriferous habit of 'Peggy Sammons'. Although slightly less hardy than *Cistus* 'Candy Stripe', 'Nepond' is still one of the more hardy *Cistus* cultivars. Zone 8a

Citrus aurantifolia 'Breegold'

D. Scholten, Boskoop, The Netherlands, 2002

Broad, upright, evergreen shrub. The foliage is glossy dark green with conspicuous, clear yellow margins.

The varying width of the colored margins gives 'Breegold' a very attractive and lively effect. Occasionally larger parts of the leaves are colored as well. The young shoots that are formed in late summer are distinctively colored dark purplish brown, which adds to the ornamental value of the plant. All parts of this lemon are fragrant when rubbed or crushed. 'Breegold' will flower with fragrant white flowers, but it will carry fruits only in the mildest climates. In these climates it can be grown outdoors, but in most northern European and U.S. areas it is not hardy enough and must be kept as a patio plant. 'Breegold' was found as a sport on *C. aurantifolia*, in a private garden in New Zealand. Zone 9

Citrus aurantifolia 'Breegold' RONALD HOUTMAN

Citrus 'Variegated Columbia 1970'

Evergreen shrub that grows to about 3 m high with a broad, upright habit. The elliptic leaves are lustrous green with yellow margins. All parts of the plant spread a pleasant fragrance when rubbed or crushed. Like most *Citrus* cultivars, the fragrant flowers are white. In warm climates they will be followed by variegated fruits. Zone 9

Citrus 'Variegated Columbia 1970' RONALD HOUTMAN

Clerodendrum bungei 'Pink Diamond'

Eijkenboom Nursery, Kaulille, Belgium, 1994

Of only two winter-hardy *Clerodendrum* species, *C. bungei* usually behaves as a perennial or subshrub. Only in mild climates it will grow as a shrub. All parts of this suckering plant spread a typical fragrance, faintly resembling peanut butter. This fragrance is even stronger in the other species, *C. trichotomum*. The opposite leaves are grayish green, with irregular light gray and white margins. The flowerheads, which can grow up to about 12 cm in diameter, appear in late summer. In August and September the purplish pink flowers open and add to the playful effect of this nice plant. Zone 7

Clerodendrum bungei 'Pink Diamond' RONALD HOUTMAN

Clerodendrum trichotomum 'Carnival'

United Kingdom, before 1996

Handsome shrub with a broad, upright habit. The leaves are broad ovate and up to 20 cm long. They are medium green with broad, irregular yellow margins. Occasionally there are some lighter green to yellowish green blotches in the leaves. All parts of the plant spread a typical and strong fragrance, which is not

Clerodendrum trichotomum 'Carnival' RONALD HOUTMAN

Clethra alnifolia 'Creel's Calico' GERT FORTGENS

Cleyera japonica 'Tricolor' RONALD HOUTMAN

appreciated by all people. The flowers open in broad cymes during late summer. The individual flowers are creamy white with light pinkish red calyces. 'Carnival', sometimes offered as 'Harlequin' or 'Variegatum', is an attractive variegated shrub. It was named only a few years ago, but hopefully will soon be more widely available. Zone 7a

Clethra alnifolia 'Creel's Calico'

Very unusual deciduous shrub with a dense and fairly upright habit at first, later becoming wider. The foliage has the same shape as the species, obovate to oblong and up to 10 cm long. The leaves are densely speckled and dotted creamy white to greenish white. The flowers are borne in racemes up to 15 cm long in late summer. They are creamy white and spread a sweet fragrance. The variegation is very unusual and curious. Zone 4

Cleyera japonica 'Tricolor'

Japan, before 1860

Small to medium-sized evergreen shrub with a rounded habit that grows to 2 m high and wide. The leaves are thick and leathery. When unfolding they are tinted pinkish red, later becoming dark green with broad creamy white margins. The bisexual flowers are pale yellow and rather inconspicuous. 'Tricolor' was first introduced into Europe by Robert Fortune, who imported it from Japan around 1860. Although it is not very hardy this plant should be more widely grown. In milder areas it can make an excellent bushy shrub. In colder areas 'Tricolor' can be used as a container plant on terraces or balconies. *Cleyera japonica* 'Tricolor' is sometimes grown under its synonym 'Variegata'. Zone 8

Coprosma

A genus of about ninety species of small trees and shrubs found in New Zealand, Australia, Tasmania, Indonesia, and the Pacific Islands, including Hawaii. All coprosmas are evergreen and carry dioecious flowers. They usually have rather thick and leathery leaves. Many species are noted for their attractive berrylike fruits, which, of course, only develop when male and female specimens are planted. In practice usually only one clone is planted, so no fruits will appear.

All variegated cultivars described here originate from New Zealand species. The approximately forty-five New Zealand species are, except for one, endemic. Some of them are referred to as mirror plant, because of the exceptionally glossy foliage. One of the advantages of *Coprosma* versus similar variegated plants is that they are very healthy and only rarely affected by pests or diseases. Another advantage of *Coprosma* is its salt and wind resistance. Most species grow in coastal areas and the cultivars derived from these species are also suitable for seaside planting.

More than twenty variegated cultivars of *Coprosma* are known. Some of these are described only briefly here. In most areas they will not be winter-hardy enough. Therefore it is not always possible to plant a *Coprosma* in the garden. However, because of the attractive colored and, in many cases, glossy foliage, they make outstanding container plants. Unless otherwise stated, all cultivars of *Coprosma* described here are hardy to zone 9.

Coprosma 'Beatson's Gold' RONALD HOUTMAN

Coprosma 'Beatson's Gold'

Beatson, Glenfield, New Zealand, before 1973

Dense shrub with a spreading habit that grows to 2 m high, but less when grown as a container plant. The spreading branches hold many small leaves that are dark green to olive green with a yellow variegation along the midrib. This variegation normally covers about two-thirds of the leaf blade. Sometimes the main vein is reddish, giving the foliage an extra effect. 'Beatson's Gold' is an attractive bushy shrub that endures pruning very well. Therefore, it can be used even in places with little room. For the best leaf coloring it must be grown in full sun. When planted in semi-shade the color will fade and the effect can be disappointing. One of the parents of this hybrid is most likely *Coprosma areolata*. Zone 8

Coprosma 'Evening Glow' RONALD HOUTMAN

Coprosma 'Evening Glow'

P. J. Fraser, Kihikihi, New Zealand, 1995

Striking evergreen with a broad, upright habit that grows to about 80 cm high. The leaves are ovate to obovate and about 3 cm long. They are very glossy and spectacularly colored green with irregular golden yellow spots and stripes. In autumn the yellow changes to orange-red to dark red. The best foliage coloring will be achieved when planted in full sun. Flowers rarely appear at a young age and are inconspicuous. 'Evening Glow' was found as a sport in *Coprosma* 'Pride', an older variegated *Coprosma*. To keep a compact plant and prevent it from becoming leggy, it is best pruned every three years.

Coprosma ×kirkii 'Kirkii Variegata' RONALD HOUTMAN

Coprosma 'Rainbow Surprise' RONALD HOUTMAN

Coprosma repens 'Exotica' RONALD HOUTMAN

Coprosma ×kirkii 'Kirkii Variegata'

New Zealand

Compact-growing shrub with a prostrate habit that will not grow more than 1 m high, but usually much wider. The leaves are oblong to nearly lanceolate and up to 3.5 cm long and 1.5 cm wide. They are leathery and glossy on both surfaces. The grayish green leaves have creamy white margins. *Coprosma ×kirkii* 'Kirkii Variegata' is widely grown and noted for its groundcover habits. In milder areas it is excellent in borders and along paths. Otherwise it is only suitable as a container plant.

Coprosma 'Kiwi Gold'

New Zealand, before 1994

Low and spreading evergreen that grows to only 50 cm high and more than 1.75 m wide. The leaves are small, about 2.5 cm long, and attractively variegated golden yellow and lime green. The variegated effect is strongly intensified by the clear yellow branches. In milder areas 'Kiwi Gold' is an excellent groundcover shrub with striking variegated foliage. Its parentage is uncertain, but *C. prostrata* appears to be one of the parents.

Coprosma 'Kiwi Silver'

New Zealand

Green and silvery white variegated, sometimes with a touch of pink.

Coprosma 'Pride'

New Zealand, before 1994

Very glossy coppery green foliage with yellow splashes, changing to orange in autumn and winter.

Coprosma 'Rainbow Surprise'

R. G. Ware, Napier, New Zealand, 1995

Compact evergreen with a broad spreading bushy habit that grows to about 60 cm high. The ovate-shaped leaves are small and have wavy margins. The leaves are dark green with relatively broad pale yellow margins. On older leaves these margins turn orange-red. In autumn the leaf color changes to dark orange-red to red with green. 'Rainbow Surprise' was found as a sport in C. 'Brunette'.

Coprosma repens 'Argentea'
New Zealand
The foliage has silvery white spots, blotches, and edges.

Coprosma repens 'Exotica'
New Zealand
Creamy white to golden yellow leaves with irregular deep green margins.

Coprosma repens 'Goldsplash'
Graeme Platt, Albany, New Zealand
Good golden yellow variegated leaves, very stable. Improvement of *C. repens* 'Variegata'. Sometimes offered under the synonym 'Taupata Gold'.

Coprosma repens 'Marble King'
New Zealand
Dark green leaves spotted lime green to yellowish.

Coprosma repens 'Marble Queen'
New Zealand
The attractive rounded leaves have irregular creamy white margins and a deep green central zone.

Coprosma repens 'Marginata'
New Zealand
Dark green foliage edged yellowish white.

Coprosma repens 'Painter's Palette'
New Zealand
Glossy dark green leaves have irregular yellow to golden yellow margins, changing bronzy orange to deep orange-red in autumn and winter.

Coprosma repens 'Picturata'
New Zealand
Glossy deep green leaves with irregularly shaped pale yellow to yellowish green central zones.

Coprosma repens 'Pink Splendour'
New Zealand
Glossy deep green leaves with creamy yellow to yellow margins. The leaves are washed pink, which intensifies during autumn and winter. 'Pink Splendour' is a very striking plant.

Coprosma repens 'Exotica' RONALD HOUTMAN

Coprosma repens 'Goldsplash' DAN HEIMS

Coprosma repens 'Marble Queen' RONALD HOUTMAN

Coprosma repens 'Picturata' RONALD HOUTMAN

Coprosma repens 'Variegata' RONALD HOUTMAN

Coprosma repens 'Silver Queen'

New Zealand

Very similar to *C. repens* 'Variegata', but appears to have branches that are slightly more arching.

Coprosma repens 'Variegata'

United Kingdom, 1866

Handsome evergreen with a spreading habit at first, later more upright. It can reach a height of about 1.5 m. The dark green and very glossy leaves are tough and leathery, broad ovate to broad oblong, and up to 9 cm long and 7 cm wide. Each leaf has a creamy yellow to yellow margin. This attractive shrub is suitable for planting in beds (groundcover) but can also be trimmed against a wall or a fence. This is one of the oldest *Coprosma* cultivars. It has a strong tendency to revert and is surpassed by other golden-variegated cultivars such as 'Goldsplash', which is more stable and has a slightly more upright habit.

Coprosma robusta 'Variegata'

New Zealand

Deep green leaves striped golden yellow in the centers.

Coprosma robusta 'Williamsii Variegata'

New Zealand

Graceful shrub with arching, almost pendulous branches. The leaves have irregular creamy white margins, whereas the central zone is dark green with lighter green and grayish blotches.

Cornus

This genus consists of about forty-five species, growing mainly in temperate regions of the Northern Hemisphere. *Cornus* is divided into nine subgenera, based on inflorescence and flower form. This explains the diversity in the various *Cornus* species. Apart from a few species, all *Cornus* have opposite leaves that hang together with xylem-thickenings when torn. A similar effect can be seen in *Eucommia ulmoides*, which is not a relative of *Cornus*.

Many cultivars of *Cornus* are variegated. Almost all species have variegated cultivars, and they usually prove quite stable. Some of these variegated *Cornus* cultivars, such as *C. alba* 'Elegantissima' and various *C. florida* cultivars, are well known and widely used. Another, *C. controversa* 'Variegata', is according to many people the most beautiful of all variegated plants.

Cornus alba

Broad, upright shrubs that will attain a height of about 2.5 to 3 m. They usually form well-branched bushes with green leaves and attractive reddish brown twigs. Several cultivars have been selected for their attractive stem color, of which *C. alba* 'Sibirica' is the best known. The flowers are inconspicuous and cream colored.

Variegated cultivars of *Cornus alba* WOUT KROMHOUT

They are followed by white, berrylike fruits. In some cultivars, for instance 'Siberian Pearls', the fruits are one of the main features.

Cornus alba has both white and yellow variegated cultivars. Most of these cultivars have colored margins, whereas the central zones are deep green or have layers of grayish, whitish, or yellowish green. Although most cultivars tend to revert to green or entirely yellow (or white), there are some newer, more stable cultivars available. Their dense but broad habit, together with the colorful foliage in summer and attractive stem colors in winter, make the variegated *C. alba* cultivars excellent landscape or amenity plants.

Cornus alba 'Bailhalo' IVORY HALO™

Bailey Nurseries, St. Paul, Minnesota, United States, before 1992

Densely branched, medium-sized shrub that grows to about 1.8 m high and wide. It has a good rounded

Cornus alba 'Bailhalo' IVORY HALO™ WOUT KROMHOUT

Cornus alba 'Cream Cracker' RONALD HOUTMAN

Cornus alba 'Gouchaultii' RONALD HOUTMAN

habit, the main difference with *C. alba* 'Elegantissima', of which 'Bailhalo' derived as a sport. The leaves, which feel somewhat papery, are light green with creamy white margins. In winter the branches are reddish brown and quite attractive. 'Bailhalo' is a more recent introduction that does not revert easily and can be considered as an improvement of the old, but still valued, 'Elegantissima'. Zone 3b

Cornus alba 'Cream Cracker'

Pannebakker & Co, Hazerswoude, The Netherlands, 1991

Medium-sized shrub with a broad rounded-upright habit that grows to 2 m high. It originated as a sport of *C. alba* 'Gouchaultii' and differs from it in foliage color. The leaves have irregular pale yellow to cream margins. They are significantly less yellow than in 'Gouchaultii', although not as white as in 'Elegantissima'. The young shoots are tinged pink, a feature inherited from 'Gouchaultii'. The branches are colored dark purplish red in winter. The foliage does not tend to revert to green or entirely yellow, as often occurs in 'Gouchaultii'. It is therefore a good substitute for the less-stable 'Gouchaultii' and a good addition in the range of variegated *C. alba* cultivars. 'Cream Cracker' was given an Award of Merit by the Royal Boskoop Horticultural Society in 1999. Zone 3b

Cornus alba 'Elegantissima'

Before 1880

Large shrub that grows to 3 m high with a broad, upright habit, eventually forming a large bush. The branches are dark reddish brown and attractive, although not as striking as *C. alba* 'Sibirica'. The foliage has broad white margins and stripes. The variegation is conspicuous, but rather irregular and sometimes the plant tends to revert to green (or entirely white leaves). Although 'Elegantissima' is slightly easier to propagate, *C. alba* 'Sibirica Variegata' is preferable to this old and well-known cultivar. Zone 3b

Cornus alba 'Gouchaultii'

A. Gouchault, Orléans, France, 1888

Broad, upright shrub with the same habit as 'Elegantissima'. Its dull green leaves have broad golden yellow margins and a conspicuous pink tinge when young. This gives quite a stunning effect. 'Gouchaultii' is a striking cultivar, but also unstable. There was no alter-

Cornus alba 'Elegantissima' RONALD HOUTMAN

Cornus alba 'Elegantissima' RONALD HOUTMAN

Cornus alba 'Sibirica Variegata' RONALD HOUTMAN

Cornus alba 'Spaethii' RONALD HOUTMAN

native for a long time, but it is now surpassed by 'Cream Cracker'. 'Gouchaultii' is similar to *C. alba* 'Spaethii', but the latter differs in having shinier green foliage. Zone 3b

Cornus alba 'Sibirica Variegata'

C. de Vos, Hazerswoude, The Netherlands, before 1867

Broad, upright shrub that grows to 2 m high with red branches in winter. Most striking is its foliage. The leaves are shiny dark green with very conspicuous, irregular silvery white margins. 'Sibirica Variegata' is somewhat similar to 'Elegantissima', but differs in more contrasting and stable foliage colors, wider leaves, and a denser habit. Therefore, 'Sibirica Variegata' is preferable to 'Elegantissima'. It also has proven to be even more hardy than other *C. alba* cultivars and can be used in areas with extreme, cold winters. Zone 3a

Cornus alba 'Spaethii'

Späth Nurseries, Berlin, Germany, 1884

Broad, upright shrub, similar to 'Gouchaultii' in height and habit. It differs in having shiny green leaf centers, whereas 'Gouchaultii' has dull green leaf centers. 'Spaethii' arose as a sport on a graft of a silver variegated form of *C. alba*. The scion died and a yellow variegated branch, later named 'Spaethii', was formed on the spot where scion and stem grew together. Like 'Gouchaultii', it is not entirely stable, therefore newer cultivars (such as 'Cream Cracker') are recommended instead of 'Spaethii'. Zone 3b

Cornus alternifolia 'Argentea'

Temple & Beard, United States, before 1900

Medium-sized shrub that grows to 3 m high (rarely taller), with a striking habit. The branches are horizontal on the main stem, giving the plant a neat appearance. The leaves are up to 9 cm long and dark green, with creamy white edges. It is the combination of leaf color and habit that makes this plant a striking one. When used in the right location, it can be highly effective as contrast against a darker background. The related *C. controversa* 'Variegata' looks similar in overall habit and color but is larger in all its features. In addition, *C. alternifolia* has pruinose young branches, which do not occur in *C. controversa*. Although 'Argentea' is hardy enough in most temperate regions, I recommend protecting young plants during frost periods. Zone 5b

Cornus capitata 'Ragdoll'

Cornus capitata is a large shrub to medium-sized evergreen tree that is closely related to *C. kousa* and the rare *C. honkongensis*. In its natural habitat (Nepal and southwestern China), it can reach a height of about 15 m. In cultivation, it is usually more shrubby and will stay much lower. The flowerheads are surrounded by four bracts of sulfur-yellow, an extraordinary color for a *Cornus*. The flowers appear in midsummer and are followed by red, strawberry-like fruits. 'Ragdoll' is a rare cultivar with dark green foliage with clear yellow margins. The colors are somewhat dull during winter, but in spring and summer it is absolutely fabulous. Zone 8

Cornus controversa 'Variegata'

James Veitch & Sons, London, United Kingdom, before 1890

This is probably the most beautiful variegated plant of all! It is a small to medium-sized tree that grows to 8 m high with a regular, broad triangular habit. As in *C. alternifolia* 'Argentea', the branches are sweeping and tabulated. The leaves have good silver margins and add very much to the overall striking effect of this plant.

Cornus controversa 'Variegata' most likely originated in Japan and was first imported as "fuiri-mizu-ki". In Europe there are several, only slightly different, clones that are known as 'Variegata'. One of these is a clone brought into the trade by Barbier in the late nineteenth century. Another clone, 'Marginata Nord', was put on the market from northern Italy; it is more vigorous

Cornus alternifolia 'Argentea' RONALD HOUTMAN

Cornus controversa 'Marginata Nord' RONALD HOUTMAN

Cornus capitata 'Ragdoll' RONALD HOUTMAN

Cornus controversa 'Variegata' GERT FORTGENS

Cornus controversa 'Variegata' WOUT KROMHOUT

than 'Variegata' and the leaves are larger. The cultivar name 'Marginata Nord' is illegitimate. It holds the Latin word *marginata*, which is not allowed according to the rules of the ICNCP. Zone 6b

Cornus florida

Broad, upright, medium-sized to large shrub that grows to 10 m high, but usually it does not reach more than about 6 m. The variegated cultivars normally grow to about 2 m high or slightly taller. In its native habitat, ranging from the eastern United States into northern Mexico, *Cornus florida* is common in open forests and along forest edges. The flowers consist of a flowerhead that is surrounded by (usually) four bracts. The flowers appear in early spring before the leaves unfold.

Although they are striking flowering shrubs, they are best used in the United States. In Europe the climatological circumstances are less suitable for these shrubs and they sometimes have proven to be difficult to establish. *Cornus florida* is highly susceptible to "cornus decline," a disease caused by a fungus named *Discula destructiva*. When plants are infected they usually first show leaf spots, but within one or a few years the entire plant can die. This should not discourage planting *C. florida* cultivars. They are first-class flowering shrubs with a great variety in leaf and flower color and also highly rated for their excellent autumn colors. Although perfectly hardy in most temperate regions, the flowers are sometimes damaged by late frosts.

Cornus florida 'Daybreak' CHEROKEE DAYBREAK™

Commercial Nursery Co. Ltd., Decherd, Tennessee, United States, before 1989

Handsome variegated cultivar with deep green leaves that have creamy white margins. In autumn the leaf color changes to a vivid pink to pinkish red. The flowers are white. This is one of the better variegated *C. florida* cultivars with healthy, rather vigorous growth. 'Daybreak' was given an Award of Recommendation by the Royal Boskoop Horticultural Society in 1993. Zone 6b

Cornus florida 'First Lady'

Boyd Nursery Co., Inc., McMinnville, Tennessee, United States, 1957

Upright shrub that is not only attractive in its variegation but perhaps even more in its autumn coloring. The leaves are brilliant deep to yellowish green with golden yellow to greenish yellow margins. The variegation is somewhat irregular—the yellow is sometimes suffused along the veins toward the center of the leaves. The white flowers are conspicuous but not richly produced. In autumn the foliage color changes to a wonderful play of colors in scarlet, chestnut-purple, pink, and yellowish green. Zone 6b

Cornus florida 'George Henry Ford'

Verkade's Nurseries, Waybe, New Jersey, United States, 1968

Rather fast-growing medium-sized shrub that grows to 3 m. The foliage is green with yellow variegation, strikingly colored orange-red to deep red in autumn. An advantage of this plant in comparison to most other *C. florida* cultivars is that 'George Henry Ford' is less sensitive to late frosts. It is sometimes offered as 'President Ford' or 'President Gerald H. Ford', which are synonyms. Zone 6b

Cornus florida 'Golden Nugget'

United States

Another cultivar with variegated leaf margins. Each leaf has a broad bronzy yellow to dark yellow margin. The flowers of 'Golden Nugget' are white. Zone 7a

Cornus florida 'Daybreak' CHEROKEE DAYBREAK™ PPH (COLLECTION OF HARRY VAN DE LAAR)

Cornus florida 'Daybreak' CHEROKEE DAYBREAK™ PPH (COLLECTION OF HARRY VAN DE LAAR)

Cornus florida 'George Henry Ford' PPH (COLLECTION OF HARRY VAN DE LAAR)

Cornus florida 'First Lady' RONALD HOUTMAN

Cornus florida 'Pink Flame' RONALD HOUTMAN

Cornus florida 'Rainbow' PPH (COLLECTION OF HARRY VAN DE LAAR)

Cornus florida 'Sunset' CHEROKEE SUNSET™ RONALD HOUTMAN

Cornus florida 'Junior Miss Variegated'

Yuzo Masuda, Japan, before 1998

Medium-sized shrub with a broad, upright habit that grows to 3 m. The very attractive foliage is speckled and striped with cream, white, and yellow. Especially on the young foliage there are flushes of pink. 'Junior Miss Variegated', which originated as a sport of 'Junior Miss', is most similar to 'Welchii', but is slightly more vigorous. The bracts of the rather large flowers are deep pink in the centers, lightening toward the edges. Zone 6b

Cornus florida 'Pink Flame'

Another cultivar whose leaves have creamy white margins. The major difference between 'Pink Flame' and the other cultivars described here is that the emerging foliage is deep pinkish red, a wonderful contrast against the variegated leaves. In autumn the leaves become dark red to deep reddish purple. Zone 6b

Cornus florida 'Rainbow'

F. Schmidt & Son, Boring, Oregon, United States, 1968

Another yellow-variegated cultivar with a broad, upright habit, but a more compact growth up to about 2.5 m. The leaves are dark green with dark golden yellow variegation. Especially during autumn, the foliage colors can be very striking. It starts with parts of dark orange to bright red, later becoming dark red to reddish purple. The yellow parts of the leaves start coloring first, and the green stays visible during autumn. 'Rainbow' is one of the most attractive variegated *Cornus* cultivars, with a well-chosen name. Zone 6b

Cornus florida 'Sunset' CHEROKEE SUNSET™

Commercial Nursery Co. Ltd., Decherd, Tennessee, United States, 1987

Splendid variegated *C. kousa* that does not only attract with its colorful foliage, but also with purplish red flowers. The foliage has striking yellow variegation and gives good autumn colors, but it is not significantly different from similar cultivars such as 'George Henry Ford' and 'Rainbow'. An advantage of 'Sunset' in comparison with some other cultivars is that the foliage does not tend to burn during hot spells in summer. The main difference is in the color of the flowers. The bracts of 'Sunset' are a splendid purplish red, although it is not very floriferous at a young age. 'Sunset' was given an Award of Recommendation by the Royal Boskoop Horticultural Society in 1993. Zone 6b

Cornus florida 'Welchii'

Cole Nursery, Painesville, Ohio, United States, 1937

Although 'Welchii' is not very different from other *C. florida* cultivars in habit and growth, it is easily distinguished by its white variegated foliage. The leaves are irregularly mottled cream to white with flushes of pink. The flowers are white. 'Welchii' can be quite an elegant variegated plant, but the leaves are often deformed, which is an unattractive sight. It is most similar to 'Junior Miss Variegated', but the latter is slightly more vigorous. Because of the deformed leaves of 'Welchii', 'Junior Miss Variegated' is a preferable cultivar. 'Welchii' is occasionally found under its synonym 'Tricolor'. Zone 6b

Cornus kousa

This native of Japan, Korea, and China is closely related to the subtropical *C. capitata* and *C. hongkongensis*. It is a large shrub to small tree that grows to 9 m high, narrow, upright when young, later becoming very broad with elegantly arching branches. The dark green leaves are broad elliptic and up to 10 cm long, usually with slightly wavy margins. The leaf colors change to red then dark purplish red during autumn. The flowers consist of a globular flowerhead with four white to almost red bracts.

Contrary to *C. florida* and its cultivars, *C. kousa* is not susceptible to "cornus decline" (see *C. florida*). In addition it is more adaptive to moist soil conditions and cool weather. For these reasons *C. kousa* is recommended instead of *C. florida*, especially in western Europe, although *C. florida* and its cultivars are generally more attractive. More than seventy cultivars of *C. kousa* are known, but only a few have variegated foliage.

Cornus kousa 'Bonfire'

Large shrub with a broad, upright habit. The leaves are grayish green with conspicuous golden yellow margins. The young growth is purplish, as are the twigs, which contrast well against the foliage. 'Bonfire' is generally regarded as one of the best golden-variegated *C. kousa* cultivars on the market. Zone 6b

Cornus florida 'Welchii' CHRIS SANDERS

Cornus kousa 'Bonfire' RONALD HOUTMAN

Cornus kousa 'Bultinck's Beauty' RONALD HOUTMAN

Cornus kousa 'Bultinck's Beauty'

Antoine Bultinck, Vliersele, Belgium, 1993

Broad, upright, large shrub with conspicuous purplish young twigs. The leaves are dark green and irregularly

Cornus kousa 'Gold Star' PPH (COLLECTION OF HARRY VAN DE LAAR)

Cornus kousa 'Pevé Limbo' RONALD HOUTMAN

marbled and blotched white. The variegation is at its strongest in the young foliage of the second growth, but in spring it is already spectacular. Older foliage tends to become entirely green, however, some variegation will be present in these leaves, too. The variegated leaves go well with the colored twigs. 'Bultinck's Beauty' was raised as a seedling of *C. kousa*. In this batch several plants were variegated, but 'Bultinck's Beauty' proved to be the best. Zone 6b

Cornus kousa 'Gold Star'

Sakata Nursery Co., Yokohama, Japan, about 1977

Vigorous, upright, large shrub that immediately attracts with its golden variegated foliage. The leaves are dark green with an irregularly shaped, relatively large, golden yellow central blotch. 'Gold Star' is a healthy and floriferous plant resembling the species in most features (except for the foliage, of course). 'Gold Star' thrives best in full sun and, although it is an excellent shrub, it tends to revert to green. Therefore, branches with entirely green leaves must be removed at an early stage. Zone 6b

Cornus kousa 'Pevé Limbo'

Piet Vergeldt, Lottum, The Netherlands, 2001

This vigorous cultivar resembles *C. kousa* 'Samzam' and 'Wolf Eyes' in some respects. It differs in being larger in all parts. The leaves can grow almost twice as large as in 'Samzam', for example. The leaves are deep grayish green with irregular creamy white, very wavy margins. In spring the margins are distinctively more yellowish cream than in 'Samzam' and 'Wolf Eyes'. 'Pevé Limbo' was discovered as a sport in *C. kousa* var. *chinensis*. Zone 6b

Cornus kousa 'Samzam' SAMARITAN™

Lake County Nursery, Inc., Lake County, Ohio, United States, before 1998

Broad, upright shrub that grows to 2.5 m high with a dense habit. 'Samzam' was discovered as a sport of *C. kousa* 'Milky Way'. It has grayish green leaves with creamy white margins. The leaf margins are conspicuously wavy, adding a lot to the elegance of this shrub. Like 'Snowboy', I recommend planting 'Samzam' in a semi-shaded location—not because it tends to burn, but in full sun leaf curl sometimes occurs. 'Samzam' is not very floriferous. The bracts are creamy white with pale greenish white margins. Both 'Samzam' and 'Wolf Eyes' are quite similar to 'Snowboy', but easier to grow and therefore recommended. 'Samzam' was given an Award of Recommendation by the Royal Boskoop Horticultural Society in 2001. Zone 6b

Cornus kousa 'Snowboy'

Sakata Nursery Co., Yokohama, Japan, about 1977

Very attractive upright, large shrub that grows to 3 m high. Due to its well-branched habit, 'Snowboy' has a compact appearance. The foliage is grayish green with striking silvery white margins. Occasionally the white parts are broader, leaving only a narrow central band of green on the leaf. The bracts (underneath the flowerheads) are whitish with pale greenish white margins.

It is a pity this first-class shrub has some disadvantages. The leaves often suffer from sunburn in late summer, therefore 'Snowboy' is best planted in a semi-shaded location. Propagation and cultivation is another problem. The success rate with grafting (or budding) usually is much lower than with similar varieties, and young plants are sometimes difficult to establish. 'Snowboy' is undoubtedly one of the most beautiful variegated dogwoods, but similar varieties such as 'Samzam' and 'Wolf Eyes' are preferable because, although perhaps slightly less beautiful, they are much stronger. Zone 6b

Cornus kousa 'Samzam' SAMARITAN™ RONALD HOUTMAN

Cornus kousa 'Snowboy' KLAAS VERBOOM

Cornus kousa 'Summergames'

Broad shrub with a somewhat irregular growth habit. Eventually it will become a large shrub to small tree. The foliage colors of 'Summergames' are quite distinct. The leaves are dark green with irregular cream margins or blotches. Throughout the plant, parts of leaves are dark purplish green. This is also the color of the young shoots. The overall appearance of 'Summergames' can be a bit loud, but it also gives this plant something extra. It is a nice addition in this group of variegated cultivars, and above all, very distinct. Zone 6b

Cornus kousa 'White Dust'

Japan, named by Masato Yokoi, before 1998

Broad, upright shrub with a habit similar to *C. kousa* 'Gold Star'. The foliage has a very curious variegation. The dark green leaves are densely covered with creamy white to yellowish dots and blotches. Some of these dots are very small, others cover larger parts of the leaf

Cornus kousa 'Summergames' RONALD HOUTMAN

Cornus kousa 'White Dust' RONALD HOUTMAN

blade. From a distance the foliage looks creamy grayish yellow, giving the plant an exclusive character. The flowers are profusely borne and have creamy white bracts. Even young plants are free-flowering. Of course, it is a matter of personal taste whether this kind of variegation is appreciated, it certainly is unusual. Zone 6b

Cornus kousa 'Wolf Eyes'

Manor View Farm, Inc., Monkton, Maryland, United States, before 1999

Broad, upright shrub that grows to 2.5 m high with a dense habit. This cultivar was selected from a range of seedlings of *C. kousa*. The leaves are grayish green with creamy white margins. The leaf margins are conspicuously wavy, which adds much to the elegance of this shrub. Like 'Snowboy', I recommend planting 'Wolf Eyes' in a semi-shaded location—not because it tends to burn, but in full sun leaf curl sometimes occurs. The flowers do not appear at a young age. The bracts are

Cornus kousa 'Wolf Eyes' RONALD HOUTMAN

creamy white with pale greenish white margins. *Cornus kousa* 'Samzam', another cultivar with silvery white leaf margins, resembles 'Wolf Eyes' in all its features. Both 'Samzam' and 'Wolf Eyes' are quite similar to 'Snowboy', but easier to grow and therefore recommended. Zone 6b

Cornus mas

Large shrub to small tree with a broad, upright, rounded habit. Older branches have attractive grayish brown exfoliating bark. A nice feature of this species is the flowering time. Usually *C. mas* flowers in late winter and early spring, before the leaves appear. The flowers are pale yellow to golden yellow and, on large specimens, a very attractive sight. In addition to a yellow-leaved cultivar, several variegated ones, and a small number of cultivars with fruits in different colors (white, yellow, and purplish red), there are some cultivars especially raised and grown for their edible fruits. In various countries liqueur is made from the fruits; in Turkey it is called *serbert*, while the French have their famous *vin de cornoulle*. *Cornus mas* and its cultivars are hardy to zone 5a.

Cornus mas 'Aurea Elegantissima'

J. & C. Lee, Isleworthy Nursery, Hammersmith, United Kingdom, 1869

Handsome medium-sized to large shrub that grows to about 3 m high. The foliage has attractive golden yellow margins with a touch of pink. Because the leaves are susceptible to sunburn during warm and sunny summers, it is better to plant 'Aurea Elegantissima' in semi-shade.

Among growers there is some discussion on the correct name for this plant. Although dendrologists and taxonomists often conclude the cultivars *C. mas* 'Elegantissima' and 'Tricolor' are similar to 'Aurea Elegantissima', various nurseries grow different plants under these names. 'Elegantissima' seems to be synonymous to 'Aurea Elegantissima'. 'Tricolor' is supposed to have tricolored leaves, and there are nurseries that grow clones with leaves that are variegated yellow and white. It is my opinion that *C. mas* 'Aurea Elegantissima' and *C. mas* 'Tricolor' are not similar, and therefore the cultivar names are not synonyms.

Cornus mas 'Aurea Elegantissima' WOUT KROMHOUT

Cornus mas 'Variegata' FA. C. ESVELD

Cornus mas 'Variegata'

United Kingdom, 1838

Like *C. mas* 'Aurea Elegantissima', but leaves with silvery white margins. The variegation is very stable and constant, which makes 'Variegata' an outstanding medium-sized to large shrub. Also 'Variegata' is noted for a free-fruiting habit. The fruits are similar to those of the species; bright red, somewhat cherrylike, and edible.

Cornus nuttallii 'Goldspot'

Doty & Doerner Nurseries, Portland, Oregon, United States, 1966

Large shrub to small tree that grows to more than 10 m. The foliage is attractively spotted yellow. It is quite a free-flowering shrub that usually flowers a second time in early autumn. The flowers are relatively large and creamy white. It does very well as a large specimen. 'Goldspot' is sometimes misspelled as 'Gold Spot'. Zone 7a

Cornus stolonifera 'Silver and Gold'

Mount Cuba Center, Greenville, Delaware, United States, 1987

Resembling *C. alba* in general appearance, 'Silver and Gold' is a broad, upright, suckering shrub that grows to about 2 m high. It originated as a sport from *C. stolonifera* 'Flaviramea' and has the same greenish yellow branches. The leaves are dark green with silvery white edges. The name 'Silver and Gold' refers to the foliage and branch colors. It is a very stable variegated plant that does not tend to revert easily. It is a great

Cornus nuttallii 'Goldspot' RONALD HOUTMAN

Cornus stolonifera 'White Gold' RONALD HOUTMAN

Cornus stolonifera 'Silver and Gold' WOUT KROMHOUT

plant for landscaping and in urban areas where unusual and sunny colors are required. Due to its extreme hardiness, it can be used widely. Zone 2

Cornus stolonifera 'White Gold'

Canada, before 1982

Broad, upright shrub with close similarity to *C. stolonifera* 'Silver and Gold'. The foliage is silvery white edged, but some leaves are spotted as well. The name 'White Gold' refers to the foliage and branch colors. Although it looks very similar to 'Silver and Gold', it is slightly less vigorous and will attain a height of about 1.75 m. Contrary to 'Silver and Gold', this plant reverts quite easily. 'Silver and Gold' is therefore to be recommended over 'White Gold'. 'White Gold' was found as a sport in *C. stolonifera* in western Canada, where this species is native. It is occasionally offered under its synonym 'White Spot' Zone 2

Cotoneaster ×*suecicus* 'Erlinda' PPH (COLLECTION OF HARRY VAN DE LAAR)

Cotoneaster ×*suecicus* 'Erlinda'

A. van Beek, Loenhout, Belgium, 1993

Creeping evergreen of only 25 cm high, but usually grown as a weeping plant on a stem. It originated as a variegated sport in *C.* ×*suecicus* 'Skogholm'. The leaves are broad elliptic to obovate, 1.5 to 1.8 cm long, and up to 1 cm wide. The young foliage is slightly pinkish, soon changing into creamy white. The leaf centers are dark green. Young leaves sometimes appear entirely creamy white, and when grown in full sun these leaves tend to burn. The small fruits are red and are not richly carried. 'Erlinda' is a striking and above all trendy plant that is very suitable for small gardens. It is also ideal as a container plant on patios or balconies. 'Erlinda' was given a Certificate of Appreciation by the Royal Boskoop Horticultural Society in 1993, followed by a Certificate of Valuation–in Gold in 1994. Zone 5b

Cotoneaster ×*suecicus* 'Juliette' RONALD HOUTMAN

Cotoneaster ×*suecicus* 'Juliette'

J. F. R. Koster, Boskoop, The Netherlands, 1996

Found as a sport in *C.* ×*suecicus* 'Erlinda', this plant has a similar habit, but is more vigorous. Like 'Erlinda', it is usually grown on a stem. 'Juliette' has a broader habit, and the leaves are larger: up to 2.5 cm long and 1.5 cm wide. The most distinctive difference, however, is the less conspicuous variegation. This gives 'Juliette' a more grayish look. Contrary to 'Erlinda' the leaves show less tendency to burn during hot and sunny

Crataegus monogyna 'Variegata' RONALD HOUTMAN

Crataegus monogyna 'Variegata' RONALD HOUTMAN

Crataegus ×media 'Gireoudii' RONALD HOUTMAN

spells. The fruits are orange-red and larger than those of 'Erlinda', and they are more richly produced, especially on established plants. 'Juliette' was given an Award of Merit by the Royal Boskoop Horticultural Society in 1998. Zone 5b

Crataegus ×media 'Gireoudii'

Späth Nurseries, Berlin, Germany, 1899

Broad, upright, large shrub to small tree that may grow to about 5 m high but usually much lower. The young leaves are obtusely lobed and attractively mottled pink and white. The unfolding shoots are pinkish red and also very attractive. Later in the season green leaves are formed. The white flowers are not very conspicuous against the young foliage, but the large, glossy, dark red fruits are quite showy. In autumn the leaves become strikingly red. 'Gireoudii' has an irregular capricious habit that makes it a plant that does not fit in every garden. The ornamental value is unrecognized, however, and this plant should be more widely grown. It is easily pruned into a more regularly shaped plant, and pruning also forces the plant to produce more of those striking young shoots.

Although 'Gireoudii' is widely known as a cultivar of *C. laevigata*, recent studies have concluded it derived from *C. ×media*, which is a hybrid between *C. monogyna* subsp. *nordica* and *C. laevigata* subsp. *laevigata*. Zone 5a

Crataegus monogyna 'Variegata'

This old variegated cultivar of the common hawthorn forms a large shrub or small tree that grows to 4 m high. The plant resembles the species in all its features, except for the white mottled foliage. The white flowers are rather inconspicuous against the white variegated foliage, but the red fruits are more attractive. Zone 5a

Cryptomeria

Interesting monotypic genus of evergreen conifers, consisting only of *C. japonica*. This large tree is native to China and Japan, where it is widely used for timber production. The wood is called *sugi*, which is also the Japanese common name for this species. More than 100 cultivars are known, but only a few are variegated.

Cryptomeria japonica 'Aureovariegata'

Japan, before 1868

Very rare cultivar with the same conical habit as the species. The foliage is lustrous dark green, variegated yellow. Brought into the European trade by Sénéclause Nurseries of Bourg Argental, France, in 1868. Zone 6b

Cryptomeria japonica 'Elegans Variegata'

Kalmthout Arboretum, Kalmthout, Belgium, before 1887

Broad, upright, shrubby conifer with a slightly irregular habit. As in the green-leaved 'Elegans', the foliage consist of soft starlike needles. 'Elegans Variegata' differs from it in having numerous silvery white variegations. Because of this variegation, it grows slightly weaker than its green-leaved counterpart. 'Elegans Variegata' is quite rare in cultivation but is occasionally offered in the trade. Zone 6b

Cryptomeria japonica 'Knaptonensis'

Isola Madre, Lago Maggiore, Italy, 1923

Densely branched conifer with an irregular but attractive habit. The compact, almost dwarfish habit is the result of its very slow growth. The foliage is dark green and heavily variegated creamy white. The variegation on young shoots is much clearer than on older branches, where it tends to become a dirty cream color. A semi-shaded location is recommended because the white parts of the plant tend to scorch during hot and sunny spells. During severe frost the variegated parts might be damaged. The variegation sometimes is slightly unstable, forming fully green branches. Keeping these aspects in mind, 'Knaptonensis' is a handsome variegated *Cryptomeria*. It was found by Murray Hornibrook on Isola Madre as a witches' broom of

Cryptomeria japonica 'Elegans Variegata' J. R. P. VAN HOEY SMITH

Cryptomeria japonica 'Knaptonensis' RONALD HOUTMAN

Cryptomeria japonica 'Nana Albospicata' J. R. P. VAN HOEY SMITH

Cryptomeria japonica 'Top Gold' RONALD HOUTMAN

×*Cupressocyparis leylandii* 'Harlequin' RONALD HOUTMAN

C. japonica 'Jindai'. He took parts of the plant back to Ireland and named it after his house (Knapton House) in Abbeyleix. Zone 6b/7a

Cryptomeria japonica 'Nana Albospicata'

Japan, before 1901

Extremely rare cultivar with an irregular dwarfish habit. The branches are very thin and nicely variegated white, almost like silver threads—a true collectors' item! This cultivar is very rare in cultivation but it must not be confused with 'Nana Albospica', a larger cultivar that is not variegated. 'Nana Albospica' has white young shoots, later fading to pale green. Zone 6b

Cryptomeria japonica 'Top Gold'

Van den Top Nursery, Barneveld, The Netherlands, 1985

Dense and compact-growing cultivar with an irregular habit. The foliage is an almost unnatural light green. Some of the young shoots are greenish yellow, whereas others emerge light green. The variegated shoots turn green in the second year (again the young shoots are variegated). This plant was discovered as a sport in *C. japonica* 'Jindai'. 'Top Gold' is a distinct new cultivar that can be used as a container plant or in the garden. Zone 6b

×*Cupressocyparis*

In 1999 a new conifer species called *Xanthocyparis vietnamensis* was discovered in Vietnam. It shows many similarities to *Chamaecyparis nootkatensis*, and it is most likely that this species will be placed in the new genus *Xanthocyparis*. These new insights will also have consequences for the hybrid ×*Cupressocyparis*, of which *Chamaecyparis nootkatensis* is one of the parents (*Cupressus macrocarpa* being the other parent). When *Chamaecyparis nootkatensis* is reclassified, the name of ×*Cupressocyparis* will change to ×*Cuprocyparis leylandii*.

×*Cupressocyparis leylandii* 'Harlequin'

The Earl of Bradford, Weston Park, Shifnel, United Kingdom, 1975

Upright cultivar with a narrow conical habit. 'Harlequin' was discovered as a sport of *C.* ×*leylandii* 'Haggerston Grey', and it has the same grayish green foliage. Small white spots are scattered throughout the foliage, giving the whole plant an even more grayish appearance. It is easily distinguished from 'Silver Dust' by its smaller patches of white and grayer foliage. Like all ×*Cupressocyparis leylandii*, it is very suitable for hedging. Zone 7a

×*Cupressocyparis leylandii* 'Jubilee'

Wansdyke Nurseries, Devizes, United Kingdom, 1977

An indistinct variegated cultivar with green foliage intermixed with pale greenish yellow branchlets. 'Jubilee' was informally distributed in the late 1970s and early 1980s by the late Humphrey Welch, who stopped growing it because it proved to be indistinct. However, the cultivar still exists and is still grown by nurserymen who got their original plants from Welch. Zone 7a

×*Cupressocyoparis leylandii* 'Jubilee' RONALD HOUTMAN

×*Cupressocyparis leylandii* 'Silver Dust'

S. G. Marsh, U.S. National Arboretum, Washington, D.C., United States, 1960

Upright tree with a good columnar habit. This cultivar will stay slightly smaller than the average green-leaved clones. The foliage is green with irregular patches of creamy white, usually larger than in 'Harlequin'. An attractive detail is that the cones of 'Silver Dust' are also variegated. 'Silver Dust' was discovered as a sport in *C.* ×*leylandii* 'Leighton Green'. It is a stable cultivar that is not uncommon in the trade. Zone 7a

×*Cupressocyparis leylandii* 'Silver Dust' J. R. P. VAN HOEY SMITH

×*Cupressocyparis leylandii* 'Sirebo'

Stichting Sierteeltpromotie Regio Boskoop, Boskoop, The Netherlands, 1992

Discovered as a sport in *C.* ×*leylandii* 'Castlewellan', 'Sirebo' becomes a stately tree with a columnar habit. Young plants are narrow and columnar. The foliage of 'Sirebo' is light green with yellow variegations scattered over the plant. 'Sirebo' is short for the foundation (*stichting* in Dutch) after which the plant was named. This organization was founded to promote the Boskoop region in general and the nursery industry in particular. Zone 7a

×*Cupressocyparis leylandii* 'Star Wars' J. R. P. VAN HOEY SMITH

×*Cupressocyparis leylandii* 'Star Wars'

A relatively new cultivar. The habit, foliage colors, and variegation are almost identical to 'Sirebo'. Zone 7a

Cupressus macrocarpa 'Greenstead Magnificent Variegated'

Drue Wholesale Nursery, Berry, Australia, 1989

Dwarf conifer with a dense and irregular habit. The foliage is bluish gray-green and heavily variegated white and cream. As the name suggests it was discovered as a sport of 'Greenstead Magnificent', a curious cultivar well worth planting in small gardens. Likewise 'Greenstead Magnificent Variegated' is very suitable for gardens of all sizes. Because of the dense and compact habit, it is also suitable for planting in arrangements on balconies or terraces. Zone 8b

Daboecia cantabrica 'Rainbow'

After 1969

Small evergreen with a dense habit that grows to 50 cm high. The small dark green leaves are mottled and speckled yellow. In spring the unfolding foliage is bronze colored. In summer and early autumn the warm purple flowers appear in upright terminal racemes and contrast well with the variegated foliage. Given the fact that many different colors are united in one plant, 'Rainbow' is a well-chosen name. All *Daboecia* thrive best in fairly moist and lime-free soil in full sun or semi-shade. When lightly pruned during midsummer, they produce new flowers and keep their compact habit. Zone 7a

Dapnhe ×*burkwoodii*

R. Aireton, Longfleet Nurseries, Poole, United Kingdom before 1935

These are interesting hybrids between *Daphne caucasica* and *Daphne cneorum*. They form dense deciduous shrubs of about 1 m high. The dark bluish green leaves are narrow oblong to oblanceolate and usually not more than 5 cm long. The flowers are pale pink to white and are richly produced in terminal clusters during April and May. They are very fragrant and noted for their fine perfume. Variegated cultivars have been developed over the years. Most of these plants have leaves with yellow to pale yellow edges, with only a few exceptions, such as 'Briggs Moonlight'. In this plant the variegation is reversed: pale yellow foliage with dark green margins.

Dapnhe ×*burkwoodii* cultivars are among the easiest daphnes to grow. They thrive best in well-drained soil in a sunny location. Because they dislike root disturbance, it is best to plant a *Daphne* at a young age, so it will not have to be transplanted after some years. Even when all the above is taken care of, daphnes still die without a visible cause. Unfortunately, this problem occurs often and we must simply accept that they are short-lived. However, the sheer beauty of *D.* ×*burkwoodii* makes it well worth planting in every garden.

Daphne ×*burkwoodii* 'Astrid'

M. van der Velde, Boskoop, The Netherlands, 1983

Well-branched, broad, upright shrub to about 1 m high. Leaves up to 6 cm long, dark bluish green with a narrow irregular bright yellow edge, later becoming paler into creamy white. 'Astrid' originated as a sport in *D.* ×*burkwoodii* (most probably 'Albert Burkwood' or 'Somerset'). It was given an Award of Merit by the Royal Boskoop Horticultural Society in 1983. Zone 6a

Daphne ×*burkwoodii* 'Briggs Moonlight'

Briggs Nursery, Olympia, Washington, United States, before 1996

Interesting cultivar with striking foliage colors. The leaves are slightly larger than in most other cultivars, but more exceptional is the color of the foliage. The leaves are creamy yellow to butter yellow with a narrow, dark green edge. 'Briggs Moonlight' originated as a sport of *Daphne* ×*burkwoodii* 'Somerset'. A similar new cultivar is 'Gold Strike', originated at Junker's Nursery in West Hatch, Taunton, United Kingdom. This plant is not widely grown yet. Zone 6a

Daphne ×*burkwoodii* 'Carol Mackie'

C. Mackie, New Jersey, United States, 1962

Another variegated sport of *D.* ×*burkwoodii* 'Somerset', originating in the United States. The leaves are dark bluish green with golden yellow margins, later turning more cream colored. This excellent cultivar has proven hardier than most other *D.* ×*burkwoodii* cultivars. Zone 6a

Daphne ×*burkwoodii* 'G. K. Argles'

Champernowne Nursery, Buckland Monachorum, Devon, United Kingdom

Exciting variegated cultivar that differs from the others in a more vigorous growth and broader leaves. The pale pinkish white flowers are also slightly larger. The leaves have attractive golden yellow margins, which

Daphne ×*burkwoodii* 'Astrid' PPH (COLLECTION OF HARRY VAN DE LAAR)

Daphne ×*burkwoodii* 'Carol Mackie' GERT FORTGENS

Daphne ×*burkwoodii* 'Briggs Moonlight' KLAAS VERBOOM

Daphne ×*burkwoodii* 'G. K. Argles' RONALD HOUTMAN

are darker than 'Astrid', 'Carol Mackie', and 'Somerset Gold Edge'. Zone 6a

Daphne ×*burkwoodii* 'Somerset Gold Edge'

Like most variegated cultivars of *D.* ×*burkwoodii*, this is also a sport of 'Somerset'. The bluish green leaves have yellow margins, later turning more creamy yellow. 'Somerset Gold Edge' is quite similar to 'G. K. Argles' in vigor, but has a more bushy habit and paler variegation. Also the flowers seem somewhat paler than in other cultivars. Although 'Somerset Gold Edge' is the correct name, it is usually listed as 'Gold Edge'. Zone 6a

Daphne ×*burkwoodii* 'Somerset Gold Edge' PPH (COLLECTION OF HARRY VAN DE LAAR)

Daphne cneorum 'Variegata' RONALD HOUTMAN

Daphne odora 'Aureomarginata' RONALD HOUTMAN

Daphne odora 'Geisha Girl' RONALD HOUTMAN

Daphne cneorum 'Variegata'

Dense, usually procumbent evergreen that will not grow higher than approximately 40 cm. In spring the fragrant pink flowers appear in dense terminal heads. The basic color of the small lanceolate leaves is dark green, sometimes slightly bluish green. Two clones seem to be available under the name 'Variegata'. One clone has leaves with creamy white to white edges. The other one has more rounded leaves with creamy yellow to cream-colored margins. Both clones are more vigorous than the species. Based on the literature, the white-variegated clone is supposed to be called 'Albomarginata', and the more yellow-variegated clone should be called 'Variegata'. However, in the trade there is much confusion and both clones are offered as 'Variegata'. The variegated *D. cneorum* is a splendid plant for rockeries and small gardens. The rich flowering habit combined with good variegated foliage (in both clones) make them superb plants. Zone 5a

Daphne odora 'Aureomarginata'

Loosely upright, evergreen shrub with comparatively thick branches. It can grow to about 2 m high but will usually not exceed 1.5 m in cultivation. The leaves are elliptic to lanceolate and up to 8 cm long. They feel rather fleshy. The glossy green leaves have irregular, narrow, yellow margins. The pale pink to pinkish white flowers appear in early spring and stand in dense terminal heads. The dark pink buds and later exteriors of the flowers give a bicolored effect to the plant. The flowers are certainly among the most fragrant of all. The combination of handsome variegated foliage and exceptionally fragrant flowers in late winter and early spring makes *Daphne odora* 'Aureomarginata' well worth planting in every garden.

The variegated cultivars of *Daphne odora* seem slightly more winter hardy than the green-leaved ones, contrary to the normal experience with variegated plants. Unfortunately, 'Aureomarginata' is not an easy plant to grow and therefore not commonly cultivated. Zone 7

Daphne odora 'Geisha Girl'

Striking cultivar with the same type of variegation as *D.* ×*burkwoodii* 'Briggs Moonlight'. The inner parts of the leaves are pale yellow to yellow, with irregular dark green margins. 'Geisha Girl' flowers in early spring with pale pink flowers, darker in bud. As with all daphnes, this is not an easy plant to grow and therefore not yet widely available. Zone 7

Daphne odora 'Variegata'

Japan, before 1800

Slow-growing cultivar of *Daphne odora* with extremely variegated leaves. The yellow to light yellow margins are conspicuously wider and darker than in 'Aureomarginata'. Unfortunately, it is a rather weak grower, which is caused by the lack of chlorophyll. 'Variegata' is even rarer than 'Aureomarginata'. Zone 7b

Daphne odora 'Variegata' RONALD HOUTMAN

Deutzia crenata 'Summer Snow'

Shibamichi Kanjiro Co., Japan, 1979

Densely branched upright, deciduous shrub. At a young age the branches are gracefully arching, later becoming more stiff and upright. The foliage is irregularly mottled cream to greenish white. The young leaves are more cream to yellowish white variegated. The overall effect this variegation creates is rather loud, but from a (short) distance it gives the shrub a gray appearance. The single white flowers appear in terminal panicles during early summer. Because of the heavy variegation they do not stand out on the shrub. 'Summer Snow' is a good shrub to combine with dark green–leaved shrubs and colorful perennials, such as *Delphinium*, *Hemerocallis*, and *Papaver*. In Japan it was traded under the illegitimate name *D. crenata* var. *variegata*. Carl. R. Hahn assigned the cultivar name 'Summer Snow'. Zone 5b

Deutzia crenata 'Summer Snow' RONALD HOUTMAN

Disanthus cercidifolius 'Ena Nishiki'

Japan

Disanthus is a monotypic genus related to *Liquidambar*. In general appearance it resembles *Cercis*. This plant,

Disanthus cercidifolius 'Ena Nishiki' RONALD HOUTMAN

Deutzia crenata 'Summer Snow' RONALD HOUTMAN

native to Japan, forms a broad medium-sized shrub up to about 3 m high and wide. The cordate leaves are relatively thick and somewhat leathery. *Disanthus cercidifolius* shows its true character best in autumn. The leaves change from deep green into stunning pink and deep crimson, easily belonging to the best fall colors of all ornamental shrubs. 'Ena Nishiki' is the first and only variegated cultivar of *Disanthus*. The leaves are green to grayish green with very conspicuous, irregular white margins. Zone 7

Elaeagnus

Small but horticulturally important genus of evergreen and deciduous shrubs. The variegated cultivars exist, without exception, in the evergreen species *Elaeagnus pungens* and the hybrid *Elaeagnus* ×*ebbingei*. These cultivars are excellent for planting in large groups or as broad hedges. Because they are extremely wind resistant and salt tolerant, they belong to the most important plants in coastal gardening. In the northern temperate zones *E. pungens* and *E.* ×*ebbingei* are the equivalent of the Mediterranean *Olea europaea* and the Australian and New Zealand *Griselinia*, *Metrosideros*, and *Olearia*. Although some variegated cultivars of *Elaeagnus* have a cream-colored variegation, no white variegation is reported. As with all variegated plants the cultivars with green leaf margins show more tendency to revert to green than the ones with variegated margins. Of course, reverted twigs and branches must be removed at an early stage.

Elaeagnus ×*ebbingei*

This hybrid originated as a seedling of *Elaeagnus macrophylla*. The late S. G. A. Doorenbos, Director of Public Parks in The Hague, sowed seeds of flowers that were pollinated by *Elaeagnus pungens*. From this hybrid four clones were distributed as *Elaeagnus* ×*ebbingei* in 1938 through M. Koster & Sons of Boskoop, The Netherlands. Two of these clones disappeared from cultivation within a decade. The two other clones, differing from each other in minor details, became commonly cultivated. Although it was clear the two clones were not the same, it was not until 1976 that H. G. Hillier proposed the cultivar names 'Albert Doorenbos' and 'The Hague'. The first one has leaves up to 16 cm long and silvery white undersides. 'The Hague' carries smaller leaves and conspicuous brownish scales on its young shoots. On older plants the differences are not so easy to observe.

Elaeagnus ×*ebbingei* 'Coastal Gold'

This evergreen shrub grows to 3 m high and 2 m wide. It has large golden yellow leaves with an irregular dark green margin. Sometimes the green invades the leaf blade up to the midrib. The leaves are conspicuously silvery gray beneath. Zone 7a

Elaeagnus ×*ebbingei* 'Gilt Edge'

John Waterer, Sons & Crisp, Bagshot, United Kingdom, 1965

Broad, upright, evergreen with glossy dark green leaves. The margins are rich golden yellow, contrasting well with the leaves. Occasionally entirely yellow leaves develop, and even more rarely entirely green leaves appear. Therefore, it is one of the most stable variegated *Elaeagnus* cultivars. Zone 7a

Elaeagnus ×*ebbingei* 'Lannou' ELEADOR™, GOLD SPLASH™

Pepiniéres Ladan S.A., Meilars, France, 1995

Upright evergreen that grows to 3.5 m high that looks very similar to 'Limelight'. The leaves are golden yellow

Elaeagnus ×*ebbingei* 'Coastal Gold' RONALD HOUTMAN

Elaeagnus ×*ebbingei* 'Gilt Edge' FA. C. ESVELD

Elaeagnus ×*ebbingei* 'Gilt Edge' RONALD HOUTMAN

Elaeagnus ×*ebbingei* 'Lannou' ELEADOR™, GOLD SPLASH™
RONALD HOUTMAN

Elaeagnus ×ebbingei 'Lemon Ice' RONALD HOUTMAN

Elaeagnus ×ebbingei 'Limelight' RONALD HOUTMAN

Elaeagnus ×ebbingei 'Variegata' RONALD HOUTMAN

with irregular dark green margins. In some leaves the green is partially absent, in some the yellow is more blotched green and not only at the margin. It is a vigorous cultivar, initially promoted as an improvement of 'Limelight', but apart from the more yellow appearance, there are only minor differences. Therefore, 'Lannou' seems to be just another variegated cultivar. Zone 7a

Elaeagnus ×ebbingei 'Lemon Ice'

E. Verweij, Reeuwijk, The Netherlands, 1999

This new cultivar originated as a sport of the well-known *E. ×ebbingei* 'Limelight'. The leaf centers of 'Lemon Ice' are pale yellow instead of the common golden yellow, as in most other *E. ×ebbingei* cultivars. This gives the leaves a vivid, somewhat silvery yellow appearance. It also has a more compact habit than 'Limelight', resulting in a bushy shrub. 'Lemon Ice' is a fine evergreen shrub and a good addition in this range. In 1999 it was given an Award of Recommendation by the Royal Boskoop Horticultural Society. Another variegated cultivar of *E. ×ebbingei* is 'Silver Lining'. It is of unknown origin, very rare, and probably no longer in cultivation. Zone 7a

Elaeagnus ×ebbingei 'Limelight'

The Netherlands

Very popular and widely grown cultivar with a broad, upright habit that grows to 3.5 m high. The leaf margins are dark green and the centers are golden yellow. The foliage is glossy, which adds to the great ornamental value of this cultivar. Although it is one of the most common variegated cultivars of *Elaeagnus ×ebbingei*, it strongly tends to revert. Regular pruning of green-leaved branches must be done to keep a variegated plant. Zone 7a

Elaeagnus ×ebbingei 'Variegata'

Perhaps the oldest variegated cultivar of this hybrid and most certainly one of the rarest in cultivation. The leaves of 'Variegata' are dark green and have a narrow cream-colored margin. Although quite stable in its appearance, it is surpassed by excellent cultivars such as 'Gilt Edge'. Zone 7a

Elaeagnus pungens 'Dicksonii'

Contrary to most other cultivars of *E. pungens*, 'Dicksonii' has a more upright habit and eventually will grow to about 2.5 m high and wide. It is also less vigorous. The leaves are dark green with golden yellow margins. These margins are very irregular in width. They may be a 2 mm wide, but sometimes they only leave about 1 cm of green along the midrib. Furthermore, the margins are less wavy than in other cultivars such 'Maculata' or 'Frederici'. It is an old cultivar of unknown origin (probably United Kingdom) and not very widely grown. The main reason for its disappearance is the fact that it has been surpassed by other cultivars. Still, 'Dicksonii' is a nice shrub that should be found in every collector's garden. *Elaeagnus pungens* 'Aurea' is sometimes used as a synonym for 'Dicksonii'; however, it is not clear whether these cultivars are the same. In any case, they are very similar and easily confused. Zone 7a

Elaeagnus pungens 'Dicksonii' CHRIS SANDERS

Elaeagnus pungens 'Frederici'

Von Siebold & Co, Leiden, The Netherlands, before 1880

Bushy evergreen shrub that grows to 3 m high, with a more compact habit than the species. The leaves are rather small, narrow, and dark green, with a large pale yellow blotch. It is much less vigorous than most other cultivars. 'Frederici' is an old, first-class cultivar, but still not widely grown. 'Frederici' was probably sent to Europe by P. F. von Siebold and introduced by his company after his death. It was named to honor of Prince Frederik, one of the sons of the Dutch King William III. Zone 7a

Elaeagnus pungens 'Frederici' FA. C. ESVELD

Elaeagnus pungens 'Goldrim'

W. J. Streng, Boskoop, The Netherlands, 1974

Evergreen, broad, upright, bushy shrub that grows to 3.5 m high with shiny foliage. The leaves have yellow edges that are narrow to rather broad and wavy. The leaf undersides have striking grayish white hairs. 'Goldrim' is an attractive cultivar that has, in contrast to *E. pungens* 'Maculata', yellow leaf edges, whereas 'Maculata' has yellow leaf centers and therefore tends to revert to green. 'Goldrim' was given an Award of Merit by the Royal Boskoop Horticultural Society in 1974. Zone 7a

Elaeagnus pungens 'Goldrim' PPH (COLLECTION OF HARRY VAN DE LAAR)

Elaeagnus pungens 'Hosuba Fukurin'

Japan, before 1996

Compact, broad, upright shrub with a vigorous but dense habit. The elliptic leaves are slightly longer than in the species. They are dark green with very conspic-

Elaeagnus pungens 'Hosuba Fukurin' CHRIS SANDERS

Elaeagnus pungens 'Maculata' RONALD HOUTMAN

uous narrow cream to light yellow margins. The margins are wavy, adding substantially to the distinctiveness of this shrub. The undersides of the leaves are, as in the species, silvery gray. It is slightly less hardy than other variegated cultivars of *E. pungens*. Zone 8

Elaeagnus pungens 'Maculata'

Germany, before 1864

Evergreen bushy shrub with a broad, upright habit that grows to 3.5 m high. The dark green foliage has large yellow tot pale yellow centers. Despite its good features, 'Maculata' strongly tends to revert to green foliage. If green leaves appear, they must be taken away immediately to preserve the good variegated foliage. This well-known and very commonly grown variegated plant is of unknown origin. James Veitch & Sons received a First Class Certificate for 'Maculata' from the Royal Horticultural Society in 1891.

'Clemson Variegated' is a more recent introduction. The leaves are wider than in 'Maculata' with very conspicuous golden yellow to clear yellow centers, leaving only a narrow band of dark green along the margins. It keeps its color very well throughout the year and will not burn in direct sunlight. 'Pacific Gold' is another variegated cultivar of *E. pungens*. It is very rare and has probably disappeared from the trade. Zone 7a

Elaeagnus pungens 'Tricolor'

The leaves of this cultivar are variegated white, yellow, and pale pinkish white. 'Tricolor' is only rarely available in the trade. Zone 7a

Elaeagnus pungens 'Variegata'

Before 1927

This is another old cultivar of unknown origin. An evergreen shrub with a bushy habit that grows to 3.5 m

Elaeagnus pungens 'Variegata' CHRIS SANDERS

high. The foliage has pale yellowish white margins. Although still available, 'Variegata' is not very widely cultivated anymore, because it has been surpassed by better cultivars such as 'Goldrim'. *Elaeagnus pungens* 'Aurea' (see under 'Dicksonii') is an old cultivar from Belgium (1864; as *Elaeagnus pungens foliis aureo-marginatis*) and is similar to 'Variegata', except for the color of the leaf margins, which are more golden yellow. Zone 7a

Eleutherococcus sieboldianus 'Aureomarginatus'

Bushy deciduous shrub with an upright habit that grows to 3 m high and wide. The branches are gracefully arching. The spiny stems are grayish and carry palmate leaves with five to seven leaflets. The leaflets have irregular yellow to pale yellow margins. *Eleutherococcus sieboldianus* 'Aureomarginatus' is a useful shrub well worth planting in places where contrast is needed. The arching branches and conspicuous variegation make it an excellent shrub for large borders and groves. The genus *Eleutherococcus* used to be named *Acanthopanax*. Zone 5b

Eleutherococcus sieboldianus 'Variegatus'

P. F. von Siebold, Leiden, The Netherlands, 1860

Bushy shrub generally similar to 'Aureomarginatus', but with cream to white variegated foliage. In many

Eleutherococcus sieboldianus 'Variegatus' RONALD HOUTMAN

Eleutherococcus sieboldianus 'Variegatus' RONALD HOUTMAN

leaves not only the margin is creamy, but the entire leaflets have turned creamy white. 'Variegatus' is just as conspicuous as 'Aureomarginatus' and can be used in the garden the same way. 'Variegatus' is an old cultivar that has been known in cultivation since the nineteenth century, and it is more widely grown and available than 'Aureomarginatus'. Zone 5b

Enkianthus campanulatus 'Tokyo Masquerade' RONALD HOUTMAN

Enkianthus campanulatus 'Tokyo Masquerade'

Wayside Gardens, Hodges, South Carolina, United States, 1995

Compact, upright, deciduous shrub that grows to about 1.5 m high. The stems are dark purplish red. The leaves are obovate to elliptic or somewhat diamond shaped and about 5 cm long. The green leaves have irregular creamy margins, which are more yellow on young leaves. In autumn, the green parts of the leaves change to a deep scarlet red, making the effect even more dramatic. The bell-shaped flowers appear in late spring. They are pinkish red but not very numerous. Although named and introduced in the United States, 'Tokyo Masquerade' was first discovered in Japan by Barry R. Yinger and imported into the United States. The main ornamental value of this flowering shrub is the striking combination of variegated foliage and colored stems. Zone 6a

Escallonia laevis 'Gold Ellen' RONALD HOUTMAN

Escallonia laevis 'Gold Ellen'

Philip Marie Moreau, Bodyke, Ireland, 1985

Attractive evergreen shrub with a dense, broad, upright habit. In time it will become a broad, flattened shrub. The ovate to obovate leaves are golden yellow with a small blotch of dark green in the center. The green blotch is variable in size. The blotch usually covers approximately 25 percent of each leaf, but often it is much smaller. Yellow-leaved branches form with regularity, thus reverting to *E.* 'Gold Brian', from which it derived as a sport. The dark pinkish red flowers open during summer. 'Gold Ellen' is an excellent plant for creating contrast in the garden. The clear foliage colors can give a surprising effect in combination with blue- or purple-flowering plants. Zone 8

Escallonia 'Silver Anniversary'

United Kingdom, about 1993

Hybrid *Escallonia* with quite a vigorous, broad, upright habit that grows to about 1.5 m. The leaves are glossy dark green with pale silvery green margins. The typical *Escallonia* flowers open during summer. They are dark pink to reddish pink. A rather unusual *Escallonia* because only a few variegated cultivars are known in the trade. Zone 8

Euonymus

A well-known genus of evergreen and deciduous shrubs to small trees. About 175 species grow in temperate regions of the Northern Hemisphere. Most of the deciduous species and cultivars have attractive fruits and autumn colors. The fruit is a three- to five-valved capsule that opens to expose usually brighter colored arils that hold the seeds. In many species the arils are orange or reddish, while the capsule is whitish to purplish.

Variegated cultivars are mainly derived from *E. fortunei* and *E. japonicus* and their cultivars. Like *Hedera*, they are notorious for their capability to form sports. Most of these sports are only slightly different or they revert to the original cultivar. The cultivars of *E. fortunei* and *E. japonicus* are widely grown in gardens, in pots, and on terraces or balconies.

Euonymus alatus 'Silver Cloud'

W. M. van Nierop, Boskoop, The Netherlands, 2003

For many years a variegated *Euonymus alatus* was growing in the garden of Wim van Nierop. Although very beautiful, it remained unnamed. When researching

Euonymus alatus 'Silver Cloud' RONALD HOUTMAN

Euonymus alatus 'Silver Cloud' RONALD HOUTMAN

Euonymus europaeus 'Aucubifolius' WOUT KROMHOUT

this book I came across this beautiful shrub and it was named 'Silver Cloud'. Van Nierop got it many years ago from a friend who found it as a chance seedling. 'Silver Cloud' is a small, finely branched shrub with a dense habit. It will reach a height of about 1 m. The obovate leaves are medium green with very conspicuous silvery white margins. The cultivar name reflects the general appearance of this attractive plant. It is not yet widely grown, but surely deserves to be. Zone 4

Euonymus europaeus 'Aucubifolius'

Germany, before 1862

Deciduous shrub that grows to about 3 m high, sometimes slightly larger. The leaves are conspicuously spotted and blotched pale yellow and white. The spots are usually quite large and sometimes cover more than half the leaf. In autumn the foliage changes to a striking purplish red. The greenish flowers are inconspicuous and the crimson to pinkish red fruits have orange arils. The cultivar name 'Aucubifolius' (sometimes misspelled as 'Aucubaefolius') suggests colorful foliage

Euonymus fortunei 'Canadale Gold' KLAAS VERBOOM

with small dots of yellow, white, and pink. The foliage is not as colorful as the cultivar name suggests. Zone 4

Euonymus fortunei

An evergreen shrub, sometimes with a scandent habit. The leaves are ovate to elliptic and usually grow to 3 cm long, but in many cultivars they are only about 2 cm long. The first growth of this species is juvenile, developing into an adult stage later. In the adult stage it will flower and produce fruits. The fruits are creamy white, and when ripe they show striking orange arils. Cultivars of this species belong to the best-known variegated plants. They are widely grown and can be used in pots and tubs on terraces and balconies, as well as in the garden or as an amenity plant. They are also very suitable for making low hedges. A naturally occurring variety, *E. fortunei* var. *radicans*, was already in cultivation in 1860. It was once defined as a separate species, *E. radicans*. This variety is reliably hardy and almost all known cultivars were derived from *E. fortunei* var. *radicans*. Unless otherwise stated, all cultivars are hardy to zone 6a.

Euonymus fortunei 'Canadale Gold'

Canadale Nurseries Ltd., Canada, 1974

This cultivar has a broad, upright habit and is densely branched with rather stiff branches. Its best feature is the relatively large leaves that are light green with yellow to pale yellow margins. Sometimes the leaf blades are also splashed yellow. 'Canadale Gold' is a popular cultivar that is excellent for the use in large plantings and as an amenity plant. It was discovered as a sport of 'Carrierei'.

Euonymus fortunei 'Emerald Delight'

Another variegated cultivar with glossy green leaves that have clear yellow to greenish yellow margins. The leaves are relatively large, not unlike the size of those of 'Silver Queen'. In habit and use 'Emerald Delight' does not differ from similar variegated cultivars.

Euonymus fortunei 'Emerald Gaiety'

Corliss Bros., Gloucester, Massachusetts, United States, 1960

'Emerald Gaiety' is perhaps the best-known silver variegated cultivar of *E. fortunei*. It has a broad, upright habit and, like 'Canadale Gold', relatively large leaves. The leaves are grayish green with irregular silvery white margins. This cultivar is quite similar to the old and also widely distributed 'Variegatus'. 'Emerald Gaiety' has larger leaves and will not grow as tall as 'Variegatus'.

Euonymus fortunei 'Emerald Delight' WOUT KROMHOUT

Euonymus fortunei 'Emerald Gaiety' RONALD HOUTMAN

Euonymus fortunei 'Emerald Jade'

Broad, upright evergreen with a dense conical habit. The leaves are glossy green with silvery white margins of irregular width.

Euonymus fortunei 'Emerald 'n' Gold'

Corliss Bros., Gloucester, Massachusetts, United States, 1967

Compact broad, upright shrub that grows to 50 cm with a bushy habit. The leaves are small and green to grayish green with golden yellow margins. During winter the foliage becomes orange-red to purplish red.

Euonymus fortunei 'Emerald Jade' WOUT KROMHOUT

Euonymus fortunei 'Emerald 'n' Gold' RONALD HOUTMAN

'Emerald 'n' Gold' is a beautiful small shrub that grows to about 50 cm high with exceptionally golden foliage. It can be used for low hedges or in small plantings. It is also excellent grown in containers.

Euonymus fortunei 'Emerald Surprise'

Broad, upright, mounded shrub that grows to about 1 m high. The leaves are relatively large and similar in size to 'Emerald Delight'. They are glossy green with broad golden yellow margins. These fade to creamy yellow with age.

Euonymus fortunei 'Gaiety Gold'

Broad, upright evergreen that grows to 1 m high or slightly more. The green leaves are relatively large with golden yellow margins. Contrary to 'Emerald 'n' Gold', it is very suitable for larger plantings. However, 'Gaiety Gold' lacks the attractive winter coloration in which 'Emerald 'n' Gold' is exceptionally striking.

Euonymus fortunei 'Emerald Surprise' WOUT KROMHOUT

Euonymus fortunei 'Gaiety Silver'

Broad, upright, bushy shrub with some resemblance to 'Emerald Gaiety' (also in its name, which can be confusing). The leaves are green and have a broad pure white edge. The overall impression of 'Gaiety Silver' is that it looks more white than other cultivars. It is a good introduction that certainly has an added value within this group of variegated cultivars.

Euonymus fortunei 'Harlequin'

Japan, before 1983

Broad but low-growing bushy evergreen that grows to about 50 cm high. Main feature is the white-speckled dark green leaves, in combination with the almost pure white to creamy white young growth. Unfortunately, 'Harlequin' is less winter hardy than the majority of cultivars, and the foliage tends to burn in dry and sunny spells. Although it is a relatively weak plant, 'Harlequin' is quite valuable as a border plant or in containers. The attractive combination of colors makes it a unique cultivar within the range of *E. fortunei* culti-

Euonymus fortunei 'Gaiety Silver' RONALD HOUTMAN

Euonymus fortunei 'Harlequin' KLAAS VERBOOM

Euonymus fortunei 'Interbolwi' BLONDY™ WOUT KROMHOUT

Euonymus fortunei 'Moonshadow' RONALD HOUTMAN

vars. 'Harlequin' was introduced into cultivation by Brookside Gardens, Maryland, United States, but it was originally discovered in Japan.

Euonymus fortunei 'Interbolwi' BLONDY™

Bolwijn Nursery, Putten, The Netherlands, 1990

Bushy upright shrub that grows to about 50 cm high. The leaves are dark green with a large golden yellow central spot, which becomes creamier on older leaves. In autumn the coloration of the edges of the central spot changes to orange-yellow. 'Interbolwi' was found as a sport in *E. fortunei* 'Sunspot'. It is excellent for the use in borders, smaller plantings, pots, and tubs.

Euonymus fortunei 'Moonshadow'

United States

A new cultivar, not unlike 'Interbolwi' in habit and color. It forms a rather low-growing bushy shrub with a broad spreading habit. Eventually it will grow to a height of about 60 cm and much wider. The leaves are creamy white with dark green margins. These green margins are slightly wider than in 'Interbolwi', but narrower than in 'Sunspot'. 'Moonshadow' is supposed to be more stable and less prone to sunburn than 'Interbolwi'.

Euonymus fortunei 'Sheridan Gold'

Relatively small and low-growing evergreen that grows to about 50 cm high and slightly wider. The young leaves are suffused golden yellow in spring. During summer they fade to green. Its variegation is

Euonymus fortunei 'Sheridan Gold' RONALD HOUTMAN

only visible in the first half of the season: during autumn and winter it is an ordinary green-leaved cultivar. 'Sheridan Gold' is not recommended for general use, but is a typical plant for the collector.

Euonymus fortunei 'Silver Queen'

France, 1914

Broad spreading to upright cultivar that can grow to 1 m or taller. The leaves are relatively large and elliptic to ovate. The centers of the leaves are grayish green, and when unfolding the margins are attractively cream to creamy yellow. Later in the season this color changes to creamy white. 'Silver Queen' arose as a sport of 'Carrierei', a green-leaved cultivar, and is unfortunately less hardy than most other cultivars of *E. fortunei*. Therefore it needs some protection during periods of severe frost. 'Silver Queen' is also slightly less easy to propagate by cuttings, which results in lower rooting percentages. Yet, this is perhaps the most beautiful *E. fortunei* cultivar. Zone 7a

Euonymus fortunei 'Silver Queen' RONALD HOUTMAN

Euonymus fortunei 'Sparkle 'n' Gold'

United States, before 1985

Broad, upright evergreen that grows to about 80 cm high. The leaves are green to grayish green with golden yellow margins, turning purplish in winter. 'Sparkle 'n' Gold' is very similar to 'Emerald 'n' Gold', but it grows slightly taller and the foliage is more yellowish.

Euonymus fortunei 'Sparkle 'n' Gold' WOUT KROMHOUT

Euonymus fortunei 'Sunshine'

Jac. Schoemaker, Boskoop, The Netherlands, 1978

Nice cultivar with a broad, upright habit that grows to about 80 cm high. The relatively large leaves are 3 to 4 cm long, grayish green with broad golden yellow margins, turning slightly lighter as the season progresses. It originated as a sport of 'Emerald 'n' Gold' and is supposed to be an improvement of this well-known cultivar. The main differences with 'Emerald 'n' Gold' are the larger leaves, stouter branches, and more intense variegation. Although it is quite distinct from 'Emerald 'n' Gold', 'Sunshine' tends to revert to it.

Euonymus fortunei 'Sunshine' RONALD HOUTMAN

Euonymus fortunei 'Sunspot'

R. Nielsen & Son, Canada, before 1980

Low and dense bushy shrub with an almost prostrate habit. The branches grow upright and spreading and are yellow to yellowish green. Unlike most other var-

Euonymus fortunei 'Sunspot' RONALD HOUTMAN

Euonymus fortunei 'Variegatus' RONALD HOUTMAN

Euonymus hamiltonianus 'Snow' RONALD HOUTMAN

iegated cultivars of *E. fortunei*, 'Sunspot' has dark green leaves with a yellow central spot or several small spots. Unfortunately, it has the tendency to revert to green. Because of its compact habit, 'Sunspot' is excellent for use in smaller borders and containers. It is one of the hardier cultivars that can be used into zone 6 (perhaps zone 5). 'Sunspot' is sometimes sold under the name 'Goldspot'.

Euonymus fortunei 'Surespot'

Brucedale Gardens, Canada, 1991

This plant originated as a sport of *E. fortunei* 'Sunspot' and was registered by the Canadian Ornamental Plant Foundation as 'Surespot'. It is supposed to have a more stable variegated character and a more compact and slower growth than its parent.

Euonymus fortunei 'Surrey Marble'

United Kingdom, before 1976

Small evergreen with a spreading upright habit that grows to about 60 cm high. The fresh green leaves are narrow elliptic and irregularly splashed and mottled white. Other leaves have white margins, even on the same plant. Although quite rare, 'Surrey Marble' is a curious variegated plant especially sought after by collectors.

Euonymus fortunei 'Variegatus'

P. F. von Siebold, Leiden, The Netherlands, 1860

Broad, upright to almost creeping evergreen that grows to 50 cm with rooting twigs. When grown against a wall it can reach a height of about 3 m. The small grayish green leaves have narrow whitish margins, which turn purplish in winter. 'Variegatus' is an old and very well-known cultivar that is widely used for low hedges and small group plantings. It was found in Japan by P. F. von Siebold, who introduced it into the Western trade. Although 'Variegatus' is often confused with 'Emerald Gaiety', there are a few distinct differences (see under 'Emerald Gaiety'). 'Variegatus' is also offered under its synonyms *E. fortunei* var. *argenteomarginatus*, var. *gracilis*, or 'Silver Gem'.

Euonymus hamiltonianus 'Rainbow'

A very rare cultivar that is almost identical in habit to *E. hamiltonianus* 'Snow'. The main difference is in the colors of the foliage: the leaves of 'Rainbow' have pale yellow to yellowish green margins and turn red to purplish red in autumn, whereas the leaves of 'Snow' usually have pure white margins. Zone 5a

Euonymus hamiltonianus 'Snow'

Y. Hirose, Japan

Variegation in the evergreen cultivars of *Euonymus* is quite common; however, it is difficult to find any variegated forms of deciduous *Euonymus*. *Euonymus hamiltonianus* 'Snow', which is actually derived from the subspecies *sieboldianus*, is one of the few. It is a shrub with an upright habit that will reach a height of about 2.5 m. The leaves are elliptic to lanceolate and have broad, usually pure white margins. On many leaves, more than half the leaf is white. The centers of the leaves are green, but look darker due to the contrast with the white margins. In autumn pale pink with orange fruits can appear, which adds even more to this colorful plant. Zone 5a

Euonymus japonicus

The Japanese spindle is a large evergreen shrub to small tree that grows to 4 m high, although it rarely reaches this height in cultivation. The leaves are narrow oval to obovate or elliptic and usually have toothed margins. They are up to 6 cm long and feel thick and leathery. The fruits, which are not often seen, are pale pink to white with orange arils. Because of their relatively strong growth and evergreen aspect, Japanese spindles are very suitable for hedging, especially in coastal areas. In northern temperate regions cultivars of this species are also very widely grown as container plants. Apart from powdery mildew, which can cause severe problems in *E. japonicus*, there are no notorious diseases to which *E. japonicus* is extremely susceptible.

In the past many variegated cultivars were introduced, often with very indistinct descriptions. This sometimes makes it difficult to identify cultivars of *E. japonicus*. Many of the variegated cultivars were introduced into the Western trade by P. F. von Siebold and herbarium specimens should be present in Leiden and Munich, but in these herbaria hardly any *E. japonicus* can be found. Some of the better documented and more common variegated cultivars are described more extensively here. Others are only briefly mentioned, because most of these are rare in cultivation. Unless otherwise stated all cultivars described here are hardy to zone 8a.

Euonymus japonicus 'Albomarginatus'

United Kingdom, before 1863

Old cultivar, originally described as botanical var. *albomarginata*. The leaves are oval with rather conspicuous obtuse tips. The leaves have narrow, clear white margins. The centers of the leaves are dull green and sometimes spotted gray. 'Albomarginatus' is one of the most commonly grown variegated cultivars of *E. japonicus*. It is sometimes referred to as 'Argenteomarginatus'

Euonymus japonicus 'Argenteovariegatus'

A cultivar with bright green leaves, with broad white margins.

Euonymus japonicus 'Albomarginatus' RONALD HOUTMAN

Euonymus japonicus 'Argenteovariegatus' RONALD HOUTMAN

Euonymus japonicus 'Aureomarginatus' MAARTEN VAN ATTEN

Euonymus japonicus 'Aureomarginatus' RONALD HOUTMAN

Euonymus japonicus 'Chollipo' RONALD HOUTMAN

Euonymus japonicus 'Aureomarginatus'

Japan, before 1861

The dark green leaves of this cultivar have clear yellow margins. P. F. von Siebold introduced this plant in Leiden, The Netherlands, between 1859 and 1861 and described it in 1863. It was already grown in Japan by that time. Although 'Aureomarginatus' is not as common as the white-margined cultivar 'Albomarginatus', it is certainly not a rare plant. The contrast between the dark green and clear yellow in the foliage makes it an attractive plant for use in containers and borders.

Euonymus japonicus 'Aureus'

France, before 1847

Nice yellow-leaved cultivar. The ovate leaves have dark green margins, contrasting well with the yellow centers. More clones are grown under this name, and many unnamed yellow variegated *E. japonicus* cultivars are supposedly 'Aureus'. Usually the petioles and stems are also colored yellow.

Euonymus japonicus 'Bravo'

W. A. Sanders, Boskoop, The Netherlands, 1989

Upright shrub with a broad pyramidal habit. The leaves are glossy dark green with narrow silvery white edges. This interesting cultivar was found in a Dutch garden under the name of *E. americanus*. The late Harry van de Laar recognized it was not even a close relative of the deciduous "true" *E. americanus*, but a cultivar of *E. japonicus*. Because there were no records about its true origin and there was no known similar variety, Sanders named it 'Bravo'. This plant closely resembles *E. japonicus* 'Chollipo' but differs slightly in its more cream-colored margins. 'Bravo' is readily available in the European trade, but is not widespread throughout the United States.

Euonymus japonicus 'Chollipo'

Chollipo Arboretum, Chollipo, South Korea, 1985

Interesting cultivar with an upright habit. The young growth is golden yellow with only a narrow band of green in the center of the leaves. Older leaves have broad, irregular yellow to golden yellow margins. The leaves are grayish green to dark green in the centers. Very distinctive and promising cultivar but, unfortunately, virtually unknown.

Euonymus japonicus 'Crispus'

This unusual cultivar has twisted and curled leaves with white margins. The foliage is also partially marbled and splashed white.

Euonymus japonicus 'Duc d'Anjou'

Gégu, Angers, France, about 1870

The leaves of this cultivar are dark green with a pale yellow or grayish center. It is an old but still quite popular cultivar, originating from the nursery of A. Leroy in Angers, France. Mr. Gégu, head gardener with this nursery, found the plant around 1870 and published the name 'Duc d'Anjou' in 1872. In 1895, the same plant was published as *E. japonicus* var. *macrophyllus viridivariegatus* by Beissner and in 1900 this variety name was reduced by Rehder into var. *viridivariegatus*. It is unclear whether there is an older description of this plant, but from reading the history this is not to be expected. Although many books list 'Viridivariegatus' as the correct cultivar name, 'Duc d'Anjou' is preferred here.

Euonymus japonicus 'Bravo' WOUT KROMHOUT

Euonymus japonicus 'Golden Maiden'

This cultivar is very similar to 'Aureus'. It forms an upright, bushy plant with golden yellow leaves with dark green margins. Like many other variegated *Euonymus*, this cultivar also has a strong tendency to revert to green.

Euonymus japonicus 'Golden Maiden' RONALD HOUTMAN

Euonymus japonicus 'Heespierrolino' PIERROLINO™

Van Heesbeen Nursery, Haarsteeg, The Netherlands, 1998

Compact dense shrub with a broad ovate habit. The foliage is dark green mottled white. The young foliage is very attractive when unfolding. It is heavily marbled white, becoming more green with age. 'Heespierrolino' is an attractive plant for use in pots and tubs but has proven rather weak in the garden.

A rare and older Japanese cultivar, named 'Izayoi', may be the same as 'Heespierrolino'. If these plants are proven to be the same, the older name, 'Izayoi', will be preserved.

Euonymus japonicus 'Latifolius Albomarginatus'

This rare cultivar has very large leaves reaching a length of 10 cm and a width of 5 cm. They are dark green with very conspicuous pure white margins. 'Latifolius Albomarginatus', sometimes offered under its

Euonymus japonicus 'Latifolius Albomarginatus' RONALD HOUTMAN

Euonymus japonicus 'Microphyllus Albovariegatus' RONALD HOUTMAN

Euonymus japonicus 'Ovatus Aureus' RONALD HOUTMAN

synonym 'Macrophyllus Albus', is one of the most striking variegated forms within this species. However, due to the large leaves it must be protected from severe frosts, which can be done by growing it against a wall facing south or west. Once settled, it will be a great showpiece in every garden.

Euonymus japonicus 'Mediopictus'

Another cultivar with oval yellow leaves edged with dark green. The petioles and stems are also yellow to yellowish green. Perhaps a synonym of *Euonymus japonicus* 'Aureus'.

Euonymus japonicus 'Microphyllus Albovariegatus'

Moser, Versailles, France, about 1888

Contrary to 'Latifolius Albomarginatus', this cultivar has almost the smallest foliage in this species. It is a small and compact bushy shrub with a somewhat *Buxus*-like appearance, due to its small leaves and dense habit. The leaves are up to 3 cm long (usually shorter) and narrow elliptic to oblanceolate. They are dark green with white edges. 'Microphyllus Albovariegatus' derived from 'Microphyllus', which was brought from Japan to Europe by P. F. von Siebold in 1830 and came into the trade under the illegitimate name 'Pulchellus', thus creating an illegitimate name for the variegated sport of it, 'Pulchellus Albomarginatus'.

Euonymus japonicus 'Microphyllus Aureovariegatus'

Has the same habit and shape of the leaf as 'Microphyllus Albovariegatus', but a different color. The foliage of this cultivar is suffused golden yellow.

Euonymus japonicus 'Microphyllus Gold Pillar'

Small plant with a narrow, upright habit, especially at a young age. Foliage is golden variegated.

Euonymus japonicus 'Microphyllus Variegatus'

Another small plant with an erect habit and small, white-margined leaves. Probably similar to 'Microphyllus Albovariegatus'.

Euonymus japonicus 'Moness' SILVER PRINCESS™

Dense upright shrub that grows to about 1 m high. It

resembles 'Microphyllus Albovariegatus', but with larger leaves.

Euonymus japonicus 'Ovatus Albus'

Leaves broad and relatively large, margined, splashed, and suffused with white, gray, and green.

Euonymus japonicus 'Ovatus Aureus'

Before 1847

Dense, broad, upright evergreen that has become the most popular cultivar of *E. japonicus*, also known as *E. japonicus* 'Aureovariegatus'. Its dark green foliage is blotched and splashed golden yellow along the margins, thus creating a most striking plant. The young growth especially is quite dramatic in its coloration. It is very suitable for planting against a wall, in borders, or in pots and tubs. I recommend planting 'Ovatus Aureus' in a sunny location, to maintain good foliage colors. A variegated cultivar named 'Marieke' is the same as 'Ovatus Aureus'.

Euonymus japonicus 'Président Gauthier'

France

Large-leaved cultivar that is more common in southern Europe than in other parts of the world. The leaves are relatively large and elliptic. They have broad yellowish white margins and grayish green centers. Only a narrow band of dark green is visible along the midrib.

Euonymus japonicus 'Président Gauthier' RONALD HOUTMAN

Euonymus japonicus 'Président Gauthier' RONALD HOUTMAN

Euonymus japonicus 'Susan' RONALD HOUTMAN

Euonymus phellomanus 'Silver Surprise' RONALD HOUTMAN

Euonymus japonicus 'Punctatus'
Leaves mottled and dotted yellow.

Euonymus japonicus 'Silver King'
Dense upright shrub with relatively large leaves that are narrow ovate to elliptic. The deep green foliage has bright silvery white margins.

Euonymus japonicus 'Silver Krista'
Jonkers Bros., Elshout, The Netherlands, 1997
Rather dense-growing cultivar with a broad, upright habit. The young leaves are yellowish white variegated, later becoming silvery white. 'Silver Krista' was found as a sport of 'Ovatus Aureus'.

Euonymus japonicus 'Silver Queen'
This is a similar cultivar to 'Silver King' and 'Moness' SILVER PRINCESS™, but the leaf edges are more cream colored.

Euonymus japonicus 'Sulphureovariegatus'
A yellow-leaved cultivar with dark green leaf margins. The leaf centers are paler yellow than in similar cultivars.

Euonymus japonicus 'Susan'
Upright cultivar with a conical habit. The leaves are dark green with narrow silvery white margins. From a short distance the whole plant appears grayish, due to the fact that the margins are rather narrow. The leaves are much larger than in 'Microphyllus Albovariegatus', but are colored in the same way.

Euonymus japonicus 'Tricolor'
The leaves of this cultivar are green and yellow variegated. The young leaves are tinged pink.

Euonymus japonicus 'Yellow Queen'
A cultivar with relatively broad ovate dark green leaves, with yellow margins.

Euonymus phellomanus 'Silver Surprise'
H. Kolster, Boskoop, The Netherlands, 1990
Broad, upright, deciduous shrub that grows to about 3 m high. The branches nearly lack the typical corky wings that characterize this species. The branches are grayish in summer, but change into soft grayish pink in

winter. The leaves are elliptic to ovate and dark green, with white margins. Unfortunately, the foliage is ruffled. Its variegation is remarkable and the coloration of the branches during winter is a unique and quite spectacular feature. Zone 6a

Fagus

This small genus consists of only a few naturally occurring large trees. Belonging to the Fagaceae (beech family), it is closely related to the genera *Castanea* and *Quercus*. All genera in this family have nutlike fruits (acorns in *Quercus*) that are enclosed or held by a cupule, which is best described as a woody cup. In *Quercus* the cupule is usually open at the top, in *Fagus* and *Castanea* it is closed.

The beech grows in western, central, and southeastern Europe; Turkey; the Caucasus; China; Japan; and the United States into Mexico. Of the approximately ten species, only *Fagus sylvatica* is commonly grown. Because it is native to Europe, it has long been cultivated, and variegated cultivars were known in the eighteenth century.

All *Fagus* are medium to large deciduous trees with a broad, upright to almost rounded crown. The leaves are placed alternately and are broad elliptic to ovate and have sinuate, somewhat wavy margins. The winter buds are narrow lanceolate, long, and pointed. Unless otherwise stated, all cultivars described here are hardy to zone 5b.

Fagus sylvatica 'Albomarginata'

About 1770

Very old cultivar, dating from the late eighteenth century. In this medium sized tree the leaves are somewhat narrower than in the species. Also the edges are more wavy and sinuate. Of course, the most distinct difference with the species is the irregular yellowish white leaf margins. In some leaves only a narrow band of green is visible around the midrib. Although it is an old cultivar, 'Albomarginata' is still quite commonly grown. When placed in semi-shade it can add a dramatic effect to large gardens and parks. It is sometimes available under the illegitimate name 'Albovariegata'

Fagus sylvatica 'Argenteomarmorata'

Späth Nurseries, Berlin, Germany, 1899

A curious tree that does not appear to be variegated when the leaves unfold in spring. The first growth consists of fully green leaves. During summer the second growth appears, and these leaves are irregularly marbled and dusted white. This can be quite attractive in contrast with the older leaves of the first growth, but it generally gives the whole plant a somewhat messy character. 'Argenteomarmorata' was introduced by the famous Späth Nursery in 1899, after they received the plant as an unnamed seedling in 1886.

Fagus sylvatica 'Bicolor Sartini'

Sartini Nursery, Piatto, Italy, 1995

This recently discovered sport of 'Purpurea Tricolor' differs from it in lacking the purple and pink in the foliage, resulting in a green-leaved beech with pale yellow margins. It is not yet widely cultivated. The cultivar name 'Bicolor Sartini', which includes the Latin word *bicolor*, is not legitimate according to the ICNCP. Perhaps it is proper to name it just 'Sartini'.

Fagus sylvatica 'Albomarginata' RONALD HOUTMAN

Fagus sylvatica 'Argenteomarmorata' PPH (COLLECTION OF HARRY VAN DE LAAR)

Fagus sylvatica 'Bicolor Sartini' JO BÖMER

Fagus sylvatica 'Feuerglut' G. DÖNIG

Fagus sylvatica 'Feuerglut'

G. Dönig, Erlangen, Germany, 1989

The young foliage of this attractive medium-sized tree is a striking pink. During late spring and summer the leaf turns dark green, but the margins are dotted and splashed pinkish red. In the center of the leaves are also small pinkish red dots. The combination of dark green and pink in the leaves make 'Feuerglut' quite a spectacular plant.

Fagus sylvatica 'Feuermarmor'

G. Dönig, Erlangen, Germany, 1991

Another beautiful variegated beech. It forms a medium to large tree that can reach a height of more than 10 m. The exfoliating foliage is dark purplish brown marbled clear reddish pink. Later in the season the leaves become less variegated and only small splashes of pink can be observed. During summer it looks like a regular brown beech from a distance, the main feature of this tree.

Fagus sylvatica 'Franken'

G. Dönig, Erlangen, Germany, 1993

This tree represents a group of variegated cultivars introduced more recently. In habit it is the same as the

Fagus sylvatica 'Feuermarmor' J. R. P. VAN HOEY SMITH

Fagus sylvatica 'Franken' JO BÖMER

species, although the leaf margins look more sinuate and slightly wavier. The new growth is spectacularly pale creamy white. When aging the leaves change into green, only slightly marbled creamy to greenish white. 'Franken' is quite a spectacular plant, especially in spring, when the leaves unfold. It was found in Berlin as a seedling of 'Marmorata' and differs from it in its better marbled foliage and orange-tinted twigs. Especially during winter, the color of the twigs is quite spectacular.

Fagus sylvatica 'Luteovariegata'

United Kingdom, about 1770

Medium-sized tree that is similar to 'Albomarginata' in habit and leaf shape, although 'Luteovariegata' is more vigorous. The leaves are green, edged with yellow. Along the secondary veins the yellow flows into the leaf blade. This effect is intensified by the pale greenish yellow veins.

Fagus sylvatica 'Marmorata'

Germany, 1903

Medium to large tree with a broad, upright habit. The leaves are dark green conspicuously striped and marbled creamy white to white. This effect is even stronger on the young foliage in spring. Occasionally the young leaves are tinged pink. A few newer cultivars, such as 'Franken' and 'Marmor Star', derived from 'Marmorata' as seedlings. These newer cultivars are preferable because the foliage colors are stronger. Zone 5b

Fagus sylvatica 'Luteovariegata' GERT FORTGENS

Fagus sylvatica 'Marmorata' RONALD HOUTMAN

Fagus sylvatica 'Marmor Star' JO BÖMER

Fagus sylvatica 'Oudenbosch' JO BÖMER

Fagus sylvatica 'Purpurea Tricolor' RONALD HOUTMAN

Fagus sylvatica 'Marmor Star'

G. Dönig, Erlangen, Germany, 1992

A rather new cultivar of *F. sylvatica*. Like 'Franken', this is a seedling of 'Marmorata', found in Berlin. 'Marmor Star' is a medium-sized tree with rather broad, light green leaves with conspicuous apiculate tips. The foliage is spectacularly creamy white marbled, contrary to 'Franken', which has more pinkish colors in its leaves. The coloration is stronger on young leaves and is V-shaped along the secondary veins, from the midrib toward the margins. From a distance 'Marmor Star' looks grayish white, making it an excellent contrast tree in larger gardens and parks.

Fagus sylvatica 'Oudenbosch'

Arboretum Oudenbosch, Oudenbosch, The Netherlands, 1996

A curious plant that was found as a seedling in a village named Oudenbosch in the south of The Netherlands. The veins are green but the parts between the veins are yellow. This gives 'Oudenbosch' a distinctive character and makes it a good addition in the range of variegated beeches.

Around 1850 a variegated form of beech was found in the Czech Republic. According to literature this cultivar must have looked very similar to 'Oudenbosch'. Most likely it has disappeared from cultivation.

Fagus sylvatica 'Purpurea Tricolor'

France, about 1885

Very attractive densely branched small to medium-sized tree. 'Purpurea Tricolor' is one of the few purple-leaved variegated beeches. The young leaves emerge deep carmine red in spring and later develop cream and pink margins. The basic leaf color changes to a more brownish purple during late spring and summer. The variegation is brighter when planted in areas with a high light intensity.

In the late nineteenth century this plant was described in several countries under several different names. Although written evidence is absent, it is plausible that the name was given to more than one clone, based on the fact that there is some variation in leaf coloration, especially in the width of the pink edge. The plant was first described in 1885 as 'Tricolor', but this name had already been given to a white variegated beech by Koch in 1873 (this plant is no longer grown). The next oldest cultivar name, 'Purpurea Tricolor', was also proposed by Bean in his *Trees and Shrubs* in 1973. In 1927 Rehder named a similar *Fagus sylvatica* var. *roseomarginata*. The name 'Roseomarginata', now a synonym for 'Purpurea Tricolor', is still widely used for this plant.

Fagus sylvatica 'Rolf Marquardt'

G. Dönig, Erlangen, Germany, 1992

Raised as a seedling of 'Marmorata' this cultivar looks quite similar to its parent. The main difference is that, in addition to the green and white, the leaves of 'Rolf Marquardt' also have yellowish stripes. Especially in spring, this cultivar is heavily variegated and very spectacular.

Fagus sylvatica 'Rolf Marquardt' JO BÖMER

Fagus sylvatica 'Silberthaler'

G. Eschrich, Recklinghausen, Germany, 1993

Nice cultivar with green leaves and white margins. The leaves are slightly smaller than in the species, which adds to the elegance of 'Silberthaler'. The foliage is not prone to sunburn during hot and sunny spells and, although it tends to revert to green, it still is worth growing.

Fagus sylvatica 'Silberthaler' JO BÖMER

Fagus sylvatica 'Silverwood'

M. Bömer, Zundert, The Netherlands, 1986

Densely branched small to medium-sized tree that grows to 10 m high. The leaf margins are conspicuously sinuate and slightly wavy. The green leaves have narrow, irregular, silvery white margins. When unfolding these margins are broader and more cream colored. This cultivar differs from 'Silberthaler' in its larger leaves and shows less tendency to revert to green, although green-leaved branches are occasionally formed.

Fagus sylvatica 'Silverwood' JO BÖMER

Fagus sylvatica 'Striata'

Germany, about 1851

Old and quite curious tree of more than 10 m high. The leaves are broader than in the species and emerge green in spring. During late spring and summer, they develop yellowish green to yellow stripes between the main veins. The precise origin of 'Striata' is unknown, but it was introduced in the trade by the German Späth Nursery in 1892. Although the variegation is very curious, it can also be regarded as a form of chlorosis, giving 'Striata' an unhealthy appearance. This cultivar

Fagus sylvatica 'Striata' RONALD HOUTMAN

Fagus sylvatica 'Viridivariegata' RONALD HOUTMAN

×*Fatshedera lizei* 'Annemieke' RONALD HOUTMAN

is not widely grown and only of little ornamental value.

Fagus sylvatica 'Viridivariegata'

P. Lombarts Nurseries, Zundert, The Netherlands, 1935

A rather peculiar variegated cultivar. The leaves are green with numerous, very small, yellowish green dots along the secondary veins. As with 'Striata', it is of little ornamental value because more beautiful variegated cultivars of *F. sylvatica* are grown.

×*Fatshedera lizei*

This intergeneric hybrid is the result of a cross between *Fatsia japonica* 'Moseri' and *Hedera hibernica*. It was developed in 1910 by the Lizé Frères (Lizé Brothers) of Nantes, France. It is a broad, upright, evergreen shrub with thick, light brown branches and brown pubescent young leaves and petioles. The clear green adult leaves are palmately lobed with three to five lobes and feel somewhat leathery. During autumn the plants can flower with numerous greenish white flowers in panicles up to about 25 cm long.

×*Fatshedera lizei* 'Annemieke'

In the United States 'Annemieke' was distributed through the J. C. Raulston Arboretum, Raleigh, North Carolina beginning in 1994. It is similar to ×*F. lizei* in every aspect, but the foliage has pale yellow splashed centers. Although the plant is not very rare, correct labeling is. Usually these plants are offered as 'Aureovariegata'. The misspelling 'Anna Mikkels' is also used more often than the correct spelling. Moreover, this plant is also known as 'Lemon and Lime'. Despite taxonomical confusions 'Annemieke' is an attractive evergreen for use in warmer temperate regions or in pots and tubs. Zone 7b

×*Fatshedera lizei* 'Variegata'

After 1910

'Variegata' is another of the few variegated cultivars of the hybrid described here. The leaves have creamy white margins. There are also plants with creamy white splashed leaf centers labeled 'Variegata'. This name is incorrect, and these must be called 'Annemieke'. Zone 7b

Fatsia japonica 'Variegata'

Japan, before 1859

Slow-growing evergreen shrub with thick branches that grows to 4 m high but usually not exceeding 2 m. Its handsome foliage consists of large, palmately lobed leaves that can reach a width of more than 30 cm. The leaves are glossy dark green with creamy white edges. This is a truly spectacular plant, best placed in semi-shade or against a wall to create a dramatic scene in the garden.

'Variegata' was introduced into Western gardens by P. F. Von Siebold, who imported it from Japan in 1859. Hirose and Yokoi (1998) mention two other *Fatsia japonica* cultivars that have been grown only very rarely: 'Murakumo Nishiki' (meaning "brocaded cluster of clouds"), which is pale yellowish green variegated, and 'Spider's Web' (named by Yoshimichi Hirose), with foliage heavily dusted white. Zone 8a

×*Fatshedera lizei* 'Variegata' RONALD HOUTMAN

Fatsia japonica 'Variegata' RONALD HOUTMAN

Forsythia

Well-known spring-flowering shrubs, some of the first to flower each spring. This genus consists of seven species. One species, *F. europaea,* is native to southeastern Europe, and the other six are native to Asia. *Forsythia* ×*intermedia,* the hybrid between *F. suspensa* and *F. viridissima,* is the best known, and cultivars derived from this hybrid are more floriferous and have more deeply colored, larger flowers.

All *Forsythia* have yellow flowers. With their foliage, the variegated *Forsythia* have extra ornamental value. *Forsythia* is best used in a semi-shaded location. They usually are quite vigorous and respond well to heavy pruning. Of course, this is best done after flowering.

Forsythia ×*intermedia* 'Dawson's Form'

Upright shrub that grows to 3 m high with gracefully arching branches. The foliage is very distinctively heavily variegated. The leaves are dark green with irregular broad pale yellow to yellow margins. In some leaves only a small part of green is visible along the central vein. 'Dawson's Form' is a very rare cultivar that deserves to be grown and used more widely. Zone 5b

Forsythia ×*intermedia* 'Dawson's Form' RONALD HOUTMAN

Forsythia ×*intermedia* 'Fiesta' RONALD HOUTMAN

Forsythia ×*intermedia* 'Golden Times' RONALD HOUTMAN

Forsythia ×*intermedia* 'Josefa' RONALD HOUTMAN

Forsythia ×intermedia 'Fiesta'

Duncan & Davies, New Plymouth, New Zealand, 1986

Low and compact shrub usually not exceeding 1 m in height. Contrary to other variegated *Forsythia*, 'Fiesta' has green leaves with yellow to creamy yellow parts in the centers. Its cultivar name, referring to the joyful leaf coloring, is very well chosen. 'Fiesta' produces good yellow flowers. It was discovered as a sport of *F. ×intermedia* 'Flojor' MINIGOLD™, which is the origin of its dwarfish habit. Although slightly prone to sunburn during warm sunny spells, it does very well in a semi-shaded location. Zone 5b

Forsythia ×intermedia 'Golden Times'

Handsome deciduous shrub with an upright and rather graceful habit due to the somewhat arching branches. It can grow to a few meters high, usually not taller than about 3 m. The most important characteristic of 'Golden Times' is, of course, its variegated foliage. The leaves are elliptic to narrow ovate and dark green, with yellow margins. The leaves tend to burn very easily when planted in a sunny location. 'Golden Times' belongs to the more floriferous of the variegated *Forsythia* cultivars. Its origin is unknown, however, the plant known as 'Golden Times' grew in The Netherlands for the first time in 1995 and the J. C. Raulston Arboretum, Raleigh, North Carolina, United States, distributed this plant in 1996 and 1997. Zone 5b

Forsythia ×intermedia 'Josefa'

A. M. Vermeulen, Boskoop, The Netherlands, 1985

Upright shrub that grows to about 1.5 m high. The leaves are dark green with creamy white margins. The yellow flowers are similar to *F. ×intermedia* 'Spectabilis', in which 'Josefa' was found as a sport, however, it is not a very floriferous plant. It also grows rather weakly and is not as easy to propagate as similar cultivars. Zone 5b

Fraxinus

Important genus of medium-sized to large trees that are exceptionally suitable for landscape plantings and as specimen trees. About sixty species grow throughout the Northern Hemisphere, but only a few are of commercial value. *Fraxinus americana, F. angustifolia, F. excelsior, F. ornus* and *F. pennsylvanica* (and their cultivars) are the most important species. Because *F. excelsior* is native to most parts of Europe, it has long been cultivated. Its first cultivars, including some variegated ones, date back to the eighteenth century.

The opposite leaves are usually pinnately compound and deciduous. *Fraxinus* produces small creamy white to white flowers in axillary or terminal racemes. The flowers themselves are unattractive, but because the plants are quite floriferous, it can be a spectacular sight to see a *Fraxinus* in full bloom. The fruits of *Fraxinus* are nutlike with a sometimes very conspicuous wing at the apex. The variegated cultivars of *Fraxinus* are of no commercial value in landscape plantings or as street trees. Although most variegated cultivars of *Fraxinus* were named more than a century ago, they are very poorly distributed. However, they are valuable park trees and every collector of variegated plants must have at least one *Fraxinus*. Members of this genus are easy to establish and reliably hardy.

Fraxinus angustifolia 'Variegata'

This species is native to southern Europe, northern Africa, and western Asia. It is a large tree that grows to about 20 m with a relatively open ovate crown.

Fraxinus angustifolia 'Variegata' PPH (COLLECTION OF HARRY VAN DE LAAR)

Fraxinus excelsior 'Argenteovariegata' PIERRE THEUNISSEN

Fraxinus excelsior 'Pendula Variegata' J. R. P. VAN HOEY SMITH

The branches are thinner and the leaves are significantly narrower than in *F. excelsior*, which is a native of parts of the same areas. The leaves are usually in whorls of three, instead the usual opposite. The pinnate leaves consist of seven to thirteen narrow lanceolate leaflets.

In 'Variegata' the light green leaflets are heavily speckled greenish white. The young branches are reddish brown, making an excellent contrast to the foliage. 'Variegata' is a beautiful tree that does not grow as large as the species. Unfortunately it is rare. Zone 6b

Fraxinus excelsior 'Argentea'

Paris, France, 1802

Very heavily variegated cultivar of the European ash that is easily distinguished by its white appearance. The leaves are very heavily variegated, and sometimes they are entirely white. When planted in the right semi-shaded location, 'Argentea' is a spectacular tree. However, it is prone to sunburn and can be rather weak. It is not common in cultivation. Zone 4

Fraxinus excelsior 'Argenteovariegata'

United Kingdom, before 1770

Medium-sized tree that grows to about 10 m with a broad crown. The leaflets usually have white margins, but variegated leaves also occur. Sometimes 'Argenteovariegata' is mixed up with 'Argentea'. 'Argenteovariegata' has less variegated foliage and, seen from a distance, it gives a grayish green appearance. Although this is an old cultivar and probably the most widely distributed variegated *Fraxinus*, it is quite rare in cultivation. Zone 4

Fraxinus excelsior 'Pendula Variegata'

C. de Vos, Hazerswoude, The Netherlands, 1887

Curious, rather slow-growing cultivar derived from *F. excelsior* 'Pendula'. The leaves are irregularly variegated. Together with its strong weeping habit, this results in an unusual tree. 'Pendula Variegata' tends to revert to green fairly easily. This cultivar is probably no longer in cultivation and is only rarely mentioned in the literature. Zone 4

Fraxinus pennsylvanica 'Albomarginata'

K. Koch, Germany, 1872

Upright, medium-sized tree with an ovate habit. The

Fraxinus pennsylvanica 'Albomarginata' GERT FORTGENS

Fraxinus pennsylvanica 'Aucubifolia' GERT FORTGENS

Fraxinus pennsylvanica 'Albomarginata' WIM SNOEIJER

leaves are light green with irregular white to cream-colored margins. The margins are quite wide and make 'Albomarginata' a distinct cultivar. Zone 4

Fraxinus pennsylvanica 'Aucubifolia'

Muskau Arboretum, Muskau, Poland, 1864

Within the genus *Fraxinus* this cultivar is unusual. Instead of the white variegation that is found in other cultivars, 'Aucubifolia' has gold-spotted leaves. Zone 4

Fraxinus pennsylvanica 'Aucubifolia Nova'

James Booth & Sons, Flottbeck, Germany, 1872

This cultivar was originally grown as 'Aucubifolia', but differs in having larger and more irregular gold spots on its leaves. Zone 4

Fraxinus pennsylvanica 'Aucubifolia Nova' RONALD HOUTMAN

Fraxinus pennsylvanica 'Variegata' PIERRE THEUNISSEN

Fuchsia 'John Ridding' FIRECRACKER™ RONALD HOUTMAN

Fuchsia magellanica 'Sharpitor' RONALD HOUTMAN

Fraxinus pennsylvanica 'Variegata'

Before 1903

One of the better variegated cultivars of *Fraxinus*. The leaves are grayish, mottled and margined creamy white. From a distance this gives a gray appearance to the tree. Zone 4

Fuchsia

Fuchsia is a genus of about 100 species, belonging to the Onagraceae (evening primrose family), a small family also including *Circaea*, *Epilobium*, *Gaura*, and *Oenothera*. *Fuchsia* is the only woody genus in this family. Species are confined to tropical Central and South America, Haiti, Tahiti, and New Zealand.

With their elegant flowers in many colors, fuchsias are very popular plants for use in pots and borders. Although most species and cultivars are frost-tender, a relatively small number of species and cultivars are hardy enough to be grown outdoors in zone 7, to which large parts of Europe and the United States belong. Most of these plants belong to the species *F. magellanica*, which grows in southern Chile and Argentina. Even more important is the winter-hardiness of this species, which is also present in numerous cultivars, of which a few are variegated. Apart from *F. magellanica* and its cultivars, 'John Ridding' and 'Tom West' are the best known variegated cultivars. Occasionally, variegated cultivars such as 'Anjo' (cream-margined foliage, poor flowering, waxy white flowers with cherry red corollas), 'Golden Lena' (yellow-variegated foliage, pale pink tubes and calyces, purple corolla), and 'Golden Marinka' (yellow-variegated foliage with reddish veins, red flowers) can be found.

Fuchsia 'John Ridding' FIRECRACKER™

John Ridding, Fuchsiavale Nurseries, Torton, United Kingdom, 1991

Discovered as a sport of 'Thalia', which was raised in 1855 with *F. triphylla* as the mother and an unknown pollinator. One of the qualities of these hybrids are the spectacular orange-red flowers that are produced in dense panicles. The individual flowers have long and narrow tubes. The leaves are broad ovate and dark green to grayish olive green. In 'John Ridding' they have irregular creamy white to white margins. Usually the leaves are tinged purple at the base when young, as is the main vein. From mid to late summer the spectacular flowers open in large, dense panicles. They add consistently to the beauty and ornamental value of 'John Ridding'. So far it has proved to be a very stable variegated cultivar. Like other *F. triphylla* hybrids, it is not hardy enough to plant outdoors, except in the mildest climates. Throughout most of Europe and the United Stated it is best treated as container plant. 'John Ridding' must be kept away from frost during winter. Zone 9

Fuchsia magellanica 'Sharpitor'

Sharpitor National Trust Garden, Devon, United Kingdom, 1973

Nice shrub with an upright habit and elegant arching branches. Although it is hardy to zone 7, it will not grow taller than about 1.5 m in this zone. In milder climates it will grow taller. The foliage has grayish and white margins, however, it reverts quite easily. This cultivar was derived from *F. magellanica* var. *molinae*, from which it inherited the pale pinkish white flowers. Zone 7

Fuchsia magellanica 'Variegata' J. R. P. VAN HOEY SMITH

Fuchsia magellanica 'Variegata'

Like 'Sharpitor', this is also an elegant shrub with arching branches. It grows to about 1.5 m high in zone 7, but will be taller in milder areas. The leaves are green, with cream to creamy white margins. 'Variegata', derived from *F. magellanica* var. *gracilis*, forms a compact shrub with a rather fine texture. The flowers have the same narrow shape as those of *F. magellanica* var. *gracilis*. They have scarlet tubes and sepals, and the corollas are violet. The flowers contrast well against the colorful foliage. Zone 7a

Fuchsia magellanica 'Versicolor'

This variegated cultivar of *Fuchsia magellanica* does not differ too much from the other two. The main distinction is the foliage coloring: the leaves of 'Versicolor' are green with pink tints and irregular white margins. The pink young leaves make 'Versicolor' a striking foliage shrub that also flowers profusely with drooping scarlet and violet flowers. Zone 7a

Fuchsia magellanica 'Versicolor' RONALD HOUTMAN

Fuchsia 'Tom West'

Auguste Miellez, Esquermes-les-Lille, France, 1853

Old variegated cultivar that was recently rediscovered and is becoming increasingly popular. It grows into a

Fuchsia 'Tom West' RONALD HOUTMAN

rather lax, bushy shrub that can also be used for trailing. The ovate leaves are dark grayish green with irregular creamy white margins, which are purple in young foliage. Occasionally the leaves have yellowish blotches as well. The flowers have the basic *Fuchsia* colors: a carmine red tube and sepals with a purple corolla. 'Tom West' is generally regarded as one of the very best variegated fuchsias. It is very stable and hardy enough for use in most temperate regions.

Auguste Miellez, who raised 'Tom West', was a nurseryman from northern France. In addition to this *Fuchsia*, he raised ninety-seven roses and a number of peonies, of which *Paeonia* 'Festiva Maxima' and *P.* 'Mme Calot' are the most famous. Zone 7a

Ginkgo

Ginkgo is a monotypic genus, belonging to the Ginkgoaceae, which is in fact the only family belonging to the Ginkgophyta, one of the four divisions in the gymnosperms (Coniferophyta, Gnetophyta, and Cycadophyta being the other three). Fossilized leaves of *Ginkgo* dated to 200 million years B.P. have been found, apparently similar to those that grow on present trees. It is native in a small area in eastern China, but some dendrologists think it is extinct in nature and has only survived through cultivation. *Ginkgo biloba* is a large tree with an open and irregular habit. Specimens occasionally produce relatively long and heavy side branches, at an angle of 90 degrees to the main stem. Still it is a beautiful and somewhat mysterious tree, easily recognized by its peculiar but very distinct foliage.

Ginkgo biloba 'Pevé Lobo' RONALD HOUTMAN

Ginkgo biloba 'Pevé Lobo'

P. Vergeldt, Lottum, The Netherlands, 2003

Raised as a seedling of *G. biloba*, this cultivar grows upright with an open and irregular habit. The foliage is striped creamy yellow to light yellow. Apart from the colors it does not differ much from that of *G. biloba* 'Variegata'. 'Pevé Lobo' is an attractive new cultivar that unfortunately has the same tendency to revert as 'Variegata'. Zone 5a

Ginkgo biloba 'Pevé Maribo' RONALD HOUTMAN

Ginkgo biloba 'Pevé Maribo'

P. Vergeldt, Lottum, The Netherlands, 2003

Small, flattened, globular plant. 'Pevé Maribo' was found as a sport in *G. biloba* 'Mariken' and has the same habit. The branches are relatively thick, and the plant is much less vigorous than the species. Likewise, the leaves are the same size as in the species, but also more leathery. They are striped light yellow. The splendid compact habit of 'Mariken' in combination with the variegated foliage make 'Pevé Maribo' a very promising new cultivar. It can be grown both as a shrub or grafted on a standard. Zone 5a

Ginkgo biloba 'Roswitha'

Rudolf Dirr, Asbach-Bäumenheim, Germany, 1992

Unique cultivar with a horizontal growth habit. The leaves are identical to those of *G. biloba* 'Variegata': striped creamy white to cream. 'Roswitha' was discovered as a sport of the green-leaved 'Horizontalis' and inherited the same distinctive habit. Although it is possible to grow 'Roswitha' as a shrub, it is preferable to graft it on a standard. Like all variegated *Ginkgo*, it is likely to revert and green-leaved branches must be taken out. Zone 5a

Ginkgo biloba 'Roswitha' JO BÖMER

Ginkgo biloba 'Variegata'

M. André Leroy Nurseries, Angers, France, 1854

Distinctive variegated cultivar of the well-known maidenhair tree. The unique fan-shaped leaves are easily distinguished from any other plant in the world. In 'Variegata' the leaves are dull green, striped cream to creamy white. The tree can reach a height of more than 8 m and has an irregular habit, caused by the lateral branches that grow almost horizontal from the main trunk. It is said that the original 'Variegata' was a female clone. However, normal green-leaved specimens occasionally produce variegated-leaved branches that are virtually indistinguishable from 'Variegata'. Over the last 150 years, various other variegated *G. biloba* were raised and offered as 'Variegata'. This means there can be some variation between these clones, in gender as well. Zone 5a

Ginkgo biloba 'Variegata' RONALD HOUTMAN

Griselinia

This small genus is closely related to *Aucuba*. Although it supposed to be placed in its own family, Griseliniaceae, *Griselinia* was long included in the Cornaceae (dogwood family). *Griselinia* consists of only six species, four endemic to Chile and two that only grow in New Zealand. In addition to the two New Zealand species, *G. littoralis* and *G. lucida*, the Chilean *G. scandens* is occasionally found in cultivation. *Griselinia* are trees that easily grow more than 15 m in height in their native environment. All species have unisexual flowers, usually on different plants.

All variegated cultivars are derived from *G. littoralis*, by far the most widely grown *Griselinia* species. It is a medium-sized tree that grows to 15 m in its native habitat, considerably lower in western Europe and the United States. It has a very distinctive short, thick trunk that is twisted and gnarled. The thick and leathery leaves are broad ovate to oblong or obovate. They are up to 12 cm long and 7 cm wide. *Griselinia littoralis* is hardy to zones 7/8 and most common in coastal areas in the United Kingdom, Ireland, and continental Eu-

Griselinia littoralis 'Bantry Bay' RONALD HOUTMAN

Griselinia littoralis 'Brodick Gold' FA. C. ESVELD

rope. It has a very high resistance to salty wind and can be used for hedging or as an amenity plant. *Griselinia littoralis* will tolerate almost any soil and situation.

Two types of variegation can be seen in *Griselinia*. Most of the variegated cultivars have colored leaf centers and green or pale green margins. 'Bantry Bay', 'Brodick Gold', 'Dairy Cream', and 'Dixon's Cream' all belong to this group. Sometimes these cultivars are erroneously referred to as 'Maculata', which is nothing more than a collective name for cultivars that have variegated leaf centers and green margins. All these cultivars originated as sports of *G. littoralis* 'Variegata', which is the main representative of the second group. The cultivars in this group have colored margins and are green or grayish green in the leaf centers. In addition to 'Variegata', 'Green Jewel' also belongs to this group. The variegated cultivars do not grow as tall as the species. They will usually not grow taller than about 4 m, even smaller when grown in containers. All *Griselinia* described here are winter-hardy to zones 7/8.

Griselinia littoralis 'Bantry Bay'

Ilnacullin, Glengariff, Ireland, 1950

Nice variegated cultivar with golden yellow to cream variegated leaves and grayish green to green margins. 'Bantry Bay' was found as a sport of the species. Murdo MacKenzie, head gardener of Ilnacullin, a small garden island in southwestern Ireland, found the variegated sport in *G. littoralis*. He cut back the green shoots for several years, until the variegated shoot became a leader. 'Bantry Bay' has proven to be more difficult to propagate than, for instance, 'Variegata'. It is also quite sensitive to cold winds and slightly less hardy than other *Griselinia* described here. Together with 'Variegata', 'Bantry Bay' is the most widely grown variegated *Griselinia* in Europe.

Griselinia littoralis 'Brodick Gold'

Brodick Castle Gardens, Brodick, United Kingdom

A good cultivar that is similar to 'Bantry Bay', except for its more golden appearance. The leaf centers are a good golden yellow and the narrow margins are pale green.

Griselinia littoralis 'Dairy Cream'

Duncan & Davies, New Plymouth, New Zealand, 1978

Very good cultivar of New Zealand origin. Although it

looks quite similar to 'Dixon's Cream', 'Dairy Cream' is said to have less of a tendency to grow reverted shoots. The leaf centers are creamy yellow, surrounded by yellowish green margins.

Griselinia littoralis 'Dixon's Cream'

Major W. G. M. Dixon, Jersey, United Kingdom

This cultivar also originated as a sport of *G. littoralis* 'Variegata'. The strongly variegated leaves only occasionally show a narrow band of deep green along the margins. The rest of the leaf is variegated creamy yellow to yellowish green. It is best grown in a semi-shaded location.

Griselinia littoralis 'Dixon's Cream' RONALD HOUTMAN

Griselinia littoralis 'Green Jewel'

Christchurch Botanic Gardens, Christchurch, New Zealand

'Green Jewel' is a very distinctive cultivar with narrower and more pointed leaves than 'Variegata'. The leaves are deep green with striking creamy yellow margins. In the green center some irregular splashes of pale green and grayish green occur. When the leaves are older, these shades disappear and the leaf centers gradually become deep green. When aging, the margins also become more cream colored instead of the yellowish colors on young leaves. 'Green Jewel' is a nice cultivar that is mainly grown in New Zealand (especially on the South Island). Although it cannot match 'Variegata' in ornamental value, it definitely should be more widely grown in Europe and the United States.

Griselinia littoralis 'Green Jewel' RONALD HOUTMAN

Griselinia littoralis 'Maculata'

This is a collective name for various variegated cultivars and probably an illegitimate name. In 'Variegata', a true cultivar, the leaves have yellow margins. In the clones known as 'Maculata' the leaves have a central variegation. Although several cultivars such as 'Brodick Gold', 'Dairy Cream' and 'Dixon's Cream' have been named, some clones remain unnamed.

A typical example of *Griselinia littoralis* 'Maculata' J. R. P. VAN HOEY SMITH

Griselinia littoralis 'Variegata'

Undoubtedly the best-known variegated cultivar of *Griselinia*. The rounded leaves are deep green with irregular creamy white to yellowish margins. In most leaves the variegation flows into the leaf center, giving the plant an even heavier variegated aspect. 'Variegata' is the oldest variegated cultivar in this genus, and many new cultivars were derived from it as sports.

Griselinia littoralis 'Variegata' RONALD HOUTMAN

Gymnocladus dioica 'Variegatus' J. R. P. VAN HOEY SMITH

Gymnocladus dioica 'Variegatus' WOUT KROMHOUT

Gymnocladus dioica 'Variegatus'

Medium-sized deciduous tree that grows to about 10 m, but usually not more than 6 m. Like the species, this variegated cultivar has the same characteristic thick branches. The large bipinnate leaves can reach a length of more than 70 cm. They are heavily speckled creamy white. The young growth is a delicious soft pink. The variegation by itself is not very beautiful, but seen from a short distance, the whole tree is striking in its appearance. This rare but spectacular variegated tree is not easy to propagate, which is the main reason it is offered only rarely. Zone 5a

Halesia monticola 'Variegata'

This is perhaps one of the most peculiar variegated plants. Young leaves of this cultivar are green with narrow creamy yellow margins. However, the yellow margins are not on the outer edges of the leaves, but are visible as narrow lines approximately 4 mm from the outer edges. As they mature the green centers turn more grayish and the variegation changes to creamy white. The outer edges stay clear green. Like the species, 'Variegata' flowers with white nodding bells in spring, followed by four-winged fruits. Contrary to *Halesia monticola* 'Yellow Blush', the variegation in 'Variegata' is much more stable. Although the name is not legitimate (it is a Latin word given to a plant after January 1, 1959), 'Variegata' is well worth growing. Zone 5

Halesia monticola 'Yellow Blush'

André van Nijnatten, Zundert, The Netherlands, 2003

Splendid small to medium-sized tree with an upright habit and spreading branches. The mountain snowdrop tree is native to the southeastern United States that grows to a height of about 10 m in its native habitat. In cultivation it usually stays smaller. In spring *Halesia monticola* flowers with nodding, bell-shaped white flowers, followed by four-winged fruits. The leaves are green, irregularly variegated clear yellow. Unfortunately, the variegation is very unstable and the foliage easily reverts to green. Zone 5b

Halesia monticola 'Variegata' RONALD HOUTMAN

Hamamelis ×*intermedia* 'Double Gold'

J. M. van Gemeren, Hazerswoude, The Netherlands, 1996

Discovered as a sport of *H.* ×*intermedia* 'Westerstede', this is one of the few variegated *Hamamelis* cultivars. It forms a broad, upright to spreading shrub with an open, flattened habit. The leaves are obovate and dull green with greenish yellow margins, especially near the leaf tips. In young leaves, the centers are bronze-green to brownish. The variegation causes leaf deformation, giving the shrub a sloppy appearance. The name refers to the winter-flowering habit: the golden yellow flowers open in late February to early March, even later than the late-flowering 'Westerstede. A true collectors' item, very rare in the trade. Zone 6b

Halesia monticola 'Yellow Blush' PIERRE THEUNISSEN

Hamamelis mollis 'Gold Edge'

Richard Nutt, United Kingdom

Relatively slow-growing deciduous shrub with a broad, upright habit. The leaves are obovate, dull green, and distinctively pubescent, especially on the

Hamamelis intermedia 'Double Gold' RONALD HOUTMAN

Hamamelis intermedia 'Double Gold' RONALD HOUTMAN

Hamamelis mollis 'Gold Edge' RONALD HOUTMAN

Hamamelis mollis 'Gold Edge' RONALD HOUTMAN

Hebe ×*andersonii* 'Anne Pimm' DAN HEIMS

undersides. The pubescence is a typical feature of *H. mollis*. All leaves have an irregular creamy to greenish yellow margin, most distinct near the tips. Like 'Double Gold', the leaves suffer from deformation caused by the variegation. 'Gold Edge' flowers in late January with dark yellow flowers, which are slightly smaller than in the species. A collectors' item that is difficult to obtain. Zone 6b

Hebe

Very important genus of shrubs belonging to the Scrophulariaceae (figwort family). All species grow in the Southern Hemisphere. More than 140 species are known, of which about 90 are endemic to New Zealand. Other species grow in the Falkland Islands, South America (mainly Chile), New Guinea, and Australia.

Hebe, which consists of all evergreen shrubs, is closely related to *Veronica*, a genus of deciduous shrubs and herbaceous plants, in which it was originally placed. *Hebe* differs from *Veronica* in that the growing shoots are always covered by leaves. Also, the ripe seed pods of *Veronica* split open vertically, whereas the seed pods of *Hebe* split horizontally. The third important difference lies in the chromosome numbers of the genera

The genus *Hebe* can be divided into two groups: hebes with leaves and the "whipcord" hebes. Whipcord hebes consist of fourteen species and some cultivars. Their general appearance resembles small cypresslike conifers. Unlike the leafy hebes, they grow in a juvenile stage (small, usually rounded leaves) at first, later producing adult foliage (the characteristic whipcords). There are no variegated cultivars within this group. The group of hebes with normal leaves is much larger and more important horticulturally. All plants in this group carry their flowers in axillary racemes, sometimes branched racemes. The flowers vary in color from white and lilac or pink to deep purple or violet-red. Of the many existing species and cultivars, only a handful are variegated.

The winter-hardiness of hebes is difficult to classify in general. Many *Hebe* species and cultivars are hardy to zone 8, but some are more frost-tender (zones 9 or 10). However, there are a number of hebes that can be planted in zone 7. In general, the smaller the leaves of a hebe, the greater the hardiness. All hebes have excellent salt and wind resistance and make superb shrubs for coastal planting. Their colorful flowers and attractive (variegated) foliage are good qualities.

Hebe ×andersonii

Usually the hybrid *H. ×andersonii* and its variegated cultivars are referred to as, for instance, *Hebe* 'Andersonii' and *H.* 'Andersonii Anne Pimm'. However, *H. ×andersonii* was originally described in 1863 as *Veronica ×andersonii*. Therefore, according to the ICNCP, the correct name for these cultivars must be *Hebe ×andersonii* 'Andersonii' and *H. ×andersonii* 'Anne Pimm'.

Hebe ×andersonii 'Anne Pimm'

A variegated cultivar of *H. ×andersonii* that is quite rare in cultivation. It is slightly less vigorous than the species (hybrid) and will attain a height of about 1.2 m. The leaves are ovate to lanceolate and up to 7 cm long and 3 cm wide. They are green with irregular cream-colored margins. The leaf surface is slightly gray-downy, giving the leaf a grayish appearance. The downy layer is easily rubbed off. 'Anne Pimm' produces purple flowers carried in dense racemes up to 8 cm long. It is about as winter-hardy as *H. ×andersonii* 'Variegata' and therefore only suitable in milder areas. Zone 9

Hebe ×andersonii 'Aurea'

Uncommon yellow-variegated cultivar that is only rarely offered in the trade. It is very similar to the better-known *H. ×andersonii* 'Variegata', but the leaves have yellow margins of varying width. The main reason it is only rarely grown is its poor winter-hardiness. Zone 10

Hebe ×andersonii 'Variegata'

New Zealand, before 1874

Rather vigorous upright evergreen, later a rounded shrub of about 1.50 m high and 1.25 m wide. The large leaves are narrow ovate to lanceolate and up to 10 cm long. They are variegated grayish green and have irregular creamy margins. During summer, light violet flowers appear in racemes up to 10 cm long, giving the shrub an even more colorful radiance. This is one of the oldest variegated plants from New Zealand. It originated as a sport in *Hebe ×andersonii* 'Andersonii'. Zone 9

Hebe 'Dazzler'

Lowaters Nursery, Warsash, United Kingdom

Compact, rather slow-growing, globe-shaped shrub that grows to 40 cm high and 50 cm wide. The narrow leaves are about 3 cm long and up to 8 mm wide. They are green with a comparatively broad creamy margin. In autumn the foliage color changes to deep burgundy. This color is kept until the average temperature rises in spring. Very good plant for use in perennial borders and in containers. Zone 8

Hebe ×franciscana 'Variegata'

Bushy shrub with a rounded habit that does not grow taller than about 1 m. The distinctively convex leaves are broad elliptic to obovate and up to 5 cm long. The leaves are medium green in the centers, surrounded by somewhat irregular creamy yellow margins, more yellow on young foliage. The flowers are pale to pinkish purple and carried in dense racemes up to 7 cm long. *Hebe ×franciscana* 'Variegata' is probably the best-known variegated *Hebe*. It is widely grown in Europe and the United States as well as in Australia and New Zealand. The good and stable foliage coloration makes it a popular shrub. Zone 8

Hebe 'Dazzler' CHRISTOPHER FAIRWEATHER

Hebe ×franciscana 'Variegata' RONALD HOUTMAN

Hebe glaucophylla 'Variegata' RONALD HOUTMAN

Hebe glaucophylla 'Variegata'

Graceful small shrub that grows to about 1 m high, forming a rounded bush. The thin twigs are brownish, especially at the nodes. The small lanceolate leaves are grayish green with creamy edges, contrasting well against the brown twigs. In summer the lilac flowers appear in short axillary racemes. This cultivar is very distinct in its small leaves. All other variegated hebes have larger leaves. Zone 8

Hebe 'Goldrush'

Joh. van Niekerk, Waddinxveen, The Netherlands, 2003

Densely branched, broad ovate evergreen, eventually reaching a height of about 50 cm. The small obovate leaves are light reddish green at first. During spring and summer they become greenish yellow to golden yellow, leaving only a narrow central band of green. In April and May the light pink flowers open in dense racemes. The flowerbuds are a deeper pink. The flowers contrast very well against the bright foliage. 'Goldrush' is the first yellow-variegated small-leaved hebe and is very popular as a container plant. Zone 8

Hebe 'Goldrush' RONALD HOUTMAN

Hebe 'Heartbreaker'

Joh. van Niekerk, Waddinxveen, The Netherlands, 2002

Compact bushy evergreen with a globular habit that grows to about 50 cm high. The lanceolate leaves are green with irregular creamy white margins. The young shoots are deep purplish pink, which creates a striking effect, especially in late winter and spring. The shoot tips are also purplish pink during winter. 'Heartbreaker' has some similarities with *H.* 'Neprock', but the variegation is brighter and the colors of the young shoots are much deeper. Zone 8

Hebe 'Heartbreaker' RONALD HOUTMAN

Hebe 'Lady Ann'

Van Vliet New Plants, Boskoop, The Netherlands, 2001

Discovered as a sport of *H.* 'Orphan Annie', this small shrub has the same flattened-globular habit. The leaves are narrow elliptic and silvery white with narrow grayish green centers. In spring the young growth is deep purple. During early summer the small flowers appear in dense panicles. Individual flowers are pink. Although 'Lady Ann' is not very floriferous, this surely adds to its ornamental value. Its main use is as a container plant for balconies and terraces. Zone 8

Hebe 'Lopen'

E. J. Goddard, Lopen Head, United Kingdom, after 1954

Discovered as a variegated sport of *H.* 'Midsummer Beauty', this interesting cultivar has the same broad, upright habit. It is an open shrub that grows to about 1.5 m high. The leaves are lanceolate to oblanceolate and up to 10 cm long. They are clear green with broad creamy white margins. Occasionally the leaves are streaked cream and light green as well. The flowers open from late June to early November. They are carried in dense racemes up to 20 cm long. Individual flowers are violet-purple, giving great contrast to the foliage. Unfortunately, the leaves of 'Lopen' are prone to sunburn. Therefore, it definitely needs a location in semi-shade. It is hardy only in the mildest climates, otherwise it is best treated as a container plant. Zone 9

Hebe 'Lady Ann' RONALD HOUTMAN

Hebe 'Neprock' PURPLE SHAMROCK™

Doug and Paulette Thomson, Irish Garden Plants, Downpatrick, Northern Ireland, 1994

This sport of *H.* 'Mrs Winder' is an attractive variety with superb variegated grayish green, cream-edged foliage. From late September until early April the foliage is purple with dark pink margins. The young leaves have creamy yellow margins and make a good display against the dark purple twigs. It forms a compact, globe-shaped shrub about 60 cm high. 'Neprock' is foremost a foliage plant. The flowers, which are not produced abundantly, are blue and stand in long racemes. Zone 8

Hebe 'Lopen' RONALD HOUTMAN

Hebe 'Orphan Annie'

Annton Nursery Ltd., Cambridge, New Zealand, 1995

Fine compact evergreen shrub that attains a height of

Hebe 'Orphan Annie' RONALD HOUTMAN

Hebe 'Neprock' PURPLE SHAMROCK™ RONALD HOUTMAN

Hebe 'Rainseiont' RAINBOW™ RONALD HOUTMAN

Hebe 'Silver Dollar' RONALD HOUTMAN

approximately 50 cm and will grow as wide. The attractive foliage is green with creamy white to pale yellow margins. Sometimes the main vein is also pale creamy yellow. In spring the young shoots are conspicuously purplish red. The flowers, also appearing in late spring, are dark pink and stand in dense axillary racemes. Zone 8

Hebe 'Rainseiont' RAINBOW™

Neil Alcock, Seiont Nurseries, Caernarfon, Wales, United Kingdom, 2003

Broad, upright, evergreen shrub with a relative dense habit that grows up to about 50 cm high. The elliptic leaves are relatively large, approximately 2.5–3.5 cm. They are green with creamy white margins and stripes in the centers. The foliage contrasts well with the purplish twigs. In June and July the small flowers open in dense racemes. They are violet-blue, fading to pale violet to white. 'Rainseiont' RAINBOW™ is a nice addition in the already large range of hebes. Like most others, it is best used as a container plant. In milder areas it will survive during winter, otherwise it must be regarded an annual. Zone 8

Hebe 'Silver Dollar'

Lowaters Nursery, Warsash, United Kingdom

A compact bushy plant that will grow to a height of about 60 cm. 'Silver Dollar' was found as a seedling and combines silvery variegated foliage with good winter colors and white flowers. In summer the leaves have narrow reddish margins and in colder periods the foliage will turn burgundy red. The white flowers open in spring in dense racemes. Zone 8

Hedera

A genus of seven to fifteen evergreen species (depending on various interpretations) belonging to the Araliaceae (aralia or ginseng family). All species grow in the Northern Hemisphere only. Although there are only a few species, the number of cultivars easily exceeds 400.

In horticulture, *Hedera* are generally divided into two groups: climbing and nonclimbing (adult types). Climbing *Hedera* are usually juvenile and therefore not flowering. The moment a part of a plant reaches its adult stage, it no longer climbs, but forms a bushy habit. The shape of the leaves changes, usually into a rhombic shape, and the plant starts producing flowers. These are borne in dense, globose umbels, followed by blackish (or yellow) fruits. Bees and bumblebees are strongly attracted to the flowers of adult *Hedera* plants.

Hedera helix, the English ivy, is the best-known species within the genus. It is native to the larger part of Europe (north to Scandinavia [60°N], east to Ukraine, and south to Cyprus and Crete). In the United States it is considered a weed due to its sometimes aggressive habit. The numerous cultivars mainly differ in leaf size, shape, and coloration. Although most of the cultivars are green leaved, a large number of cultivars have variegated foliage. Variegated cultivars can be found both in juvenile (climbing) and adult (shrubby) types. Apart from a few exceptions, almost every variegated ivy tends to revert. Some of them, such as 'Goldheart', are notorious for their reversions.

Hedera algeriensis 'Gloire de Marengo'

Pépinières Vilmorin, Paris, France, about 1883

Vigorous climber that grows to 5 m high or more and therefore suitable to cover a large wall or house. The leaves are relatively large and green to light green with grayish spots. The margins are yellowish white, especially striking on young shoots. This ivy is widely grown as a houseplant both in Europe and the United States, but it can also be grown outdoors.

Hedera algeriensis is sometimes considered a variety of *H. canariensis*, and 'Gloire de Marengo' was first described as *H. canariensis* var. *variegata* by Vilmorin. The plant had almost been forgotten when both Hillier of Winchester and Jackmans of Woking published the name 'Gloire de Marengo' in 1924. This name derived from Marengo Park in Algiers, where it was reintroduced from in the 1920s. Although the name *variegata* is older, this cultivar is commonly referred to as 'Gloire de Marengo'. Zone 8

Hedera algeriensis 'Gloire de Marengo' RONALD HOUTMAN

Hedera colchica 'Dentata Variegata'

L. R. Russell Ltd., Richmond, United Kingdom, 1907

Well-known variegated ivy with large green leaves up to 20 cm. The margins are clear creamy yellow and are not prone to sunburn during hot and sunny spells. 'Dentata Variegata' can be used as a climber or as a groundcover, retaining its variegation very well. When climbing, the

Hedera colchica 'Dentata Variegata' RONALD HOUTMAN

Hedera colchica 'Sulphur Heart' RONALD HOUTMAN

Hedera colchica 'Sulphur Heart' RONALD HOUTMAN

leaves hang down in a curious manner typical for *H. colchica* and its cultivars. The margins are slightly recurved and have only a few small teeth. Zone 7a

Hedera colchica 'Sulphur Heart'

Boot & Co Nurseries, Boskoop, The Netherlands, 1968

Splendid cultivar resembling 'Dentata Variegata' in general habit. The leaves are green to light green irregularly splashed and striped pale yellow to greenish yellow. The stripes usually run to the margins. Like 'Dentata Variegata', it is very suitable as a groundcover and hardier than other *H. colchica* cultivars. Therefore, 'Sulphur Heart' is recommended for use in colder climates. This plant is an old cultivar that was grown before World War II as *H. colchica dentata aureo-striata*. However, this name was never published and is therefore illegitimate. In 1968 it was named 'Sulphur Heart' by the late Harry van de Laar, two years prior to 'Paddy's Pride', which later proved to be the same. Zone 6b

Hedera helix 'Adam'

Before 1968

Rather compact bushy ivy with comparatively small leaves (only 3 to 4 cm long). The leaves are three-lobed and light green to grayish green with creamy white margins. The central lobe is slightly curved sideways, which is a typical characteristic of this cultivar. It also has a cordate leaf base, making 'Adam' distinguishable from 'Eva', its more creamy yellow counterpart. This is a juvenile, climbing cultivar. Zone 6

Hedera helix 'Angularis Aurea' WOUT KROMHOUT

Hedera helix 'Angularis Aurea'

United Kingdom, 1890

Splendid yellow-variegated juvenile ivy cultivar that derived from the green-leaved 'Angularis'. The three-lobed leaves are about 5 cm long with broad wedge-shaped lobes. Often the lateral lobes are very shallow. The leaves are glossy dark green and heavily blotched and dotted bright to light yellow. Young leaves are entirely green at first, becoming more variegated with age. During winter the leaves turn dark green with purplish spots. Zone 6

Hedera helix 'Argentea Variegata RONALD HOUTMAN

Hedera helix 'Argentea Variegata'

United Kingdom, before 1770

The leaves of this old and nearly forgotten cultivar are quite variable in size and variegation. Usually the leaves are shallowly lobed (three lobes), but many unlobed, broad ovate to almost deltoid leaves exist as well. They are dark green with irregular, broad, white margins. But again, in many leaves larger parts are variegated. 'Argentea Variegata' is very prone to sunburn, but it keeps its color well when planted in a shaded location. Therefore it is excellent for planting against a north-facing wall or fence. During severe winters the leaves might be damaged by frosts. Zone 7

Hedera helix 'Aureovariegata' RONALD HOUTMAN

Hedera helix 'Aureovariegata'

United Kingdom, before 1770

The name 'Aureovariegata' was first mentioned, without description, by Weston in 1770. In 1942 this name was used collectively to define all golden-variegated *H. helix*, which are virtually indistinguishable from one another. The leaves of 'Aureovariegata' are relatively large, up to 5 cm. They usually have three shallow lobes. They are green with butter-yellow margins. Occasionally the leaves have yellow patches. Because the

Hedera helix 'Blushing Cream' RONALD HOUTMAN

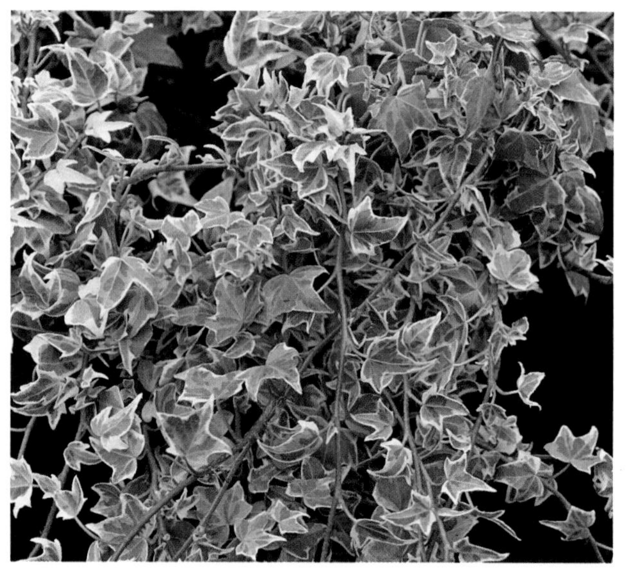
Hedera helix 'Carine' RONALD HOUTMAN

Hedera helix 'Cavendishii' RONALD HOUTMAN

name 'Aureovariegata' is used for this clone, other names have disappeared into synonymy. These include 'Aurea Maculata', 'Chrysophylla', and 'Hibernica Aureomarginata'. Zone 7

Hedera helix 'Blushing Cream'

Hanno Hardijzer, Boskoop, The Netherlands, 1996

Beautiful variegated ivy that was discovered as a sport of 'Clotted Cream'. 'Blushing Cream' differs in having extremely wrinkled leaf margins. The colors are almost identical: light green with broad creamy white margins. During winter the margins turn red, which is quite attractive. Zone 7

Hedera helix 'Caecilia'

Rogmans, Geldern, Germany, 1976

Cultivar with both attractively colored and nicely shaped leaves, resembling 'Parsley Crested' in general habit. It derived from the Danish cultivar 'Harald' and has the same leaf coloration. The 3 to 4 cm long leaves are usually five-lobed with obtuse lateral lobes and a central lobe almost twice as long. The grayish green markings are lighter, and the leaves have irregular creamy yellow to creamy white margins. The margins are wrinkly and wavy, making 'Caecilia' a joyful cultivar. Sometimes the name is misspelled as 'Sicelia' or 'Sicilia'. Zone 6

Hedera helix 'Carine'

A. W. van Bockel, Boskoop, The Netherlands, 1999

Compact cultivar that originated as a sport of *H. helix* 'Kolibri'. The three-lobed leaves are about 3 cm long with a rather narrow central lobe. They are dark grayish green with lighter parts. The margins are clear creamy white. Due to its good branching habit, the variegation is even more spectacular. Originally 'Carine' was grown as a houseplant, but it can be used as a garden plant as well. Zone 7

Hedera helix 'Cavendishii'

United Kingdom, before 1790

This old cultivar is still one of the best variegated ivies. It is a plant of moderate growth but it is well branched. The leaves are three-lobed (occasionally five-lobed) to deltoid, very uniform with an equilateral central lobe, and up to about 4 cm long. The grayish green to green leaves have narrow silvery white to ivory white margins. 'Cavendishii' is an outstanding cultivar. It is not an extremely strong grower and almost never reverts to green. Due to its long existence plants are grown under one of the many synonyms, such as 'Argentea Elegans', 'Marginata', 'Marginata Elegantissima', or 'Marginata Minor'. Usually 'Cavendishii' changes into the adult stage when quite young. Therefore, there are a number of adult clones available. They are usually sold under names such as 'Cavendishii' (adult), 'Arborea Variegata'. Two named cultivars that arose as adult clones from 'Cavendishii' are 'Ghost' and 'Ice Cream'. Zone 6

Hedera helix 'Clotted Cream'

Hanno Hardijzer, Boskoop, The Netherlands, 1985

Another attractive cultivar with wrinkly and wavy leaf margins resembling 'Parsley Crested'. The five-lobed leaves are about 4 cm long and have a significantly longer central lobe. 'Clotted Cream' is most similar to 'Caecilia' and even supposed to be synonymous with it, but it is definitely not the same plant: 'Caecilia' was named almost ten years prior to 'Clotted Cream'. 'Clotted Cream' is a valuable cultivar that can be used as groundcover as well as for climbing in a trellis or against a wall. Zone 6

Hedera helix 'Clouded Sky'

Attractive cultivar closely resembling 'Angularis Aurea'. The young leaves are a dark glossy green, becoming bright yellow with age. Occasionally entirely yellow leaves are formed. 'Clouded Sky' is excellent as a groundcover because it does not climb much. Especially in semi-shade or in combination with shrubs or conifers, it makes a dramatic scene. Zone 6

Hedera helix 'Elfenbein'

Stauss Bros., Au i. d. Hallertau, Austria, 1977

'Elfenbein' (meaning "ivory") is a rather slow-growing ivy that is best described as a variegated counterpart of 'Parsley Crested'. The name obviously refers to the ivory white to creamy yellow marginal variegation. The leaves are five-lobed, usually heavily curled and twisted. The leaf edges are strongly sinuate and crinkled. Due to its irregular growth habit, 'Elfenbein' does not make a good container plant. It is recommended as a garden plant. Zone 6

Hedera helix 'Clotted Cream' RONALD HOUTMAN

Hedera helix 'Clouded Sky' RONALD HOUTMAN

Hedera helix 'Eva' RONALD HOUTMAN

Hedera helix 'Glacier' RONALD HOUTMAN

Hedera helix 'Golden Eclipse' RONALD HOUTMAN

Hedera helix 'Eva'

Tage Melin, Hjallese, Denmark, 1960

The three-lobed leaves of 'Eva' are grayish green to dark green with yellowish white margins. 'Eva' was discovered as a variegated sport of 'Harald', another variegated Danish cultivar discovered by Melin of Hjallese. 'Eva' is much smaller in all its parts than 'Harald'. Both 'Eva' and 'Harald' are not as winter-hardy as most other variegated ivies described here. Therefore, they have become very popular as container plants. Zone 7

Hedera helix 'Glacier'

Weber Nurseries, Los Angeles, California, United States, 1943

Very popular variegated ivy that is widely grown throughout the world. It is suitable both as a container plant and as a garden plant. It forms a well-branched climbing or groundcover shrub with three-lobed leaves. The leaves are medium green to grayish green with a narrow grayish to a silvery white edge. Various other variegated ivies have been derived from 'Glacier', because it rarely reaches its adult stage. Older plants can reach an adolescent stage, in which they form sports quite easily. 'Glacier' is a good cultivar that can be used for small to medium-sized plantings, as well as for climbing in large trees. Zone 6

Hedera helix 'Golden Eclipse'

A. W. van Bockel, Boskoop, The Netherlands, 1999

Discovered as a sport of 'Sagittifolia' and differing from it in having golden yellow leaf margins. The similarity with 'Sagittifolia' is very clear, because the central lobe of the usually three-lobed leaf is significantly longer than the lateral lobes. 'Golden Eclipse' was discovered in 1999, but the name was given on August 11, 2000, when a full solar eclipse was seen in western and central Europe. It is very suitable as a container plant, but not hardy enough to be grown outdoors in colder areas. Zone 7

Hedera helix 'Golden Inge'

Frode Maegaard Nurseries, Ringe, Denmark, 1987

Striking Danish cultivar that was first introduced as a container plant but has proven to be an excellent garden plant as well. The leaves are three-lobed but the lobes are very shallow, often resulting in almost triangular leaves. They are dark green and heavily splashed and mottled clear yellow to creamy yellow. The leaf edges are strongly wavy to almost crinkly. Although originally named 'Golden Inge', it is often sold as 'Golden Ingot'. Inge is a popular girls' name in Scandinavia, but when first brought into the United Kingdom the tag was misread as 'Golden Ingot'. It is an excellent shrub for groundcover that holds its strong color even in the shade. Zone 6

Hedera helix 'Golden Wedding'

Jan Willem Wezelenburg, Hazerswoude, The Netherlands, 1998

Approximately fifty years after the famous 'Goldheart' was found, this arborescent (adult) ivy was derived from it. The leaves have the same striking color as its parent: dark green with a striking golden yellow blotch in the center. Contrary to 'Goldheart', 'Golden Wedding' has a nonclimbing habit and the leaves have a different shape. It forms a dense bushy shrub that grows to about 1 m high. The leaves are diamond-shaped to narrow diamond-shaped. 'Golden Wedding' tends to produce some juvenile growth every now and then, as well as green-leaved shoots. I recommend cutting these out when noticed. By giving the plant less nitrogen (which promotes the growth of juvenile shoots), this can partially be avoided. Zone 6

Hedera helix 'Goldheart'

Italy, about 1950

Healthy climbing or groundcover ivy with dark green three-lobed leaves. The leaf centers are irregularly spotted clear yellow, contrasting very well against the dark green. Many plants with a variegated leaf center are less stable than those with a marginal variegation. 'Goldheart' is no exception to this, and the plant easily reverts to green, especially after pruning.

'Goldheart' is perhaps the best-known variegated ivy. Its exact origin is still a mystery, but certainly it was first introduced as 'Oro di Bogliasco' in Italy in the 1950s. In the 1950s and 1960s it showed up in European gardens under various names, such as 'Jubiläum Goldherz', 'Jubilee', and 'Goldherz'. After a Royal Horticultural Society show in the United Kingdom it was published as 'Goldheart' in the RHS proceedings (1970). The plant readily became very popular under this name, despite its original Italian name. In plant catalogs from southern Europe it is still listed as 'Oro di Bogliasco'. Zone 6

Hedera helix 'Golden Inge' RONALD HOUTMAN

Hedera helix 'Golden Wedding' RONALD HOUTMAN

Hedera helix 'Goldheart' PPH (COLLECTION OF HARRY VAN DE LAAR)

Hedera helix 'Harald' RONALD HOUTMAN

Hedera helix 'Ice Cream' RONALD HOUTMAN

Hedera helix 'Little Diamond' RONALD HOUTMAN

Hedera helix 'Harald'

Tage Melin, Hjallese, Denmark, about 1958

Nice ivy with three-lobed leaves that are grayish green with white to creamy white margins. Only a few years after 'Harald' was introduced, Melin found a sport in 'Harald' in which all parts are smaller. He called it 'Eva'. Both 'Eva' and 'Harald' are slightly less winter-hardy than most other variegated ivies. Therefore, they have become very popular as container plants. Since its introduction in the late 1950s 'Harald' has been regularly offered under synonyms such as 'Esther' and 'Ingrid'. Zone 7

Hedera helix 'Ice Cream'

H. Kolster, Boskoop, The Netherlands, 1999

Dwarf shrub with a dense and compact habit that eventually will reach about 150 cm in height. It was found as an adult form of 'Cavendishii' on a wall in France by Wim van der Poel of Boskoop, The Netherlands. The leaves are narrow diamond-shaped and grayish green with narrow silvery green to ivory green margins. In late summer the small greenish flowers open in globular umbels. Zone 6

Hedera helix 'Kolibri'

Brokamp Nursery, Ramsdorf, Germany, 1975

'Kolibri' is a dense groundcover or hanging shrub that derived as a sport from 'Harald'. The leaves are three-lobed but quite variable in lobe size. Some leaves are triangular, whereas others are deeply lobed with a very pronounced central lobe. The leaves are dark green with grayish green parts. The margins are irregularly blotched and spotted silvery white. On some leaves the variegation is not confined to the margins: they are light gray to grayish white in the centers as well. 'Kolibri' means hummingbird in German and Dutch. It probably refers to the joyful coloration of the leaves and elegant habit. This plant is best grown in pots or tubs, because it is less winter-hardy than other variegated ivies. Zone 7/8

Hedera helix 'Little Diamond'

United States, 1960

Popular ivy with a dense habit suitable for the rock garden as well as groundcover for smaller gardens. The leaves are quite distinctly shaped. They are usually unlobed and 3 to 4 cm long. As the leaves have acute tips and attenuate bases, they are truly diamond shaped. Sometimes branches with normal *Hedera helix* leaves appear. These are dark green with grayish green spots and lighter green main veins. The leaves have narrow creamy white to clear white margins. 'Little Diamond' is sometimes offered as 'Kleiner Diamant' in central Europe and German-speaking countries. Zone 6

Hedera helix 'Luzii'

Ernst Luz, Stuttgart-Fellbach, Germany, 1951

Well-branched ivy with the usual five-lobed (sometimes three-lobed) leaves with more pronounced central lobes. The leaves are green to grayish green and densely speckled and mottled yellowish green. Although it was first introduced in 1951 (as 'Luzii') it was first correctly published in 1970. In the meantime various synonyms showed up, such as 'Lutzei' and 'Marmorata'. 'Luzii' is a great plant for indoors, but can also be grown in the garden, although it will be less speckled. Zone 7

Hedera helix 'Masquerade' RONALD HOUTMAN

Hedera helix 'Masquerade'

Hermann Königer, Aalen, Germany, 1955

This ivy derived from *H. helix* 'Luzii' and varies from it only in having a denser pattern of speckles on its leaves. On different plants, even on different branches on one plant, the density of speckles varies. Therefore, it can be questioned whether 'Masquerade' can still be regarded a cultivar. It is also sold as 'Marmorata', which, in turn, is also a synonym for 'Luzii'. Zone 7

Hedera helix 'Microphylla Picta'

Haage & Schmidt, Germany, 1862

Yet another variegated ivy that was nearly forgotten. For a long time 'Microphylla Picta' was very rare and only grown in Germany by Brother Ingobert Heieck, who grew a large number of ivies in the garden of Neuburg Abbey near Heidelberg. In 1968 some plants were collected from the Canary Islands. These were named 'Tenerife', but after thorough study it became clear these plants are 'Microphylla Picta'. The usually three-lobed leaves of 'Microphylla Picta' are relatively small and green to grayish green. The margins are creamy yellow to cream colored, usually with some small dots on the edges. Zone 6

Hedera helix 'Microphylla Picta' RONALD HOUTMAN

Hedera helix 'Midas Touch' CHRISTOPHER FAIRWEATHER

Hedera helix 'Sagittifolia Variegata' RONALD HOUTMAN

Hedera helix 'Sulphurea' GEORGE OTTER

Hedera helix 'Midas Touch'

Frode Maegaard Nurseries, Ringe, Denmark, 1987

Another nice Danish cultivar that is very suitable for growing as a container plant, as well as in the garden. The leaves are distinctly three-lobed, sometimes with two small lobes at the base. They are medium green with irregular, comparatively large, golden yellow blotches. It is the combination of these colors that gives the dramatic effect to the whole plant. 'Midas Touch' was originally named 'Golden Kolibri'; due to preclusion by the ICNCP it was renamed 'Midas Touch'. Zone 6

Hedera helix 'Mint Kolibri'

Frode Maegaard Nurseries, Ringe, Denmark, 1986

'Kolibri', which is a popular and widely grown ivy, is the source of various new cultivars that derived from it as branch sports. 'Mint Kolibri' is a very distinct plant. The silvery white variegation is covered with a grayish green transparent overlay, giving the foliage a soft, almost olive green appearance. 'Mint Kolibri', also known as 'Minty', makes a good houseplant, but is also very suitable for growing in pots. Zone 7

Hedera helix 'Sagittifolia Variegata'

Contrary to its name, this cultivar has more resemblance with 'Königer's Auslese' than with 'Sagittifolia'. The leaves are usually deeply five-lobed with narrow lobes and a distinctly elongated central lobe. Some leaves nearly lack lateral lobes and do only consist of the central lobe, thus creating a lanceolate leaf. The leaf base is remarkably heart-shaped. The foliage is green and grayish green with irregular creamy white margins. Sometimes white to cream mottled leaves appear. Zone 6

Hedera helix 'Sulphurea'

United Kingdom, before 1872

The leaves of 'Sulphurea' have the regular ivy shape. They are three-lobed to five-lobed with a distinct middle lobe. The leaves are about 6 cm long and 7 cm wide. 'Sulphurea' is not a very conspicuously variegated ivy. The leaves are light grayish green with narrow sulfur-yellow to cream-colored margins. This quite vigorous grower is very suitable as a groundcover as well as a climber, and it can be used both in full sun or in shaded locations. It is sometimes regarded as a cultivar of *Hedera hibernica*, the Atlantic ivy. Zone 7

Hedera helix 'Tricolor'

England, before 1866

Old and very distinct cultivar that is less vigorous than most other garden ivies. The leaves are rather small (2 to 4 cm long) and triangular to shallowly three-lobed (sometimes five-lobed). They are deep green to grayish green with lighter veins and irregular creamy yellow margins. The petioles are attractively colored reddish purple. During autumn and winter the color of the margins changes to pink or deep purple, depending on weather conditions. 'Tricolor' is still a popular cultivar that is widely used for growing on low walls or fences as well as small group plantings. It is also known under its synonyms 'Marginata Rubra', 'Microphylla Variegata', and 'Silver Queen'. Zone 6

Hedera helix 'Tricolor' RONALD HOUTMAN

Hedera helix 'Yab Yum'

Hanno Hardijzer, Boskoop, The Netherlands, 1995

Nice cultivar that was found as a sport in 'Sulphurea'. The leaves are variable in size and shape, but usually have three to five lobes. They have an average length of 4 cm and normally are slightly wider. The margins are wavy to crinkly. The most exceptional feature of 'Yab Yum' is its heavily variegated foliage. The leaves are light green with creamy white to greenish white spots. It is a new climbing ivy suitable for growing against a low wall or fence. It does not grow very vigorously and therefore 'Yab Yum' can also be used as a container plant. Zone 6

Hedera helix 'Yab Yum' RONALD HOUTMAN

Hibiscus syriacus 'Meehanii'

France, before 1867

Of *Hibiscus syriacus*, the woody mallow, only a few variegated cultivars are known. 'Meehanii' seems to originate from France and is one of the best known. It forms a dense bushy shrub that grows to about 1 m tall. The leaves are obovate and are usually shallowly three-lobed near the top. They are light green with creamy white to yellowish white margins. The single flowers are lilac-purple with dark red centers. In bud they have a more intense coloration. Although it is one of the better flowering variegated cultivars, the color does not suit the foliage, according to some people. It is a matter of personal taste whether people like this combination. Zone 6b

Hibiscus syriacus 'Meehanii' PPH (COLLECTION OF HARRY VAN DE LAAR)

Hibiscus syriacus 'Purpureus Variegatus'

Jacob-Mackoy, Liège, Belgium, 1865

Another cultivar with creamy white to yellowish white edged leaves. Contrary to 'Meehanii' the leaves are grayish green and the variegated margins are narrower, thus giving the whole plant a less variegated appearance. The double flowers open very late in the season. In fact, in many temperate regions they do not open at all. Due to the rather cool summers and lower temperatures during September the flowerbuds remain closed. 'Purpureus Variegatus' usually grows in areas that are in zone 7 or cooler. Because of the poor flowering habit in combination with the less attractive foliage, 'Meehanii' is preferred. Zone 6b

Hibiscus syriacus 'Purpureus Variegatus' MARCO HOFFMAN

Hoheria populnea 'Alba Variegata' RONALD HOUTMAN

Hoheria populnea 'Alba Variegata'

Duncan & Davies, New Plymouth, New Zealand, before 1959

Hoheria is a small genus of small to medium-sized trees that are endemic to New Zealand. The alternate leaves change from juvenile to adult. The juvenile leaves are cut and deeply toothed, the adult being only shallowly toothed to almost entire. Older trees develop beautiful reticular bark structures that gave *Hoheria* the common names lacebark and ribbonwood. The flowers of *H. populnea* open in autumn. They are carried in loose cymes. Individual flowers are pure white with conspicuous purplish stamens and styles. *Hoheria populnea* only grows on the North Island of New Zealand and is generally regarded as the most beautiful species of this genus.

The oldest variegated cultivar in *Hoheria* is *H. populnea* 'Variegata'. This cultivar dates back to 1926 and has green leaves blotched yellow to yellowish green. It is sometimes referred to as 'Aurea Variegata', but this is a name given illegitimately for the same cultivar and dates back to about 1945. The superb 'Alba Variegata' was discovered as a sport of 'Variegata'. The dark green leaves have splendid creamy white margins. Because the variegation is very stable and extremely pronounced, 'Alba Variegata' is one of the best variegated small trees for use in milder climates. Zone 8b

Hydrangea

Very popular summer-flowering shrubs or climbers. *Hydrangea macrophylla* and its cultivars are the best-known representatives of this genus, but cultivars of *H. paniculata* and *H. quercifolia* are becoming increasingly popular. Given the number of cultivars, only a relative few have variegated foliage. Like their green-leaved counterparts, they thrive in almost any soil, as long as it is well drained and not too dry.

Hydrangea anomala 'Firefly'

United States

This first variegated climbing *Hydrangea* actually derived from *H. anomala* subsp. *petiolaris*, better known by its previous name *H. petiolaris*. It is a vigorous climber that grows to about 5 m high. The broad ovate leaves are a dark glossy green with bold creamy yellow to yellow margins. In early summer the white flowers open in flattened cymes. Zone 6a

Hydrangea macrophylla

The hortensias are a very important group of summer-flowering shrubs. Usually the leaves are ovate to broadly ovate or obovate and fresh green. The flowers appear in two basic inflorescence types: globe shaped (or semi-globe shaped) mopheads and flattened lacecaps. In a lacecap the flowers in the center are fertile, surrounded by sterile flowers along the margin of the inflorescence. In mopheads most fertile flowers are transformed into sterile flowers, thus needing more room to develop. Flower colors range from pure white to deep purplish red, but through adding sulfur or aluminum sulfate some pink-flowering cultivars can be forced to flower with blue flowers. When the pH is about 7 or higher, the flowers of these cultivars will emerge in good pink colors. *Hydrangea macrophylla* is widely used in gardens and parks throughout the world. The majority of the more than 500 cultivars have green leaves. Only a small number of cultivars have variegated foliage. All are hardy to zone 6a.

Hydrangea anomala 'Firefly' WOUT KROMHOUT

Hydrangea macrophylla 'Lemon Wave'

Cultivar that reaches a height of about 1.5 m. The rather large leaves are less elliptic and more rounded than in the typical *H. macrophylla*. They resemble 'Quadricolor', but the margins are relatively broad and have larger yellow parts. The flowers appear in nearly flat lacecaps and are pinkish. 'Lemon Wave' is a quite uncommon cultivar, mainly because 'Quadricolor' and 'Tricolor' are more widely grown. 'Lemon Wave' is easily distinguished from 'Quadricolor' by lacking cream in the foliage.

Hydrangea macrophylla 'Lemon Wave' FA. C. ESVELD

Hydrangea macrophylla 'Quadricolor'

Dense and bushy shrub of about 1.5 m tall. The leaves are dull green with grayish green and have irregular creamy white margins. Parts of the margins are spotted

Hydrangea macrophylla 'Quadricolor' FA. C. ESVELD

Hydrangea macrophylla 'Tricolor' J. R. P. VAN HOEY SMITH

Hydrangea macrophylla 'Tricolor' WOUT KROMHOUT

creamy yellow to golden yellow. The pink flowers appear in flattened lacecaps. 'Quadricolor' is an old cultivar that has proven to be a remarkably stable cultivar. It is often mislabeled 'Tricolor', but is easily distinguished from it by its yellow spots along the margins.

***Hydrangea macrophylla* 'Tricolor'**

Japan, before 1844

Forms a dense shrub of about 1.75 m high. The leaves are green with irregular white margins and occasionally white spots in the centers as well. 'Tricolor' is a rather unstable cultivar and will form green leaves at some point. The flowers appear in lacecaps and are pinkish to pinkish white. They usually look a bit washed out. Although 'Tricolor' is a very commonly used name for variegated *H. macrophylla* cultivars, several different cultivars are sold under this name, including 'Variegata', a synonym for 'Tricolor'. Very often 'Tricolor' is confused with the more stable and better cultivar 'Quadricolor', which can be distinguished from it by its yellow spots along the margins.

***Hydrangea scandens* 'Fragrant Splash'**

Masato Yokoi, Japan

Also known as *H. luteovenosa* 'Variegata', this is a bushy shrub reaching about 2 m in height. The leaves are ovate to narrowly elliptic and up to 5 cm long. They are dark green with irregular patterns of clear yellow to creamy yellow splashes. 'Fragrant Splash' needs a place in full sun or semi-shade. It is less winter-hardy than most other, more common, species and cultivars. Therefore it should only be used in places with a milder climate. Zone 8b

***Hydrangea scandens* 'Konterigi Ki Nakafu'**

Broad, upright shrub that grows to a few meters high, but usually not exceeding 1.5 m. The leaves are elliptic with entire margins and are about 5 cm long. 'Konterigi Ki Nakafu' has a most extraordinary variegation. The young foliage is light green, quickly turning blackish green in late spring. A sparse variegation of small yellowish blotches can be observed in both young and mature leaves. 'Konterigi Ki Nakafu' is a most peculiar variegated plant. It can be grown in full sun, as well as in semi-shade. When grown in full shade, the yellowish blotches will disappear. Zone 7b

Hypericum

This large and versatile genus belongs to the Clusiaceae (garcinia family). More than 350 species grow in temperate regions in Europe and North America, as well as in mountainous areas in tropical and subtropical regions. Almost all species have yellow or yellowish flowers. The cultivars of *H. androsaemum* and *H. ×inodorum* are widely used as ornamentals, but they have an even better reputation when grown for their fruits. These are cut and sold with flowers in bouquets. Very few cultivars are variegated, but these three are absolutely worthwhile growing.

Hydrangea scandens 'Konterigi Ki Nakafu' RONALD HOUTMAN

Hypericum androsaemum 'Mrs Gladis Brabazon'

John Colleran, Japanese Garden, Tully, Ireland, 1982

Broad, upright, deciduous shrub, reaching a height of about 60 cm. The gracefully arching branches make it an elegant shrub. The ovate leaves are 5 to 9 cm long and heavily dotted and speckled cream, white, and pink. Young foliage is more pinkish than are mature leaves. Also noteworthy is that most seedlings of this cultivar have variegated foliage as well. In fact, this cultivar derived from *Hypericum androsaemum* f. *variegatum*. The flowers are bright yellow and approximately 2.5 cm wide. They are followed by berrylike fruits that are clear red at first, but turn black later. Especially in spring and early summer 'Mrs Gladis Brabazon' makes a splendid scene in a border or large pot. However, the leaves are very prone to sunburn and will be damaged severely when not protected during hot and sunny spells.

The name 'Mrs Gladis Brabazon' is sometimes misspelled as 'Gladys Brabazon', however, the Irish spelling is correct. Although it is given as 'Gladis Brabazon' in most publications, the originally published name, which is the only correct name, is 'Mrs Gladis Brabazon'. Zone 7b

Hypericum androsaemum 'Mrs Gladis Brabazon' WOUT KROMHOUT

Hypericum ×inodorum 'Autumn Surprise'

Hulsdonk Garden Centre, Zundert, The Netherlands, 2002

Broad upright shrub with gracefully arching branches. The ovate leaves are heavily splashed creamy white, especially near the margins. In autumn the color changes to dark greenish purple with purplish red splashes. This coloration is very spectacular. During late June and July the yellow flowers open in loose terminal and axillary cymes. They contrast well against the varie-

Hypericum ×inodorum 'Autumn Surprise' RONALD HOUTMAN

gated foliage. The fruits are brownish and rather inconspicuous against the foliage. The branches of 'Autumn Surprise' are long-lasting when used as cut foliage. Zone 7

Hypericum ×*moserianum* 'Tricolor'

J. J. Moser, Versailles, France, 1887

Semi-evergreen to evergreen shrub that grows to about 60 cm high with overhanging branches. The leaves are narrowly ovate and 4 to 6 cm long. They are dark green, speckled pink and white. Usually the variegation is confined along the margins, but whole leaves are also variegated. The flowers are borne during summer and are relatively large, about 5 cm wide. 'Tricolor' is an attractive shrub that is best planted in a sheltered but sunny location. With its overhanging branches, it is excellent for use on slopes or in containers. Zone 7a

Hypericum ×*moserianum* 'Tricolor' RONALD HOUTMAN

Ilex

The genus *Ilex*, commonly referred to as holly, has many variegated cultivars. Traditionally the genus is divided into two subgenera; subgenus *Ilex* with evergreen foliage and subgenus *Prinus* with deciduous foliage. Most *Ilex* species and cultivars belong in the subgenus *Ilex*, as well as the majority of the variegated cultivars. The most commonly grown species are *I. aquifolium*, *I. opaca*, and *I. crenata*.

Ilex aquifolium, the English or common holly, is a native of Europe and very widely grown. More than 100 cultivars have been named, many of them variegated. In this book only the most important variegated cultivars of *I. aquifolium* will be mentioned.

Ilex opaca, the American holly, is the American counterpart of *I. aquifolium*. It is a variable species that grows in the eastern United States. Over the years, more than 500 cultivars have been named. Although it is very hardy, it is best grown in a continental climate. Therefore, it is less popular than *I. aquifolium* in western Europe.

Ilex crenata, the Japanese holly, lacks spiny leaves. The leaves are usually small and rounded. More than 150 cultivars of *I. crenata* have been named, with many of them exhibiting dwarf growth. Only a handful of *I. crenata* cultivars are variegated.

In addition there are various hybrids. The most important are *I.* ×*altaclerensis*, Highclere holly (*I. aquifolium* × *I. perado*), and *I.* ×*meserveae*, blue holly (*I. rugosa* × *I. aquifolium*). Another popular hybrid in the United States is *I.* ×*attenuata*, Topel holly (*I. cassine* × *I. opaca*).

Ilex ×*altaclerensis* 'Belgica Aurea'

M. Koster & Son, Boskoop, The Netherlands, before 1908

Old but still widely grown cultivar with a broad, upright to conical habit, which is typical for *I.* ×*altaclerensis*. The distinct flat leaves are elliptic to narrowly elliptic, sometimes lanceolate. They are shiny dark green with pale yellow margins. On young leaves the margins are golden yellow. The margins are usually entire, but sometimes have a few small spines along the upper half of the leaf blade. Although 'Belgica Aurea' is a female clone, it usually does not set fruit. Awarded a First Class Certificate by the Royal Boskoop Horticultural Society in 1908. Zone 7b

Ilex ×*altaclerensis* 'Camelliifolia Variegata'

United Kingdom, before 1865

An old but rare variegated cultivar. The leaves are elliptic to elliptic-oblong, usually with entire or sparsely spined margins. They have dark green centers with broad creamy yellow margins. Occasionally only a narrow streak of green is visible in a leaf or leaves are half or entirely yellow. Although 'Camelliifolia Variegata' is female, it is not a richly fruiting cultivar. As the name suggests, it was discovered as a sport of 'Camelliifolia'. Zone 7b

Ilex ×*altaclerensis* 'Golden King'

J. Munro, Bangholm Nursery, United Kingdom, 1884

Large shrub with the typical broad, upright habit of *I.* ×*altaclerensis*. The convex ovate-oblong leaves are relatively large, up to 10 cm long and 6 cm wide. They are glossy dark green with irregular golden yellow margins, on older leaves turning creamy yellow. The leaf edges are usually entire and only occasionally have a few small spines. Despite its name, this is a female cultivar. The fruits are clear red but are not carried in great numbers. 'Golden King' is a very popular variegated holly and therefore widely grown, especially in Europe. Its good color and fine habit are responsible for its success. It is also offered under the incorrect name *I. aquifolium* 'Golden King'. Zone 7b

Ilex ×*altaclerensis* 'Howick'

Howick Estate, Howick, United Kingdom, before 1987

Despite its naming in the 1980s, this form was already known before 1900. It is a broad, upright, evergreen shrub of 3 to 5 m in height and equally wide. The leaves

Ilex ×*altaclerensis* 'Belgica Aurea' RONALD HOUTMAN

Ilex ×*altaclerensis* 'Camelliifolia Variegata' RONALD HOUTMAN

Ilex ×*altaclerensis* 'Howick' RONALD HOUTMAN

Ilex ×*altaclerensis* 'Golden King' RONALD HOUTMAN

Ilex ×altaclerensis 'Howick' RONALD HOUTMAN

Ilex ×altaclerensis 'Lawsoniana' RONALD HOUTMAN

do not differ very much from 'Golden King'. They are dark green to dark olive green and have narrow yellow margins, later turning creamy yellow. The edges are slightly recurved, giving the leaves a somewhat bullate appearance. 'Howick' is a female cultivar, but it usually only carries sparse orange-red fruits. It is sometimes offered as 'Hendersonii Variegata'. Zone 7b

Ilex ×altaclerensis 'Lawsoniana'

Lawson Co., Edinburgh, Scotland, United Kingdom, about 1869

Broad, upright, evergreen shrub resembling 'Howick' in habit, but more like 'Golden King' in leaf shape and coloration. Mainly differs from the latter in more mottled variegation instead of a marginal variegation. The leaves often revert to green. Like the other variegated cultivars of *I. ×altaclerensis*, 'Lawsoniana' is also a female cultivar. The fruits are red, but often only sparsely produced.

This cultivar was raised by Hodgins Nursery of Cloughjordan, Ireland, in the first half of the nineteenth century, but is still quite common in cultivation. William Hodgins discovered it as a sport of 'Hendersonii', and 'Lawsoniana' tends to revert to this cultivar every now and then. 'Lawsoniana' was introduced by Lawson around 1869. Zone 7b

Ilex ×altaclerensis 'Ripley Gold'

T. Sparkes, North Ripley, United Kingdom, 1980

Another female cultivar of the Highclere holly. This cultivar originated as a sport of 'Golden King' but has a closer resemblance to 'Lawsoniana'. The leaves have the same coloration, but the leaf margins are twisted. 'Ripley Gold' can be planted both in the sun or in the shade, as it keeps its color well, an advantage over several other variegated cultivars. At Dargle Cottage, Enniskerry, Ireland, a similar variegated sport on 'Golden King' was discovered by Dr. Neil Murray of Regional Nursery, Dundrum. It was named 'Lady Valery' in 1988. Zone 7b

Ilex aquifolium 'Angustimarginata Aurea'

United Kingdom, 1863

A male cultivar with relatively narrow elliptic leaves. These are dark olive green to dark green with yellow to greenish central blotches. The margins are finely serrate with short spines. The young branches are dark purple, contrasting well against the foliage.

This cultivar was known as 'Angustifolia Aurea Marginata' or 'Myrtifolia Elegans'. According to Fred C. Galle, recent studies have proven 'Angustimarginata Aurea' did not derive from 'Angustifolia' or 'Myrtifolia'. Therefore, the new cultivar name 'Angustimarginata Aurea' was given by Susyn Andrews of the Royal Botanic Gardens of Kew in the late 1990s. However, according to the ICNCP this new cultivar name is not legitimate because it is in Latin. Zone 7a

Ilex aquifolium 'Argentea Marginata'

Lawson Co., Edinburgh, Scotland, United Kingdom, about 1869

Upright shrub with a broad pyramidal habit. After many years it can reach 8 m in height. The leaves are broad elliptic to oblong and glossy dark green with broad cream-colored margins. The leaves have slightly wavy margins and five to seven spines on each side. The young shoots are tinted somewhat pinkish. 'Argentea Marginata' is a female cultivar that produces red fruits very freely during autumn. It is an old, but still very popular cultivar. It is easy to grow from cuttings, which adds to its popularity in the trade. The most commonly used synonyms for this cultivar are 'Albomarginata' and 'Argenteovariegata'. Other, less commonly used synonyms are 'Argentea Marginata Major', 'Silver Beauty' (United States), and 'Silver Princess' (United States). Zone 7a

Ilex aquifolium 'Argentea Marginata Pendula'

Messrs. Perry, Banbury, United Kingdom, 1859

Broad, upright shrub with somewhat sinuous main branches and weeping lateral branches. At an older age it forms a large and broad mounded shrub. Apart from

Ilex aquifolium 'Argentea Marginata Pendula' PIERRE THEUNISSEN

Ilex ×*altaclerensis* 'Ripley Gold' RONALD HOUTMAN

Ilex aquifolium 'Angustimarginata Aurea' FA. C. ESVELD

Ilex aquifolium 'Argentea Marginata' RONALD HOUTMAN

Ilex aquifolium 'Argentea Marginata Pendula' J. R. P. VAN HOEY SMITH

Ilex aquifolium 'Aurea Marginata Pendula' RONALD HOUTMAN

its peculiar weeping habit and slightly larger leaves, this cultivar is almost identical to 'Argentea Marginata'. The branches are purplish, as opposed to green in 'Argentea Marginata'. It is a female cultivar, richly carrying its red fruits in autumn. Because it is an old cultivar, many synonyms appeared in the trade. The most widely used synonyms are 'Argentea Pendula', 'Albomarginata Pendula', 'Perry's Weeping', and 'Silver Weeping'. Zone 7a

Ilex aquifolium 'Aurea Marginata Pendula'

Waterer's Nursery, Bagshot, United Kingdom, about 1875

Broad, upright shrub with a beautiful pendulous habit. Older plants form large and broad mounded shrubs. The oval to elliptic leaves are dark green with clear golden yellow margins. The leaves have five to seven spines on each side. As in many of the English holly cultivars, the stems are purplish. The inconspicuous flowers are followed by vivid red berries, giving great contrast to the variegated foliage. Zone 7a

Ilex aquifolium 'Aurifodina' RONALD HOUTMAN

Ilex aquifolium 'Aurifodina'

United Kingdom, 1863

This old and almost forgotten female cultivar is sometimes referred to as smudge holly. The leaves are medium green to olive green and heavily variegated grayish yellow to yellowish green. The margins are also yellowish green. The relatively large ovate to ovate-oblong leaves are up to 6.5 cm long, on young plants even longer. They are quite flat and spiny. 'Aurifodina' is quite rare in the trade, but can occasionally be found at arboreta, botanic gardens, and old estates. Zone 7a

Ilex aquifolium 'Crispa Aureo Picta' RONALD HOUTMAN

Ilex aquifolium 'Crispa Aureo Picta'

United Kingdom, before 1854

Dense male shrub with a broad, upright habit and dark purple twigs. The leaves are elliptic but heavily twisted and contorted. They always have a spine at the tip. Besides this one spine, however, some leaves have entire margins and others have only a few spines. Occasionally some small spines are formed on the leaf blade, such as in 'Ferox' and similar cultivars. In fact, 'Crispa Aureo Picta' derived from 'Ferox Aurea' as a sport. The leaves are dark green, irregularly blotched clear yellow to greenish yellow in the centers and occasionally with some smaller blotches near the tips. It is not a rare plant, but is still quite unusual in the trade. The typically shaped and colored foliage makes 'Crispa Aureo Picta' a holly well worth planting, not only a plant for the collector. Zone 7a

Ilex aquifolium 'Crispa Aureo Picta' RONALD HOUTMAN

Ilex aquifolium 'Elegantissima'

United Kingdom, before 1863

Broad, upright shrub. The leaves are broad elliptic and dark green, occasionally mottled grayish green in the centers. The regularly spined margins are clear creamy white. It is a male cultivar, so no fruits will appear. 'Elegantissima' is again an old cultivar that still is quite uncommon. This fact is strange, because it most certainly is quite stable and of great ornamental value. However, the choices in variegated *Ilex* are extremely wide. Zone 7a

Ilex aquifolium 'Elegantissima' RONALD HOUTMAN

Ilex aquifolium 'Ferox Argentea' RONALD HOUTMAN

Ilex aquifolium 'Ferox Argentea'

United Kingdom, 1662

The variegated hedgehog holly is a rather strange but attractive shrub with a broad conical habit. Its leaves are shiny dark green, with regular yellowish white margins. The ovate leaves are smaller than in other cultivars: 3 to 5 cm long. They have very wavy margins that are heavily spined. The spines are not only on the margins but also on the upper side of the leaf blade. Most of the spines are yellowish white. The pedicels and young branches are distinctively colored dark purple, adding much to the dramatic color and texture of this fine cultivar. 'Ferox Argentea' is a sterile male cultivar and will not set fruits. It is also not suitable as pollinator for other (female) cultivars. 'Ferox Argentea' is the variegated cultivar that derived from the old, green-leaved 'Ferox', the hedgehog holly. In fact, 'Ferox' is the oldest known named cultivar within the genus *Ilex*. Zone 7a

Ilex aquifolium 'Ferox Aurea'

United Kingdom, before 1760

This cultivar is similar to 'Ferox Argentea', but differs in leaf coloration. The leaves have the same shape and spiny aspect, but they are dark green to dark olive green with a conspicuous golden yellow blotch in the center. The spines are green. 'Ferox Aurea' is far less popular than 'Ferox Argentea' and therefore rather unusual in the trade. Zone 7a

Ilex aquifolium 'Golden Hedgehog'

Rather slow-growing small shrub with an untidy habit. The shape and size of the leaves are similar to 'Ferox

Ilex aquifolium 'Ferox Aurea' RONALD HOUTMAN

Ilex aquifolium 'Golden Hedgehog' RONALD HOUTMAN

Argentea' and 'Ferox Aurea', but the variegation is the opposite: the leaves have dark green centers and conspicuous yellow margins. In young leaves the centers are light green, whereas the margins are yellowish green. Unfortunately, 'Golden Hedgehog' is a weak-growing plant and it will stay a dwarfish shrub. Zone 7a

Ilex aquifolium 'Golden Milkboy'

Hillier & Sons, Winchester, United Kingdom

Broad, upright shrub with an irregular pyramidal habit. This male cultivar has spiny dark green leaves with slightly wavy margins. The centers have large, irregular, light greenish yellow blotches. Although it is a male cultivar, it does not flower very well and is therefore not a good pollinator for female plants. It looks very much like 'Golden Milkmaid', a female clone with the same characteristics. Very often these two cultivars are mixed up in nurseries. Zone 7a

Ilex aquifolium 'Golden Milkboy' RONALD HOUTMAN

Ilex aquifolium 'Golden Milkmaid'

United Kingdom, before 1750

This is the female counterpart of 'Golden Milkboy' and is very similar to it. The leaves have the same spiny and wavy margins and central blotch. The main difference is that 'Golden Milkmaid' is a female cultivar that can carry red fruits. These contrast well against the light colors of the variegated leaves. Both 'Golden Milkboy' and 'Golden Milkmaid' are unstable in their variegation and will easily revert to green. Zone 7a

Ilex aquifolium 'Golden Milkmaid' PIERRE THEUNISSEN

Ilex aquifolium 'Golden Queen'

United Kingdom, before 1867

Large upright shrub that grows to 8 m with a broad pyramidal habit. The fresh green leaves are relatively large, up to 10 cm. They have broad clear yellow margins. Occasionally half the leaf or a whole leaf is colored yellow. In coloration, 'Golden Queen' is one of the most beautiful variegated hollies, but because of its inferior winter-hardiness it has been surpassed by 'Madame Briot', which has a close resemblance to 'Golden Queen'. Despite the name indicating a female cultivar, this is a male clone. Zone 7b

Ilex aquifolium 'Golden Queen' FA. C. ESVELD

Ilex aquifolium 'Golden van Tol'

W. Ravestein & Sons, Boskoop, The Netherlands, 1969

Broad pyramidal to almost rounded shrub with the same habit as the illustrious 'J. C. van Tol'. Because

Ilex aquifolium 'Golden van Tol' PIERRE THEUNISSEN

Ilex aquifolium 'Gold Flash' RONALD HOUTMAN

Ilex aquifolium 'Handsworth New Silver' RONALD HOUTMAN

'Golden van Tol' derived from 'J. C. van Tol', it is similar in all its features, except for the leaf coloration. The leaves are dark green with light yellow to dark yellow margins. 'Golden van Tol' has become one of the most widely grown variegated hollies, especially in Europe, where cultivars of *I. aquifolium* are more common than in the United States. Like 'J. C. van Tol', this cultivar is also a hermaphrodite, red fruits are richly carried without the need of a pollinator. The Royal Boskoop Horticultural Society awarded 'Golden van Tol' a First Class Certificate in 1969. Zone 7a

Ilex aquifolium 'Gold Flash'

Bos & Hoogenboom/Th. J. Nieuwesteeg, Boskoop, The Netherlands, 1978

Upright shrub, usually with a broad pyramidal habit. The leaves are dark green, with irregular clear yellow blotches. 'Gold Flash' was found as a sport in 'J. C. van Tol', one of the most popular green-leaved hollies in cultivation. Like its parent, 'Gold Flash' has the same somewhat convex leaf blade with nearly spineless margins. Although it is a female cultivar, there is no need to plant a male clone next to it because it is self-pollinating. 'Gold Flash' has proven to be a very hardy cultivar, but it reverts to green very easily. It was raised many years before its introduction in 1978, and in the United Kingdom it was occasionally sold as 'Bosgold'. Zone 6

Ilex aquifolium 'Handsworth New Silver'

Fisher & Holmes, Handsworth Nurseries, United Kingdom, before 1850

Broad pyramidal, upright shrub. The leaves are elliptic-oblong and regularly spined along the margins. They are dark green, sometimes with grayish green spots in the center. The margins are clear creamy white to light yellowish white. 'Handsworth New Silver', also known as 'Handsworth Silver', has proven to be one of the best white-variegated cultivars. The variegated foliage contrasts well against the purplish young shoots of this fine cultivar. During autumn the red fruits give it an extra value. Zone 7a

Ilex aquifolium 'Ingramii'

Fisher & Holmes, Handsworth Nurseries, United Kingdom, before 1875

Broad, upright shrub that grows to about 3 m with an irregular habit. The leaves are relatively small, 3 to 4 cm long, and flat. They are ovate and the slightly wavy margins have about nine small spines on each side. The olive green to dark green leaves are heavily speckled greenish white to cream. No pattern can be detected in the variegation. Young shoots are pink to pinkish white. Due to its difficult propagation, 'Ingramii' is not very commonly grown. However, it is a remarkable variegated cultivar that is also suitable for the smaller garden. 'Ingramii' is a male cultivar and will therefore not set fruit. Zone 7b

Ilex aquifolium 'Ingramii' FA. C. ESVELD

Ilex aquifolium 'Laurifolia Aurea'

United Kingdom, before 1867

The variegated laurel-leaf holly is another reasonably nice variegated *Ilex*. It forms a broad, upright shrub. Apart from an occasional small spine near the tip of the leaf, the elliptic leaves are not spined. They are dark green with distinctive creamy yellow margins. 'Laurifolia Aurea' is a male cultivar, so no fruits develop. Like so many of the variegated hollies, 'Laurifolia Aurea' has become rare in cultivation. Zone 7a

Ilex aquifolium 'Laurifolia Aurea' RONALD HOUTMAN

Ilex aquifolium 'Lurida Variegata'

A cultivar with relatively large, broad, elliptic to oblong leaves. These are regularly spined, especially in the upper half of the leaf. The variegation of 'Lurida Variegata' is usually confined to the margins of the leaves. This is an old and almost forgotten cultivar of *Ilex*. Zone 7a

Ilex aquifolium 'Madame Briot'

France, 1866

Broad, upright, large shrub to small tree that grows to 7 m high and wide. The leaves are similar to those of

Ilex aquifolium 'Madame Briot' KLAAS VERBOOM

Ilex aquifolium 'Lurida Variegata' RONALD HOUTMAN

Ilex aquifolium 'Maderensis Variegata' RONALD HOUTMAN

Ilex aquifolium 'Myrtifolia Aurea Maculata' RONALD HOUTMAN

Ilex aquifolium 'Myrtifolia Aurea Marginata' RONALD HOUTMAN

the species and have about seven spines on each side. They are dark green with irregular clear yellow margins. Although it is a female cultivar, it will usually not carry many of its red fruits. 'Madame Briot' is an old cultivar but undoubtedly the best yellow-variegated holly there is. It is widely grown and readily available. Zone 7a

Ilex aquifolium 'Maderensis Variegata'

United Kingdom, before 1868

Broad and comparatively low-growing shrub that reaches about 3 m high and more than 4 m wide. The ovate to obovate leaves are dark green with an irregular yellow to pale yellow central blotch. They are regularly spined, but not sharp to the touch. Green shoots often arise and, if not taken out, the plant easily reverts to green. The stems are purplish. Unlike its green namesake 'Maderensis', this is not a cultivar of *I.* ×*altaclerensis*. It is sometimes listed as *I.* ×*altaclerensis* 'Maderensis Variegata', but has proven to be a true *I. aquifolium*. Zone 7a

Ilex aquifolium 'Myrtifolia Aurea Maculata'

United Kingdom, before 1875

Upright shrub that grows to 2.5 m with a narrow pyramidal habit. The lanceolate to narrow ovate leaves are regularly spined with approximately seven spines, pointed forward on each side. The leaves are dark green with a small yellow blotch in the center. This cultivar is male, so no fruits are set. It is a rare cultivar that is not often grown. Zone 7a

Ilex aquifolium 'Myrtifolia Aurea Marginata'

Paul, United Kingdom, 1863

Like 'Myrtifolia Aurea Maculata', this is a narrow pyramidal shrub that grows to 2.5 m high. It is similar in all its features, but the leaves have narrow yellow margins. It is also rare in cultivation and seldom offered. Zone 7a

Ilex aquifolium 'Ovata Aurea'

United Kingdom, before 1854

Relatively small broad shrub that grows to 2 m high and wide. The leaves are distinctly ovate with six small spines on each side. They are dark green with clear yellow margins. The stems are purple, contrasting well against the leaves. 'Ovata Aurea' is an old cultivar that is not widely grown. This is a pity, because it is a nice and hardy variegated holly, especially for the smaller garden. Zone 7a

Ilex aquifolium 'Pyramidalis Aurea Marginata'

J. van der Kraats, Boskoop, The Netherlands, 1910

Large broad pyramidal upright shrub that grows to about 8 m high. This cultivar is very similar to the well-known 'Pyramidalis'. Leaves lanceolate-ovate to elliptic, with only one or two spines on each side. On older plants the margins are usually entire. The leaves are glossy dark green with narrow yellow margins. 'Pyramidalis Aurea Marginata' is a female clone that can carry masses of lively red fruits. Zone 7a

Ilex aquifolium 'Ovata Aurea' RONALD HOUTMAN

Ilex aquifolium 'Rubricaulis Aurea'

Continental Europe, before 1867

Broad, upright shrub with a somewhat gloomy appearance, mainly due to the dark purplish black twigs and dark olive green leaves. They are flat, ovate, and have about six small spines on each side, with narrow, dark greenish yellow margins. The fruits are red and often carried in large quantities. However, a male plant must be placed nearby for pollination. 'Rubricaulis Aurea' is an old and widespread cultivar that is not the most beautiful of the variegated hollies, but is especially planted for its good winter hardiness. Zone 6b

Ilex aquifolium 'Pyramidalis Aurea Marginata' PIERRE THEUNISSEN

Ilex aquifolium 'Scotica Aureopicta'

Cheshunt Nurseries, United Kingdom, before 1850

A large shrub, usually with a globular to flattened globular habit that grows to 7 m high and more than 8 m wide. The typically shaped leaves are ovate and usually spineless. They are very wavy to twisted. The leaves are dark green to dark yellowish green with irregular central blotches. Although 'Scotica Aureopicta' is a female cultivar, it rarely sets fruit. Within the range of variegated hollies, this is quite a peculiar cultivar. However, it tends to revert to green very easily and therefore needs some maintenance. Zone 7a

Ilex aquifolium 'Rubricaulis Aurea' RONALD HOUTMAN

Ilex aquifolium 'Silver Milkboy'

Hillier & Sons, Winchester, United Kingdom

Broad, upright shrub that grows to about 4 m high. Heavily branched with a dense habit, due to the relatively slow growth. The elliptic leaves are very wavy, often almost twisted. They have four or five large, sharp

Ilex aquifolium 'Silver Milkmaid' KLAAS VERBOOM

Ilex aquifolium 'Silver Milkboy' KLAAS VERBOOM

Ilex aquifolium 'Silver Milkmaid' KLAAS VERBOOM

spines on each side. The dark green to dark olive green leaves have pale yellow blotches in the centers. 'Silver Milkboy', which rarely flowers, was introduced as a male clone, but later appeared to be female. Zone 7b

Ilex aquifolium 'Silver Milkmaid'

United Kingdom, before 1820

Dense shrub with the same features and qualities as 'Silver Milkboy'. In fact, this female clone is much older than its (apparently) male counterpart. The dark orange-red fruits are borne profusely on 'Silver Milkmaid'. Both 'Silver Milkboy' and 'Silver Milkmaid' tend to revert to green and are not hardy enough in most parts of Europe and the United States. Zone 7b

Ilex aquifolium 'Silver Queen'

United Kingdom, before 1863

Beautiful upright shrub with a pyramidal habit. Eventually, it will reach a height of about 6 m with a width of approximately 3 m and stays slightly smaller than similar cultivars. The leaves are broad ovate and dark green with irregular creamy white margins. 'Silver Queen' is very similar to 'Argentea Marginata' and 'Handsworth New Silver', but differs in having lilac-pink young foliage. It has been surpassed by these cultivars, however, because 'Silver Queen' is less hardy. This male cultivar will not set fruit. Young plants need some support when developing a central leader. Zone 7b

Ilex aquifolium 'Silver van Tol'

B. Blanken, Boskoop, The Netherlands, 1977

Similar to 'Golden van Tol', but with conspicuous silver-margined leaves, this cultivar is especially attractive during winter. The leaves are also slightly more convex than in 'Golden van Tol' and 'J. C. van Tol'. Like these, 'Silver van Tol' is a hermaphroditic cultivar that will give fruits without pollen from another holly. The Royal Boskoop Horticultural Society gave 'Silver van Tol' an Award of Merit in 1977. Zone 7a

Ilex aquifolium 'Silver Queen' RONALD HOUTMAN

Ilex aquifolium 'Watereriana'

John Waterer, Sons & Crisp, Bagshot, United Kingdom, before 1863

This is an old and quite unusual variegated holly cultivar. It is a relatively slow-growing shrub with a dense habit. The leaves are oval to broad elliptic and dark green to dark olive green. They have irregular, narrow clear yellow margins. Occasionally half of the leaf or the entire leaf is yellow. It is a male cultivar, so no fruits are produced. Zone 7a

Ilex aquifolium 'Silver van Tol' PIERRE THEUNISSEN

Ilex aquifolium 'Whitesail'

J. S. Wieman, Portland, Oregon, United States, 1960s

This broad and somewhat irregular upright cultivar was raised as a seedling of 'Handsworth New Silver'. The dark green leaves have conspicuous pale yellowish white to light yellow margins. The leaves have four or five spines on each side, but leaves with six or seven smaller spines are not unusual. The stems are purple and contrast well against the foliage. The fruits of this

Ilex aquifolium 'Whitesail' RONALD HOUTMAN

Ilex aquifolium 'Watereriana' RONALD HOUTMAN

Ilex cornuta 'O. Spring' RONALD HOUTMAN

Ilex crenata 'Luteovariegata' RONALD HOUTMAN

Ilex crenata 'Shiro Fukurin' RONALD HOUTMAN

female cultivar are dark orange-red. Although they go beautifully with the foliage, it is a pity they are not richly produced. Zone 7a

Ilex cornuta 'O. Spring'

T. Dodd Jr., Mobile, Alabama, United States, late 1950s

Somewhat irregular, upright shrub that eventually becomes a large bushy shrub of about 3 m in height. The leaves are very distinct, both in shape and in coloration. They are usually convex, oblong, and have one to four spines on each side. The leaves are dark green with lighter green to grayish green and yellow spots. This irregular variegation gives 'O. Spring' a very informal character. The leaves tend to burn during sunny spells in winter. Unfortunately, this attractive plant is less hardy than most of the *I. aquifolium* cultivars and therefore less suitable for planting in northwestern Europe and other colder areas. Zone 7b

Ilex crenata 'Luteovariegata'

Japan, 1863

Small dense shrub with an irregular upright habit. The leaves are narrow elliptic to lanceolate. They are dark green and irregularly spotted yellow to light yellow. 'Luteovariegata' was introduced by Carl Ivanovich Maximowicz, who got the plant from Japan in 1863. It took until 1957 before it was introduced into the American nurseries. This was done by Frank Meyer, who brought a plant from the Royal Botanic Gardens of Kew. In the trade, various plants go under the name 'Luteovariegata'. Sometimes it is 'Aureovariegata', differing in having smaller blotches and speckles of yellowish white on the leaves. Zone 6

Ilex crenata 'Shiro Fukurin'

Japan, before 1957

Several white variegated clones are known in the trade under this Japanese name, meaning "white margin." These plants all have dark green leaves, sometimes striped lighter green, with irregular creamy white margins. The leaves are only very slightly convex to flat. Zone 7a

Ilex crenata 'Snowflake'

Nakada Nursery, Angyo, Japan

Somewhat irregular, upright, bushy shrub. Leaves dark green with irregular creamy white margins. Some leaves are partially creamy white or entirely white. The leaves are ovate to broad ovate and up to 3 cm long. This clone was obtained from the Nakada Nursery in 1957 by J. L. Creech. To highlight the good qualities of this clone, it was named 'Snowflake' by T. R. Dudley & G. K. Eisenbeiss in 1966. Although this cultivar is named, it is quite possible that other plants going under the name 'Shiro Fukurin' are exactly the same. Zone 7a

Ilex crenata 'Wiesmoor Silber' RONALD HOUTMAN

Ilex crenata 'Wiesmoor Silber'

Wiesmoor, Germany, 1975

Nice bushy shrub, only 1.5 m high with an irregular broad, upright habit. The leaves are similar to *I. crenata* 'Convexa', a very well-known green-leaved cultivar of Japanese holly. The leaves are elliptic, approximately 2.5 cm long, and strongly convex. They are grayish green with conspicuous white margins. All variegated Japanese hollies are less suitable for hedging or large group plantings, but they will add to every garden with their bright leaf colors. They are very suitable for smaller gardens. Zone 7a

Ilex ×*meserveae* 'Golden Prince' RONALD HOUTMAN

Ilex ×*meserveae* 'Golden Prince'

G. S. Kuijf, Boskoop, The Netherlands, 2002

Every now and then variegated sports arise in blue holly cultivars. 'Golden Prince' was discovered as a sport in 'Blue Prince' and has the same broad, upright habit and slightly irregular growth. The ovate leaves are not sharp to the touch. They are dark olive green with very conspicuous, broad, golden yellow margins. Like 'Blue Prince', the young stems are purplish and contrast well against the foliage. It is a new plant that is not readily available in the trade yet. Zone 6a

Jasminum officinale 'Argenteovariegatum' RONALD HOUTMAN

Jasminum officinale 'Argenteovariegatum'

Moderate to vigorous deciduous climber that grows to 10 m high. The opposite leaves are imparipinnate and consist of five to seven, occasionally nine, elliptic to oblong-elliptic leaflets. These are dull dark grayish green with irregular light creamy white margins. The flowers of 'Argenteovariegatum' are white and very fragrant. Unfortunately, they are not very conspicuous against the variegated foliage. Because it is a sun-loving climber, it is best planted against a wall facing west or south and is very suitable for growing over a trellis or fence. Zone 8a

Jasminum officinale 'Aureovariegatum'

1770

Similar to 'Argenteovariegatum' in habit and leaf shape. The dark green leaves are heavily splashed and blotched with golden yellow. It makes an excellent shrub for covering fences, walls, or old sheds. It does not flower as easily as the species or the white-variegated cultivar, but above all 'Aureovariegatum' must be regarded as a foliage plant. It can create a dramatic effect, especially a combination with blue or purple-flowered perennials such as *Campanula* or *Delphinium*. It is also known as 'Aureum'. Zone 8a

Jasminum officinale 'Aureovariegatum' RONALD HOUTMAN

Juniperus

With about sixty species and many more cultivars, *Juniperus* is one of the largest conifer genera. The many species and cultivars in cultivation vary from dwarf shrubs to groundcovers and trees. Some have an attractive habit, and the foliage colors are among the best of all conifers. Many species of *Juniperus* have variegated cultivars. The majority are derived from *J. chinensis*, the Chinese juniper, and *J. communis*, the common juniper. Recently some taxonomical changes have been made. The variegated cultivars of *J. davurica* now belong to *J. chinensis* and some cultivars of *J. virginiana* now belong to *J. scopulorum*. Most variegated cultivars of *Juniperus* are quite stable and well worth

Juniperus chinensis 'Expansa Aureospicata' KLAAS VERBOOM

using in the garden. They are generally not rare in cultivation.

Juniperus chinensis 'Expansa Aureospicata'

United States, 1938

Dense and low-growing shrubby conifer forming a good groundcover. Eventually it will grow to a height of about 1 m but much wider. The foliage is dark green and heavily speckled golden yellow, especially on the younger growth. 'Expansa Aureospicata' is widely grown and readily available. It is a valuable variegated conifer that can be used in both mass plantings or as a specimen plant in the smaller garden. Due to a taxonomical error in the late 1940s, 'Expansa Aureospicata' and 'Expansa Variegata' were long regarded as cultivars of *J. davurica*. Later studies have proven they are cultivars of *J. chinensis*. Zone 5a

Juniperus chinensis 'Expansa Aureospicata' RONALD HOUTMAN

Juniperus chinensis 'Expansa Variegata'

United States, before 1939

This cultivar is similar to 'Expansa Aureospicata'. The variegation is more cream-colored and the whole plant is less variegated. The variegated parts can be damaged during severe frosts, but the plant will usually recover the next spring. 'Expansa Variegata' can be used in ways similar to 'Expansa Aureospicata'. Zone 5a

Juniperus chinensis 'Expansa Variegata' RONALD HOUTMAN

Juniperus chinensis 'Japonica Variegata'

France, 1867

Medium-sized conifer with a broad habit, attaining a height and width of about 2 m. The foliage is dull green to grayish green and covered with small creamy white spots. 'Japonica Variegata' has proven quite stable over the years, which is why it is still grown. The name holds a contradiction, meaning "variegated Japanese Chinese juniper." However, the name is old and therefore legitimate. Zone 5a

Juniperus chinensis 'Japonica Variegata' RONALD HOUTMAN

Juniperus chinensis 'Kaizuka Variegated'

Monrovia Nurseries, Azusa, California, United States, 1958

Beautiful upright conifer with an irregular habit. The branches grow in several directions, but always more or less upright. This leads to a very informal but distinguished habit. The foliage is dark green with numerous small creamy white branchlets. 'Kaizuka Variegated' is a good cultivar with a sparkling variegation. It is quite stable and will stand a lot of sunlight without

Juniperus chinensis 'Kaizuka Variegated' RONALD HOUTMAN

getting burned. It is also described as 'Variegated Kaizuka', a synonym. Zone 5a

Juniperus chinensis 'Plumosa Aureovariegata'

Germany, before 1873

Compact and densely branched conifer that grows to about 2.5 m high and wide. The plume-shaped spreading branches are slightly decurved at the top, thus creating an elegant habit. It is less vigorous than its green-leaved and yellow-leaved counterparts. The foliage is dark green and irregularly but distinctly golden yellow variegated. 'Plumosa Aureovariegata' is an old cultivar that is quite common in cultivation. Zone 5a

Juniperus chinensis 'Variegata'

United Kingdom, before 1865

Elegant conifer with an upright and conical habit. The foliage has an attractive bluish green color intermixed with pale yellow branchlets. The effect of these foliage colors is very strong in combination with pink or blue flowering plants. Plants named 'Albovariegata', 'Argentea', 'Argenteo-variegata', and 'Stricta Variegata' are identical to 'Variegata', and are therefore synonyms. Zone 5a

Juniperus chinensis 'Plumosa Aureovariegata' RONALD HOUTMAN

Juniperus chinensis 'Variegata' RONALD HOUTMAN

Juniperus communis 'Constance Franklin' RONALD HOUTMAN

Juniperus communis 'Spotty Spreader' RONALD HOUTMAN

Juniperus communis 'Aureovariegata'

Germany, before 1891

Uncommon variegated conifer with an upright, conical habit. The foliage is tipped golden yellow, as are some individual needles. This old cultivar is rare in cultivation. Zone 3

Juniperus communis 'Constance Franklin'

E. C. Franklin, Earley, United Kingdom, 1982

Large shrub to small tree with a columnar habit. From a distance, this cultivar shows some similarity to the well-known *J. scopulorum* 'Skyrocket' (*J. virginiana* 'Skyrocket'). The foliage has the same grayish green color, but is speckled creamy white. 'Constance Franklin' was discovered as a sport of *J. communis* 'Hibernica'. It is available in the trade, but not on a large scale. Zone 3

Juniperus communis 'Spotty Spreader'

M. Droogh, Boskoop, The Netherlands, 1990

Discovered as a sport of *J. communis* 'Repanda', this conifer has the same procumbent habit. With its spreading branches, 'Spotty Spreader' is very suitable as a groundcover, especially when planted in small groups. In time, it can reach a height of about 30 cm, but it will grow much wider. The foliage is dull dark yellowish green with some yellowish variegation in it. It is not a very pronounced variegation, but in this case it adds to the usefulness as a groundcover. 'Spotty Spreader' is not prone to sunburn, and it is readily available. Zone 3

Juniperus communis 'Tage Lundell' J. R. P. VAN HOEY SMITH

Juniperus communis 'Tage Lundell'

Tage Lundell, Helsingborg, Sweden, 1970

Interesting conifer with a narrow, upright habit, becoming broad columnar after several years. The foliage

Juniperus conferta 'Brookside Variegated' RONALD HOUTMAN

Juniperus conferta 'Sunsplash' J. R. P. VAN HOEY SMITH

Juniperus horizontalis 'Andorra Variegated' J. R. P. VAN HOEY SMITH

is bluish green and sharp to the touch. It is densely covered with small yellowish branchlets. 'Tage Lundell' closely resembles an old cultivar named 'Suecica Variegata', which is no longer in cultivation; the only difference is that the variegated parts in 'Suecica Variegata' are slightly larger. Zone 3

Juniperus conferta 'Brookside Variegated'

United States, before 1988

The shore juniper is native to northern Japan and Sakhalin. There it forms dense, low-growing plants with a spreading to creeping habit. This makes *J. conferta* and most of its cultivars excellent for groundcover. They look like *J. communis*, but the needles are distinctively longer. The native habitat of *J. conferta* is confined to the coastal areas of the above mentioned places. Therefore it is less hardy than *J. communis* and its cultivars.

Only a few variegated cultivars of the shore juniper are known. The best-known of these is 'Brookside Variegated'. It forms a dense creeping shrub with bluish green foliage, spotted yellow. Another variegated cultivar of *J. conferta* is 'Sunsplash'. This plant also originated in the United States (before 1995). It differs from 'Brookside Variegated' in having complete golden yellow branchlets intermixed with green-leaved branchlets. Zone 6a

Juniperus horizontalis 'Andorra Variegated'

Italy, before 1999

Unlike most cultivars of *J. horizontalis*, this plant does not have a creeping habit. Both the green-leaved 'Andorra Compact' and its variegated counterpart have a broad spreading-upright habit. They form flattened bushy conifers with a broad inverted triangular habit. As the name suggests, 'Andorra Variegated' was discovered as a sport of 'Andorra Compact'. The foliage of 'Andorra Variegated' is green with small cream-colored spots. During winter the green changes to peculiar lilac-brown colors. The variegation is less distinctive during these months, but still visible. Like 'Andorra Compact', this is a healthy cultivar and well worth planting. This plant was first reported in Italy, where it was sold as 'Andorra Variegata' and 'Andorra Variegated'. According the ICNCP the first of these names is illegitimate. The correct cultivar name must therefore be 'Andorra Variegated'. Zone 4

Juniperus horizontalis 'Variegata'

United States, 1932

Low-growing cultivar with a creeping to decumbent habit. The foliage is an attractive bluish green with cream-colored branchlets. 'Variegata' is a vigorous grower that is very suitable as a groundcover. Because variegated sports occasionally arise in other cultivars of *J. horizontalis*, there is more than one clone on the market. These might be slightly different from each other. Zone 4

Juniperus ×media 'Blue and Gold'

United States, before 1984

Rather vigorous conifer with a broad spreading-upright habit. It was discovered as a sport of *J. ×media* 'Pfitzeriana' and has the same general appearance. The foliage has a strong bluish green color, beautifully intermixed with light yellow branchlets. 'Blue and Gold' is very stable and will stand full sun without burning. It is one of the better variegated conifers and is readily available. Zone 4

Juniperus ×media 'Milky Way'

Konijn Nurseries, Heemstede, The Netherlands, 1968

Compact conifer with elegant spreading branches and decurving tips. The foliage is green, variegated creamy

Juniperus horizontalis 'Variegata' RONALD HOUTMAN

Juniperus ×media 'Blue and Gold' RONALD HOUTMAN

Juniperus sabina 'Variegata' J. R. P. VAN HOEY SMITH

Juniperus scopulorum 'Moonglow Variegated' RONALD HOUTMAN

white. 'Milky Way' was raised in the 1940s, but it was not named until 1968. Zone 4

Juniperus sabina 'Variegata'

Before 1775

Another old variegated cultivar of a juniper species native to Europe. It forms a bushy plant with a broad spreading-upright habit. The plumelike foliage is green with white variegated branchlets. As with other old variegated conifer cultivars, there is more than one clone on the market. These usually differ only in detail. However, plants going under 'Variegata' might not be similar to the type described and shown here. Zone 4

Juniperus scopulorum 'Moonglow Variegated'

United States

Splendid upright conifer with a narrow columnar habit. It resembles *J. scopulorum* 'Skyrocket' (*J. virginiana* 'Skyrocket') in habit, but is not as narrow. 'Moonglow Variegated' maintains a compact and closed habit, unlike 'Skyrocket', even at an older age. The foliage of 'Moonglow Variegated' is attractively bluish gray, heavily spotted cream to creamy yellow. The effect thus created is absolutely fabulous and makes it one of the most beautiful variegated conifers. Zone 5a

Juniperus squamata 'Floreant'

W. M. van Nierop, Boskoop, The Netherlands, before 1998

Discovered as a sport of *J. squamata* 'Blue Star', this cultivar has the same flattened globular habit. The needles have the typical appearance of the juvenile *Juniperus* foliage, but are intense greenish blue. Small branchlets of creamy yellow are intermixed in the foliage. This cultivar was named after the Boskoop Soccer Club;

Juniperus squamata 'Floreant' RONALD HOUTMAN

however, it was published misspelled as 'Floriant'. According the ICNCP a misspelled cultivar name can be changed into the correct spelling, and the correct name is 'Floreant'. Zone 6a

Juniperus squamata 'Golden Flame'

L. Konijn & Co, Reeuwijk, The Netherlands, before 1968

Uncommon conifer with an irregular broad, upright habit. The habit was inherited from *J. squamata* 'Meyeri', from which 'Golden Flame' was derived as a sport. The branch tips are attractively decurved. Like 'Floreant', the needles are an attractive greenish blue, intermixed with small light yellow branchlets. Although it was introduced in 1968, it was first described by Gerd Krüssmann in 1979. Zone 6a

Juniperus squamata 'Gold Flash' J. R. P. VAN HOEY SMITH

Juniperus squamata 'Gold Flash'

Cedar Lodge, New Plymouth, New Zealand, 1986

A cultivar similar to 'Golden Flame' in general habit, but with a slightly more spreading habit and larger variegated parts. The branch tips are attractively decurved. 'Gold Flash' is sometimes spelled as 'Golden Flash'. A third cultivar that also derived from *J. squamata* 'Meyeri' is 'Gold Tip'. This cultivar is almost indistinguishable from 'Gold Flash'. Zone 6a

Juniperus squamata 'Gold Tip' J. R. P. VAN HOEY SMITH

Kadsura japonica 'Fukurin'

Relatively slow-growing, evergreen, twining shrub that grows to about 3.5 m high. Leaves narrow ovate to lanceolate and somewhat leathery. They are medium green with irregular creamy white to yellowish white edges. The flowers, which are solitary during summer and early autumn, are creamy yellow to light yellow. They are not very showy and most of the flowers are covered by the leaves. The flowers can be followed by scarlet berries. A cultivar named 'Variegata' is most likely similar to 'Fukurin', if not identical. Other variegated cultivars are 'Chirimen' (leaves irregularly marbled and streaked creamy white) and 'Tricolor' (leaves with yellow and cream speckles and streaks). *Kadsura japonica* and its cultivars will usually drop their leaves during winter, except in milder areas. Zone 7b

Kadsura japonica 'Fukurin' RONALD HOUTMAN

Kerria japonica 'Aureovariegata'

Before 1914

Densely branched, broad, bushy shrub that will attain a height of about 1.75 m. The rounded branches mainly appear from the base. They are bright green. The ovate leaves are dull green with yellow margins. The single golden yellow flowers stand solitary and appear in spring. Occasionally some flowers appear during autumn. All *Kerria* are very suitable for landscaping. They can be planted singly and in large groups. Due to their suckering habit, they will form dense bushes where weeds have little chance of establishing. Zone 5

Kerria japonica 'Picta'

Japan, before 1844

Perhaps the best-known variegated cultivar of *Kerria japonica*. It is very similar to 'Aureovariegata', but will stay smaller, about 1.5 m high. The leaves are grayish green with conspicuous narrow white margins. 'Picta' is a poor-flowering cultivar, which is compensated by its variegated foliage. It is very suitable for landscaping. The rather grayish foliage makes it a useful shrub for mass plantings or as a broad hedge. 'Picta' was introduced into Western trade by P. F. von Siebold in 1860. Zone 5

Kerria japonica 'White Cloud'

Relatively low-growing (to about 1.5 m), bushy shrub with a broad habit. The most interesting feature of

Kerria japonica 'White Cloud' RONALD HOUTMAN

Kerria japonica 'Picta' RONALD HOUTMAN

'White Cloud' is the white flowers. Like the species, these appear during spring and early summer. The leaves are speckled and mottled white, which makes the flowers less conspicuous. 'White Cloud' can be used in the same way as other *K. japonica* cultivars. Zone 5

Lavandula ×*intermedia* 'Burgoldeen' GOLDBURG™

Gert van den Burg, Maasdijk, The Netherlands, 1998

Compact and bushy evergreen shrub that grows to about 70 cm high. The leaves are narrow elliptic to linear and grayish green with conspicuous creamy yellow margins. The light blue flowers are carried in upright spikes that appear in August and September. This is not a very floriferous cultivar. Due to the variegated foliage it tends to grow less vigorously than similar green-leaved cultivars, such as 'Dutch'.

'Burgoldeen', which originated as a sport of *L.* ×*intermedia* 'Dutch', is one of the very few variegated lavenders in the world. It is well worth growing in any garden where a southern atmosphere is desired. It prefers a dry and sunny location. During moist winters 'Burgoldeen' can be severely damaged or die when the soil is not dry enough. Apart from this minor disadvantage, it is a wonderful and unique variety to grow. *Lavender* ×*intermedia* 'Walvera' WALBERTON SILVER EDGE™ is another variegated lavender. This is similar to 'Burgoldeen', but the foliage has silvery white margins. Zone 6b/7

Lavandula ×*intermedia* 'Burgoldeen' GOLDBURG™
CHRISTOPHER FAIRWEATHER

Lavatera arborea 'Variegata'

Slender deciduous shrub or small tree with an open and upright habit and stout branches. The palmate leaves are dark green, strikingly variegated white to cream. The amount of white in the foliage can vary. Sometimes the leaves are almost entirely green with some small variegated parts, whereas other plants are heavily variegated. The deep pinkish purple flowers open from late spring into summer. They have deep purple veins, especially at the base of the petals, which contrasts splendidly with the foliage. Even though it is usually short-lived, 'Variegata' is easily propagated by softwood cuttings. In colder areas it can be used as an annual. Excellent for planting in perennial borders. Zone 8

Lavatera arborea 'Variegata' RONALD HOUTMAN

Leucothoe walteri 'Rainbow' RONALD HOUTMAN

Leucothoe walteri 'Tricolor' RONALD HOUTMAN

Ligustrum japonicum 'Silver Curls' GERT FORTGENS

Leucothoe walteri 'Rainbow'

Girard Bros., Geneva, Ohio, United States, 1949

Broad, spreading, upright, evergreen shrub that will usually not grow taller than 1 m and wider than 1.5 m. The gracefully arching branches hold leathery leaves, ovate to ovate-lanceolate and up to 15 cm long. The leaves are dark green marbled white, yellow, and pale pink. During autumn the leaves turn darker reddish tones. Like most members of Ericaceae (heather family), *Leucothoe* thrives best on humus-rich soil. *Leucothoe walteri* is best planted in semi-shade, under trees with a transparent crown or in woodland settings.

Surprisingly, both Girard Bros. of the United States and Hillier & Sons of Winchester, United Kingdom, claim to have found 'Rainbow'. The American clone is often referred to as 'Girard's Rainbow'. Whether these cultivars are exactly identical is not clear, but they certainly look very similar. Various books and articles add to the confusion by naming one as a synonym for the other. Zone 6a

Leucothoe walteri 'Tricolor'

Very rare variegated counterpart of the well-known 'Rainbow'. The leaves are dull green to yellowish green, with irregular creamy margins and stripes. The young shoots are coppery orange to bronze, which is perhaps the only positive feature of this plant. During warm and sunny spells the foliage easily scorches, and it is therefore necessary to plant 'Tricolor' in semi-shade. This cultivar is easily surpassed by 'Rainbow', which is recommended in every respect. Zone 6

Ligustrum

Relatively small genus belonging to the Oleaceae (olive family) and closely related to *Syringa*. The approximately fifty species grow mainly in Europe and Asia, but some are also native to northern Africa and Australia. Privets are widely used, and the variegated cultivars, especially, are highly ornamental. In addition to the attractive foliage, they are usually very floriferous and the flowers are followed by berries. The fragrance of the flowers is not appreciated by everyone, however. *Ligustrum*, especially *L. ovalifolium* and *L. vulgare*, is excellent for hedging. Other species and cultivars are used as specimen plants or in group plantings.

Ligustrum japonicum 'Silver Curls'

Trompenburg Arboretum, Rotterdam, The Netherlands, 1993

Rather curious plant with thick, leathery foliage. The margins are very wavy, which causes the leaf blade to curl. The leaves are glossy green with a narrow, cream-colored central spot. It will grow into a dense and bushy, slightly irregular shrub. Because 'Silver Curls' is not hardy, it is best used as a patio plant. In milder climates it can make a nice garden shrub. 'Silver Curls' was discovered as a sport in *L. japonicum* 'Variegatum' by Gert Fortgens, Curator of the Trompenburg Arboretum in Rotterdam. *Ligustrum japonicum* 'Jack Frost' is another variegated variety. The leaves are less curled and grayish green with irregular creamy white margins. Zone 8

Ligustrum japonicum 'Variegatum' MARCO HOFFMAN

Ligustrum japonicum 'Variegatum'

United Kingdom, 1885

Densely branched, broad, upright, evergreen shrub that eventually reaches a height of about 2 m. The leaves are ovate to lanceolate, up to 8 cm long, and slightly rugose. They have a green center and narrow creamy white to pale greenish white margins. In midsummer the shrub flowers richly with masses of creamy white flowers in dense panicles, followed by dark purplish black fruits.

The American cultivar 'Silver Star' is most likely a synonym for 'Variegatum'. This cultivar is sometimes incorrectly called *L. texanum* 'Silver Star'. Another variegated cultivar from the United States is 'Silver Tint Waxleaf'. Whether this patented cultivar is the same as 'Silver Star' is uncertain. If so, 'Silver Star' must be regarded as a trademark, not as a cultivar name. Zone 8a

Ligustrum lucidum 'Excelsum Superbum' RONALD HOUTMAN

Ligustrum lucidum 'Excelsum Superbum'

United Kingdom

Very attractive large evergreen shrub to small tree. In milder climates it can easily reach a height of more than 8 m. However, in most northern European countries and throughout the United States, 'Excelsum Superbum' will stay shrubby. The long acuminate ovate leaves are up to 12 cm long, thick, and leathery. The dark green leaves are heavily speckled and have creamy white and yellow margins. Young foliage is more yellowish. In late summer masses of small white flowers appear in large panicles up to 20 cm long, followed by dark bluish black berries. Another yellow

Ligustrum lucidum 'Tricolor' FA. C. ESVELD

Ligustrum lucidum 'Tricolor' RONALD HOUTMAN

Ligustrum lucidum 'West Hatch Glory' DAN HEIMS

variegated cultivar of *L. lucidum* is 'Aureovariegatum'. It has dark green, yellow variegated leaves, but is inferior to 'Excelsum Superbum'. Zone 8b

Ligustrum lucidum 'Tricolor'

Around 1895

Another remarkably attractive variegated evergreen privet. Like 'Excelsum Superbum', 'Tricolor' will become a large shrub to small tree that grows to 9 m. The leaves are slightly smaller, about 10 cm long. The young foliage is soft pink. When aging the leaves turn dark green with yellowish and white speckles and margins. The variegated evergreen privets described here thrive well in a sunny or semi-shaded location. They can be used to contrast against green-leaved plants. Zone 8b

Ligustrum lucidum 'West Hatch Glory'

Junker's Nursery, West Hatch, Taunton, United Kingdom, early 1990s

A splendid cultivar with large glossy leaves that are clear green with broad golden yellow margins, later fading into cream. The young growth is quite spectacularly tinted orange-pink, adding to the variegation. 'West Hatch Glory' is a colorful shrub that is very effective in between dark green-leaved shrubs or purple-flowering perennials. Its main advantage over other *Ligustrum* cultivars is that the variegation is very different in color. However, it is not totally stable in its variegation and green-leaved branches must be removed. 'West Hatch Glory' was discovered as a chance sport in *L. lucidum*. Zone 8

Ligustrum ovalifolium 'Argenteum'

United Kingdom, 1914

Semi-evergreen to deciduous upright shrub that grows to about 2.5 m tall. Leaves drop from November to February, depending on the weather. Leaves irregularly bullate, ovate-lanceolate, to lanceolate and green to grayish green with narrow white margins. On young leaves the margins are more yellowish. The small white flowers are carried in short panicles during midsummer (July and August) followed by black fruits. Due to the white variegated foliage, the flowers are quite inconspicuous. 'Argenteum' is less stable than 'Variegatum' and the irregular bullate leaves do not add to its value. However, it is whiter and therefore

Ligustrum ovalifolium 'Argenteum' MARCO HOFFMAN

adds to the range of variegated privets. 'Argenteum' can be used for hedging or planted as a single specimen. Zone 7a

Ligustrum ovalifolium 'Aureum'

The Netherlands, 1860

The golden privet is an evergreen to semi-evergreen shrub that grows to about 2.5 m. Leaves drop from November to late March, although this cultivar is usually evergreen and will only shed its foliage in cold climates. It has the same broad, upright habit as 'Argenteum', but differs in leaf color and leaf shape. The leaves are ovate to oblong with clear yellow margins, and some leaves are entirely yellow. The white flowers appear in relatively large panicles up to 8 cm. Contrary to 'Argenteum', they contrast well against the yellow variegated foliage. In autumn the blackish globular fruits look good with the foliage. As with 'Argenteum',

Ligustrum ovalifolium 'Argenteum' MARCO HOFFMAN

Ligustrum ovalifolium 'Aureum' MARCO HOFFMAN

Ligustrum ovalifolium 'Little Gold Star' RONALD HOUTMAN

this cultivar easily reverts to green and these branches must be removed when observed. Like all *L. ovalifolium* cultivars, 'Aureum' is excellent for hedging, and it can be used in mixed plantings or for topiary. Zone 7a

Ligustrum ovalifolium 'Little Gold Star'

André van Nijnatten B.V., Zundert, The Netherlands, 1991

Densely branched, rounded shrub that grows to about 1.5 m high and wide. Smaller in all its features than the other variegated *L. ovalifolium*. Leaves ovate to elliptic, up to 4.5 cm long, dark green with broad light yellow margins. 'Little Gold Star' produces small flowers in small panicles, rarely followed by black fruits. It is an attractive new cultivar which, because of its smaller habit, is very suitable for small gardens. Grafted on a standard, it makes a great and highly fashionable plant. 'Little Gold Star' was raised as a seedling of *L. ovalifolium* 'Aureum'. Zone 7a

Ligustrum ovalifolium 'Variegatum'

Before 1906

Strong-growing, broad, upright shrub that grows to 3 m high. It has a semi-evergreen habit and leaf drop occurs from November to February. It is very similar to 'Aureum', but the leaves have pale yellow margins. On older leaves the margins are whiter. Its variegation is quite stable and even, more stable than *L. ovalifolium* 'Argenteum', with less bullate leaves. However, the variegation is whiter in 'Argenteum', and for the color alone 'Argenteum' is preferable over 'Variegatum'. The flowers are carried in about 8 cm long panicles during July and August. They are followed by blackish fruits. 'Variegatum' is suitable for hedging, mixed plantings, or topiary. 'Variegatum' is often offered as *L. ibolium* 'Variegatum', but due to the glabrousness of all parts, it definitely belongs to *L. ovalifolium*. Zone 7a

Ligustrum ovalifolium 'Variegatum' MARCO HOFFMAN

Ligustrum tschonoskii 'Glimmer'

Trompenburg Arboretum, Rotterdam, The Netherlands, 2003

Broad, upright, deciduous shrub with a rounded habit that grows to about 2 m high with elegantly arching branches. The ovate to broad elliptic leaves are up to about 8 cm long and slightly pubescent. They are light greenish yellow with small green centers. The creamy white flowers open in June and early July. 'Glimmer' was discovered as a sport of *L. tschonoskii* in 1991, but it took until February 2003 before it was named. Therefore, it is not yet available, which will change in the coming years. Zone 6

Ligustrum tschonoskii 'Glimmer' GERT FORTGENS

Ligustrum sinense 'Variegatum' RONALD HOUTMAN

Ligustrum vulgare 'Argenteovariegatum' RONALD HOUTMAN

Ligustrum vulgare 'Aureovariegatum' MARCO HOFFMAN

Ligustrum vulgare 'Aureovariegatum'

United Kingdom, 1770

Broad, upright, deciduous shrub that grows to 2.5 m high. The leaves drop in late autumn, usually early November. They are fairly large, up to 9 cm, and oblong to obovate. They are speckled and splashed yellow to greenish yellow. Unfortunately, this cultivar produces green-leaved branches very easily. Besides the variegated foliage, which is interesting for collectors, 'Aureovariegatum' is of little ornamental value. A white-variegated form is called 'Argenteovariegatum'. Except for the color of the variegation it is similar to 'Aureovariegatum'. Both variegated cultivars of *L. vulgare* are rare in cultivation and of far less ornamental value than the variegated cultivars of *L. ovalifolium*. Zone 5a

Liquidambar

Small genus of trees belonging to the Hamamelidaceae (the witch hazel family). The only species that has variegated cultivars is *L. styraciflua*, the American sweet gum. It is a medium-sized to large tree that grows to 30 m in the wild or to 20 m in cultivation. The leaves are usually five-lobed. The flowers and fruits of *Liquidambar* are inconspicuous and of no ornamental value; however, the corky bark, attractive five-lobed leaves, and good autumn colors make *Liquidambar* attractive trees. Furthermore, they are strong and healthy and make great street trees. Although various clones have been named, it appears only a few actually differ from one another.

Liquidambar styraciflua 'Aurea'

Before 1880

Striking medium-sized tree with a broad pyramidal to conical habit. Like the species, this cultivar gets a corky bark and branches with age. The leaves are five-lobed, but the three middle lobes are usually more developed than the two at the leaf base. Young leaves are slightly pinkish when unfolding. Mature leaves are glossy dark green with irregular clear yellow blotches. This gives the tree a greenish yellow appearance, especially from a distance. Despite the name 'Aurea', this cultivar is variegated and definitely not yellow-leaved.

There is a lot of confusion regarding the correct name for this attractive variegated tree. 'Variegata' is now regarded a synonym for 'Aurea'. The American cultivar 'Goduzam' GOLD DUST™ is most probably the same as 'Aurea' as well. However, several clones of 'Aurea' can be found. These originated when nurserymen started propagating branches with a more intense variegation. Zone 5b

Liquidambar styraciflua 'Aurea' RONALD HOUTMAN

Liquidambar styraciflua 'Aurea' KLAAS VERBOOM

Liquidambar styraciflua 'Aurea' RONALD HOUTMAN

Liquidambar styraciflua 'Golden Treasure' PPH (COLLECTION OF HARRY VAN DE LAAR)

Liquidambar styraciflua 'Silver King' RONALD HOUTMAN

Liquidambar styraciflua 'Golden Treasure'

Before 1994

Slow-growing small tree with an irregular broad pyramidal habit. The five-lobed leaves are dark green with very conspicuous golden yellow margins. In autumn the color changes to deep burgundy red with dark yellow to orange margins. Because of its smaller habit, this wonderful cultivar is also suitable for smaller gardens. Zone 5b

Liquidambar styraciflua 'Silver King'

Before 1994

Medium-sized tree with the same habit as 'Aurea'. The five-lobed leaves are green to grayish green with creamy white margins, which gives the whole tree a grayish appearance. In autumn the color changes to pinkish rose tints, together with the green and white variegation. Some plants labeled 'Variegata' that also have leaves with white margins are actually 'Silver King'. More often, however, these are yellow variegated plants that should be named 'Aurea'. 'Silver King' can be used as is 'Aurea', and it makes an excellent specimen tree for medium-sized gardens to large parks. Zone 5b

Liriodendron

The two species of this genus grow into tall trees, easily reaching 20 m or so. The peculiarly shaped leaves are very characteristic for this genus: broad, four-lobed, and with a very distinct wide emarginate apex. *Liriodendron* belongs to the Magnoliaceae (magnolia family), and the relation is best observed when looking at the flowers. The common name tulip tree derived from the conspicuous, large, tuliplike flowers, which open in June. The flowers are approximately 5 cm wide, yellowish orange, and without fragrance. All variegated cultivars are derived from *L. tulipifera*, native to eastern North America. No variegated cultivars derived from the Chinese *L. chinense*.

Liriodendon tulipifera 'Aureomarginatum'

Germany, before 1865

Large tree with a broad, upright to broad pyramidal crown. The leaves are green with broad golden yellow margins, especially in spring and early summer. Later in the season they become more greenish yellow. This cultivar usually flowers very freely. Several slightly dif-

Liriodendron tulipifera 'Aureomarginatum' RONALD HOUTMAN

Liriodendron tulipifera 'Purgatory' JO BÖMER

ferent clones seem to be present in the trade. One of these was trademarked MAJESTIC BEAUTY by Monrovia Nurseries of Azusa, California, United States. As a specimen tree 'Aureomarginatum' can become one of the most striking variegated trees. Zone 5b

Liriodendron tulipifera 'Mediopictum'

This large tree has the same habit and characteristic leaf shape as 'Aureomarginatum'. The leaves are green with a greenish yellow to creamy green blotch in the center. It is not as free flowering as 'Aureomarginatum', but still worthwhile planting for its great foliage. Both 'Aureomarginatum' and 'Mediopictum' are good alternatives to the green-leaved species. Zone 5b

Liriodendron tulipifera 'Purgatory'

M. Bömer, Zundert, The Netherlands, 1996

Large tree with the same habit as the species. The light green leaves are irregularly variegated with light yel-

Liriodendron tulipifera 'Aureomarginatum' WOUT KROMHOUT

Liriodendron tulipifera 'Mediopictum' PPH (COLLECTION OF HARRY VAN DE LAAR)

low. In many leaves 50 percent of each leaf is variegated, but leaves with less variegation also exist. Although not entirely stable, it is worthwhile growing this peculiarly variegated tree. The nursery of Bömer is located in the Vagevuurstraat, freely translated from the Dutch as Purgatory Street, hence the name of this plant. Zone 5b

Lonicera

About 180 species of *Lonicera* shrubs and climbers exist throughout the Northern Hemisphere. Some shrubs, such as *L. nitida*, are small, whereas *L. tatarica* can grow into large bushes. The climbing species are usually very vigorous and can easily reach a height of more than 4 m. In most species the opposite leaves are deciduous, but some are evergreen. *Lonicera* flowers tend to be colorful and fragrant. They are tubular with a lobed corolla.

Lonicera ×*italica* 'Sherlite' Harlequin™ RONALD HOUTMAN

Because it is a diverse genus, the uses of *Lonicera* are also versatile. The lower evergreen shrubs, such as *L. nitida* and *L. pileata*, are very suitable for hedging. The larger shrubs are commonly used in groups or mixed plantings by local authorities or along roads. The variegated shrubby cultivars are of more ornamental value and are well suited to a private garden, as are the climbing cultivars.

Lonicera canadensis 'Marble King'

Norseco, Inc., Laval, Québec, Canada, 1996

Broad, upright, deciduous shrub that grows to about 1.5 m high and 1 m wide. Very free branching, thus creating a bushy habit. The opposite leaves are ovate to ovate-oblong and have an average length of 6 cm. They are dull green and heavily mottled creamy white to yellowish white. The creamy white flowers fade to yellowish and are followed by red berries. 'Marble King' is a very hardy shrub for landscape uses or as contrast plant against green-leaved shrubs. Zone 3

Lonicera ×*italica* 'Sherlite' Harlequin™

O. Messenger, Ipswich, United Kingdom, 1984

Deciduous twining shrub that is less vigorous than the well-known *L. periclymenum* (European honeysuckle). Eventually it will reach about 8 m in height. The opposite leaves are elliptic to oblong and about 7 cm long. The margins are usually entire, but many leaves are pinnately lobed, resembling oak leaves. These oaklike leaves mostly arise on young and vigorous shoots. All leaves are dull green to grayish green and have narrow creamy white margins. The variegation is not very distinct, and the whole plant appears more grayish than variegated. The flowers open in early summer and are of the typical honeysuckle shape. They are light purplish on the outside and creamy to creamy yellow inside. The flowers are not as fragrant as those of *L. periclymenum*, spreading only a faint fragrance. 'Sherlite' is an attractive variegated climber for use on trellises, fences, and walls. Zone 6

Lonicera japonica 'Aureoreticulata'

Japan, before 1860

Vigorous twining shrub that grows to about 2 m high. The leaves are relatively small, orbicular to oblong with entire margins, and green with clear yellow to pale yellow veins. Like 'Sherlite', this cultivar also forms oaklike leaves on young and vigorous shoots. The white flowers fade to yellowish and appear during early summer, in June and July. This attractive climber is less hardy than the species and will die back in severe winters. It usually will regrow and, because it is vigorous, the damage is soon camouflaged. Like so many plants, P. F. von Siebold introduced this plant into the Western trade. Zone 6b

Lonicera japonica 'Maskerade'

P. van Manen, Ederveen, The Netherlands, 2002

Deciduous climber that grows to about 4 m high. The leaves are dark green with narrow creamy white margins. As the leaves age, the margins become more narrow. The flowers open in July, August, and early September. They are pale rosy red on the outside and much lighter, almost white, inside. The flowerbuds are rosy red. Like all *L. japonica*, the flowers open in pairs. 'Maskerade' was discovered as a sport in *L. japonica* 'Halliana'. Zone 6a

Lonicera japonica 'Mint Crisp'

Matt Lohan, Carbury, County Kildare, Ireland, 1999

Like all cultivars of *L. japonica*, this also is a vigorous, semi-evergreen twining shrub. It will attain a height of about 3.5 m. The ovate leaves are light green and heavily mottled creamy white to white. In autumn, the leaf colors change into pinkish tints. The flowers open from early summer into midsummer, are white, and turn yellow with age. 'Mint Crisp' is very suitable for covering walls, trellises, or fences. Especially good with red- or purple-flowering shrubs or perennials; also very effective against red brick. Zone 6b

Lonicera nitida 'Lemon Beauty'

K. Meijnen, Dessel, Belgium, 1994

Elegant small evergreen shrub that grows to about 1 m. The main branches are spreading and gracefully arching to almost horizontal. The opposite leaves are about 1.2 cm long and about half as wide. They are glossy green with relatively broad creamy yellow margins. 'Lemon Beauty' was found as a sport in *L. nitida* 'Elegant' and resembles this cultivar in habit. It is a remarkably fresh-looking shrub that is suitable for mass plantings, but can also be grown in a large pot on a terrace or balcony. It was given an Award of Merit by the Royal Boskoop Horticultural Society in 1995. Another

Lonicera japonica 'Maskerade' RONALD HOUTMAN

Lonicera japonica 'Mint Crisp' RONALD HOUTMAN

Lonicera nitida 'Lemon Beauty' GERT FORTGENS

Lonicera nitida 'Silver Beauty' RONALD HOUTMAN

variegated cultivar is 'Stone Green', named after an estate in the United Kingdom. Zone 7a

Lonicera nitida 'Silver Beauty'

Darthuizer Nurseries B.V., Leersum, The Netherlands, 1991

Like 'Lemon Beauty', this plant was also found as a sport in *L. nitida* 'Elegant' and has the same elegant habit and small leaves. The leaves are narrow-elliptic and grayish green with white margins. Occasionally green-leaved branches are formed. These must be removed to keep the plant variegated. 'Silver Lining' is a similar cultivar whose dark green leaves have silvery white margins. It will grow to about 1.2 m. Both cultivars described here can be used in the same ways as 'Lemon Beauty'. Zone 7a

Lophomyrtus 'Gloriosa'

Small shrub with a dense habit that grows to about 1 m. The twigs are attractively colored purple, which contrasts very well against the variegated foliage. The leaves are green with irregular, but relatively large, yellow centers. 'Gloriosa' is only hardy in mild areas and therefore only suitable as a container plant in colder climates. Zone 9

Lophomyrtus ×*ralphii* 'Little Star'

Small shrub with a dense ovate habit that grows to about 1 m. The opposite leaves are pinkish grayish

Lophomyrtus 'Gloriosa' RONALD HOUTMAN

Lophomyrtus ×*ralphii* 'Little Star' RONALD HOUTMAN

green with relatively conspicuous pinkish cream margins. Although 'Little Star' is a frost-tender shrub, this should not prevent anyone from using it in the garden. As a container plant it can make a splendid addition to the patio or balcony. The little orbicular leaves are of a fine texture and go well with many other shrubs.

Lophomyrtus ×*ralphii* is a naturally occurring hybrid between *L. bullata* and *L. obcordata,* native in New Zealand. It is regularly found in areas where both parent species meet. There are several other cultivars of *L.* ×*ralphii* on the market. These include 'Multicolor' (sometimes misspelled 'Multicolour'), an illegitimate name for a cultivar with variegated centers in the leaves; 'Sundae', variegated yellow and reddish; and 'Technicolor', with dull yellow variegated foliage that is also blotched brownish, orange, and pink. Zone 9

Luma apiculata 'Glanleam Gold'

Glanleam House, Valentia Island, County Kerry, Ireland, 1957

Small tree with a narrow, upright habit. Older bark becomes a shiny light reddish brown, young shoots are purplish red. The small leaves are dark green with creamy white margins. Young leaves are tinted pinkish. The white flowers appear during midsummer and are sometimes produced in abundance. 'Glanleam Gold' is an attractive cultivar. Though often sold as small container plant or houseplant, it can reach more than 7 m in height in milder climates. 'Glanleam Gold'

The original tree of *Luma apiculata* 'Glanleam Gold' RONALD HOUTMAN

Luma apiculata 'Glanleam Gold' RONALD HOUTMAN

Lycianthes rantonnetii 'Variegatum' RONALD HOUTMAN

Magnolia grandiflora 'Anne Pickard' RONALD HOUTMAN

Magnolia grandiflora 'Variegata' GERT FORTGENS

was raised as a seedling, being the only variegated plant in a batch of thousands of seedlings at Glanleam House. The original tree still grows in the garden, and it is more than 7 m high. *Luma apiculata* is sometimes referred to as *Myrtus apiculata* or *M. luma*. Zone 8b

Lycianthes rantonnetii 'Variegatum'

Broad, upright shrub with a flattened-rounded habit. The broad ovate leaves are grayish green, with irregular white margins. This contrasts very well to the bright purple flowers that are produced throughout summer. *Lycianthes* was long included in *Solanum*, but this was recently corrected. Due to its tenderness, this member of the Solanaceae (potato family) is mainly known as a container plant. 'Variegatum' works well on every terrace, patio, or balcony. Zone 10

Magnolia grandiflora 'Anne Pickard'

A. A. Pickard, Magnolia Gardens, Canterbury, United Kingdom, 1968

Medium-sized to large evergreen tree with an irregular, broad, upright habit. The broad oblong to obovate leaves are very thick and leathery. They are glossy dark green above and brown tomentose beneath. 'Anne Pickard' was discovered as a sport of 'Saint George', which was also raised by Pickard. 'Saint George', a green-leaved cultivar, shows better hardiness than the average *M. grandiflora*. The flowers usually have more than the average fourteen tepals of *M. grandiflora*. 'Anne Pickard' is similar to 'Saint George', except for the variegated foliage. Zone 7

Magnolia grandiflora 'Variegata'

Collective name for several variegated clones of the southern magnolia. The large leathery leaves of these plants are often irregularly margined or mottled and splashed with creamy white. Usually these clones do not remain stable, and the variegation disappears within a few years. It is a matter of taste whether people like these unstable clones. Zone 7b

Magnolia virginiana 'Mattie Mae Smith'

John Allen Smith, Chunchula, Alabama, United States, 1995

Beautiful large shrub to small tree with an irregular, narrow, ovate, upright habit. The foliage of the swamp laurel or sweet bay is almost evergreen and spreads a nice lemony fragrance when crushed. The leathery leaves of 'Mattie Mae Smith' are oblong-lanceolate to ovate-lanceolate. They are dark green, with irregular but attractive clear golden yellow to dark greenish yellow margins. The variegation covers approximately 50 percent of the leaf surface. The flowers, which open in late spring, are creamy white, up to about 4 cm, and up to 8 cm across. They are lemon scented as well. 'Mattie Mae Smith' is by far the most attractive variegated *Magnolia*. It is a pity that this plant is not hardy enough for colder climates. Zone 8

Mahonia aquifolium 'Versicolor'

Upright evergreen shrub that grows to about 1.5 m. To maintain a dense and well-branched plant, it is necessary to prune the oldest branches every two or three years. Otherwise it will become a loose and leggy plant. The attractive pinnate leaves are light green and heavily speckled and mottled yellow. Occasionally an orange blotch is visible in older leaves. 'Versicolor' is a true collectors' item and not suitable for the general public. *Mahonia aquifolium* is known for its good yellow flowers, dense habit, and healthy dark green foliage; the green-leaved cultivars 'Apollo' and 'Atropurpurea' are recommended over 'Versicolor'. Zone 5

Malus 'Dovar'

IVT, Wageningen, The Netherlands, 1971

Small tree that grows to 4 m with an irregular upright habit. The leaves are yellow to greenish yellow with some white streaks and margins. In late April and early May, the purplish flowerbuds open white. They are followed by orange-blushed deep yellow fruits. 'Dovar' (a combination of "John *Do*wnie" and "*var*iegated") was raised from a batch of grafts of 'John Downie' that had been treated with X-rays. After research, it was evident that the mutation is not caused by a virus (see Appendix A). Apart from the variegated leaves, 'Dovar' differs from its parent in somewhat weaker growth and slightly fewer fruits that ripen a week later in the season. Some green-leaved branches have been reported. It is a very rarely grown cultivar, probably only existing in one or two collections. Zone 5

Metasequoia glyptostroboides 'White Spot'

About 1997

One of the very few variegated *Metasequoia glyptostroboides* cultivars. It forms a large tree with the same

Magnolia virginiana 'Mattie Mae Smith' WIM RUTTEN

Mahonia aquifolium 'Versicolor' RONALD HOUTMAN

Malus 'Dovar' PIERRE THEUNISSEN

Metasequoia glyptostroboides 'White Spot' RONALD HOUTMAN

Metrosideros kermadecensis 'Variegata' RONALD HOUTMAN

Metrosideros umbellata 'Harlequin' RONALD HOUTMAN

narrow pyramidal habit as the species. The deciduous pinnate leaves are lively light green variegated silvery white. In some leaves a few leaflets are variegated, but whole leaves are also sometimes white. Even though the variegation is very irregular, it seems stable. 'White Spot' is not a very distinctive variegated plant. Seen from a distance it looks more like a light green–leaved plant than a variegated plant. It is a true collectors' item with little commercial or ornamental value. 'Jack Frost' is another variegated cultivar. The base of some needles is white. It is less variegated than 'White Spot', however, and therefore less recommended. Zone 5b

Metrosideros kermadecensis 'Variegata'

New Zealand

A large tree, reaching a height of more than 15 m in its native habitat, but only a large shrub in cultivation. The elliptic to ovate leaves are up to 5 cm long and dull green with broad creamy white margins. The undersides are densely white pubescent. The scarlet bottlebrush flowers open in winter.

This plant was long thought to be a cultivar of *M. excelsa*, but differs from that species in a slightly different leaf shape and smaller leaves. The leaves of *M. excelsa* are elliptic-oblong and 5 to 10 cm long. All *Metrosideros* are only suitable for the mildest areas. In colder climates they are only grown as container plants, but are still very attractive. Zone 9

Metrosideros umbellata 'Harlequin'

J. Cartmann, Christchurch, New Zealand, 1992

Metrosideros umbellata is easily distinguished from other *Metrosideros* species by its narrower, lanceolate leaves that have more or less pointed tips. In 'Harlequin' the leaves are glossy green with very conspicuous yellow margins. The flowers are an unusual brilliant red color, contrasting well against the foliage and giving the plant a tropical appearance. 'Harlequin' makes an excellent container plant in most temperate regions, except for the mildest climates, where it can be grown in the garden.

In addition to the cultivars of *M. kermadecensis* and *M. umbellata* described here, there are several more variegated *Metrosideros* cultivars. These include *M. kermadecensis* 'Lewis Nicholls' (leaves blotched yellow), 'Red and Gold' (leaves with golden yellow margins), and 'Sunninghill' (leaves with a large creamy central spot), as well as *M. carminea* 'Carousel' (leaves with yellow margins). Zone 9

Microbiota decussata 'Sinclair'

Terry Sinclair, Wales, United Kingdom, 1992

Low groundcover conifer with a procumbent habit. The dense foliage resembles *Thuja* (hence the reference to *Biota*, the old name for *Thuja*). In summer it is green, but during winter the foliage changes to brownish purple-green. The foliage of 'Sinclair' has attractive yellow variegation. It is an extremely hardy plant with good groundcover qualities. Occasionally other variegated clones of *Microbiota*, usually illegitimately called 'Aureovariegata' or 'Variegata' are offered. These seem to be similar to 'Sinclair'. If these cultivars differ from 'Sinclair', a new cultivar name must be given to these plants. Zone 3

Microbiota decussata 'Sinclair' KLAAS VERBOOM

Myrtus communis 'Variegata'

1597

Within the species *M. communis*, there are two slightly different variegated cultivars. The first described here is the most widely grown. 'Variegata' is a medium-sized, densely branched evergreen shrub with a broad, upright habit. When grown against a south-facing wall, this shrub can eventually attain a height of about 1.5 m. The aromatic ovate to ovate-lanceolate leaves are glossy and dark with narrow creamy white margins. The solitary white flowers are borne freely during summer. The second variegated cultivar belongs to the subspecies *tarentina* and it is also known as 'Variegata'. This cultivar is smaller in all its features and is only rarely available in the trade. 'Variegata' can be planted in the garden only in the mildest climates. Like the green-leaved species, this cultivar thrives very well in windy seaside areas. In colder areas, it can only be used as a container plant. Zone 8b

Myrtus communis 'Variegata' WIM SNOEIJER

Olearia arborescens 'Variegata'

New Zealand

Broad, upright, evergreen shrub with an irregular habit. This variegated cultivar is less vigorous than the species and will not grow any taller than about 3 m. The alternate leaves are ovate, occasionally with a few distinct teeth. They are dull green, irregularly blotched, and streaked grayish green and creamy white. The small, white, daisylike flowers appear in axillary and

Olearia arborescens 'Variegata' RONALD HOUTMAN

Olearia traversii 'Tweedledum' RONALD HOUTMAN

Olearia traversii 'Variegata' RONALD HOUTMAN

Orixa japonica 'Variegata' RONALD HOUTMAN

terminal panicles during May and June. Within the woody members of Asteraceae (daisy family) only a few variegated plants exist; all of these are *Olearia*. *Olearia arborescens* 'Variegata' is the most stable of these cultivars, but still tends to revert quite easily. These green-leaved shoots must be removed. Zone 8b

Olearia traversii 'Tweedledee'

New Zealand

Olearia traversii is a highly wind-resistant small tree that is much planted in coastal areas such as Cornwall and western Ireland. It forms a dense shrubby tree that grows to 6 m high. This variegated cultivar is less vigorous, but will eventually reach more than 3 m. The stems are square and the opposite, ovate-oblong leathery leaves are grayish green with irregular greenish yellow margins. Leaves with variegated centers are also formed. The undersides of the leaves have a silvery pubescence, which is absolutely striking when moved by the wind. The greenish flowers are inconspicuous because they lack ray florets. 'Tweedledee' is an unstable cultivar that reverts very easily. Zone 9

Olearia traversii 'Tweedledum'

New Zealand

Like 'Tweedledee', but with the variegation in the leaf centers. Because these two cultivars are very similar, it is probably better to call all three variegated *Olearia traversii* cultivars 'Variegata', the oldest legitimate name. Zone 9

Olearia traversii 'Variegata'

This evergreen shrub does not differ very much from the two other cultivars of *O. traversii*. The leaves are irregularly variegated, both at the margins and in the leaf centers. It is very unstable and only interesting for collectors. It is highly uncertain whether 'Tweedledee' and 'Tweedledum' can be retained as separate cultivars. They too are very unstable and often different patterns of variegation exist on the same plant. Zone 9

Orixa japonica 'Variegata'

Orixa is a monotypic genus belonging to the Rutaceae (rue family). The only species, *O. japonica*, is a deciduous shrub with a broad spreading-upright habit. All parts of the plant are strongly aromatic. This smell is not regarded as pleasant by most people. The small greenish white flowers are inconspicuous but are borne profusely on older plants.

Orixa japonica 'Variegata' is a medium-sized shrub that grows to about 3 m high with an open habit. The silvery green leaves have broad creamy white margins. Older plants can be attractive when in full bloom during spring. 'Variegata' is easy to grow, but not very attractive, except for a short period during spring. It is only rarely offered in the trade. Zone 6a

Osmanthus

Osmanthus is a small genus of evergreen shrubs belonging to the Oleaceae (olive family). The leaves of all species are opposite, and the campanulate to tubular flowers, usually white or yellowish, have four corolla lobes.

Osmanthus heterophyllus, the holly olive, is perhaps the best-known species. In fact, it is the only species within the genus that holds variegated cultivars. Although looking superficially like *Ilex*, *Osmanthus heterophyllus* is easily distinguished by its opposite leaves. All cultivars described here form dense shrubs with a rounded habit. They can grow to a height of 3 to 5 m. The leaves are elliptic to elliptic-oblong or ovate-elliptic and usually have two to four teeth on each side. Older plants usually have entire leaves. The flowers appear in axillary and terminal clusters during early autumn. With an average diameter of 7 mm, the leaves are relatively small, but they are pleasantly fragrant. All cultivars described here are hardy to zone 7a.

Osmanthus heterophyllus 'Aureomarginatus' RONALD HOUTMAN

Osmanthus heterophyllus 'Goshiki' GEORGE OTTER

Osmanthus heterophyllus 'Aureomarginatus'

Before 1877

The leaves of this old cultivar are glossy yellow-green bordered with yellow. There is not a lot of contrast between the different colors in the leaf, which is why this is not a very distinct variegated cultivar. Due to the popularity of white variegated cultivars and the tricolored 'Goshiki', 'Aureomarginatus' is not a widely grown plant.

Osmanthus heterophyllus 'Goshiki'

Japan

Striking form with heavily variegated tricolored foliage. The young foliage emerges in pinkish tints, soon becoming heavily mottled and speckled with different shades of green and yellow.

In 1980 Barry R. Yinger introduced this plant from Japan, and most probably it has been in cultivation in Japan for many more years. It became well known as 'Tricolor', but because this Latin name was given after January 1959, it was invalid. After research it became clear the older Japanese name 'Goshiki' (meaning "five colors") is the only valid name for this attractive cultivar. It is now widely used as a garden plant and as a container plant. It is also suitable for hedging and group plantings.

Osmanthus heterophyllus 'Kembu'

Japan, before 1982

With a maximum height of about 1 m, 'Kembu' is smaller than the other *O. heterophyllus* cultivars. It forms a dense, rounded bush. The leaves are nearly spineless or

Osmanthus heterophyllus 'Kembu' RONALD HOUTMAN

Osmanthus heterophyllus 'Variegatus' RONALD HOUTMAN

have very few spines. They are also smaller than in other cultivars of the species. The leaves have narrow creamy white margins. 'Kembu' is a nice semi-dwarf shrub suitable for the smaller garden. It was first introduced in the Western trade at the Floriade 1982 in Amsterdam, The Netherlands, where it was shown in the Japanese exhibition. The cultivar name 'Kembu' (meaning "sword dance") was assigned by Barry R. Yinger.

Osmanthus heterophyllus 'Variegatus'

Japan, before 1860

Old and well-known variegated cultivar of *O. heterophyllus* that was imported from Japan by P. F. von Siebold. It forms a densely branched shrub about 3 m high. The leaves are slightly smaller than those of the species and dark green with creamy white margins. This cultivar is recommended and regarded to be very stable: it hardly ever reverts to green.

Pachysandra terminalis 'Silver Edge'

Creeping evergreen subshrub that grows to 20 cm high. The fleshy branches ascend from a rootstock. The leaves are clustered at the branch tips. They are diamond-shaped to obovate with the upper half toothed. The light green leaves have narrow silvery white to creamy white margins. The terminal spikes consist of small creamy white flowers and are produced during early spring on the previous year's wood. 'Silver Edge' is a handsome low-growing plant that is particularly suitable for groundcover. It thrives best in moist, humus-rich soil in semi-shade; when planted in full sun or poor soil, the leaves readily turn yellowish. Whether 'Silver Edge' is similar to 'Variegata' is not certain. It appears to have lighter green foliage, whereas 'Variegata' has grayish green variegated leaves. Some authors, however, treat it as a synonym for 'Variegata'. Zone 5b

Pachysandra terminalis 'Variegata'

Japan, before 1859

Like 'Silver Edge', but the leaves are grayish green and have irregular narrow creamy white margins. All *P. terminalis* cultivars are valuable groundcovers, but the variegated cultivars grow slightly slower than the green-leaved ones. 'Variegata' was introduced into Western cultivation by P. F. von Siebold, who brought it from Japan in 1859. Zone 5b

Parrotia persica 'Lamplighter'

Stephen Taffler, Berkhamsted, United Kingdom

The Persian ironwood is a small tree with a rounded crown, beautiful exfoliating bark, and fantastic autumn colors. It is a close relative of *Hamamelis*, and the leaves somewhat resemble *Hamamelis virginiana*. 'Lamplighter' combines the good qualities of the species with nice variegated foliage. The green leaves have broad creamy white margins. In autumn the leaves are flushed red and purple, adding to the value. 'Lamplighter' is not an easy plant to establish. It needs a semi-shaded or shady location. Because of its variegation, it is less vigorous than the species. Once the plant is established, strong-growing green-leaved branches are occasionally formed. 'Lamplighter' is less vigorous than the species and will remain a medium-sized to large shrub. Zone 5

Pachysandra terminalis 'Variegata' RONALD HOUTMAN

Parrotia persica 'Lamplighter' RONALD HOUTMAN

Philadelphus coronarius 'Variegatus'

United Kingdom, before 1770

Densely branched compact shrub that grows to about 1.75 m with a bushy, broad, upright habit. The leaves on nonflowering shoots are up to 9 cm long. Those on flowering shoots are smaller, usually not longer than 5 cm. The ovate to broad lanceolate leaves are a dull medium green, with white to creamy white margins. Occasionally 'Variegatus' produces entirely white leaves. The pleasantly fragrant flowers are single and pure white and have an average diameter of 3.5 cm. They are carried in short racemes with five to nine flowers. The cultivar named 'Bowles' Variety' has proven to be the same as 'Variegatus'. Zone 5a

Philadelphus 'Innocence'

Lemoine, Nancy, France, 1928

Broad, upright shrub, with roughly the same habit as *P. coronarius* 'Variegatus'. The leaves are ovate and distinctly toothed with five to six teeth on each side. They are light green and heavily streaked and mottled greenish yellow to yellow. The single to semi-double flowers are very fragrant and are produced profusely. 'Innocence' can be used as a specimen or in mixed groups. Besides the variegated foliage, the richly produced fragrant flowers are also a reason for planting this exceptional shrub. Zone 6

Philadelphus coronarius 'Variegatus' RONALD HOUTMAN

Philadelphus 'Innocence' RONALD HOUTMAN

Photinia davidiana 'Palette' RONALD HOUTMAN

Photinia glabra 'Parfait' CHRISTOPHER FAIRWEATHER

Photinia davidiana 'Palette'

A. A. M. Vissenberg, Zundert, The Netherlands, 1980

Dense, rather narrowly upright evergreen shrub that grows to about 3 m. It grows more weakly than the species and will not grow as tall. Young foliage is reddish pink, later turning light green with creamy white and pinkish streaks and blotches. The branches are reddish brown, contrasting well against the colorful foliage. 'Palette' is a very conspicuous variegated shrub that tends to suffer from leaf burn during warm and sunny spells. It is best planted in a semi-shaded location. It can create a wonderfully blended hedge, but is also very suitable as a specimen in both smaller and larger gardens. The species *P. davidiana* is often referred to as *Stranvaesia davidiana*. According to the latest research, however, this species is now included in *Photinia*. Zone 7a

Photinia glabra 'Parfait'

Sakata Nursery Co., Japan, 1979

Evergreen shrub with an upright habit that grows to about 3 m. The elliptic to lanceolate leaves are bronzy pink at first, turning green with grayish green during summer. The margins are dark pink when young, later turning light pink to creamy white. This stable cultivar was introduced in the Western trade by Barry R. Yinger, who also assigned the cultivar name 'Parfait'. This cultivar is also known under a range of synonyms, including 'Pink Lady', 'Roseomarginata' (or 'Rosea Marginata'), and 'Variegata'. Zone 8a

Picea glauca 'Arneson's Blue Variegated'

R. L. Fincham, Coenosium Gardens, Sandy, Oregon, United States, 1989

Small conifer with a very compact and dense growth and an irregular conical habit. The needles are attractive bluish green, irregularly variegated with green branchlets. The result is one of the most peculiar variegated plants, as far as color is concerned. The slightly irregular growth habit is very beautiful. However, the variegation is highly unstable and plants easily turn into entirely blue-leaved specimens. 'Arneson's Blue Variegated' was given an Award of Recommendation by the Royal Boskoop Horticultural Society in 1991. Zone 3

Pieris

A small genus belonging to the Ericaceae (heather family) and consisting of only seven species. Only *P. floribunda, P. formosa,* and *P. japonica* and its cultivars are of ornamental value, although a couple of hybrids between *P. japonica* and other species are grown.

All *Pieris* are evergreen shrubs, usually growing to about 3 m high, but occasionally more than 3 m. In spring the creamy white to white flowers appear in terminal (paniculate) racemes. They superficially resemble *Convallaria,* hence the common name lily-of-the-valley bush. *Pieris* thrive best in peaty, humus-rich soil in semi-shaded locations. They are very suitable for mass planting in woodland gardens. Many of the cultivars, the variegated ones included, are smaller and also popular in small gardens or as container plants on balconies and terraces. All *Pieris* cultivars described here are hardy to zone 6b.

Pieris 'Flaming Silver'

A. J. Kuijf & Son, Boskoop, The Netherlands, 1985

Compact evergreen shrub that grows to 1 m in height. Young leaves are brilliant red, fading to salmon-pink

Picea glauca 'Arneson's Blue Variegated' RONALD HOUTMAN

Pieris 'Flaming Silver' RONALD HOUTMAN

Pieris japonica 'Astrid' FA. C. ESVELD

Pieris japonica 'Astrid' RONALD HOUTMAN

Pieris japonica 'Carnaval' RONALD HOUTMAN

and finally becoming dark green with creamy white margins in early summer. The creamy white flowers open in April and are carried in arching racemes up to 7 cm long. 'Flaming Silver' was raised as a sport of *P.* 'Forest Flame', which is a hybrid between *P. formosa* var. *forrestii* and *P. japonica*. 'Flaming Silver' did not only inherit the strikingly colored young foliage from 'Forest Flame', but it did inherit the susceptibility for late frosts. Frosts can seriously damage the young foliage, however, the plant will always recover. It is very similar to *Pieris* 'Mouwsvila', but the margins of 'Flaming Silver' are narrower and the whole plant looks less bright. The Royal Boskoop Horticultural Society awarded 'Flaming Silver' an Award of Merit in 1985, followed by a First Class Certificate in 1986.

Pieris japonica 'Astrid'

W. Gijsen, Rijkevorsel, Belgium, 2000

Nice variegated *Pieris* that was discovered as a sport in *P. japonica* 'Red Mill'. Like this cultivar, 'Astrid' has a broad, upright habit. The leaves are similar in shape to 'Red Mill'. Occasionally they are slightly bent, a feature in 'Red Mill'. The young leaves are deep purplish red. Mature leaves are dark green with creamy margins. 'Astrid' differs significantly from other variegated *Pieris* cultivars by its more cream-colored leaf margins, instead of the silvery or white margins in other cultivars. The warm colors of the young growth add to the ornamental value of this plant. It was given an Award of Recommendation by the Royal Boskoop Horticultural Society in 2001.

Pieris japonica 'Carnaval'

G. van Santvoort, Someren, The Netherlands, 1992

Compact, relatively narrow, upright evergreen shrub. Eventually it can reach a height of 1.5 m. The young foliage is deep chestnut-brown at first, soon becoming dark red. Later in spring the leaves turn dark green with irregular creamy white to silvery white margins. White flowers in slightly drooping racemes up to 12 cm open in April. 'Carnaval' originated as a sport of *P. japonica* 'Mountain Fire' and is easily recognized by the same, rather narrow, upright habit. Unfortunately, this variegated plant tends to produce green-leaved branches. 'Carnaval' is excellent as a container plant, but will also do well in the garden. It was awarded a First Class Certificate by the Royal Boskoop Horticultural Society in 1999.

Pieris japonica 'Little Heath'

P. Foley, Little Heath Nursery, Berkhamsted, United Kingdom, about 1976

Very distinctive variegated cultivar with a rounded compact habit that grows to 1 m high. The leaves are relatively short and therefore look wider than in other *P. japonica* cultivars. They are green with broad creamy white margins. Young foliage is reddish brown. 'Little Heath' is not very floriferous. The flowers are white and carried in slightly drooping, short racemes of about 3 cm. Green-leaved shoots sometimes appear, and these must be removed. It was in that manner that 'Little Heath Green', the green-leaved sport of 'Little Heath', was discovered. In fact, this is one of the very few examples whereby the variegated plant was named before the green-leaved variant. This rather droll plant has become one of the most popular variegated *Pieris* cultivars for growing as a container plant.

Pieris japonica 'Variegata'

Japan, before 1860

Compact evergreen shrub with a dense habit that grows to about 1 m high and wide. In milder areas it can grow larger, up to 2 m. The leaves are green with irregular creamy white margins. The young leaves are only slightly bronze. The flowers are creamy white and carried in relatively short racemes. During winter the flowerbuds are light red. 'Variegata' was introduced into the Western trade in 1860 by P. F. von Siebold. Synonyms for 'Variegata' include *P. japonica* var. *albomarginata*, 'Elegantissima', 'Variegata Nana'.

Pieris japonica 'Carnaval' RONALD HOUTMAN

Pieris japonica 'Variegata' WOUT KROMHOUT

Pieris japonica 'Little Heath' MARCO HOFFMAN

Pieris japonica 'White Rim' RONALD HOUTMAN

Pieris 'Mouwsvila' HAVILA™ RONALD HOUTMAN

Pieris 'Robinswood' RONALD HOUTMAN

Pieris japonica 'White Rim'

Mayfair Nurseries, Hillsdale, New Jersey, United States, 1948

This is most probably a renamed clone of *P. japonica* 'Variegata', of which a few more clones seem to be in cultivation. It closely resembles 'Variegata', but differs in its pinkish young foliage and more yellowish cream margins on young leaves. During winter the flower-buds are more reddish than 'Variegata'. This cultivar is sometimes offered as 'Gold Rim'.

Pieris 'Mouwsvila' HAVILA™

J. J. M. Mouws, Zundert, The Netherlands, 1987

Very similar to *P.* 'Flaming Silver' and also discovered as a sport of *P.* 'Forest Flame'. 'Mouwsvila' mainly differs in having broader creamy white margins, which gives the plant a brighter appearance. It was given an Award of Merit by the Royal Boskoop Horticultural Society in 1988. However, it has proven less healthy than 'Flaming Silver' and regularly forms brown leaves that die off.

Pieris 'Robinswood'

United Kingdom, about 1970

Like 'Flaming Silver' and 'Mouwsvila' HAVILA™, this English cultivar was also discovered as a sport in *P.* 'Forest Flame'. The green leaves have cream margins, and the young shoots are deep red. Although 'Robinswood' has a less bright appearance than the two other cultivars mentioned here, the plant has a good upright habit. Eventually it will grow into a dense, medium-sized shrub with an irregular broad conical habit.

Pinus

The pine trees, belonging to the important family Pinaceae, form the largest genus of conifers. Depending on the classification used, the number of *Pinus* species ranges from about 70 to more than 100. Pines mainly grow in temperate regions across the Northern Hemisphere, ranging from real dwarf plants only suitable for rock gardens to large trees. Some species are important trees for forestry. Some species, mainly *P. parviflora* and *P. thunbergii*, are very popular for growing as bonzai. This has resulted in a huge number of cultivar names, most of which are very difficult to verify.

The needles of *Pinus* are usually longer than in other conifer genera and in some species very soft to the touch. Needles are grouped in fascicles, varying from one to five needles per fascicle. Generally, *Pinus* species and cultivars make impressive trees or attractive shrubs. The habit of some cultivars is irregular and capricious, adding to the slight mystique surrounding these wonderful garden plants. Throughout the world their ornamental value is highly rated, both the plain-colored species and cultivars as well as the variegated ones.

Most variegated cultivars of *Pinus* are derived from *P. mugo*, the dwarf mountain pine, *P. parviflora*, the Japanese white pine, and *P. thunbergii*, the Japanese black pine. Some cultivars are variegated in having yellow or creamy branchlets. Others have bicolored needles with variegated bases or tips. These so-called dragon's eye pines are very popular in Japan, and many of these cultivars were named there. The cultivars with variegated needles are usually more stable than those with variegated branchlets. In addition to the cultivars described here, there are many more variegated *Pinus*, most being uncommon to very rare.

Pinus cembra 'Aureovariegata'

Sénéclause Nurseries, Bourg Argental, France, 1868

Relatively compact conifer with a narrow conical habit. The long, soft needles are in groups of five. The foliage is green and in part golden yellow. This yellow is at its brightest during winter. 'Aureovariegata' is a nice old cultivar that is still in cultivation, although rare. Zone 3

Pinus densiflora 'Oculus-draconis'

Japan, 1890

Large shrub to small tree with a rather open, irregular habit. The needles are grouped in pairs, approximately 10 cm long, and relatively soft to the touch. They are grayish green with two light yellow spots: a large spot at the base and a smaller spot in the middle of each needle. Seen from above it looks like two yellow rings against a grayish green background, making it a typical dragon's eye pine. This cultivar, as well as *P. thunbergii* 'Oculus-draconis', are old Japanese cultivars and quite common in cultivation. Zone 6b

Pinus densiflora 'White Band'

A dense, rather slow-growing small tree with a slightly irregular habit. The branches are densely packed with

Pinus densiflora 'Oculus-draconis' RONALD HOUTMAN

Pinus densiflora 'Oculus-draconis' J. R. P. VAN HOEY SMITH

Pinus densiflora 'White Band' J. R. P. VAN HOEY SMITH

Pinus leucodermis 'Aureospicata' J. R. P. VAN HOEY SMITH

Pinus mugo 'Chameleon' RONALD HOUTMAN

Pinus mugo 'Frosty' RONALD HOUTMAN

needles in fascicles of two. Some needles are dark grayish green, others are entirely creamy yellow. The effect is as curious as it is beautiful. In some branches the proportion between green and variegated needles is equal. In other branches the green leaves are on one side, while the variegated ones are on the other side. Zone 6b

Pinus koraiensis 'Variegata'

Japan, 1880

The soft needles of this upright conifer are partially light yellow to entirely yellow. These are intermixed with grayish green needles with a typical silvery undertone. This old cultivar is most likely no longer in cultivation. Zone 4

Pinus leucodermis 'Aureospicata'

Hermann A. Hesse Nurseries, Weener, Germany, 1955

A slow-growing conifer with a broad conical habit. In time it will become a small tree. The needles, grouped in pairs, are 6 to 8 cm long and rather stiff. They are dark green with cream-colored to light yellow tips.

'Aureospicata' is the only variegated cultivar belonging to *P. leucodermis*, a beautiful tree with a conical habit. This species is native to southeastern Europe, especially the Balkan region. It is very closely related to *P. heldreichii*; some authors regard *P. leucodermis* a natural variety of it. 'Aureospicata' is not widely grown, however, it is still in cultivation. Zone 6a

Pinus mugo 'Chameleon'

Vic van Lier, Meyel, The Netherlands, 2003

Another cultivar of *P. mugo* with a relatively dense, but somewhat irregular, low-growing habit. This habit makes it valuable as a rock garden plant. The needles are about 4 cm long and dark green. They are tipped clear yellow, making it a dragon's eye pine. During winter the yellow tips change into deep red, hence the name 'Chameleon'. This plant was found in a batch of seedlings, attracting attention with its variegated foliage. Although only recently brought into cultivation, 'Chameleon' looks very promising and will be worthwhile growing in any garden. Zone 3

Pinus mugo 'Frosty'

P. Vereijken, Vianen (NBr.), The Netherlands, 2003

Dense conifer with a flattened globular habit. The needles are about 3.5 cm long and in pairs in fascicles. They are not very stiff to the touch, but certainly not soft either. The foliage is grayish green, regularly intermixed with pale creamy white needles. This cultivar was found in 1988 in a batch of seedlings of *P. mugo*, but it took until 2003 before the plant was named. 'Frosty', with its pale grayish cream appearance, is certainly unique in the range of variegated pines, but whether it is of commercial value remains a question. In any case, it is very interesting to the collector. Zone 3

Pinus mugo 'Kokarde' RONALD HOUTMAN

Pinus mugo 'Kokarde'

Reinold Nurseries, Dortmund, Germany, 1952

Rather open and irregularly branched conifer that grows to about 1.5 m high and little wider. The needles are in pairs. They are dark green and conspicuously spotted yellow with one yellow spot at the base and one at the tip. When viewed from above two yellow circles are visible. Unfortunately, this cultivar has a rather untidy habit and the needles tend to burn during warm and sunny spells. 'Kokarde' is therefore best grown in semi-shade. Zone 3

Pinus mugo 'Marand' RONALD HOUTMAN

Pinus mugo 'Marand'

André van Nijnatten, Zundert, The Netherlands, 1984

Broad and upright with an irregular and rather open habit. The needles, placed in pairs, are light green with a pale yellow base; this is another cultivar of the dragon's eye type. 'Marand' looks less washed out during winter, when the foliage colors intensify. Its loose, irregular habit and washed out color during summer make it less recommendable as a garden plant, however. Other cultivars, such as 'Pal Maleter', are of more ornamental value. Zone 3

Pinus mugo 'Pal Maleter' RONALD HOUTMAN

Pinus mugo 'Pal Maleter'

A. J. A. van der Poel, Hazerswoude, The Netherlands, 1965

Broad, upright, relatively fast-growing, bushy conifer. During summer the needles are green, but in winter the color changes dramatically, becoming dark green with clear yellow tips. They will stand full sun without getting burned. 'Pal Maleter' was raised as a seedling of *P. mugo* and it is probably the best variegated cultivar of this species. During summer it does not look washed out, like some other *P. mugo* cultivars. During winter it shows a bright variegation. It is easy to grow and has a good habit. Zone 3

Pinus mugo 'Sunshine' J. R. P. VAN HOEY SMITH

Pinus mugo 'Sunshine'

The Netherlands, 1992

Another dragon's eye cultivar of *P. mugo*. It forms a rather upright, bushy conifer with an irregular habit. The needles are dark green with yellow tips or yellow spots near the tips. The foliage colors are much better in winter than in summer. 'Sunshine' is not yet widely distributed. Zone 3

Pinus nigra 'Stanley Gold'

Stanley & Sons Nurseries, Boring, Oregon, United States, before 1996

The Austrian pine is a large tree that grows to 40 m high in its native habitat—southern Europe and Turkey. It forms a broad conical crown at a young age, later becoming more or less umbrella shaped. The needles are in pairs, up to 12 cm long, dark green, and relatively stiff to the touch. 'Stanley Gold' is an American cultivar that develops into a medium-sized tree. The foliage is dark green with clear yellow variegations. It is heavily variegated. Zone 5b

Pinus nigra 'Stanley Gold' J. R. P. VAN HOEY SMITH

Pinus parviflora 'Fukai' RONALD HOUTMAN

Pinus parviflora 'Fukai' RONALD HOUTMAN

Pinus parviflora 'Ogon Janome' J. R. P. VAN HOEY SMITH

Pinus parviflora 'Tani Mano Uki' RONALD HOUTMAN

Pinus parviflora 'Fukai'

Tage Lundell, Helsingborg, Sweden, before 1975

Small conifer with a dense pyramidal habit. In ten years it will attain a height of about 1 m. The needles are relatively short, about 4 cm long. They are soft to the touch and placed in groups of five. The color of the upper half of the needles is dark bluish green, and the lower half is light yellow to creamy yellow. Especially in spring this gives 'Fukai' a splendid appearance. The needles do not burn during spring, but in a warm and sunny autumn they might be slightly damaged. 'Fukai' is very popular among collectors of variegated plants and dwarf conifers. It is relatively easy to propagate and suits every garden. Zone 5b

Pinus parviflora 'Ogon Janome'

United States, 1976

A compact and low-growing shrubby conifer of irregular habit. Eventually it will grow into a large, broad, spreading-upright shrub. The needles are dark green with clear yellow bases. 'Ogon Janome' is very similar to *P. parviflora* 'Oculus-draconis', if not identical. If proven similar, the cultivar name 'Oculus-draconis' has priority, as it was published earlier (1890). Both plants are not common in cultivation, but certainly worth growing more widely. Zone 5b

Pinus parviflora 'Tani Mano Uki'

Before 1990

Irregular conifer with a broad pyramidal habit. The grayish green needles have a beautiful silvery white variegation. Entirely variegated needles are also formed. 'Tano Mano Uki' is a nice variegated cultivar, but not very widely grown. Although it was introduced in the United States in 1990, it was probably raised in Japan. Zone 5b

Pinus peuce 'Aureovariegata' RONALD HOUTMAN

Pinus peuce 'Aureovariegata'

The Netherlands, 1968

Relatively narrow, upright conifer with a slender conical habit. Eventually it will form a tree that grows to about 10 to 15 m. The dark green to dark grayish green needles are in groups of five, up to 10 cm long, and relatively stiff to the touch. *Pinus peuce*, the Balkan pine or Macedonian pine, is native in a relatively small area in the Balkan region (Bosnia, Albania, Macedonia, and the north of Greece). Some branchlets of young shoots carry clear golden yellow needles. The effect is very beautiful. Fully grown specimens show their variegation on several places in the tree, giving it an informal appearance. The Latin cultivar name 'Aureovariegata' first arose in The Netherlands in 1968. If no publication of this plant was made prior to 1959, according to ICNCP rules this epithet is illegitimate and a new cultivar name must be given. Zone 6a

Pinus strobus 'Bergman's Variegated' J. R. P. VAN HOEY SMITH

Pinus sylvestris 'Barry Bergman' J. R. P. VAN HOEY SMITH

Pinus strobus 'Bergman's Variegated'

R. L. Fincham, Coenosium Gardens, Sandy, Oregon, United States, 1983

Pinus strobus, the eastern white pine, is native in eastern North America, ranging from Canada into the Allegheny Mountains. In Europe it is called Weymouth pine, after Lord Weymouth, who planted many trees throughout the United Kingdom in the eighteenth century. It is a large tree with a broad conical habit and in its native habitat it can grow to 50 m high. In cultivation it usually stays smaller, but will still be an impressive tree. The needles are in fascicles of three, up to 14 cm long, and very soft to the touch. 'Bergman's Variegated' is a cultivar of the dragon's eye type. The foliage is soft bluish green and each needle has a light yellow upper half. During summer the foliage can look a bit washed out, but in winter the coloration becomes stronger. Zone 4

Pinus sylvestris 'Barry Bergman'

United States, 1986

Pinus sylvestris is native throughout Asia and northern Europe, south to Spain and the Caucasus. In the United Kingdom it is confined to Scotland, hence the name Scots pine. Depending on the geographical origin, it will grow into a tree of 10 m to more than 30 m high, usually with a slender pyramidal habit. One of the great advantages of *P. sylvestris* is its superb winter hardiness up to zone 2. The needles are relatively soft to the touch, approximately 6 cm long, and bluish to grayish green. They are grouped in pairs.

Many cultivars have derived from *P. sylvestris*, ranging from small to medium-sized shrubs with a broad, flattened habit to large trees. Very few cultivars of *P. sylvestris* are variegated. 'Barry Bergman' is an upright cultivar with a broad pyramidal habit. It will develop into a medium-sized tree. The foliage is dark bluish green, intermixed with branchlets consisting of silvery white needles. Unfortunately, the variegated foliage is prone to sunburn. Apart from this aspect, it is a typical collectors' plant and less suitable as an ornamental conifer. 'Barry Bergman' is sometimes spelled as 'Barrie Bergman', but it is unclear which spelling is correct. Because it was named in the United States, the American spelling is used in this book. Zone 2

Pinus thunbergii 'Aocha Matsu'

Japan, before 1985

The Japanese black pine, *Pinus thunbergii*, is native to coastal areas in Japan and South Korea. It forms a large tree that grows to 40 m with a broad pyramidal habit. The needles are in pairs, up to 12 cm long, dark green, stiff, and sharp to the touch. The terminal buds are conspicuously colored grayish white.

'Aocha Matsu' is a broad pyramidal shrubby tree that stays considerably smaller than the species. The needles are partly variegated. Some are striped, others are entirely clear golden yellow. Occasionally whole branchlets consist of variegated needles. Although 'Aocha Matsu' was raised in Japan, it was introduced into the Western trade by Iseli Nurseries of Boring, Oregon, United States. It is an attractive conifer with strong foliage colors. This cultivar is not widely distributed, but still recommended. Zone 6a

Pinus thunbergii 'Aocha Matsu' KLAAS VERBOOM

Pinus thunbergii 'Beni Kujaku'

R. L. Fincham, Coenosium Gardens, Sandy, Oregon, United States, 1989

This cultivar is similar to 'Oculus-draconis' but differs in slower growth and slightly different foliage colors. 'Beni Kujaku' is less vigorous than 'Aocha Matsu' and will maintain a shrubby habit. Being of the dragon's eye type, the needles are striped yellow. Usually a small yellow spot is visible at the base of each needle together with a second, larger spot in the middle. Like 'Aocha Matsu', it was originally raised in Japan, but named and introduced in the United States. Zone 6a

Pinus thunbergii 'Beni Kujaku' J. R. P. VAN HOEY SMITH

Pinus thunbergii 'Luteolineata'

A cultivar of unknown origin that looks very similar to 'Aocha Matsu' in foliage colors, but the yellow is slightly lighter. It has a broad, upright habit. The cultivar name 'Luteolineata' could not be traced and might be illegitimate. This cultivar is not recommended over 'Aocha Matsu'. The foliage colors are paler and it is not easy to propagate. Zone 6a

Pinus thunbergii 'Luteolineata' J. R. P. VAN HOEY SMITH

Pinus thunbergii 'Oculus-draconis'

Japan, 1890

Well-known variegated conifer and probably the best example of a dragon's eye pine. It is a broad, upright, small tree with a slightly irregular, broad, pyramidal habit. The bicolored needles are dark green with a light yellow lower half. According to literature, 'Janome Matsu' is a synonym; however, plants sold as 'Janome Matsu' seem to have a slightly better variegation than those offered as 'Oculus-draconis'. Together with *P. densiflora* 'Oculus-draconis' this is one of the most widespread variegated *Pinus* cultivars. Zone 6a

Pinus thunbergii 'Shirome Janome'

Japan, 1890

Beautiful example of yet another dragon's eye pine. The needles are attractively striped yellow. In addition to a yellow base, the needles sometimes have a second

Pinus thunbergii 'Oculus-draconis' J. R. P. VAN HOEY SMITH

Pinus thunbergii 'Shirome Janome' J. R. P. VAN HOEY SMITH

Pinus thunbergii 'Shirome Janome' J. R. P. VAN HOEY SMITH

yellow marking in the middle. It is very similar to 'Oculus-draconis', and according to some authors identical. Zone 6a

Pinus thunbergii 'Variegata'

Japan, 1890

A group of variegated cultivars is summarized under this epithet (occasionally seen as *P. thunbergii* var. *variegata*). These range from yellow-variegated plants to almost white-variegated clones. In the trade 'Variegata' is usually a yellow-variegated conifer with a broad pyramidal habit. Its needles are partially or entirely yellow, often in branchlets with entirely yellow foliage. White-variegated cultivars should go as 'Albovariegata'. 'Variegata' is similar to 'Luteolineata', but easier to propagate. Zone 6a

Pinus wallichiana 'Zebrina'

Croux & Son, Sceaux, France, 1874

Graceful tree with a broad columnar habit. The long and soft needles droop elegantly and are in groups of five. They are bluish green with usually one and occasionally a few light yellow stripes below the tips or in the middle. During winter the colors intensify and the plant looks far better than in summer. The species *P. wallichiana* is sometimes offered under the illegitimate names *P. excelsa* or *P. griffithii*. 'Zebrina' is a handsome tree that, although not widely grown, is well worth planting. Zone 7a

Pittosporum

Interesting genus of approximately 200 species that originate from various parts of the Southern Hemisphere. Together with eight other genera, they form the small family Pittosporaceae (pittosporum family). *Pittosporum* grows in Australia, New Zealand, and southern and eastern Asia, as well as on Pacific Islands (especially Hawaii). The flowers are solitary or in clusters, corymbs, or umbels. They are usually yellowish to cream colored and fragrant. *Pittosporum* is a versatile genus with quite a few variegated cultivars. Most of these derived from *P. tenuifolium*. Relatively few of the available cultivars are described here. Although unsuitable to grow outdoors in colder climates, they make excellent container plants. Unless otherwise stated, all *Pittosporum* are hardy to zone 8b.

Pinus thunbergii 'Variegata' J. R. P. VAN HOEY SMITH

Pinus wallichiana 'Zebrina' J. R. P. VAN HOEY SMITH

Pittosporum crassifolium 'Variegatum'

New Zealand

Very fine shrub with exceptionally good and stable variegated foliage. The leaves are grayish green with conspicuous narrow creamy white margins. 'Variegatum' is very suitable as a container plant in colder climates. In milder areas it can be planted in the garden, where it can grow to about 2 m high. The variegated

Pittosporum crassifolium 'Variegatum' RONALD HOUTMAN

Pittosporum eugenioides 'Variegatum' RONALD HOUTMAN

leaves go very well with purple-leaved plants such as *Phormium* or blue- or purple-flowering perennials. Zone 9

Pittosporum eugenioides 'Variegatum'

New Zealand, before 1882

Medium-sized to large shrub with a broad, dense habit. It can attain a height of about 3 m. The leaves are ovate to oblong and up to 10 cm long, glossy dark green above, with broad creamy white margins. In May the pale yellow, very sweetly scented flowers appear in terminal clusters. *Pittosporum eugenioides* 'Variegatum' is regarded as one of the most beautiful variegated shrubs for mild climates. Zone 8

Pittosporum 'Garnettii'

Buxtons Nursery, Christchurch, New Zealand, before 1957

Rather narrow, upright, evergreen shrub with a conical to columnar habit. The leaves are ovate to elliptic and up to 5 cm long. They are grayish green with irregular creamy white margins, occasionally with some pinkish to red dots. This interesting and widely available plant was thought to be a cultivar of *P. tenuifolium*, but is now considered a hybrid between *P. tenuifolium* and *P. ralphii*. A seedling of 'Garnettii' was raised by F. J. Saunders of Invercargill, New Zealand, and named 'Saundersii'. This cultivar only differs from 'Garnettii' in its more compact habit and slightly rounder leaves.

Pittosporum heterophyllum 'La Blanca'

A. M. M. Vergeer, Boskoop, The Netherlands, 2003

Dense evergreen shrub with a broad compact habit that grows to 1.5 m. The leaves are relatively small and variable in shape. They are ovate, obovate, lanceolate, or oblanceolate and approximately 3.8 cm long. The leaves are distinctly convex. They are grayish green, with creamy white margins. The small flowers stand in axillary or terminal clusters are pale yellow and sweetly scented. 'La Blanca' was originally found as a sport in *Pittosporum heterophyllum* by W. M. van Nierop. It seems hardier than might be expected based on the literature. Zone 7b/8a

Pittosporum 'Mystery'

Graham Hutchins, County Park Nursery, Hornchurch, United Kingdom, 1998

Several clones of *P. tenuifolium* 'Variegatum' were available in the trade. After study, it became clear one of these is a cultivar of hybrid origin. According to the ICNCP, it could not be named *P.* 'Variegatum', so it was renamed 'Mystery' by Mr. Graham Hutchins. 'Mystery' differs from other clones in having slightly larger leaves that lack wavy margins and are almost flat. They are grayish green with conspicuous creamy white margins.

Pittosporum ralphii 'Variegatum'

A very fine variegated *Pittosporum*. The leaves of 'Variegatum' are dull green with broad, irregular, creamy white margins. In many leaves the variegation is not confined to the margins, but the whole leaf blade is mottled. The effect this gives is slightly less neat. 'Variegatum' is said to be susceptible to the *Pittosporum* chermit. In colder climates, where this plant is only used as a container plant, this pest is of no threat to *Pittosporum*.

Pittosporum tenuifolium

A variable species that grows throughout New Zealand. It is a small evergreen tree with thin leaves and relatively thin twigs. Two subspecies are recognized. *Pittosporum tenuifolium* subsp. *tenuifolium* has relatively small, thin leaves with an average length of about 5 cm. The margins are usually undulate. The second is

Pittosporum 'Garnettii' RONALD HOUTMAN

Pittosporum heterophyllum 'La Blanca' RONALD HOUTMAN

Pittosporum ralphii 'Variegatum' RONALD HOUTMAN

Pittosporum 'Mystery' RONALD HOUTMAN

Pittosporum tenuifolium 'Elizabeth' RONALD HOUTMAN

Pittosporum tenuifolium 'Golden Princess' RONALD HOUTMAN

P. tenuifolium subsp. *colensoi*, with larger (approximately 8 cm) leaves that are usually less undulate. The flowers of *P. tenuifolium* are very dark purplish black.

As to be expected from a variable species like this, many cultivars have derived from it. Several hybrids between *P. tenuifolium* and *P. ralphii* and *P. crassifolium* have been recorded as well—some with green or yellow foliage and variegated cultivars. Without exception, these cultivars are extremely ornamental in their foliage and/or habit. In mild areas they can be planted in the garden, but in colder areas they should be treated as container plants. No matter the climate, *P. tenuifolium* is well worth using in any garden.

Pittosporum tenuifolium 'Elizabeth'

United Kingdom

Handsome shrub with a dense, broad, upright habit. The foliage is grayish green with cream margins, occasionally tinged pink. During winter the leaves are tinted more pinkish, adding some extra ornamental value.

Pittosporum tenuifolium 'Golden Princess'

Graham Hutchins, County Park Nursery, Hornchurch, United Kingdom, 1999

Medium-sized shrub with an elegant upright habit. In general appearance, this cultivar is similar to 'Stirling Gold', but its habit is neater. The small, broad, ovate leaves are clear yellow to clear greenish yellow, with narrow green margins. From a distance it looks a yellow-leaved plant. The blackish purple branchlets go very well with the bright foliage. 'Golden Princess' was discovered as a sport of *P. tenuifolium* 'Silver Princess', which in its turn, was raised as a seedling of 'Silver Queen' by Graham Hutchins in 1988. 'Silver Princess' is very similar to 'Silver Queen', but the leaves have a slightly pinkish tinge.

Pittosporum tenuifolium 'Gold Star'

Excellent small to medium-sized shrub with a dense habit that grows to about 1.5 m. The undulate leaves are dark green with irregular golden yellow to chartreuse centers, an effect very conspicuous in the young foliage. When the leaves age they become greener, leaving only a narrow golden yellow blotch around the midrib. In some cases only the midrib is variegated.

Pittosporum tenuifolium **'Irene Paterson'**

G. Paterson, Dunedin, New Zealand, 1970

Striking cultivar with a dense upright habit, eventually reaching a height of 2.5 m. The leaves are broad elliptic to obovate and have an average length of 3 cm. The young leaves are almost completely white with some small green speckles. When maturing, they turn dark green speckled with creamy white. During winter the foliage develops a pinkish to reddish tint. The leaf blades rather than the margins are conspicuously wavy. 'Irene Paterson' is a beautiful shrub and one of the most popular variegated cultivars within the genus.

Pittosporum tenuifolium **'Marjorie Channon'**

R. W. Channon, United Kingdom, before 1974

Like 'Elizabeth', this is an excellent broad, upright shrub with a dense, conical habit that grows to about 3 m high. The leaves are elliptic to ovate and grayish green with creamy white margins. The margins are almost not wavy. Contrary to 'Elizabeth', the foliage is only very slightly pink tinged during winter.

Pittosporum tenuifolium 'Gold Star' RONALD HOUTMAN

Pittosporum tenuifolium 'Irene Paterson' RONALD HOUTMAN

Pittosporum tenuifolium 'Marjorie Channon' RONALD HOUTMAN

Pittosporum tenuifolium 'Silver Queen' CHRIS SANDERS

Pittosporum tenuifolium 'Silver Queen' CHRIS SANDERS

Pittosporum tenuifolium 'Silver Queen'

Slieve Donard Nursery, Newcastle, Northern Ireland, 1910

Broad, upright shrub with an ovate habit that grows to a about 3 m high. The green to grayish green leaves are broad elliptic with irregular creamy white margins. The foliage is suffused with a silvery sheen, especially during autumn and winter.

In New Zealand a similar form was described as 'Argenteum'. This cultivar is probably no longer in cultivation, and it remains uncertain whether it is identical to 'Silver Queen'. 'Silver Queen' produces numerous seedlings, but almost all are lacking chlorophyll and soon die. In 1976 a seedling raised in Castlefreke, Ireland, was named 'Kilkeran Silver'. It is more dwarfish than 'Silver Queen', about 1 m in six years, and the leaves are smaller and much lighter. *Pittosporum tenuifolium* 'Variegatum' is also quite similar to 'Silver Queen', but differs in having a more compact habit and more wavy leaf margins. It also lacks the typical silvery sheen on the foliage during winter. 'Silver Queen' is a very popular cultivar in Europe but less common in New Zealand.

Pittosporum tenuifolium 'Stirling Gold'

Dawn Nurseries, Auckland, New Zealand, before 1987

Medium-sized shrub (to small tree in warm regions) with an elegant habit, due to the somewhat loose growth and relatively small leaves. The ovate to broad oval leaves are up to about 1.5 cm long with conspicuous undulate margins. They are green with a large light yellow to greenish central variegation. Older leaves are almost entirely green with only a pale whitish midrib. The thin branchlets are blackish purple, contrasting

Pittosporum tenuifolium 'Stirling Gold' RONALD HOUTMAN

Pittosporum tenuifolium 'Stirling Mist' RONALD HOUTMAN

Pittosporum tenuifolium 'Variegatum' RONALD HOUTMAN

well against the foliage. 'Stirling Gold' was discovered as a sport of *P. tenuifolium* 'James Stirling'.

Pittosporum tenuifolium 'Stirling Mist'

Like 'Stirling Gold', this is a loosely upright shrub with an elegant habit. The ovate leaves are dull green with cream-colored, crenate margins. In cold weather the margins become pink. This can be very attractive, especially in spring.

Pittosporum tenuifolium 'Variegatum'

Similar to 'Silver Queen', but differing enough to be quite easily distinguished from it (see 'Silver Queen'). It forms a dense, bushy, medium-sized shrub with a broad ovate habit. The foliage is grayish green with beautiful creamy white margins. Several clones are available, one of which proved to be of hybrid origin. It was named *P.* 'Mystery'. Like *P. eugenioides* 'Variegatum' and *P. crassifolia* 'Variegatum', this is a very handsome shrub and also very stable in its variegation.

Pittosporum tenuifolium 'Wendle Channon'

R. W. Channon, United Kingdom, before 1972

This cultivar is nearly identical to 'Marjorie Channon', but differs from it in having creamy yellow leaf margins.

Pittosporum tenuifolium 'Wendle Channon' RONALD HOUTMAN

Pittosporum tobira 'Variegatum'

Broad, upright shrub, often with stiff erect branches. It can reach a height of a few meters, but often stays under 1.5 m. The relatively large leaves (up to 10 cm long) are obovate with rounded tips. They are glossy dark grayish green with conspicuous creamy white

Pittosporum tobira 'Variegatum' RONALD HOUTMAN

Platanus ×acerifolia 'Suttneri' RONALD HOUTMAN

Podocarpus nivalis 'Killworth Cream' RONALD HOUTMAN

margins. The sweetly scented flowers appear during spring. They open white, but fade to yellow. 'Variegatum' is an excellent garden plant for milder climates but in colder areas is only suitable as a container plant.

Platanus ×acerifolia 'Suttneri'

Before 1896

Platanus ×acerifolia, the London plane tree, is a large tree that is used widely throughout the Western world. The attractive exfoliating bark and large palmately lobed leaves are very distinct. 'Suttneri', the only variegated cultivar in the genus, has green leaves that are irregularly speckled creamy white. Young leaves are lighter green to pinkish and show less variegation. People may argue about the beauty of this tree when viewed at close range, but a fully grown specimen is always regarded to be very beautiful. Like the species, 'Suttneri' will easily reach a height of more than 15 m. Zone 6a

Podocarpus nivalis 'Killworth Cream'

United Kingdom

Small evergreen conifer with a compact, broad spreading habit. Eventually it will develop into a low, flattened bushy plant of about 50 cm high. The foliage consists of small needles that are up to 1 cm long and 3 mm wide. They are linear to linear-oblong. The needles are light olive green with cream-colored margins. These margins are relatively wide, so that only a narrow green center can be seen. The plant has a washed-out appearance and is primarily a collectors' item. It is relatively new and its sensitivity to sunburn or winter hardiness have not yet been tested. Zone 7b/8

Populus candicans 'Aurora'

Treseder's Nursery, Truro, United Kingdom, before 1954

Large tree that can easily grow taller than 15 m. It has a broad crown and large leaves on thick, stout branches. The ovate leaves are up to 15 cm long—on young shoots of pruned trees, sometimes more than 20 cm. The young foliage is tinged pink at first, later predominantly cream colored with numerous green spots. During summer the leaves turn entirely green. The trees often do not show their variegation the first year after transplanting. To maintain the variegated character, they are best pruned hard each year, preferably in March.

There is some confusion regarding the correct

name of this tree. In addition to the name *P. candicans* 'Aurora', it can also be found as *P. balsamifera* 'Aurora', *P. candicans* 'Variegata', and *P. ×jackii* 'Aurora' This tree is common in Europe; especially in the United Kingdom and Ireland, it is hugely popular and widely planted in both private gardens and parks. Zone 2

Potentilla fruticosa 'Abbotswood Silver'

Liss Forest Nurseries, Greatham, United Kingdom, 1988

Dense, upright, deciduous shrub. 'Abbotswood Silver' is one of the larger *Potentilla fruticosa* cultivars. Eventually it can reach a height of about 1 m. The imparipinnate leaves consist of five to seven small leaflets. They are dark blue-green edged silvery white. The pure white flowers appear in masses from mid-May into October. The variegation is not very stable, and the combination of foliage colors and flower color is not impressive, to say the least. The whole plant is dull and slightly boring. However, it is one of the very few variegated *Potentilla fruticosa* and therefore a true collectors' item. Zone 3

Populus candicans 'Aurora' RONALD HOUTMAN

Potentilla fruticosa 'Chilo'

A. A. Harkes, Hazerswoude, The Netherlands, 1995

Small, bushy shrub with a dense habit that grows to about 50 cm. The divided leaves usually have five or seven small leaflets. These are grayish green with rather inconspicuous cream to yellowish margins. The variegation is at its best during spring, but in summer it tends to fade. A disadvantage of 'Chilo' is that the variegation strongly tends to revert.

'Chilo' is very floriferous, with relatively small golden yellow flowers that open from late spring to early autumn. It is suitable as a rock garden plant, but can also be used in small plantings. When a rich-flowering cultivar with yellow flowers is wanted, however, various green-leaved cultivars are recommended over this shrub, for example, 'Dart's Golddigger', 'Living Daylight', and 'Medicine Wheel Mountain', the last being one of the best. Zone 3

Potentilla fruticosa 'Chilo' RONALD HOUTMAN

Prunus

Large and very important genus, both as ornamental trees and shrubs and for growing fruit. It consists of about 400 species and many more cultivars. As with other genera from the Rosaceae (rose family), *Prunus* contains relatively few variegated cultivars. Japanese cherries are the most important as ornamental trees, but no variegated cultivars exist. Most variegated cultivars exist within the evergreen species, such as *P. laurocerasus*.

Prunus cerasifera 'Hessei'

H. A. Hesse, Weener, Germany, about 1906

Deciduous, rather weak-growing, upright shrub to a small tree, rarely exceeding 5 m in height. The dark purplish brown twigs and branches are irregularly thorned. The leaves are elliptic to ovate, but the majority are irregularly incised and partly deformed. They

Prunus cerasifera 'Hessei' RONALD HOUTMAN

Prunus laurocerasus 'Green Jade' RONALD HOUTMAN

are purplish red with yellow to light green teeth along the margins. Some leaves are partially yellow or cream colored. 'Hessei' is a peculiar shrub, only of interest for collectors. It looks too unhealthy for the majority of people to become a bestseller. Zone 5a

Prunus laurocerasus 'Green Jade'

Originally thought to be a synonym for 'Marbled White', but this cultivar is slightly different. The young twigs are distinctly light greenish white, whereas those of 'Marbled White' are light green. Also, the leaves are light green to yellowish green marbled cream and make a paler impression than those of 'Marbled White'. The history of 'Green Jade' is unclear. However, it is supposed to be from Castlewellan Gardens in Castlewellan, Northern Ireland—the same origin as another variegated clone called 'Castlewellan', which is the same as 'Marbled White'. Occasionally 'Marbled White' and 'Green Jade' are mixed in cultivation. Zone 7a

Prunus laurocerasus 'Marbled White'

France, 1811

Broad, upright evergreen. Once established it can reach more than 3 m in height. The leaves are elliptic to lanceolate and grayish green, marbled white and cream. The leaf blade is often somewhat bullate. The plant rarely flowers. It can be used for hedging or planted as a specimen and is also popular as cut-foliage.

Although originally grown as 'Variegata', it was clear that various clones of the variegated cherry laurel were in circulation. To sort things out, this clone, the most widely grown, was named 'Marbled White' by Roy Lancaster, then curator of the Hillier Gardens & Arboretum in Ampfield nr. Romsey, United Kingdom, in 1986. 'Castlewellan' is another variegated clone that makes this problem more complicated. Given the name, this cultivar originated in Northern Ireland, but the background remains unclear. It is said that the plant grown at Hillier came from Castlewellan Gardens. In that case it is identical to 'Castlewellan', a name given later to the same plant. A third name that circulates is 'Marbled Dragon'. Michael Dirr (1998) suggests it is probably identical to 'Marbled White', but mentions bronze variegated young foliage. 'Marbled White' lacks this quality. 'Green Marble' is another variegated cultivar with dark green leaves that are spotted white. It was rediscovered by Stephen Taffler in Helensburgh,

Scotland, and distributed through The Plantsmans Nursery before 1978. Because 'Marbled White' has become the best-known variegated *P. laurocerasus*, various other variegated clones now go under this name. Zone 7a

Prunus laurocerasus 'Taff's Golden Gleam'

P. Taffler, Berkhamsted, United Kingdom

A golden-variegated cultivar that is rather unstable.

Prunus laurocerasus 'Taff's Golden Gleam' RONALD HOUTMAN

Prunus laurocerasus 'Marbled White' RONALD HOUTMAN

Prunus laurocerasus 'Marbled White' RONALD HOUTMAN

Prunus lusitanica 'Variegata' RONALD HOUTMAN

Pseudopanax lessonii 'Gold Splash' RONALD HOUTMAN

Pseudowintera colorata J. R. P. VAN HOEY SMITH

The leaves are irregularly blotched and striped yellow to cream. Two other yellow-variegated cultivars are 'Golden Splash' and 'Strangford Gold'. 'Golden Splash' is an American cultivar that seems more stable than 'Taff's Golden Gleam'; however, this plant also reverts quite easily. It forms a dense and flattened bushy shrub. 'Strangford Gold' is a relatively new cultivar from Ireland. It has roughly the same golden yellow variegation, but the growth habit is more upright, thus forming a broad bushy shrub. Zone 7a

Prunus lusitanica 'Variegata'

1865

Large evergreen shrub to small tree with a dense, broad, conical habit. The long, acuminate, ovate leaves are up to about 10 cm long. They are dark green with irregular narrow creamy white margins. During winter the white margins often turn pinkish, influenced by lower temperatures. 'Variegata' makes a fine specimen shrub, but is also very suitable for hedging. It is especially recommended for milder areas with hot summers, because it is less hardy than *P. laurocerasus*. Zone 8a

Pseudopanax lessonii 'Gold Splash'

Duncan & Davies, New Plymouth, New Zealand, 1975

Large evergreen shrub with thick erect main branches that grows to 3 m high. The beautifully shaped palmately divided five-lobed leaves are very leathery. They are dark green, blotched and marbled bright yellow. 'Gold Splash' originated as a sport of *P. lessonii* and is only hardy in mild climates. There it is best grown in a warm and sheltered location. Otherwise it is best used as a container plant or in a greenhouse. There is some interest in growing 'Gold Splash' for cut-foliage. Zone 9

Pseudowintera colorata

New Zealand

Small to medium-sized shrub that grows to 2.5 m in its native habitat, but smaller in cultivation. The leathery, broad ovate to obovate leaves are up to 7 cm long and half as wide. They are yellowish green, flushed pink, with dark red speckles and purplish margins. The undersides are distinctively bluish gray to gray. The small clustered flowers are yellowish green. *Pseudowintera colorata* is one of the very few variegated woody plants that grow wild. It is only suitable for the mildest climates. In other areas, it must be grown in conservatories or as a container plant. Zone 9

Pyracantha

Small genus of six thorny shrubs, native to Europe (one species) and Asia. *Pyracantha* belongs to the Rosaceae (rose family), subfamily Maloideae, and is closely related to *Cotoneaster*, *Crataegus*, and *Photinia*. Fire thorns are widely used in Europe and especially popular in France, where they are planted along roads and for hedging. They are also very suitable for growing against walls or fences. Their main ornamental value is the colorful fruits, which vary from light yellow to deep red. The fruits ripen during late summer and contrast well with the variegated foliage of the cultivars described here. Later in autumn they are eaten by birds, mainly blackbirds and thrushes.

Pyracantha 'Cadvar' SAPHYR PANACHE™

West End Nurseries, Paignton, United Kingdom, and INRA, Angers, France, 2001

Broad, upright shrub with a conical habit. The obovate to elliptic leaves are dark green with creamy white to greenish white margins. The flowers, which open in May and June, are cream-colored and are followed by orange-red fruits. 'Cadvar' was tested for susceptibility to fireblight and proved to be nearly resistant. It is a distinct addition in the range of variegated *Pyracantha*. Zone 7

Pseudowintera colorata J. R. P. VAN HOEY SMITH

Pyracantha 'Harlequin'

The leaves of this variegated fire thorn emerge pink with a white variegation, later becoming green with white margins. During cold weather the white changes to pink. Like all *Pyracantha*, this cultivar also flowers white. The fruits are bright orange-red. Its resistance to fireblight and scab is unknown. Zone 8

Pyracantha 'Mohave Silver'

Arendsnest Nursery, Boekel, The Netherlands, 1983

Medium-sized shrub with thorny branches and a broad, upright habit. It is densely branched and will attain a height of approximately 3 m. The lanceolate to oblanceolate leaves are lustrous dark green with silvery white margins. 'Mohave Silver' originated as a sport of 'Mohave' and differs only in the leaves being slightly smaller and with silvery white margins. It is

Pyracantha 'Cadvar' SAPHYR PANACHE™ RONALD HOUTMAN

Pyracantha 'Sparkler' PIERRE THEUNISSEN

Quercus cerris 'Argenteovariegata' RONALD HOUTMAN

Quercus cerris 'Aureovariegata' GERT FORTGENS

not very susceptible to fireblight, but very prone to scab. Zone 7b

Pyracantha 'Sparkler'

G. Hutchins, County Park Nursery, Hornchurch, United Kingdom, 1979

Broad spreading-upright shrub that grows to about 2 m high. The dark green leaves are obovate to oblanceolate and heavily mottled white and gray. Lower temperatures cause the foliage to become pink-tinged during autumn and winter. This striking cultivar originated as a sport of *P.* 'Harlequin', found by Graham Hutchins in 1979, but put on the market by Hopleys Plants Ltd. of Much Hadham, United Kingdom, in 1984. It has a much denser habit than the other variegated *Pyracantha* described here. Although it is very beautiful, it is rather weak and frost tender. 'Sparkler' must therefore be protected during winter. Zone 8

Quercus

The oak is probably the best-known of all trees. The genus is represented in most parts of the Northern Hemisphere, south to western tropical South America and northern Africa. Although there are approximately 600 species of oak found in the wild, only a handful of variegated cultivars exist, and most of these derived from European species. It is not unusual for the first growth to be green in these cultivars. During the second growth, emerging in June and July, the leaves are variegated.

Quercus cerris 'Argenteovariegata'

Germany, 1864

Magnificent tree with an irregular rounded crown. The leaves of this variegated turkey oak are oblong and shallowly lobed. They are dark green with very conspicuous, broad, irregular, creamy white margins. Occasionally the creamy white margins are so wide as to leave only a narrow green stripe in the center of the leaf. The acorns are half enclosed by the cups, which are densely covered with large but narrow scales. This white-variegated turkey oak is one of the most beautiful variegated trees. When planted in the right location it can create a dramatic effect in any garden or park. It is not rare in the trade, but certainly not widely available either. It is also known under the synonyms 'Argenteomarginata' and 'Variegata'. Zone 6a

Quercus cerris 'Aureovariegata'

The Netherlands, before 1867

Medium-sized tree that is very similar to 'Argenteovariegata'. The leaves have the same shape, but the margins are yellow instead of white. It is a rare cultivar that reverts very easily and therefore not worthwhile growing commercially. However, its rarity makes 'Aureovariegata' a true collectors' item. Zone 6a

Quercus cerris 'Marmorata' JO BÖMER

Quercus cerris 'Marmorata'

Small to medium-size tree with an unusual variegation. The leaves are light green and irregularly blotched yellow. In some leaves the variegation is nearly absent, in other leaves it covers most of the leaf. During late summer and early autumn the variegation fades to pale creamy white. 'Marmorata' is an old and rare cultivar of unknown origin. Zone 6a

Quercus palustris 'Carnival' J. R. P. VAN HOEY SMITH

Quercus palustris 'Carnival'

André van Nijnatten, Zundert, The Netherlands, 2003

Quercus palustris is a large, straight-trunked tree that grows to 30 m or higher. The leaves are broad ovate with acute lobes. *Quercus palustris* is famous for its orange-red to brownish red autumn colors. With its heavily variegated foliage, 'Carnival' immediately attracts attention. The leaves, having the same shape and size as the species, are extremely densely spotted creamy white to cream. Usually the speckles are very small, but occasionally larger dots develop.

Contrary to the name (*palustris* means "growing in swamps"), *Q. palustris* is not very adaptable to wet soil. In such locations, *Q. coccinea* is recommended. This species has the same leaf shape and fabulous autumn colors, although no variegated cultivars are derived from it. 'Carnival' was raised as a seedling in the 1990s, but got its name when put into cultivation in 2003. Zone 5a

Quercus robur 'Albomarmorata' KLAAS VERBOOM

Quercus robur

The English oak is native to western, central, and eastern Europe, where it is an important forest tree. *Quercus robur* is a large tree that grows to about 40 m (occasionally higher) with a relatively short stem and rounded crown. The leaves are obovate to oblong with three to six rounded lobes on each side. The leaves have a short petiole, and the grouped fruits have long stalks. A number of variegated cultivars have derived

Quercus robur 'Argenteomarginata' RONALD HOUTMAN

Quercus robur 'Argenteopicta' RONALD HOUTMAN

Quercus robur 'Castle Howard' JO BÖMER

from *Q. robur*. Most of these cultivars were named in the nineteenth century. At present the majority of these are rare in the trade, if not disappeared. Unless otherwise noted, all *Q. robur* are hardy to zone 5a.

Quercus robur 'Albomarmorata'

The Netherlands, before 1867

The leaves of this old cultivar are dark green, marbled white. The leaves that emerge during summer (the second growth) are more conspicuously variegated than those in spring. 'Albomarmorata' has nearly disappeared from cultivation.

Quercus robur 'Argenteomarginata'

Germany, before 1864

Like many of the variegated oaks, 'Argenteomarginata' in very rare in cultivation. The leaves are not deeply lobed and often deformed. They are dark green with a narrow whitish margin.

Quercus robur 'Argenteopicta'

Germany, before 1864

A cultivar very similar to 'Albomarmorata', but the leaves that unfold in spring are only sparsely speckled white. The emerging foliage of the second growth is almost entirely white. During hot and sunny spells the foliage tends to burn. It is occasionally found as 'Picta', which is a synonym.

Quercus robur 'Argenteovariegata'

Germany, about 1810

Another old cultivar very similar to 'Albomarmorata'. The leaves are relatively large and quite heavily speckled white. They are often slightly deformed. During summer the second growth is more heavily speckled. A very distinctive feature of 'Argenteovariegata' is that the branches and branchlets are striped as well.

Quercus robur 'Aureobicolor'

Germany, before 1864

A very rare cultivar that has most likely disappeared from cultivation. In spring the foliage is only slightly spotted pale yellow to creamy. The second growth consists of heavily yellow variegated leaves, often tinted reddish.

Quercus robur 'Castle Howard'

Castle Howard, Malton, United Kingdom

A splendid form, not only in its variegated foliage but also in having colored twigs. The first leaves are moderately variegated. They are green, sparsely margined and speckled creamy white. The second growth in early summer is more spectacular. The leaves are heavily speckled and blotched creamy white to white, later becoming greener. The young twigs are deep brownish red, contrasting very well with the variegated foliage. The twigs keep their color during winter. This tree was named after the place it was raised, Castle Howard. The original tree is still growing at the estate.

Quercus robur 'Fürst Schwarzenberg' JO BÖMER

Quercus robur 'Fürst Schwarzenberg'

Eisenberg Nursery, Czechoslovakia, before 1884

Relatively densely branched, broad, upright tree with a conical habit. The leaves have the normal shape of the species, but usually only three to five lobes on each side. In the first growth the leaves are entirely green, but the leaves of the second growth are heavily variegated. They are heavily splashed and mottled with creamy yellow at first. With age, the color changes to creamy white. 'Fürst Schwarzenberg' is one of the better variegated oaks, the more so because the tree's habit is superior to the other cultivars.

Quercus robur 'Maculata' RONALD HOUTMAN

Quercus robur 'Maculata'

C. de Vos, Hazerswoude, The Netherlands, about 1867

An old and rare variegated oak. The foliage of 'Maculata' is green in spring. When the second growth emerges in June and July, the leaves are conspicuously speckled yellowish.

Quercus robur 'Pulverulenta' JO BÖMER

Quercus robur 'Pulverulenta'

This cultivar is very similar to *Q. robur* 'Argenteopicta', especially during summer. In spring some differences can be observed. The young leaves are slightly reddish at first, but soon change to green with a yellow variegation. As a tree 'Pulverulenta' has a slightly broader habit than 'Argenteopicta'. Like most of the variegated oaks, this is also a rare cultivar, only occasionally available in the trade.

Quercus rubra 'Vana'

Quercus rubra, the northern red oak, is a large tree with a rounded crown that grows to about 25 m. It shows

Quercus rubra 'Vana' J. R. P. VAN HOEY SMITH

Rhamnus alaternus 'Argenteovariegata' RONALD HOUTMAN

Rhamnus frangula 'De Wildert' RONALD HOUTMAN

some superficial similarities with *Q. palustris*, but the leaves are distinctively larger and more shallowly lobed. Like *Q. palustris*, this species often produces attractive dark red to reddish brown autumn colors. 'Vana' is unusual in being the only recorded variegated cultivar of this species. The young shoots are reddish, soon changing into a heavily variegated green. The leaves are very densely spotted and blotched cream to light yellow-cream. Zone 5a

Rhamnus alaternus 'Argenteovariegata'

Medium-sized evergreen shrub with a regular, conical habit. Fast-growing when young, and becoming a tidy shrub that grows to 3 m tall. The leaves are elliptic to ovate with sparsely serrate margins. They are green with grayish spots and irregular white margins. The small yellowish green flowers are inconspicuous; they are followed by clear red fruits resembling those of a holly but slightly smaller. 'Argenteovariegata' forms a very spectacular variegated shrub when placed in a sheltered location. The leaves are very consistently variegated and the shrub does not tend to revert to green. The red fruits make a fine contrast against the foliage. Zone 7b

Rhamnus frangula 'De Wildert'

M. M. Bömer Nursery, Zundert, The Netherlands, 2003

Rhamnus frangula is medium-sized to large deciduous shrub with an ovate habit that grows to about 4.5 m. It is native to large parts of Europe, but also grows in Asia Minor and northern Africa. The deep green leaves are elliptic to obovate. The inconspicuous greenish flowers open from May to September in axillary clusters. They are followed by glossy red berries that soon become black. The leaves of 'De Wildert' are irregularly blotched clear yellow. This contrasts well with the black berries. This cultivar is not yet available in the trade. Zone 3

Rhododendron

About 850 species of *Rhododendron* are known, mainly growing in the Northern Hemisphere. About 150 species are endemic in New Guinea. Most of the other species can be found in the Himalaya and other mountainous areas in Asia, but some are native to North America and Europe.

This genus can be roughly divided into two groups:

the lepidote and elepidote species and cultivars. In the lepidote group, the leaves and sometimes the petioles, flowers, and branches are covered with small scales. This group consists of the majority of the small-leaved species, cultivars, and hybrids, and they are both evergreen and deciduous. All so-called azaleas also belong to the lepidote group. Species and cultivars of the elepidote group lack scales. All large-flowering hybrids belong to this group. They are usually evergreen shrubs with large, colorful flowers.

Although there are more than 1000 *Rhododendron* cultivars and hybrids, only a few have variegated foliage. In addition to the plants described here, several other variegated cultivars exist, including 'Claydian Variegated', a sport of 'Madame Masson', with dark green, white-margined leaves and white flowers with a golden flare. Toward the end of the twentieth century, several variegated Japanese azaleas were raised in the United States. One of the best known is 'Silver Sword', with dark green leaves and white margins. The flowers are a brilliant rosy pink. 'Brianne' and 'The Robe' are very similar to 'Silver Sword'; all three were derived from 'Girard's Rose'. Other variegated cultivars include 'Red Ruffles Variegated', 'Southern Belle', and 'Silver Streak', the last with white-margined foliage and purple flowers, an attractive combination.

Rhododendron 'Blattgold'

D. G. Hobbie, Linswege-Westerstede, Germany, 1994

A member of the Ponticum group. Broad, spreading-upright, evergreen shrub that grows to 1 m high and 1.2 m wide. The undulate leaves are narrow-elliptic to lanceolate. They are glossy dark green with large light yellow blotches in the center. The shape and size of the blotches is irregular, in some leaves only a narrow dark green margin is visible. The flowers, which appear from late May into June, are bright lilac-pink with a brownish yellow blotch. 'Blattgold' arose as a branch sport in *R.* 'Goldflimmer' and differs from it in having larger yellow centers in the leaves. 'Blattgold' is more stable in its variegation than 'Goldflimmer'. Zone 6b

Rhododendron 'Blattgold' J. R. P. VAN HOEY SMITH

Rhododendron 'Goldflimmer'

D. G. Hobbie, Linswege-Westerstede, Germany, 1955

A member of the Ponticum group. Dense, broad, spreading-upright, evergreen shrub of about 1 m high and 1.2 m wide. The leaves are elliptic to lanceolate

Rhododendron 'Goldflimmer' FA. C. ESVELD

Rhododendron 'Hot Shot Variegated' J. R. P. VAN HOEY SMITH

Rhododendron ponticum 'Variegatum' RONALD HOUTMAN

Rhododendron 'President Roosevelt' RONALD HOUTMAN

and, although they are not undulate, they are slightly lumpy. They are glossy dark green with irregular narrow golden yellow central blotches and streaks. 'Goldflimmer' flowers in late spring, from late May to mid-June. The flowers are deep lilac-pink blotched with brownish yellow. Although 'Goldflimmer' was raised in 1955, it was not until 1983 that Hachmann Nurseries introduced this cultivar. 'Sunsplash' is a similar cultivar that was raised by Malcolm Whipple of Long Island, New York, United States. Zone 6b

Rhododendron 'Hot Shot Variegated'

P. Girard, Geneva, Ohio, United States, 1976

Low shrub with a broad spreading growth and a flattened globular habit. This Japanese azalea will reach a height of about 50 cm, but will become more than 60 cm wide. The leaves are light green with clear white margins. The flowers, which open in June, are bright orange-red. They make 'Hot Shot Variegated' a very colorful plant for some time. After flowering the foliage is again the main ornamental trait. 'Hot Shot Variegated' was discovered as a sport of 'Girard's Hot Shot', a cultivar also bred by Girard. It is occasionally offered as 'Girard's Variegated Hot Shot' and is widely grown both in Europe and the United States. Zone 7

Rhododendron ponticum 'Variegatum'

Before 1900

Handsome variegated *Rhododendron* with a broad, upright habit. It will grow to about 3 m high. The lanceolate to oblanceolate leaves are glossy dark green, with creamy white margins. The flowers, which open from mid-May into June, are mauve to purplish pink. This variegated cultivar of the very common *R. ponticum* is the best-known variegated *Rhododendron*. A yellow-variegated cultivar, 'Aureovariegatum', also exists, as well as a cultivar with leaves spotted yellow, called 'Aucubifolium'. Zone 6b

Rhododendron 'President Roosevelt'

Before 1900

A member of the Ponticum group. Broad, upright, evergreen shrub that grows to 2 m in height, sometimes slightly higher. The elliptic leaves are dark green and have an irregular light green, yellowish green, and yellow center. The flowers are mauve-red, blotched whitish to pale yellow. Like all variegated elepidote

Rhododendron, it thrives best in a humus-rich, preferably peaty, soil. 'President Roosevelt' is best planted in semi-shade, but will also do well in full sun. In deep shade, the plant becomes less floriferous. 'President Roosevelt' is similar to 'Goldflimmer', but is more floriferous and has much better flowers. It is, however, unstable and green-leaved branches must be removed. Furthermore, is it a rather weak grower with branches that break quite easily from the rootball. Zone 7

Rhododendron **'Salmon's Leap'**

Dense, compact, evergreen Japanese azalea that grows to about 50 cm. The leaves are dark green with irregular silvery white margins. This is especially stunning in spring, later in the season the colors tend to fade a little. 'Salmon's Leap' flowers in May with good deep pink to purplish pink flowers. It is best grown in a semi-shaded location. Zone 7b

Rhododendron **'Silver Queen'**

United States, about 1988

Evergreen Japanese azalea with a flattened and spreading habit. Eventually it will grow about 40 cm high and much broader. The leaves are elliptic and relatively narrow. They are dark grayish green with silvery white margins. The pinkish red flowers appear in spring, contrasting well against the variegated foliage. 'Silver Queen' is easy to grow and can be used in the garden as well as indoors. Zone 7

Rhododendron 'Silver Queen' RONALD HOUTMAN

Ribes americanum **'Variegatum'**

An easy-to-grow shrub with a broad, upright habit. The leaves are three-lobed to five-lobed and clear green, with a creamy white mottled variegation evenly distributed over the leaves. The small yellowish white flowers appear in small clusters, but are no match for the dramatic variegation of the foliage. This very stable variegated plant should be used more widely. It can be grown in full sun as well as in semi-shade and contrasts well with red- or yellow-flowering perennials, as well as shrubs with dark green leaves such as *Elaeagnus* ×*ebbingei* or *Rhododendron*. Zone 3

Ribes americanum 'Variegatum' RONALD HOUTMAN

Ribes sanguineum **'Pulborough Scarlet Variegated'**

As the name suggests, this cultivar was found as a sport in the well-known 'Pulborough Scarlet'. It has

Ribes sanguineum 'Pulborough Scarlet Variegated' RONALD HOUTMAN

Rosa 'Verschuren' RONALD HOUTMAN

Rosa wichuraiana 'Variegata' GERT FORTGENS

Rosa wichuraiana 'Variegata' RONALD HOUTMAN

the same deep pinkish red flowers and neat growth. However, the leaves are heavily mottled with light yellow. It is best used in a perennial border or as a contrast plant in a semi-shaded location. Unfortunately, the name is illegitimate and needs to be changed. Zone 6

Rosa

Although the rose is generally known as the "queen of shrubs," it is certainly not the "queen of variegated shrubs." Considering that there are more than 25,000 named rose cultivars, the number with variegated foliage is negligible—a reason why these few are quite desired by collectors.

Rosa 'Cocty' CURIOSITY™

Cocker & Sons, Aberdeen, Scotland, United Kingdom, 1971

A hybrid tea rose that was discovered as a sport of *Rosa* 'Cleopatra'. The leaves are dull dark green with creamy white to white speckles and small blotches. The young shoots are reddish brown, which contrasts well against the variegated foliage. The double flowers are purplish red with yellow. They are about 10 cm wide, fragrant, and open from early summer to autumn. 'Cocty' is the best variegated rose of the three mentioned here. Its variegation is acceptable and the flowers are very attractive. Zone 4

Rosa 'Verschuren'

Verschuren, Haps, The Netherlands, 1904

Old and sometimes forgotten variegated hybrid tea rose. The foliage is green with an irregular creamy yellow to cream variegation. The flowers have the classical broad urn shape of a hybrid tea. They are salmon pink, fading into light pink, slightly fragrant, semi-double, and about 10 cm wide. Flowers open from early summer to early autumn. Although this rose is about as good as 'Cocty', the flowers are of a less intense color. Zone 5

Rosa wichuraiana 'Variegata'

Vigorous rambling rose that can reach a height of more than 5 m. The long and arching branches are clear green and sparsely covered with sharp spines. The white flowers open in June and July. They are about 4 cm wide and fragrant. The relatively small, somewhat elderlike leaves are irregularly spotted white. These contrast well against the pinkish young shoots of the plant. During autumn the foliage becomes slightly more pinkish. Zone 6

Rosmarinus

Small genus of Mediterranean evergreen shrubs that are widely known and commonly used as kitchen herbs. However, they can also be used as ornamental shrubs. The linear to narrow lanceolate leaves are strongly aromatic. Usually the flowers are lilac-blue, but in some cultivars they are pink or white. Although the main flowering period is from late March to late May, scattered flowers open throughout the season until late September. When used in the kitchen, a variegated rosemary can add a little extra color to your meals.

Rosmarinus officinalis 'Golden Rain'

Upright, aromatic, evergreen shrub with a dense habit that grows to about 2 m. The opposite leaves are narrow lanceolate and strongly aromatic when rubbed. They are dark green irregularly splashed with yellow. The lilac-blue flowers mainly appear from late March to late May, but scattered flowers open throughout the season until late September. Zone 7

Rosmarinus officinalis 'Variegatus'

Old and relatively unknown cultivar. It is an upright shrub that will reach a height of about 70 cm. The leaves are narrow lanceolate, deep green, and irregularly spotted clear yellow. Another old and disappeared cultivar, 'Foliis Aureis', is similar to 'Variegatus', according to literature. As in all *Rosmarinus*, the foliage is fragrant, which is one of the added values of this genus. Although not easy to find, 'Variegatus' is available in the trade. Zone 7b

Rosmarinus officinalis 'Wolros' SILVER SPIRES™

Mayfields Nursery, Sutton Green, Guildford, United Kingdom, 1992

Rather vigorous broad, upright shrub that grows to about 1 m high. The narrow lanceolate leaves are grayish green with conspicuous silvery white margins. The flowers are lilac-blue and appear in spring and early summer. Like all *Rosmarinus* cultivars, it is susceptible to rot during wet periods in winter.

In the seventeenth century a silver-variegated rosemary (*R. officinalis* 'Foliis Argenteis') was known, but over the years it disappeared entirely. Around 1986 Christine Wolters of the Mayfields Nursery found a variegated sport *R. officinalis*. When it became clear this was the first silver-variegated *Rosmarinus* for many centuries, it was named. Unfortunately, 'Wolros' has proven to be a rather weak plant that easily drops it leaves. It is also quite unstable. The green-leaved branches are, of course, stronger than the variegated ones. If not removed, the entire plant will revert to green within a few seasons. Zone 7b

Rosmarinus officinalis 'Variegatus' RONALD HOUTMAN

Rubus fruticosus 'Variegatus'

The common European blackberry or bramble is a bushy scrambling shrub that is native to large parts of northwestern Europe, where it is very common in open woodland, fallow fields, and along roads and railways. It is a highly variable species that is now divided into many microspecies.

In 'Variegatus', the usually very prickly branches have imparipinnate leaves that consist of five leaflets. These are dark green with irregular white margins. On many leaflets the variegation is not confined to the

Rubus fruticosus 'Variegatus' RONALD HOUTMAN

Rubus microphyllus 'Variegatus' WOUT KROMHOUT

Ruta graveolens 'Variegata' RONALD HOUTMAN

margins, and larger parts are white. The small white to light pink flowers are followed by edible blackberries. Although 'Variegatus' grows slightly weaker than the species, it is an aggressive shrub. Still, the combination of variegated foliage and edible dark purplish red to blackish purple fruits is quite interesting. Although not widely grown, it is ideal for planting in a neglected corner of the garden. Zone 5b

Rubus microphyllus 'Variegatus'

Dense suckering deciduous shrub attaining a height of about 1.5 m, but it will grow much wider. The prickly stems hold palmately three-lobed leaves, occasionally with five lobes. These are green, irregularly marbled creamy white and light pink. The flowers, opening in May and June, are white and often followed by yellow fruits. Despite its prickly stems, this variegated plant is recommended, but its hardiness leaves much to be desired. Zone 9

Ruta graveolens 'Variegata'

Small evergreen shrub of about 1 m high. Its pinnate aromatic leaves are attractive, almost fern shaped. They are bluish grayish green, variegated creamy white. The combination with greenish yellow flowers, which open during summer, is noteworthy. Rue has been used as a medicinal and kitchen herb for a long time. However, the whole plant is phototoxic, and people who are sensitive to *Ruta* can experience serious skin rash. 'Variegata' can also be used as a garnish. Zone 6b

Salix

Large and important genus of trees, large shrubs, and creeping shrubs. The genus consists of about 400 species, mainly native to the Northern Hemisphere, but some are found in the Southern Hemisphere. *Populus* and *Salix* together form the Salicaceae (willow family). In many areas *Salix* species are important plants in the landscape. The smaller, sometimes creeping shrubs and dwarf shrubs are very suitable as ornamentals in gardens and rock gardens, giving a "natural" touch to the garden.

All species of *Salix* are dioecious, meaning male and female flowers grow on separate plants. Often the silvery to grayish catkins, in which the individual flowers are carried, are among the first harbingers of spring. When the individual flowers open, the greenish, yellow, reddish, or blackish anthers or stigmata can be seen. Despite the large number of species, only a few variegated cultivars have been named.

Salix cinerea 'Tricolor'

Germany, about 1772

Salix cinerea is native to Europe, northwestern Asia, and northern Africa. It will develop into a large shrub to small tree about 5 m high. The species itself has no merit in the garden. The two variegated cultivars, however, offer great possibilities as ornamental shrubs. 'Tricolor' has a shrubby, broad, upright habit and will not grow as tall as the species, only about 3 m. The green, oblanceolate leaves are heavily speckled and mottled white, cream, and yellow, often with reddish tints. Young foliage is tinted pink. 'Tricolor' is of ornamental value, but long forgotten by the trade. It is best pruned hard each year to keep well-variegated young shoots. Zone 3

Salix cinerea 'Tricolor' RONALD HOUTMAN

Salix cinerea 'Variegata'

Germany, before 1770

Large shrub to small tree that grows to about 4 m high. The species is native to Europe and northwestern Asia and will grow to about 5 m tall. The branches are dark brown to blackish brown. The leaves are elliptic to obovate and up to 9 cm long, but usually not larger than 7 cm. They are irregularly variegated creamy white. Silvery gray catkins appear in late winter and early spring. This large shrub is rare in cultivation and of little ornamental value. 'Tricolor' is preferable. Zone 4

Salix cinerea 'Variegata' GERT FORTGENS

Salix integra 'Flamingo'

P. Bontekoe, Boskoop, The Netherlands, 2002

This cultivar was found as a sport in *S. integra* 'Hakuro Nishiki'. It differs from 'Hakuro Nishiki' in its slightly darker pink young shoots and greener mature leaves. 'Flamingo' is therefore less prone to sunburn during early summer. The twigs are also thicker, which makes the plant easier to handle during transport. The morphological differences between 'Flamingo' and 'Hakuro Nishiki' are minimal, but 'Flamingo' seems easier to grow. Zone 6a

Salix integra 'Flamingo' RONALD HOUTMAN

Salix integra 'Hakuro Nishiki' RONALD HOUTMAN

Salix integra 'Hakuro Nishiki'

Japan, before 1979

Densely branched medium-sized shrub that grows to about 3 m high, eventually forming a rounded bush. The thin twigs are reddish green during summer, becoming attractively more orange during winter. The thin leaves are oblong and often placed opposite or nearly opposite. In spring the new growth is pale pink to whitish pink. Young leaves are almost white at first, later they turn light green, conspicuously and heavily mottled white. Some leaf burn can occur during spring, when the leaves are very white. During warm and sunny spells in the summer, the leaves tend to turn green, thus protecting themselves against damage. The catkins are grayish and rather inconspicuous.

This graceful willow was introduced from Japan by the late Harry van de Laar in 1979. A Boskoop grower hit upon the idea of grafting it on a standard, and since then it has become an absolute bestseller in Europe, especially in The Netherlands and the United Kingdom. 'Hakuro Nishiki' is probably planted in a garden in every street in The Netherlands as well as in cemeteries. Dutch nurserymen and dendrologists often refer to 'Hakuro Nishiki' as "Harry's willow" to honor

Salix integra 'Hakuro Nishiki' RONALD HOUTMAN

the man who did so much for the Dutch horticulture. Zone 6a

Salvia officinalis 'Icterina'

Germany, 1864

Low, bushy, semi-evergreen shrub or subshrub that rarely exceeds 80 cm in height. The handsome opposite leaves are oblong to lanceolate. They are light green, variegated yellow. The light blue flowers appear rarely. 'Icterina' is a handsome shrub that is not only of ornamental value, but also in use as a kitchen herb, its taste being slightly milder than the species. Like the variegated rosemary, it can also be used for garnish. 'Icterina' is occasionally offered as 'Aurea', which is, in fact, a yellow-leaved cultivar. Zone 7a

Salvia officinalis 'Icterina' RONALD HOUTMAN

Salvia officinalis 'Tricolor'

France, 1896

Low subshrub that reaches 50 cm and grows slower than 'Icterina'. The handsome foliage unfolds grayish green and is speckled white, purple, and pink. The lilac-blue flowers appear in early summer and contrast well against the leaves. 'Tricolor' is rather tender and certainly not as strong as 'Icterina'. It is, however, well worth planting in any perennial border. Zone 7a

Sambucus

Relatively small genus of approximately forty species of perennials, shrubs, and small trees. The opposite leaves are imparipinnate. The flowers (usually white) appear in broad cymes or panicles, followed by red or black berrylike fruits. Some species are valued for their fruits; over the years, several cultivars have been developed for their larger and abundantly produced fruits. Most people think of *Sambucus* as weeds and find them unattractive, dull, and boring. However, there are quite a few cultivars of elder with good ornamental value, and these prove that *Sambucus* is more than a wild bush.

Sambucus nigra

All variegated *Sambucus* described here belong to *S. nigra*, the black elder. This large shrub to small tree can reach a height of about 6 m. The bark gets corky with age, and the opposite, imparipinnate leaves consist of five leaflets, occasionally seven. The creamy white flowers are followed by black fruits. In addition to the plants described here, a number of variegated cultivars of *S. nigra* have been named more recently, including 'Robert Piggin' (splashed creamy white), 'Bimble' (splashed pale yellow), and 'Din Dryfol' (splashed pale yellow). All *S. nigra* cultivars described here are hardy to zone 5.

Sambucus nigra 'Aureomarginata' RONALD HOUTMAN

Sambucus nigra 'Aureomarginata'

Germany, before 1867

The leaflets of this cultivar are dark green, with broad, clear yellow margins. C. de Vos mentioned 'Aureomarginata' in *Sieboldia* (April 14, 1877) and recom-

Sambucus nigra 'Madonna' FA. C. ESVELD

Sambucus nigra 'Marginata' RONALD HOUTMAN

Sambucus nigra 'Pulverulenta' HENNY KOLSTER

mended it over 'Aureomaculata', a long forgotten cultivar with yellow mottled leaves. It sometimes reverts, but this should not be a reason for neglecting this handsome shrub.

Sambucus nigra 'Madonna'

M. Slappendel, Boskoop, The Netherlands, 1986

Broad, upright shrub that grows to about 3 m high. The leaves are light green to grayish green with irregular broad yellow margins. Mature leaves have creamy white margins. 'Madonna' seems more stable in its variegation than 'Aureomarginata'. Occasionally yellow-leaved branches form, but these will not affect the stability of the shrub in a negative way. Moreover, 'Madonna' has broader and brighter colored leaf margins. It is therefore to be recommended over 'Aureomarginata'.

Sambucus nigra 'Marginata'

United Kingdom, about 1770

A medium-sized shrub that is very similar to 'Aureomarginata', but differs in having creamy white margins on the leaflets. The young foliage has yellow margins, which makes this shrub very similar to 'Aureomarginata' is spring. Later in the season, the differences become clearer. 'Marginata' is a relatively floriferous cultivar, especially noteworthy when in fruit. The shiny black fruits contrast extremely well against the white variegated foliage. This cultivar is also known as 'Albovariegata', 'Argenteomarginata', and 'Variegata'.

Sambucus nigra 'Pulverulenta'

United Kingdom, before 1850

Broad, upright shrub that grows more weakly than the species. The leaves are conspicuously and heavily mottled white. 'Pulverulenta' is an attractive medium-sized shrub with handsome foliage. Due to its weaker growth, it will not grow higher than about 3 m. Occasionally green-leaved branches arise, and these must be removed. This old cultivar is most probably similar to 'Albopunctata', however, some authors regard it as a different cultivar.

Schizophragma hydrangeoides 'Moonlight'

Barry R. Yinger, Lewisberry, Pennsylvania, United States, 1996

Climbing deciduous shrub, resembling *H. anomala* subsp. *petiolaris* in general habit. It was found in the

Sambucus nigra 'Albopunctata' RONALD HOUTMAN

Schizophragma hydrangeoides 'Moonlight' RONALD HOUTMAN

wild in Japan by Barry Yinger. 'Moonlight' is a vigorous, but noninvasive climber that grows to about 10 m or slightly higher. The broad ovate to almost rounded leaves have coarsely serrate margins and acute tips. 'Moonlight' has a reticulate variegation. Apart from the midrib and veins, the leaves are silvery grayish green. The veins are a deep, dark green. The effect is truly amazing. In autumn the foliage turns deep yellow. The flowers open in flattened heads with the fertile flowers in the center and creamy white sterile bracts at the margins. The bracts are long-stalked, creating very elegant inflorescences. 'Moonlight' is a superb climber that is recommended for a semi-shaded location. When considering planting a *Hydrangea anomala* subsp. *petiolaris*, try something else: *Schizophragma hydrangeoides* or this variegated cultivar. Zone 6

Sciadopitys verticillata 'Variegata'

Japan, before 1862

The Japanese umbrella pine is an impressive tree. In its native habitat it can attain a height of more than 30 m. The foliage consists of two types of needles: small scale-shaped needles are adpressed against the branches and at the base of the so-called double-needles. These are lengthwise connate, up to 12 cm long, and glossy dark green. 'Variegata' is an old Japanese cultivar that was introduced into cultivation by P. F. von Siebold in 1862. In this cultivar the green needles are intermixed with clear yellow needles. It is not very easy to propagate, but still a curious plant that is a must for every collector. Zone 7a

Sciadopitys verticillata 'Variegata' J. R. P. VAN HOEY SMITH

Sequoia sempervirens 'Variegata'

Croux & Son, Sceaux, France, before 1890

The coast redwood is a large evergreen conifer that can reach a height of more than 100 m. The foliage consists of dark green pinnate leaves. 'Variegata' is a curious cultivar with bluish green leaves irregularly variegated white and yellowish. Due to this variegation and the lack of chlorophyll, the leaves are deformed, which gives the tree an untidy appearance. It is a fast-growing, densely branched tree, and the branchlets are usually shorter than in the species. 'Variegata' is an old cultivar that was discovered in a French nursery by Abel Carrière before 1890. It is rare in cultivation, and only interesting for collectors. When ornamental value counts, a green-leaved cultivar such as *S. sempervirens* 'Cantab' is highly recommended. It has a more compact habit than the species and is therefore more suitable for garden use.

Sequoiadendron giganteum 'Argenteum'

United States, 1891

The big tree, or Wellingtonia, is an extremely large tree that is native to California, United States. In their natural habitat, trees can reach a height close to 100 m. The foliage consists of small, scale-shaped needles resembling *Cryptomeria*. It is dark green to bluish green and rough to the touch. The bark of *Sequoiadendron* is soft and spongy. There are several very similar cultivars of *Sequoiadendron* with white-variegated foliage, including the old cultivar 'Argenteum'. It is a strong-growing tree with irregular silvery white foliage. It is an uncommon cultivar, rarely available in the trade. Zone 7a

Sequoiadendron giganteum 'Aureovariegatum'

Lough Nurseries, Cork, Ireland, 1856

An old cultivar with an irregular yellow variegation,

usually in the smaller twigs. Probably no longer in cultivation. Zone 7a

Sequoiadendron giganteum 'French Beauty'

A new cultivar with heavily variegated foliage. The branchlets are light bluish green intermixed with clear white parts. It remains a bushy, broad, upright shrub for a long time, eventually becoming a medium-sized to large tree. Zone 7a

Sequoiadendron giganteum 'Variegatum'

France, 1867

This old silvery white variegated cultivar is very similar to 'Argenteum'. Likewise, it is rare in cultivation. Zone 7a

Solanum dulcamara 'Variegatum'

United Kingdom, before 1850

Solanum dulcamara, bittersweet or climbing nightshade, is a vigorous climbing subshrub that is native to Europe and western Asia, but naturalized in the United States. It is widely regarded as a weed. 'Variegatum' is far less vigorous than the species and will only grow about 1.5 m high. The leaves are ovate to oblong and dark green with broad, creamy white margins. On some leaves the variegation is not confined to the margins, and leaves are partially white. The flowers are light violet-blue with conspicuous yellow anthers in the center. They open in midsummer and are followed by clear red berries. Both flowers and fruits contrast very well against the variegated foliage. The fruits are highly toxic, so keep these out of reach of children. 'Variegatum' is a wonderful and very modest climber that fits in every garden. Zone 5b

Sophora japonica 'Variegata'

Japan, before 1850

Rather weak and slow-growing small tree with an irregular broad crown. The leaves are imparipinnate and consist of thirteen to seventeen leaflets. The leaflets are ovate to elliptic, dark green, and heavily mottled white, especially along the margins. This variegated tree is highly recommended for collectors and other people who desire variegated trees, but is of little ornamental value. Zone 6a

Sequoiadendron giganteum 'French Beauty' RONALD HOUTMAN

Sequoiadendron giganteum 'Variegatum' J. R. P. VAN HOEY SMITH

Solanum dulcamara 'Variegatum' WIM SNOEIJER

Sophora japonica 'Variegata' RONALD HOUTMAN

Sophora japonica 'Variegata' RONALD HOUTMAN

Sorbus aucuparia 'Pendula Variegata'

Before 1887

Curious weeping tree with variegated foliage. It has a strong weeping habit and does not develop a central leader. Eventually it will reach a height of about 3 m. The imparipinnate leaves consist of nine to fifteen leaflets, which are green and irregularly mottled yellow. 'Pendula Variegata' is a very rare tree and probably no longer grown. It is of little ornamental value. Zone 4

Sorbus aucuparia 'Variegata'

United Kingdom, before 1821

This is a broad, upright, small tree that grows to about 5 m high. The leaves are green and irregularly mottled yellow. Like 'Pendula Variegata', this is also a very rare tree, only of interest for collectors. In the literature this cultivar also occurs as 'Luteovariegata', a synonym. Zone 4

Spiraea thunbergii 'Mount Fuji'

Japan

Densely branched medium-sized shrub that grows to about 1 m high. The leaves are narrow lanceolate and 2.5 to 3 cm long. They are clear green, with irregular silvery white margins. In many leaves half of the leaf blade is white. The young leaves are pinkish variegated, giving a special touch to the spring foliage. The variegation is quite unstable, and 'Mount Fuji' easily forms green-leaved branches. In late spring the white flowers open in sparsely flowering umbels. The individual flowers are white. 'Mount Fuji' was imported from Japan and introduced into the Western trade by Adrian Bloom, who named it. Zone 5

Sorbus aucuparia 'Variegata' J. R. P. VAN HOEY SMITH

Spiraea thunbergii 'Mount Fuji' in summer RONALD HOUTMAN

Spiraea thunbergii 'Mount Fuji' in spring RONALD HOUTMAN

Spiraea ×*vanhouttei* 'Catpan' Pink Ice™

Small shrub usually not reaching more than 1 m in height. The leaves are obovate to rhomboidal with a few small teeth near the tip. In spring the leaves are pink at first, later changing to creamy white. The adult foliage is clear green and heavily variegated white. 'Catpan' is prone to sunburn, especially in spring when the young foliage is almost entirely creamy white. It is best planted in a location where it is protected from intense sunlight. To keep 'Catpan' variegated, reverted shoots must be removed. Zone 6

Stachyurus chinensis 'Joy Forever'

L. A. Terlouw, Leusden, The Netherlands, 1995

Deciduous shrub to about 2.5 m high. The short acuminate, ovate leaves are dark green, sometimes with yellowish green spots. The margins are clear greenish yellow, later becoming yellow to creamy yellow. 'Joy Forever' flowers like the species, with small greenish yellow flowers in axillary pendulous racemes. This cultivar grows less strongly than the species and has proven to be quite stable. It does not revert to green,

Spiraea ×*vanhouttei* 'Catpan' Pink Ice™ RONALD HOUTMAN

Stachyurus chinensis 'Joy Forever' RONALD HOUTMAN

Stachyurus chinensis 'Magpie' RONALD HOUTMAN

but occasionally shoots with entirely yellow leaves are formed. It is a nice variegated shrub that originated from a mutated cutting. An entirely golden-leaved shrub derived from 'Joy Forever' was recently named 'Goldbeater' by Rein and Mark Bulk from Boskoop, The Netherlands. Zone 7b

Stachyurus chinensis 'Magpie'

Hillier & Sons, Winchester, United Kingdom, 1948

Deciduous shrub that can reach a height of about 2 m, but if trained against a wall or building it can grow higher. The leaves are dull green with broad, creamy yellow margins. Occasionally entirely creamy white–leaved shoots appear; however, these die quickly because they lack chlorophyll. 'Magpie' flowers during late winter with pale greenish yellow flowers, borne in axillary pendulous racemes. It is not a strong plant and, especially at a young age, it needs protection during early frosts. Very suitable for growing against a west- or south-facing wall. Although it is generally placed with *Stachyurus praecox* in the United Kingdom, the pistil styles of the flowers of 'Magpie' are as long as the petals, a typical feature of *S. chinensis*. Zone 7b

Stachyurus praecox 'Marginatus'

Japan, before 1959

Contrary to *S. chinensis*, *S. praecox* is native to Japan. It forms a large and broad shrub that grows to about 4.5 m high. The branches are usually reddish brown to greenish, whereas they are purplish in *S. chinensis*. One of the best methods to tell these species apart is that the pistil style in a *S. praecox* flower is shorter than the petals. In *S. chinensis* the pistil style is as long as the pet-

Stachyurus chinensis 'Magpie' RONALD HOUTMAN

Stachyurus praecox 'Marginatus' RONALD HOUTMAN

als or longer. 'Marginatus' is a very rare cultivar that originates from Japan. The ovate to narrow ovate leaves are medium green, with yellow to greenish yellow margins. The flowers are light yellow and open in March. It appeared that 'Marginatus' had disappeared, but recently some plants were imported into The Netherlands from Japan. Zone 7a

Symphoricarpos orbiculatus 'Foliis Variegatis' RONALD HOUTMAN

Symphoricarpos orbiculatus 'Foliis Variegatis'

United Kingdom, around 1837

Small to medium-sized shrub with a compact rounded habit. It is dense, broad, and upright and grows to about 1.5 m. The ovate leaves are 2 to 4 cm long and heavily mottled yellow. Usually they also have yellow margins. 'Foliis Variegatis' is a widely grown attractive shrub that can be used in a shady as well as a sunny location. When planted in a shady location, it tends to revert more often than in full sun. Otherwise, 'Foliis Variegatis' is a problem-free shrub. Good for planting in small groups if contrast is needed in the larger garden. It is often sold as 'Variegatus', which in fact is the same plant. Zone 4

Symphoricarpos orbiculatus 'Taff's Silver Edge'

Stephen Taffler, Berkhamsted, United Kingdom

This shrub has the same habit as 'Foliis Variegatis', but differs in leaf colors. The leaves are grayish green with very narrow silvery white margins. Due to these colors and the relatively small size of the leaves, the plant looks very elegant. It was renamed by Stephen Taffler because the original name, 'Albovariegatus', was illegitimate. Zone 4

Symphoricarpos orbiculatus 'Taff's Silver Edge' PPH (COLLECTION OF HARRY VAN DE LAAR)

Syringa emodi 'Aureovariegata' RONALD HOUTMAN

Syringa emodi 'Aureovariegata' RONALD HOUTMAN

Symphoricarpos orbiculatus 'Taff's Variegated'

Stephen Taffler, Berkhamsted, United Kingdom

Unusual small to medium-sized shrub, not differing much from the other two variegated *S. orbiculatus* cultivars in habit and size. The leaves, however, are very different. They are clear green and irregularly blotched yellow. This cultivar is more unstable than the other variegated *Symphoricarpos* and will revert more easily. Zone 4

Syringa emodi 'Aureovariegata'

Before 1877

Compact upright shrub with a broad ovate habit that grows to about 3 m high. It is densely branched, and the main branches grow rather tightly upright. The leaves are broad oblong-elliptic and up to 20 cm long, even larger on young plants. They are medium green with broad, soft greenish yellow margins. During spring the margins are clear yellow. The pale lilac flowers appear in erect panicles in early June, and they fade to white. This variegated Himalayan lilac is a very distinct deciduous shrub. The greenish yellow variegation is pleasant and fits easily in any garden plan. It is sometimes called 'Variegata'. Zone 5a

Syringa vulgaris 'Aucubaefolia'

Large shrub to small tree and one of the very few known variegated cultivars of *S. vulgaris*, the common lilac. It derived as a sport of *S. vulgaris* 'President Grevy'. The leaves are heavily mottled cream and yellow. The semi-double, pale lilac-colored flowers open in May, giving a nice contrast against the foliage. Variegated forms are occasionally found in various cultivars of *S. vulgaris*. Usually they prove unstable or have no ornamental value. Two other named variegated cultivars of *S. vulgaris* are 'Dappled Dawn' and 'Wittbold's Variegated'. 'Dappled Dawn' is very similar to 'Aucubaefolia', but the flowers are single instead of semi-double. Zone 4

Tasmannia aromatica 'Suzette'

Bluebell Nurseries, Blackfordby, United Kingdom, 2000

Tasmannia aromatica was formerly known as *Drimys lanceolata* or *Drimys aromatica*, but is now included in *Tasmannia*. It is native to southeastern Australia and Tasmania, where it can grow into a large shrub or small tree up to 8 m high. 'Suzette' is a broad, upright, evergreen shrub with a dense habit that grows to about 2 m high. The lanceolate to narrow obovate leaves are dark green, irregularly mottled clear yellow. When crushed, they spread an aromatic scent. The purplish twigs contrast very well with the variegated foliage. The creamy white flowers open in late winter. Because it is not hardy enough in most temperate regions, 'Suzette' is best treated as a container plant. Zone 8b

Taxus

Only seven species of *Taxus* are known. Together with *Torreya*, this small genus belongs to the family Taxaceae (yew family). One of the features of this family are the fleshy coats (arils) surrounding the seeds. In *Taxus* the fleshy arils that enclose the seeds are open at one end. In *Torreya* they fully enclose the seeds. They are usually colored red. All parts of *Taxus*, except the fleshy arils, are poisonous.

The variegated *Taxus* described here all belong to *Taxus baccata*. This species is native to Europe, northern Africa, Asia Minor, and the Caucasus region. It has been cultivated for many centuries and plays an important role in various popular beliefs. A number of cultivars give a yellow or greenish yellow impression. Closer inspection shows these are actually variegated. The majority of these cultivars, if not all, have green needles with variegated margins. Unless otherwise stated, all cultivars described here are hardy to zone 6a.

Taxus baccata 'Adpressa Variegata'

Glasnevin Botanic Garden, Dublin, Ireland, 1860

Broad, upright conifer with a bushy but irregular habit. Its branches grow in a typical ascending manner. The needles are up to 1 cm long and 4 mm wide, which is shorter and wider than in other cultivars. They are light green to olive green with light greenish yellow margins. The margins are about 1 mm wide, leaving only a narrow green stripe in the center of the leaf. Like many *Taxus* cultivars, 'Adpressa Variegata' does not appear variegated, but more like a light green bush. It is uncertain whether 'Adpressa Variegata' was actually raised at the botanic garden of Glasnevin or was only distributed from there. Apart from the above it is a nice bushy plant that is not widely grown, although it has certainly not disappeared.

Syringa vulgaris 'Aucubaefolia' RONALD HOUTMAN

Tasmannia aromatica 'Suzette' G. C. STOLWIJK & CO. B.V.

Taxus baccata 'Adpressa Variegata' RONALD HOUTMAN

Taxus baccata 'Aldenham Gold' RONALD HOUTMAN

Taxus baccata 'Andrea' RONALD HOUTMAN

Taxus baccata 'Aldenham Gold'

Kenwith Nurseries, Great Torrington, United Kingdom, 1988

Beautiful cultivar with a relatively narrow, upright habit. The foliage is attractively variegated creamy yellow, leaving only a very narrow dark green stripe in the center of each needle. The informal columnar habit adds much to the lively appearance of 'Aldenham Gold'. It is one of the better yellow-variegated *T. baccata* cultivars.

Taxus baccata 'Andrea'

W. J. van der Werf, Boskoop, The Netherlands, 1994

Like many of the *T. baccata* cultivars, this is also a yellow-variegated plant with an informal columnar habit. The margins of each needle are clear greenish yellow, and the center consists of a narrow green stripe. 'Andrea' has a very yellow appearance. It will stand full sun without being damaged.

Taxus baccata 'Baricio'

A broad, shrubby conifer with a spreading-upright habit, eventually becoming much wider than high. The foliage is clear green intermixed with golden yellow needles. Occasionally shoots with only yellow needles appear. However, it is a very unstable cultivar and entirely green-leaved shoots appear more often. If not removed, the whole plant will revert to green in a couple of seasons. Zone 6b

Taxus baccata 'David'

M. M. Bömer Nursery, Zundert, The Netherlands, 1987

Raised in 1967 as an improvement of *T. baccata* 'Stan-

Taxus baccata 'Baricio' RONALD HOUTMAN

Taxus baccata 'David' RONALD HOUTMAN

dishii', this cultivar has the same broad columnar habit. It is a relatively slow-growing plant with yellow-variegated foliage. Each needle is green, with clear greenish yellow margins. Like similar cultivars, the overall appearance of 'David' is yellow. 'David' is not susceptible to sunburn and seems hardier than 'Standishii'.

Taxus baccata 'Fastigiata Aureomarginata'

Fisher, Son and Sibray, Handsworth Nurseries, Sheffield, United Kingdom, 1881

The habit of this cultivar is narrow columnar at first, but with age it will grow much wider. Eventually 'Fastigiata Aureomarginata' can attain a height of about 8 m and a width of more than 12 m. The foliage is dark olive green, with greenish yellow margins. It is an old cultivar that is widely grown throughout the world. Because of its eventual size, 'Fastigiata Aureo-

Taxus baccata 'David' RONALD HOUTMAN

Taxus baccata 'Fastigiata Aureomarginata' J. R. P. VAN HOEY SMITH

Taxus baccata 'Goldener Zwerg' RONALD HOUTMAN

marginata' is not recommended for small gardens in urban areas.

Taxus baccata 'Goldener Zwerg'

Another greenish yellow variegated cultivar with an upright growth habit. *Zwerg* means "dwarf" in German, and as the name suggests it is a rather weakly growing cultivar that stays considerably smaller than similar varieties. The habit is not as tidy as 'Aldenham Gold' or 'Standishii', and the plant makes a somewhat untidy impression. Like 'Fastigiata Aureomarginata', the leaves are dark green with greenish yellow margins. They also seem relatively wide, due to the fact that they are slightly shorter than in similar cultivars.

Taxus baccata 'Krzysztof'

Poland

Very narrow, upright cultivar with a columnar habit. The relatively long needles are dark green with dis-

Taxus baccata 'Krzysztof' RONALD HOUTMAN

Taxus baccata 'Pimpf' RONALD HOUTMAN

tinctive yellow margins. This beautiful new cultivar from Poland is little known, but certainly needs to be grown more widely.

Taxus baccata 'Pimpf'

Germany

Another greenish yellow variegated cultivar that grows narrow and upright. Young plants have a narrow columnar habit, but with age they will become broader. However, 'Pimpf' will not grow as wide as 'Fastigiata Aureomarginata'. 'Pimpf' means "little boy" in German, referring to the relatively slow growth of the plant, although it is certainly not a dwarf. It is a nice cultivar with a very yellow appearance.

Taxus baccata 'Standishii'

United Kingdom, 1908

With its strong fastigiate habit, 'Standishii' is one of the best variegated *Taxus* cultivars around. The habit stays columnar, even when more than fifty years old. The plant will get wider, of course, but it will never become bushy. The leaves are green with broad yellow margins. Unfortunately, it is susceptible to sunburn during hot and sunny spells. It is also slightly less winter hardy than other *Taxus* cultivars. When looking only at these two criteria, 'Standishii' is surpassed by 'David'. For many years 'Standishii' has been extremely popular and therefore widely grown. It is an excellent cultivar and highly recommended. Zone 6b

Taxus baccata 'Standishii' RONALD HOUTMAN

Taxus baccata 'Variegata' J. R. P. VAN HOEY SMITH

Thuja occidentalis 'Argentea' J. R. P. VAN HOEY SMITH

Taxus baccata 'Variegata'

United Kingdom, 1770

A broad, upright, shrubby conifer with a slightly irregular, flattened habit. The main branches grow at an average angle of about 50 degrees from the base of the plant. The foliage is green with a narrow silvery white margin on each needle. Occasionally the needles are slightly deformed, due to the lack of chlorophyll in the margins. The original 'Variegata' is supposedly not in cultivation anymore. However, following the description of *T. baccata* 'Argentea', it seems this cultivar is identical to 'Variegata'. Therefore, it is highly probable that these two nearly forgotten cultivars are one and the same. If so, the newer epithet 'Argentea' will be regarded a synonym of the older name 'Variegata'.

Thuja

A small genus consisting of only six species, of which only three are commonly grown. *Thuja occidentalis*, the eastern arborvitae or white cedar, and *T. plicata*, the western red cedar, are both native to North America. *Thuja orientalis*, the Oriental or western arborvitae, is native to Southeast Asia. According to some scientific research *T. orientalis* is placed in a separate genus, *Platycladus*. However, not all taxonomists agree with this, and the classification of this species remains arguable. It is also referred to as *Biota orientalis*, which is a generally accepted synonym. In this book cultivars of this species are described under *Thuja*.

The common name arborvitae (meaning "tree of life") was given with reference to a French voyage led by Captain Jacques Cartier in 1535. He and his crew remained in their ships on the frozen St. Lawrence River, Canada. The crew suffered badly from scurvy, a then unknown disease, caused by a vitamin C deficiency. Twenty-five crewmembers died. When all but three men were ill, the locals showed Cartier how to make an extract of the bark of a tree they called *anedda*, which was native to the region. This extract cured all the ill crewmembers within a fortnight. In 1542 the name *arbre de vie* was used for the first time, referring to a specimen of *T. occidentalis* planted in the royal garden at Fontainebleau. In 1583 the name is also used by Dodonaeus in one of his books. Although the story of Cartier is long-forgotten, the name *arborvitae* remains connected with *Thuja*.

The foliage of *Thuja* consists of small, scaly leaves.

These are very densely arranged and adpressed against the branchlets. The foliage is usually strongly scented. Many cultivars have derived from these three species. Some of these are very suitable for hedging, others become small bushy shrubs and are to be used in small gardens.

Several variegated cultivars are derived from the three *Thuja* species mentioned here. Most of these are upright, medium-sized to large shrubs. When used for hedging, their variegation will add to the ornamental value of the hedge. Of course, they are also excellent when planted as single specimens.

Thuja occidentalis 'Argentea'

France, 1855

An old and rare cultivar with a dense pyramidal habit. The foliage is green and heavily variegated white. The overall appearance of 'Argentea' is light greenish white. In the United Kingdom a cultivar called 'Variegata' was named in 1850. This has disappeared, and it is uncertain whether it was identical to 'Argentea'. Zone 3

Thuja occidentalis 'Beaufort' J. R. P. VAN HOEY SMITH

Thuja occidentalis 'Beaufort'

W. Haalboom Nurseries, Driebergen, The Netherlands, 1963

'Beaufort' derived from *T. occidentalis* 'Argentea' as a sport and is therefore similar in foliage colors. Seen from a distance, however, the foliage looks slightly lighter than in 'Argentea'. These cultivars mainly differ in habit. 'Beaufort' is less vigorous and has a broad conical habit with a rounded head, whereas the head of 'Argentea' is acute. 'Beaufort' is not rare in the trade, and it is an excellent replacement for the nearly forgotten 'Argentea'. Zone 3

Thuja occidentalis 'Cristata Argenteovariegata'

1949

A very rare conifer with a relatively slender, narrow conical habit. The cristate foliage arrangement is very typical of 'Cristata Argenteovariegata' and related cultivars and gives the plant an informal character. Unfortunately, the plant has the tendency to become leggy with age. The foliage is medium green and moderately splashed with creamy white branchlets, especially in the young growth. This cultivar has nearly disappeared from cultivation. Zone 3

Thuja occidentalis 'Cristata Argenteovariegata' RONALD HOUTMAN

Thuja occidentalis 'Perk Vlaanderen'

Konijn Nurseries, Reeuwijk, The Netherlands, 1971

Splendid cultivar with a broad conical habit. The glossy dark green foliage is heavily variegated greenish yellow. The origin of this cultivar is still unknown, but it was named after the Director of Parks of the city of Utrecht, The Netherlands. 'Perk Vlaanderen' is certainly one of the best cultivars within the genus *Thuja*. Although it is available in the trade, it is not commonly grown. Zone 3

Thuja occidentalis 'Spotty Smaragd'

A. M. M. Vergeer, Boskoop, The Netherlands, 2002

This cultivar was discovered as a sport in *T. occidentalis* 'Smaragd' (also known as 'Emerald'). 'Spotty Smaragd' has the same compact conical habit and medium green foliage. The green foliage is intermixed with light creamy white branchlets. It is a healthy conifer suitable for planting in both sunny and semi-shaded locations. Zone 3

Thuja occidentalis 'Wansdyke Silver'

H. J. Welch, Wansdyke Nurseries, Devizes, United Kingdom, 1961

Compact conifer with a dense, broad pyramidal habit that grows to about 2 m high. The green foliage is heavily but irregularly variegated creamy white. 'Wansdyke Silver' was found as an unnamed plant in a neglected nursery in Surrey, United Kingdom, by the late H. J. Welch and W. Archer. Even after closer inspection the plant could not be named, causing Welch and Archer to name the plant after Welch's nursery. 'Wansdyke Silver' is one of the few smaller variegated *Thuja*. Therefore, it is one of the few cultivars that can be grown in smaller gardens. Zone 3

Thuja orientalis 'Aureovariegata'

M. Dauvesse Nurseries, France, 1865

Old cultivar with a broad columnar habit, which later becomes pyramidal. The foliage is clear yellowish green with an irregular golden yellow variegation. Its

Thuja occidentalis 'Spotty Smaragd' RONALD HOUTMAN

Thuja occidentalis 'Wansdyke Silver' RONALD HOUTMAN

character is similar to the species, but 'Aureovariegata' is less vigorous. It is certainly not a small plant, but will easily reach a height of about 3 m. Thanks to the relatively narrow habit, 'Aureovariegata' is suitable for all except the smallest gardens. Zone 6b

Thuja orientalis 'Dogmersfield'

Whitewater Nurseries, Hook, United Kingdom, 2003

Upright conifer with a narrow columnar habit when young, later becoming narrowly pyramidal. Its delicate foliage structure was inherited from *T. orientalis* 'Conspicua', from which it was raised as a seedling. The foliage is dark bluish green intermixed with cream to creamy yellow branchlets. This cultivar is not yet available in the trade. Zone 6b

Thuja orientalis 'Flame'

Spicer Nurseries, Lutterworth, United Kingdom, before 1993

Upright conifer with a pyramidal habit. It is not very vigorous, but eventually it will attain a height of about

Thuja orientalis 'Dogmersfield' RONALD HOUTMAN

Thuja orientalis 'Aureovariegata' RONALD HOUTMAN

Thuja orientalis 'Flame' RONALD HOUTMAN

2 m. The foliage is yellowish green, variegated with small tufts of yellow. These are irregularly spread through the plant, but mostly on younger foliage. Zone 6b

Thuja orientalis 'Fleck'

'Fleck' was discovered as a sport of *T. orientalis* 'Aurea Nana', but has a narrower habit and an acute head. The foliage is irregularly spotted yellow to yellowish green. Zone 6b

Thuja plicata 'Cuprea'

W. H. Rogers, Red Lodge Nursery, Chandlers Ford, United Kingdom, around 1930

Dense and slow-growing shrubby conifer with a broad conical habit at first, later becoming a broad, mounded plant. The foliage is green with a distinct greenish yellow variegation. Depending on the season, the foliage colors change into deep yellowish green or bronze-green. Although not a true dwarf conifer, 'Cuprea' will not grow taller than approximately 1 m. Zone 6a

Thuja plicata 'Doone Valley'

R. S. Corley, High Wycombe, United Kingdom, 1970

Interesting cultivar with a slightly irregular but narrow pyramidal habit. The foliage is light green with a conspicuous golden-bronze variegation. With its informal habit, 'Doone Valley' is a distinct cultivar, although it is not widely available. I recommend it be planted as a specimen plant. Zone 6a

Thuja plicata 'Zebrina'

United Kingdom, 1923

Large vigorous tree with a dense conical habit. Eventually it will grow almost as high as the species, which grows to about 15 m. The foliage is dark green and very conspicuously striped clear golden yellow. The cultivar name 'Zebrina' is very well chosen, because the foliage is as striped as a zebra (apart from the colors, of course). 'Zebrina' is one of the best variegated conifers and also one of the most widely grown. It can be used as a specimen plant, but is also very suitable for hedging. When using 'Zebrina', however, one must bear in

Thuja orientalis 'Fleck' KLAAS VERBOOM

Thuja plicata 'Cuprea' RONALD HOUTMAN

mind that it really is a vigorous cultivar and it needs enough space to develop. Zone 6a

Thuja plicata 'Zebrina Extra Gold'

Ireland, 1987

Discovered as a sport of 'Zebrina' and similar in habit and foliage structure. As the name suggests, this cultivar has exceptionally strong variegation that gives the plant a very yellow appearance. It can be used in the same way as 'Zebrina'. Occasionally plants of 'Zebrina Extra Gold' are incorrectly labeled 'Irish Gold'. The true 'Irish Gold' has a similar habit, but its foliage is entirely golden yellow. It can be distinguished from 'Zebrina Extra Gold' because almost no green foliage is present. However, due to slight variations in colors, some plants tend to look almost identical and mistakes are easily made. Zone 6a

Thujopsis dolabrata 'Variegata'

Japan, before 1861

Broad, pyramidal, shrubby conifer with a dense, somewhat informal habit. The scaly foliage is distinctively adpressed and the branchlets are very flattened. The foliage is lively dark green intermixed with a clear white variegation. Depending on the variegation in the cuttings taken, the degree of variegation in different

Thuja plicata 'Zebrina' RONALD HOUTMAN

Thuja plicata 'Doone Valley' RONALD HOUTMAN

Thuja plicata 'Zebrina Extra Gold' J. R. P. VAN HOEY SMITH

Thujopsis dolabrata 'Variegata' RONALD HOUTMAN

plants can vary. 'Variegata' was introduced in Europe in by P. F. von Siebold. It is a splendid variegated conifer that is widely available. Zone 6b

Thymus

Large, interesting genus of herbs and small shrubs, consisting of more than 150 species. They mainly grow in temperate regions in Europe and Asia. All species are evergreen and have aromatic foliage. The flowers are typical for members of the Lamiaceae (mint family), to which *Thymus* belongs. A short tubular corolla ends in five short lobes, two on the upper side and three slightly longer lobes on the underside. The corolla is usually purple, pink, or white. Because most thymes are small, occasionally creeping, shrubs, they are best used in small gardens or rockeries. Some are very floriferous, adding to the ornamental value. They are also popular as kitchen herbs. A number of variegated cultivars are named, most of which derived from

Thymus ×*citriodorus* 'Silver Queen' MARCO HOFFMAN

T. ×*citriodorus,* a hybrid between *T. pulegioides* and *T. vulgaris.* This hybrid arose in The Netherlands in 1596 and is commonly grown in Europe.

Thymus ×*citriodorus* 'Archer's Gold'

This rare cultivar is very similar to *Thymus* 'Doone Valley', although less floriferous. It forms a broad spreading subshrub of about 25 cm to 30 cm high. The fragrant foliage is green with clear golden yellow tips. The flowers are light lilac-purple. Zone 7a

Thymus ×*citriodorus* 'Golden King'

More or less upright subshrub to about 25 cm high. The ovate leaves are 1 cm long, light green with narrow yellow margins. When bruised they smell heavily of lemon. The light purplish pink flowers appear in upright spikes during July and August. 'Golden King' superficially resembles *Thymus* 'Doone Valley', but differs in its more upright habit, slightly larger leaves, and light flowers. The leaves of 'Golden King' have yellow margins, whereas those of 'Doone Valley' have yellow tips. Zone 7a

Thymus ×*citriodorus* 'Silver Queen'

Upright, small shrub that grows to 30 cm high. The small ovate leaves are about 6 mm long and have revolute edges. They are green, with silvery white to creamy white margins. The flowers open from June to August, are light purplish pink, and are carried in upright spikes. Various white-variegated clones are available in the trade, including 'Argenteovariegatus', 'Argenteus', and 'Silver Posie'. These have proven very difficult to distinguish from each other, and according to the latest research all except 'Silver Posie' are considered synonyms of 'Silver Queen'. Zone 7a

Thymus 'Doone Valley'

W. Archer, United Kingdom, before 1992

Relatively vigorous mat-forming subshrub that grows to 20 cm high with procumbent-ascending stems. The small ovate leaves are 7 mm long and dark green with yellow tips. During the vegetative state the leaves are strongly variegated, but when flowering they turn almost entirely green. When bruised, the foliage spreads a strong lemon scent. The flowers appear in upright spikes during summer. They are purplish pink with darker spots. Despite the fact that it is only moderately

Thymus ×*citriodorus* 'Archer's Gold' MARCO HOFFMAN

Thymus ×*citriodorus* 'Golden King' GERT FORTGENS

Thymus 'Doone Valley' MARCO HOFFMAN

Thymus vulgaris 'Silver Posie' RONALD HOUTMAN

Tilia cordata 'Mixed Emotions' RONALD HOUTMAN

Torreya nucifera 'Argentea Variegata' RONALD HOUTMAN

winter-hardy and tends to die back after some years, 'Doone Valley' is a very popular thyme hybrid. Its richly produced flowers and good mat-forming habit are its main advantages. It occasionally is sold under its previous name *T.* ×*citriodorus* 'Doone Valley'. Another named variegated cultivar, 'Gold Edge', is rarely offered. It differs from 'Doone Valley' in having yellow-margined foliage. Zone 7b

Thymus praecox 'Goldstream'

Mat-forming subshrub with procumbent branches that grows to about 10 cm high. The small ovate leaves are about 7 mm long and green, with yellow tips. The flowers, which lack anthers, appear in July and August and are carried in upright spikes. When in flower, the leaf color often changes to green. 'Goldstream' resembles 'Doone Valley', but is less coarse in habit and the flowers are lighter. Moreover 'Goldstream' is more winter-hardy. Zone 6b

Thymus vulgaris 'Silver Posie'

'Silver Posie' is very similar to 'Silver Queen', but it differs in having more lanceolate and narrower leaves. Both are difficult to tell apart and are often mixed up in the trade. A good way to tell these two cultivars apart is by the fragrance. 'Silver Posie', being a cultivar of *Thymus vulgaris*, has the typical thyme scent, whereas 'Silver Queen', being a cultivar of *T.* ×*citriodorus*, has the lemony scent typical of this hybrid. 'Silver Posie' is also available as 'Argenteovariegatus' or 'Argenteus'. Zone 7a

Tilia cordata 'Mixed Emotions'

C. van der Wurff, Heeze, The Netherlands, 2003

This peculiar tree was raised as a seedling of *T. cordata* on Van der Wurff's nursery in 1988. He planted the variegated seedling, and after fifteen years grafted the first scions. The original tree is about 4 m high and is expected to grow into a medium-sized tree with a broad ovate habit. It is less vigorous than the species, mainly caused by the variegation. The heart-shaped leaves are medium green, irregularly but heavily mottled and blotched creamy white. The variegation is at its best in spring, later in the season it becomes less conspicuous. Over the years 'Mixed Emotions' has proven to be quite stable, only rarely reverting to green. Zone 4

Torreya nucifera 'Argentea Variegata'

Unusual medium-sized tree with an irregular pyramidal habit. Young plants tend to grow very shrubby. The needles of *Torreya* are up to about 3 cm long and very sharp to the touch. In 'Argentea Variegata' they are almost entirely silvery white, leaving only a very narrow stripe of dark green in the center. Unfortunately, the needles are very susceptible to sunburn and 'Argentea Variegata' should be planted in a shaded location. It is less hardy than the species and must be protected during severe cold. The cultivar name 'Argentea Variegata' could not be traced and may be illegitimate. 'Variegata', a yellow-variegated cultivar is occasionally offered as well. It is less susceptible to sunburn than 'Argentea Variegata'. Zone 7b/8

Torreya nucifera 'Argentea Variegata' KLAAS VERBOOM

Trachelospermum asiaticum 'Tricolor'

Before 1885

Trachelospermum asiaticum is a beautiful species, resembling the more common *T. jasminoides*, but differing in having smaller leaves and flowers and pointed calyx lobes. It grows vigorously and densely and is capable of covering walls and fences. 'Tricolor' is a self-clinging, dwarf climbing plant that reaches a maximum height of about 1 m, although it usually will not exceed 50 cm. The small narrow elliptic leaves are dark green and attractively variegated cream with pinkish red tints. The pink becomes stronger in autumn and winter, and the young foliage in spring is almost entirely pinkish red at first. The fragrant flowers are white and open in midsummer.

'Tricolor' is hardy only in mild climates and is an ideal container plant. When it can be grown outdoors, however, it is a very good small climber. It is best planted in a sheltered location against a south- or southwest-facing wall. The first year after planting it is slow to establish, but after a year or two it is a healthy, well-growing shrub. When the soil is moist enough, it is not susceptible to sunburn. Zone 8a

Torreya nucifera 'Variegata' J. R. P. VAN HOEY SMITH

Trachelospermum jasminoides 'Variegatum'

Before 1885

Evergreen twining shrub that grows to about 6 m high. The opposite leaves are elliptic-oblong and leathery. They are dark green with grayish and whitish spots and distinctive creamy white margins. During winter they are tinted crimson, influenced by dropping tem-

Trachelospermum jasminoides 'Variegatum' RONALD HOUTMAN

Ugni molinae 'Flambeau' RONALD HOUTMAN

Ulmus minor 'Argenteovariegata' RONALD HOUTMAN

peratures. The flowers, which are carried in axillary and terminal racemes, open in July. They are pure white, sweetly fragrant, and, with their somewhat twisted petals, they resemble a ship's rudder. This beautiful climber is best planted against a south-facing wall. In less mild areas, it must be planted in the conservatory. Zone 8b

Ugni molinae 'Flambeau'

Hanno Hardijzer Nursery, Boskoop, The Netherlands, 2002

Spreading bushy shrub with elegantly arching branches. It can reach a height of more than 1.5 m, but will usually stay smaller. The opposite leaves are ovate and dull grayish green with cream-colored margins. Almost year-round, but most strong in autumn, the young growth is attractively colored purple. In most temperate regions it is not hardy enough to plant outdoors, but 'Flambeau' is an excellent container plant for balconies and terraces. *Ugni molinae* is sometimes offered under its old name *Myrtus ugni*, which is now regarded to be a synonym. Zone 9

Ulmus

Small genus of trees and large shrubs belonging to the Ulmaceae (elm family). Most species and derived cultivars are important as street trees, landscape trees, and for their timber. The leaves of many species are rough to the touch and have an unequal leaf base. Only a few variegated elms exist. Unfortunately, *Ulmus* has a bad name because it is host to Dutch elm disease (*Ophiostoma ulmi* s.l.). In the 1970s and 1980s this beetle-borne fungal disease killed hundreds of thousands of elms throughout Europe and the United States. Biologists are still searching for a cultivar that is 100 percent resistant to this terrible disease.

Ulmus minor 'Argenteovariegata'

United Kingdom, about 1670

Large shrub to medium-sized tree, closely resembling *U. minor* 'Variegata'. The ovate leaves are 5 to 8 cm long with white speckles and veins. (The mottles and dots in the foliage of 'Variegata' are much smaller and the veins are green to grayish green, not white.) *Ulmus minor* 'Argenteovariegata' is also known as *U. procera* 'Argenteovariegata'. Zone 5a

Ulmus minor 'Silvery Gem' PIERRE THEUNISSEN

Ulmus minor 'Silvery Gem'

Fa. P. G. Zwijnenburg, Boskoop, The Netherlands, 1965

Densely branched medium-sized shrub, eventually becoming a small shrubby tree, not more than 4 m high. The ovate leaves are grayish green with conspicuous narrow silvery white margins. The effect of the variegated foliage is quite dramatic, especially in spring. Later in the season it fades a bit. Zone 5a

Ulmus minor 'Variegata' RONALD HOUTMAN

Ulmus minor 'Variegata'

France, 1772

Large shrub, eventually a medium-sized tree that grows to about 5 m or higher. The leaves are conspicuously larger than those of 'Silvery Gem' and heavily mottled and speckled grayish white and white. Although 'Variegata' occasionally reverts to green, the foliage is quite stable. Large specimens of this cultivar give a grayish impression from a distance, only when observed at close range can the mottled foliage be seen.

Ulmus minor 'Variegata' RONALD HOUTMAN

'Variegata' is still often sold under its older names, now synonyms: *U. carpinifolia* 'Pulverulenta' and *U. carpinifolia* 'Variegata'. Zone 5a

Ulmus parvifolia 'Frosty'

Japan, before 1978

Although this cultivar may look like a small shrub at first, it will grow into a large shrub of more than 5 m in height. The elliptic to ovate leaves are green, and the teeth along the serrate margins are silvery white. The name 'Frosty' is well chosen because the plant almost looks touched by a light frost in the morning. Zone 5b

Ulmus parvifolia 'Geisha'

Japan

Relatively low shrub, closely resembling 'Frosty' but smaller. The leaves have the same marginal variegation that is confined to the teeth along the margins, except in 'Geisha' the variegation is creamy white, on young foliage more cream. Over the years several variegated cultivars of *U. parvifolia* were brought into the Western trade from Japan. They are sometimes sold as bonzai trees, but most of them do not even come close. They can be used for bonzai, Of course, but besides a few (green-leaved) exceptions, *U. parvifolia* cultivars are definitely not dwarf shrubs. 'Geisha' is one of the smaller cultivars. Zone 5b

Vaccinium vitis-idaea 'Dolinda'

The Netherlands, before 1980

Dense, evergreen shrub that grows to about 30 cm

Ulmus parvifolia 'Frosty' FA. C. ESVELD

Ulmus parvifolia 'Geisha' PPH (COLLECTION OF HARRY VAN DE LAAR)

high. The obovate leaves are somewhat convex and have slightly revolute margins. They are glossy dark green, irregularly blotched white. The small campanulate flowers open pale pink, quickly fading to white. They appear in May and June and are followed by globular, clear red fruits. 'Dolinda' is best used for small group-plantings in peat gardens and heather gardens. Zone 2

Vaccinium vitis-idaea 'Dolinda' ARJAN LAROS

Viburnum

Large and important genus of ornamental shrubs and small trees consisting of about 230 species and 350 hybrids and cultivars. All *Viburnum* carry opposite leaves and all except one section of this genus flower in flattened or globular cymes. The fruit is a fleshy drupe, usually designated as a berry. As with many large genera represented in this book, *Viburnum* contains relatively few variegated cultivars. Most of these are not well known and rather unstable in their variegation. The two variegated cultivars of *V. tinus* are among the most stable and best known within the genus.

Viburnum ×*carlcephalum* 'Van der Maat'

P. de Frankrijker & Son B.V., Boskoop, The Netherlands, 1998

Deciduous, broad, upright, bushy shrub that grows to about 2 m high. The broad ovate leaves, which are 5 to 12 cm long, are rather dull green and heavily mottled yellow in an irregular pattern. The variegation is very unstable and reverts very easily. The flowers are carried in globular cymes and open during April and May. The cymes are up to 18 cm in diameter, and individual flowers are slightly larger than in *V.* ×*carlcephalum*, usually more than 1.5 cm. They are very fragrant. This cultivar was discovered as a sport of *V.* ×*carlcephalum* in 1974, but was named in 1998. Until then it was sold under the invalid names 'Variegatum' and 'Maat Select', neither of which follow the rules of the ICNCP. Zone 6a

Viburnum ×*carlcephalum* 'Van der Maat' RONALD HOUTMAN

Viburnum lantana 'Variegatum'

United Kingdom, about 1770

Large deciduous shrub that grows to 4 m high. The ovate to broad leaves are about 6 to 10 cm long and irregularly variegated creamy yellow. Young foliage has more yellow variegation. The cream colored flowers are held in flattened cymes up to 10 cm in diameter. They open in May and June. Like *V.* ×*carlcephalum* 'Van

Viburnum lantana 'Variegatum' GERT FORTGENS

Viburnum opulus 'Kaleidoscope' RONALD HOUTMAN

der Maat', 'Variegatum' is also an unstable cultivar and less interesting for anyone but a collector. Zone 4

Viburnum opulus 'Kaleidoscope'

Monksilver Nursery, Cottenham, United Kingdom, 1985

Joe Sharman, owner of Monksilver Nursery, found this cultivar in a batch of seedlings. 'Kaleidoscope' is a fairly upright, deciduous shrub with the same habit and leaf shape as the species. The three- to five-lobed leaves are irregularly blotched and striped creamy yellow to greenish yellow with pink. Unfortunately, 'Kaleidoscope' is apt to revert to green. Zone 4

Viburnum rhytidophyllum 'Variegatum'

Chenault Nurseries, Orléans, France, before 1935

Rather curious, upright, evergreen shrub that will grow slightly less tall than the species, which grows to a height of about 3 m. The large lanceolate leaves are somewhat narrower and more convex than in the species. They are up to 20 cm long and creamy yellow to pale yellow variegated when unfolding. At maturity they become irregularly mottled cream to creamy white. Some leaves are partially cream, whereas in others the green dominates. Although the flowerbuds are already visible in winter, the flowers open in May and June. They are carried in flattened cymes, cream colored, and followed by red fruits, later turning black. This large shrub looks somewhat pitiful with its hanging foliage and irregular variegation. Its variegation is not as unstable as in *V.* ×*carlcephalum* 'Van der Maat', but green-leaved branches arise regularly. Zone 6b

Viburnum rhytidophyllum 'Variegatum' RONALD HOUTMAN

Viburnum tinus 'Bewley's Variegated'

United States, before 1995

Compact evergreen shrub that grows to about 3 m high. The leaves are ovate to obovate and somewhat irregularly shaped. They are dark green with broad irregular creamy yellow margins, becoming yellowish cream on older leaves. The flowers, which open from mid-November until late April, are white and carried in flattened cymes. The flowers are followed by dark blackish blue fruits, which are persistent until the following spring. 'Bewley's Variegated' closely resembles 'Variegatum', but it has irregularly shaped leaf margins and slightly more yellowish variegation. Although not very winter-hardy shrubs, *V. tinus* and its cultivars have become hugely popular as container plants recently. In slightly milder climates, they are widely used in gardens and public areas. Zone 8a

Viburnum tinus 'Variegatum'

Before 1850

The dark green leaves of this old cultivar have narrow cream to creamy white margins. It closely resembles

Viburnum tinus 'Variegatum' RONALD HOUTMAN

Viburnum tinus 'Bewley's Variegated' RONALD HOUTMAN

Vinca major 'Reticulata' WIM SNOEIJER

Vinca major 'Surrey Marble' WOUT KROMHOUT

Vinca major 'Variegata' GERT FORTGENS

'Bewley's Variegated', but differs in having entire leaf margins and a more whitish variegation. Zone 8b

Vinca

Small genus of seven species of herbs, subshrubs, and shrubs, usually with a vigorous and trailing habit. In gardens, *Vinca* is commonly represented by two species: *V. major* and *V. minor*. The opposite leaves of both species are entire and the flowers are blue, except some pink- and white-flowering cultivars. They are best planted in moist soil in a semi-shaded location, but will also do very well in full shade.

Vinca major is a vigorous evergreen subshrub with strongly trailing procumbent shoots. It will grow to 30 cm high. The blue flowers are 3 to 4 cm wide. It is an excellent groundcover for large areas. *Vinca minor* is a smaller, procumbent evergreen that grows to about 20 cm high. The violet-blue flowers are 2 to 3 cm wide. *Vinca minor* and its cultivars are excellent groundcovers for both large and small areas. It is also worth planting in small gardens. Both species contain variegated cultivars, which have one great advantage over the green-leaved forms: the blue to lilac-blue flowers contrast very well with the foliage.

Vinca major 'Maculata'

The green leaves of this rare cultivar have greenish yellow central blotches. The flowers are similar to those of the species and open in late spring and early summer. 'Maculata' is quite effective when planted in large groups. It is also known as 'Aureomaculata' and 'Oxford'. Zone 7a

Vinca major 'Reticulata'

Germany, before 1847

The leaves of this old cultivar are dark green with clear yellow veins. Especially striking during spring, later in the season the veins become more greenish, which makes 'Reticulata' less distinct. Flowers like the species. Zone 7a

Vinca major 'Surrey Marble'

This interesting cultivar arose as a sport in *V. major*. It has attractive yellow and green marbled foliage and is easily distinguished from other cultivars by its pinkish to pinkish red stems. Zone 7a

Vinca major 'Variegata'

United Kingdom, about 1700

An old cultivar that is easily distinguished by its broader leaves that are dark green with bold cream to creamy white margins. The leaves contrast well with the blue flowers, which are nicely placed above the foliage. Zone 7a

Vinca major 'Wojo's Gem'

United States, before 2000

Low-growing plant with a creeping habit, also suitable for hanging baskets. The leaves are broad, elliptic, and cream colored, with dark green margins. Apart from the leaf size, this cultivar is similar to *V. minor* 'Illumination', but the leaf centers are golden yellow in 'Illumination'. 'Wojo's Gem' has the same possibilities as 'Illumination', but is more susceptible to sunburn. Therefore, I recommend planting it in a shady or semi-shaded location. Zone 7b

Vinca major 'Wojo's Gem' RONALD HOUTMAN

Vinca minor 'Alba Variegata'

A rare cultivar with white-margined leaves. It is very similar to *V. minor* 'Argenteovariegata', but differs in having white flowers. Thus, the contrast between the flowers and foliage is negligible. This cultivar has a very white appearance, which is sometimes required in garden architecture. Zone 5a

Vinca minor 'Argenteomarginata'

About 1770

Low, procumbent subshrub with good groundcover qualities. Unfolding foliage is grayish to gray white at first, later becoming green with irregular white margins. It is also known as 'Variegata', but this synonym is invalid, because it was used for both the white variegated and the yellow variegated forms of *V. minor*. This cultivar is often referred to as *V. minor* 'Argenteovariegata', but this may be a different plant because some authors note it is abundantly flowering, whereas 'Argenteomarginata' is a very poorly flowering cultivar, to say the least. Zone 5b

Vinca minor 'Argenteovariegata'

United Kingdom, before 1850

Closely resembling 'Argenteomarginata', but differing in a more free-flowering habit. The leaves have narrow white margins. When not in flower, 'Argenteovariegata' is indistinguishable from 'Alba Variegata' (which has white flowers). 'Argenteomarginata is also referred to as 'Variegata'. Zone 5b

Vinca minor 'Argenteovariegata' GEORGE OTTER

Vinca minor 'Aureovariegata'

United Kingdom, about 1770

Old, attractive cultivar with greenish yellow unfolding leaves. During spring the foliage color changes to green with light yellow blotches. Moderately floriferous with deep violet-blue flowers during late spring and summer. Zone 5b

Vinca minor 'Aureovariegata' RONALD HOUTMAN

Vinca minor 'Illumination' KLAAS VERBOOM

Vinca minor 'Illumination' WIM SNOEIJER

Vinca minor 'Illumination'

C. A. Hensler, Newport, Washington, United States

A new cultivar with the same creeping habit as the other cultivars described here. The leaves are attractively variegated with clear golden yellow centers and dark green margins. They are very lustrous, adding much to the overall appearance of this plant. During summer 'Illumination' flowers with violet-blue flowers. Although 'Illumination' is not very floriferous, the flowers make an excellent contrast to the foliage. Like so many variegated plants, this cultivar has the tendency to revert, and green-leaved branches must therefore be removed. Otherwise, it is a splendid groundcover shrub and certainly a good addition to the range of variegated *Vinca*. It can also be grown in hanging baskets. Zone 7a

Vinca minor 'Sebastian'

K. Kulas, K. Brzegu, Poland, 1991

Moderately vigorous subshrub that originated as a sport of *Vinca minor*. Its small leaves are bright green with a rather inconspicuous yellowish green center. This makes 'Sebastian' quite a distinct cultivar. With its less variegated appearance, it also attracts people that usually not like to use variegated plants. Very suitable as a groundcover for small areas. Zone 5b

Vinca minor 'Sterling Silver'

Before 1998

Nice addition in the range of variegated periwinkles. 'Sterling Silver' is a dense prostrate evergreen shrub, ideal as a groundcover. The leaves are green with conspicuous silvery white margins. The rich violet-blue flowers open in May and June, contrasting very well against the foliage. It is a very floriferous cultivar and therefore recommended. Zone 5b

Vinca minor 'Sebastian' RONALD HOUTMAN

Weigela

Medium-sized to large deciduous shrubs that are widely used and loved for their abundant flowering and often colorful foliage. The opposite leaves are ovate to elliptic and 5 to 10 cm long. They are usually green, but various cultivars have yellow, purple, or variegated foliage. The flowers, which open from late April into June, are attractive and colorful. Although most of the species and cultivars produce white, pink, purple, or red flowers, one or two yellow-flowering species exist as well. They are trouble-free shrubs that will thrive in any fertile soil and are best planted in full sun. In the shade, they flower less abundantly.

Weigela 'Brigela' FRENCH LACE™ RONALD HOUTMAN

Weigela 'Brigela' FRENCH LACE™

André Briant Nurseries, St. Barthelemy d'Anjou, France, 1999

Rather vigorous shrub with a broad, somewhat flattened habit that grows to about 2.5 m high and about 3.5 m wide. The elliptic to ovate leaves are dark green with irregular deep yellow margins. Later in the season the margins turn slightly more creamy yellow. 'Brigela' was discovered as a sport in *W*. 'Bristol Ruby' and has the same flower color: dark pinkish red on the outside and slightly lighter on the inside. The flowers go very well with the yellow-variegated foliage. 'Brigela' is perhaps the best yellow-variegated *Weigela* on the market. Zone 6

Weigela 'Cappuccino' RONALD HOUTMAN

Weigela 'Cappuccino'

Bert Verhoef, Hazerswoude, The Netherlands, 2002

Broad-spreading deciduous shrub. The leaves are light olive green with darker yellowish green tips. The main veins and secondary veins are lighter than the leaves. The combination of different shades of yellowish green make 'Cappuccino' a rather peculiar, but certainly not ugly, shrub. The foliage colors provide many possibilities for stunning combinations. Almost all colors seem to go very well with 'Cappuccino'. Zone 6a

Weigela 'Courtatom' COULEUR D'AUTOMNE™ GERT FORTGENS

Weigela 'Courtatom' COULEUR D'AUTOMNE™

INRA, Angers, France, 1981

Vigorous shrub with a broad habit that grows to about 3.5 m high. The leaves are green with broad light green margins. In many leaves more than half of the leaf is variegated. In autumn the foliage becomes brilliant purple-red. 'Courtatom' flowers in early summer with light, almost whitish pink flowers, quickly changing to deep pink. Zone 6

Weigela florida 'Caricature' RONALD HOUTMAN

Weigela florida 'Sunny Princess' PPH (COLLECTION OF HARRY VAN DE LAAR)

Weigela florida 'Suzanne' PPH (COLLECTION OF HARRY VAN DE LAAR)

Weigela florida 'Caricature'

H. Kolster, Boskoop, The Netherlands, 1978

Large shrub with a broad, upright habit that grows to 2.5 m or higher. The name is very well chosen: this shrub immediately attracts attention with its bold foliage. The leaves are very large, up to 20 cm, and conspicuously convex. They are light green with narrow, irregular, creamy yellow margins, more yellowish on young foliage. Because of the relatively heaviness of the leaves the twigs are bent, resulting in arching branches and eventually an irregular growing habit. 'Caricature' is not a very floriferous cultivar. The flowers are pale pinkish purple and open in mid-spring. This plant should be planted more widely, if only to bring more fun to the garden. It is not commonly grown, but certainly a collectors' item. Zone 6a

Weigela florida 'Sunny Princess'

Bert Verhoef, Boskoop, The Netherlands, 1992

Originally discovered as a sport of the winter-hardy *W. florida* 'Pink Princess' and having the same clear purplish pink flowers, purple-red in bud. 'Sunny Princess' forms a broad, upright, bushy shrub that grows to about 2 m high and wide. The ovate leaves are green, with irregular greenish yellow margins. In autumn they become more reddish. Due to the soft colors of the variegated foliage, 'Sunny Princess' can be widely used for group plantings or for giving a certain accent in the garden. 'Sunny Princess' was given an Award of Recommendation by the Royal Boskoop Horticultural Society in 1994. Zone 5b

Weigela florida 'Suzanne'

Dense, bushy shrub that grows to about 1.75 m high. The leaves are dark green with very conspicuous narrow cream-colored margins. The flowers are pink. 'Suzanne' is a pretty plant with a fresh appearance, due to the good contrast between the leaf centers and margins. Zone 6a

Weigela florida 'Variegata'

Japan, before 1853

Very similar to 'Nana Variegata', but more upright in its habit. 'Variegata' will eventually grow to about 1.5 m high, considerably lower than the species. The pink flowers contrast well against the foliage. Although it easily reverts to green foliage, 'Variegata' is still one of the most widely used variegated flowering shrubs.

This cultivar was introduced by P. F. von Siebold in 1853, who found this shrub in Japan. However, over the years several clones of 'Variegata' seem to have been named, some more stable than others. This is due to the fact that green-leaved *Weigela* now and then produce variegated shoots. These were propagated vegetatively and then put on the market as 'Variegata'. Old cultivars such as 'Kosteri Variegata' and 'Sieboldii Variegata' are very similar and nearly forgotten. Zone 6a

Weigela 'Looymansii Variegata'

Looymans, Oudenbosch, The Netherlands

Broad shrub with the same somewhat spreading habit as the other variegated *Weigela* described here. The leaves are green with conspicuous silvery white margins. The pink flowers open in late spring. Because 'Looymansii Variegata' tends to become somewhat loose with age, it is not a good cultivar. Therefore, I recommend planting one of the newer variegated *Weigela*, which stay more compact and are usually more stable. Zone 6

Weigela 'Nana Variegata'

Belgium, 1861

Relatively low, broad, spreading-upright shrub, usually not growing much higher than about 1 m. The young leaves are green with yellow margins, later becoming yellowish cream. The flowers are light pink but do not add much to the nicely colored foliage. Zone 6a

Weigela 'Olympiade' BRIANT RUBIDOR™

André Briant Nurseries, St. Barthélèmy d'Anjou, France, before 1989

With its denser and more compact habit than other cultivars, as well as the very yellow foliage, 'Olympiade'

Weigela florida 'Variegata' RONALD HOUTMAN

Weigela 'Looymansii Variegata' KLAAS VERBOOM

Weigela 'Nana Variegata' PPH (COLLECTION OF HARRY VAN DE LAAR)

Weinmannia racemosa 'Harlequin' RONALD HOUTMAN

Yucca filamentosa 'Bright Edge' GERT FORTGENS

Weigela 'Olympiade' BRIANT RUBIDOR™ RONALD HOUTMAN

is very distinct. It is a broad, upright shrub that grows to 1.5 m high. The leaves are a splendid yellow with just a small green blotch in the centers. Many leaves are entirely yellow. 'Olympiade' was discovered as a sport of *W.* 'Bristol Ruby', from which it inherited the intense ruby red flowers. The dramatic combination of almost entirely golden yellow foliage and red flowers might be too much for some people. During the first years this cultivar was sold in the United Kingdom it was renamed 'Rubigold' by Blooms of Bressingham. Zone 6a

Weinmannia racemosa 'Harlequin'

Cedar Lodge Nurseries, New Plymouth, New Zealand, 1997

Weinmannia racemosa is one of the approximately 200 species of this mainly tropical genus of evergreen trees and shrubs belonging to the Cunoniaceae (cunonia family). Other species of *Weinmannia* grow in tropical South America, Madagascar, Malaysia, and the Pacific islands. *Weinmannia racemosa* is one of the few species suitable for growing in temperate climates—indeed these are only for the mildest climates.

It is a large shrub to small tree that grows to about 3 m. As in several other genera, the plants have a juvenile and adult stage. When juvenile the leaves of *W. racemosa* are usually trifoliate or three-lobed, occasionally simple. In adult shrubs the leaves are ovate to oval. The white flowers open in slender racemes during summer. 'Harlequin' is a beautiful cultivar with joyfully colored foliage. The leaves are green, with conspicuous deep red margins. Young foliage has cream to light yellow margins. Although not hardy in most temperate regions, 'Harlequin' makes an excellent container plant. Zone 9

Wisteria floribunda 'Nishiki'

Japan, before 1887

Peculiar variegated cultivar of the Japanese *Wisteria*. It is a twining deciduous shrub that grows to about 5 m high. The imparipinnate leaves consist of eleven to seventeen leaflets. These are light green, irregularly mottled and speckled creamy white. During summer the foliage becomes greener. In late May to early June the pale violet-purple flowers open in hanging racemes. These are relatively short, approximately 15 cm. *Wisteria floribunda* 'Mon Nishiki', 'Nishiki Fuji' and 'Variegata' are synonymous with 'Nishiki', a rare cultivar. Zone 6b

Yucca

Interesting evergreen plants with stout, swordlike leaves that form large tufts. Yuccas are of major architectonical value because they are among the few winter-hardy plants that can create a subtropical effect in the garden. This means they should not be planted in any garden, but need to be carefully planned. The flowers are carried in terminal panicles often densely crowded with flowers. About forty species are found throughout North America and Central America. Only a few are cultivated on a large scale. Numerous variegated cultivars have been reported, of which only a few are mentioned here. All yuccas prefer well-drained soil and a sunny location, and it is important the soil does not stay too wet during winter.

Yucca filamentosa 'Bright Edge'

New Zealand, before 1986

Relatively slow-growing cultivar that reaches about 75 cm high. The upright green leaves are striped grayish and have narrow golden yellow margins. The flowers open in July and are creamy white. Zone 5a

Yucca filamentosa 'Variegata'

Before 1870

The name 'Variegata' is commonly used for various variegated clones of *Y. filamentosa*. The only characteristic these clones have in common is that they have grayish green leaves with creamy yellow to creamy white centers. The colors usually are less intense than in 'Bright Edge'. When a yellow-variegated cultivar is wanted, 'Bright Edge', a reliably hardy *Yucca*, is recommended over 'Variegata'. Zone 5a

Yucca flaccida 'Golden Sword'

Clump-forming plant with spreading narrow lanceolate leaves. Contrary to *Y. filamentosa* 'Bright Edge', 'Golden Sword' has yellow leaves with green margins. Like *Y. filamentosa*, *Y. flaccida* is also a stemless species. This means the clumps are formed directly on the ground instead of on a short stem. Zone 5b

Yucca gloriosa 'Variegata'

Before 1850

Small treelike plant, developing a short stem up to 2.5 m. The narrow lanceolate leaves are up to 1 m long and usually sharp-pointed. The leaves are grayish green with irregular yellow stripes and margins. On older leaves the yellow fades to creamy white. The flowers

Yucca filamentosa 'Variegata' J. R. P. VAN HOEY SMITH

Yucca flaccida 'Golden Sword' GERT FORTGENS

Zelkova serrata 'Goshiki' KLAAS VERBOOM

Yucca gloriosa 'Variegata' GERT FORTGENS

are carried in long upright panicles. They open in August and September and are white to slightly pink tinged. *Yucca recurvifolia* 'Marginata' is very similar but has shorter inflorescences and flowers in July and August. In *Y. recurvifolia* 'Variegata' the margins are green and the centers are yellowish. Zone 7b

Zelkova serrata 'Goshiki'

Japan, before 1976

Interesting elmlike tree that stays considerably smaller than the species. It can attain a height of about 10 m, but usually will not grow taller than 5 m or so. The elliptic leaves are deep green and conspicuously mottled yellow to cream. A cultivar called 'Pulverulenta' was imported from Japan by a Dutch grower. The original plant is no longer grown, but the description makes it seem similar to 'Goshiki'. Zone 6a

Zelkova serrata 'Variegata'

Small tree that grows to about 5 m high. The leaves resemble those of *Z. serrata* 'Goshiki', but are dark green with very narrow but quite distinct creamy white to white margins. Both *Zelkova serrata* cultivars described here are quite rare and not widely available. Zone 6a

Zelkova serrata 'Variegata' CHRIS SANDERS

APPENDICES

APPENDIX A
Variegation in Plants

Ben J. M. Zonneveld

Institute of Biology
Clusius Laboratory
Leiden, The Netherlands

In this work, a plant is called variegated if it has different colors on a single leaf. As foliage plants, variegated plants usually arouse more interest than plain green ones, irrespective of the cause of variegation. The underlying cause, however, is important for choosing the proper means of propagation. A large body of literature on this subject has been published (Winkler 1907; Tilney-Basset 1963; Steward and Dermen 1979).

First, readers should understand some basic concepts regarding plant genetics. Like all organisms, plants are built of cells. Each cell has a nucleus, which contains the hereditary material, or DNA. DNA is composed of a long series of the four bases adenine (A), thymine (T), cytosine (C), and guanine (G) that come together in a double-helical molecule. The DNA in the nucleus is bundled into small packets called chromosomes. The chromosomes contain genes, which are made up of specific combinations of these bases. Within a plant's DNA, there are about 25,000 genes that code for all of that plant's characteristics.

Before discussing variegation, the concept of apical organization must be mentioned. In the shoot apex there is an apical dome, or meristem, consisting of three (or two in conifers) cell layers, as elucidated by Satina et al. (1940) in *Datura*. These layers, noted L1, L2, and L3 starting from the outside, cover each other like a glove on the entire plant. The L1, usually a single-cell layer, gives rise to the epidermis. The L2, a single-cell layer below the epidermis, gives rise to all egg cells and pollen. The L3 forms the remainder of the plant and is the only layer present in the roots. Therefore, a truly variegated plant cannot be grown from root cuttings because these contain only one layer.

Another way of naming apical structure is to consider the L1 + L2 as forming the tunica and the L3 as forming the corpus. The tunica divides mainly sideways, whereas the corpus cells divide in all directions and form the bulk of the plant. The same meristem organization can be found in the lateral buds. Only when a mutation (a spontaneous change in the genetic material) takes place in the meristem can a variegated plant arise.

The Relationship between Nuclear and Chloroplast Mutations

The green color in plants is determined by the color of the chloroplasts, small particles responsible for converting carbon dioxide to sugars. This green color can vary with the species, growth circumstances, and the specific combination of chloroplast products and those of nuclear genes. Chloroplast and mitochondria contain their own circular piece of DNA, a remnant of the time they were free-living organisms. During evolution most of the genes of the chloroplast migrated to the nucleus. Of the 1000 or so genes involved with the functioning of the chloroplasts, 900 are now coded for by nuclear genes and only about 100 by genes still on the chloroplast DNA itself.

In a diploid plant, during formation of egg cells and pollen, the amount of nuclear DNA is halved, with each pollen and egg cell containing a single chromosome set (haploid). After the fusion of pollen and egg cells during fertilization, the original chromosome number is restored, resulting in a diploid organism with two chromosome sets. Therefore, in a diploid organism each gene is present twice, one from the seed parent and one from the pollen parent.

This is not true for cytoplasmic inheritance, as exemplified by chloroplasts. First there can be a large number of chloroplasts in a cell—from one or two to a few thousand. In an average *Hosta* cell, there are about ten to thirty chloroplasts; a fraction of these are found in the egg cell but not in the pollen. In most plants, chloroplasts can only be inherited from the seed-bearing parent; only in about 10 percent of species does the pollen parent also contribute chloroplasts (Corriveau and Coleman 1988). The products of chloroplast genes are mainly involved in protein synthesis and photosynthesis. A yellow color in plants can be caused by nuclear, chloroplast, or mitochondrial mutations.

According to the investigations of Vaughn et al. (1978), yellow hostas have a defect in the p700 protein complex. A mutation in a single nuclear gene results in a change in a single protein of this complex. The same mutation is probably responsible for all other yellow-leaved plants. Most mutations leading to changes in the chloroplast are lethal, and offspring with these mutations do not survive. The p700 mutation changes the structure of the chloroplast (lowered granula stacking and dilated thylakoid membranes), in such a way that chloroplasts in the cytoplasm produce a yellow leaf color.

Yellow color due to a mutation in chloroplast DNA (cytoplasmic yellow) is probably only found in a chimeral situation and usually turns white during the growing season. These plants have a different type of mutated chloroplast, with magnograna making the chloroplast nonfunctional (Vaughn et al. 1978). Both in *Zea mays* and *Oenothera* cases have been described where a nuclear gene causes mutations in the chloroplast DNA. These, in turn, can be transmitted maternally, independent of the nuclear mutation. These are called plastome mutator genes.

Yellow Leaf Color

Plants with entirely and mostly permanent yellow leaves are often encountered in conifers, but also in leafy trees. They cannot be considered as variegated, however, having a uniform color. Although yellow leaves are not variegated, I would like to say something about them because the color yellow is present in almost all true variegated, or chimeral, plants.

Yellow shoots can arise for at least two reasons, excluding those that are purely based on environmental conditions. A yellow shoot can arise on a green plant by mutation. In that case, the shoot can usually be grown as a separate plant. In contrast, a yellow branch on a variegated plant in most cases will not survive on its own. This is due to the fact that mutations in different genes are involved. A common example of a mutation that leads to a yellow plant is *Ulmus hollandica* 'Wredei'. This mutation is a nuclear encoded, heterozygous mutation (that is, each of the two gene copies is different) dominant for the yellow color, but recessive for its lethal character. Dominant yellow means that if one of the two genes in a pair is mutated to yellow, the leaf will become yellow. Recessive lethal means that, if only one gene in a pair is mutated, the lethality of the mutation is not expressed and the plant is perfectly viable; however, if both genes are mutated to yellow, this is lethal for a plant, unless the mutation is present in a chimera.

Entirely yellow plants can give rise to leaves with a green margin, resulting in a chimeral variegation. Such a green-margined plant can produce an entirely green branch or a branch with an inverted (that is, a yellow-centered) variegation due to chimeral rearrangement. Green branches can also be produced directly from yellow ones, as seen in *Ulmus hollandica* 'Wredei'. In the latter case, however, these are not due to a chimeral rearrangement, but due to a mitotic recombination changing the genotype of the plant (see below). In these entirely yellow plants, all cells have the same genetic constitution and will give rise to 50 to 60 percent yellow seedlings. Yellow branches on a variegated plant usually do not survive separately. They are the final stage of plants that started with a yellow leaf margin or center and have a different genetic background.

Natural Variegation

Some plants show natural and permanent leaf variegation. In these cases, nearly all plants of that species show the variegation. They can be grown 100 percent true to type from seed. Such plants are not considered here as truly variegated because they are not chimeras. Examples are the yellow spots in *Dracaena surculosa*, the whitish spots on *Pulmonaria*, and the dark leaf rings in *Pelargonium*. Another example is the shiny part on some leaves of *Begonia* species, where air appears locally between the epidermis and the underlying tissues.

In natural variegation, all cells of the plant have the same genotype, which is why they can be grown true from seed. The different colors on a leaf in a naturally variegated plant are the result of differential gene expression, in other words, a gene is only active in certain tissues or leaf parts. For example, flower pigments are only found in the flower not in the leaves, a wax layer is found on the leaf but not on the roots, even though genes for these characters are contained within all of the plant's cells.

Environmental Variegation

Several environmental factors may result in more or less variegated plants. A shortage of trace elements may result in a yellow margin in *Buxus*. Some plants show different leaf colors due to spraying, a toxic compound in the soil, or insect damage. Of course, this is not true variegation. Transplanting or removing the culprit may solve the problem.

Another type of variegation, often a streaked or spotted pattern, can be due to a virus. Often plants with virus are stunted, but sometimes the effect is pleasing. A well-known example of viral variegation is *Aucuba japonica* 'Variegata', although this cultivar is usually considered by nurserymen to be truly variegated.

A special case of environmental variegation is plants that only show deviant leaf colors during part of the year. This often appears in new growth in spring. A good example is found in some *Picea* cultivars that produce yellow shoots in spring that later turn green. This is most likely due to a gene involved in chloroplast functioning that is sensitive to low temperatures. It is also possible that the colored band(s) on the leaves of some *Pinus* cultivars, referred to as "dragon's eyes," are due to temperature or light effects, but this has to be investigated.

Some plants have new growth that is red in spring. This is found naturally in some plants and it can be increased by selection, as in *Pieris* 'Forest Flame'. In other cases the red, or even black, color is due to a mutation resulting in increased anthocyanin production. A good example is *Corylus maxima* 'Purpurea' in which new growth starts black but greens up later. This is a nonchimeral variegation with a defect or change that is present in all cells but only expressed in new growth under certain light or temperature conditions. In some trees, such as the purple beech (*Fagus sylvatica* f. *purpurea*), the black color is more permanent.

Occasionally, in crosses between species unstable situations arise when the part of the nuclear DNA derived from the pollen parent must cooperate with the maternal chloroplast genes. Such hybrids may be more sensitive to environmental stresses like heat and light. This might give rise to permanent unstable characteristics, resulting in yellow patches or entirely yellow leaves. If the seedlings survive, reshuffling of the DNA might lead to a greener and vital plant.

True or Chimeral Variegation

All true variegated plants are chimeras, that is, they contain genetically different cell layers. All chimeras arise when a cell undergoes a mutation. This mutated cell divides and then results in a partly or totally genetically different cell layer. These are called mericlinal chimeras if only part of a single layer is affected and sectorial chimeras if parts of all layers are affected. These partial chimeras, in turn, can lead to the much more stable periclinal chimeras, in which all cells of a single layer are genetically different from the rest of the plant. These genetic differences can be due to a nuclear or a cytoplasmic mutation.

Chimeras are only visible if they affect the leaf color or any other visible trait. However, more types of chimeras mosaics exist. For example, the presence or absence of hairs/spines as in thornless *Rubus* and the hairless peaches called nectarines. The presence of two different species in a single plant is called a graft chimera. A well-known example is +*Laburnocytisus*, a combination of a *Cytisus* and a *Laburnum*.

Chimeras, even periclinal chimeras, are nearly always unstable to a certain extent and often have green or yellow branches. The resulting deviating branches are called *sports* or *bud variants* and are rarely mutations (see below). In most cases seeds will produce nearly all green or all yellow/white seedlings, depending on the genotype of the L2.

Of course, some of the above categories can be combined in a single plant. An *Aucuba* with yellow spots from a virus, as found in most, can develop yellow margins. A purple beech can at the same time have a true variegation, such as *Fagus sylvatica* 'Purpurea Tricolor'.

Explanation of True Variegation

The number of layers involved in building monocots, dicots, and conifers

Plants are built from different layers that are more or less independent from each other. In plain green plants (and in natural variegation) all cell layers are genetically identical. A mutation can arise in each of these layers. If one of the layers mutates, the resulting plant is a chimera. To explain the different branches that might arise from such a chimera, different aspects of the structure of monocots, dicots, and conifers will be discussed.

Monocots. In this book, monocots are only represented by *Yucca*, but variegation is very common in herbaceous monocots such as *Hosta* and *Sanseveria*. Monocots are plants that germinate from seed with a single seed lobe (cotyl) that extracts its food from the endosperm. They are also characterized by the fact that the L1 not only forms the epidermis but also a significant part of the margin of the leaf. Moreover, the L1 or epidermis of monocots has chloroplasts in all cells. The result is that in plants such as *Yucca filamentosa* 'Variegata' or *Sanseveria trifasciata* 'Laurentii' the yellow margin of the leaf is formed by the L1. The L2, from which the gametes arise, only forms a single layer in the leaf and is rarely visible.

Dicots. Most plants in this book are dicots, which have two seed lobes. The main food reserve is not in the endosperm but in the seed lobes. Contrary to the monocots the dicots have no chloroplasts in the epidermal cells, apart from the stomata. Also the L1 does not contribute markedly to the margin of the leaf: it is more or less a colorless outer covering. In dicots it is the L2 that contributes to the margin of the leaf. Therefore, in *Hedera helix* 'Goldheart' the green margin of the leaf is from the L2, not from the L1. The yellow center of the leaf is formed by the L3, and in this case the color is not strongly influenced by the covering with a single green layer of the L2. Because seedlings are always derived from the L2, we only get green seedlings from dicots with a white or yellow center and white or yellow seedlings from dicots with a white or yellow edge.

Conifers. Conifers with scaly foliage have only two cell layers. Some genetically yellow plants give rise to 50–60 percent yellow offspring. These completely yellow conifers are not considered to be truly variegated. Another possibility is that one of the two layers is yellow or white, and in most cases only the second, inner layer is yellow/white (Pohlheim 1971). The plant may look a bit more yellow or bluish and might give rise to entirely yellow/white branches. In these cases the yellow or white branch rarely survives independently and these plants cannot be grown as such from seeds. Some *Taxus* cultivars have a seemingly yellow leaf margin, but it is a yellow leaf that starts to green up early from the main vein and ends as a fully green leaf. This suggests a two-layered meristem here as well.

The relationship between the terms "mutation" and "sport"

The terms *mutation* and *sport* are often used interchangeably. However, a mutation is a heritable change in the DNA of an organism. A sport is a shoot that deviates from the parent plant, irrespective of the cause. A sport can arise due to several different causes: chimeral rearrangement, that is, an exchange of cells between layers; mitotic recombination, an exchange of parts of chromosomes; a rare mutation, a change in the DNA; or loss or gain of whole chromosomes or sets of chromosomes.

Chimeral rearrangement. Again, monocots and dicots have a three-layered structure, and the layers cover each other like a glove. A chimeral rearrangement is an exchange of cells from one layer to another in the meristem of a leaf bud. Alternatively, but with the same result, a new leaf bud may start from only two layers. An example is a yellow-margined *Euonymus fortunei* producing a completely yellow branch. A chimeral rearrangement can only take place when the plant is already a chimera and a plant can only be a chimera if a mutation has taken place before.

Recombination or crossing-over. The exchange of part of a chromosome during mitosis in the plant body is called mitotic recombination, or somatic crossing-over (Marcotrigiano 1997). Diploid plants contain two copies of each gene. If a mutation arises in only one copy of a gene pair, we usually don't see anything unless the gene is dominant, like most mutations leading to a yellow leaf. Therefore, a yellow plant has in each cell a dominant gene for yellow and a recessive gene for green chloroplasts. If parts of chromosomes are exchanged (that is, crossing-over occurs) the result can be a purely green cell and a double yellow (that is, white) cell. One of these cells may be lost, and the surviving cell can lead to an entire layer. If this happens in a leaf bud of a yellow plant, it can lead to a green (white) center or margin in the plant. In a green margin, the gene for yellow has recombined with the gene for green, resulting in a cell with two green genes. In a white margin of a yellow plant, the gene for yellow is present twice due to recombination. This recombination in a yellow plant can thus result in a plant with green or white borders in the leaves. Thus, a mutation leading to an entirely yellow plant can in turn give rise to a sport with a green margin or center or an entirely green branch due to somatic crossing-over. The latter is often seen in *Ulmus hollandica* 'Wredei'.

Mutation. Mutation, a spontaneous or induced change in DNA, is a rare process: a single gene has approximately a one in 100,000 chance of mutating. In plants DNA can be found in the nucleus, in chloroplasts, and in mitochondria.

A mutation can take place in a leaf bud—a somatic mutation, that is, one that affects only the branch involved—usually leading to a change in part of that organism. Nuclear mutations can be inherited from both parents, whereas cytoplasmic mutations in the DNA of chloroplast or mitochondria can, with a few exceptions, only be transmitted via the maternal parent (seed parent). If a leaf changes from green to yellow, it can be caused indirectly by a nuclear mutation or directly by a mutation in the chloroplast DNA. So, the fact that the chloroplast is in the cytoplasm does not mean that a change in its color can be transmitted to offspring via cytoplasmic inheritance. On the contrary, the change from green to an entirely yellow branch is mostly due to nuclear mutation.

Mutations seem to arise often in tissue culture, partly due to the fact that culture is a very unnatural environment. If a plant is vegetatively propagated for a long time, mutation frequency will increase due to the accumulation of many small mutations. In natural seed formation, however, most deleterious mutations are purged during formation of pollen and egg cells.

Back mutation. If a mutant mutates back to the wild type, a back mutations has occurred. Back mutations are nearly as rare as the frequency of the original, or forward, mutations. An entirely green branch from a green-margined plant is usually not a back mutation but a chimeral rearrangement. An entirely green branch from a yellow plant is not mutated back either (or rarely so) but the result of the much more frequent somatic crossing-over or somatic recombination. A green branch from a chimera reverts by a reshuffling of cells (chimeral rearrangement to the original green plant), whereas a green branch from a yellow plant gives rise to green plants due to breakage and reunion of chromosomes (recombination). In the latter case, the resulting green plants are not identical to the original plant and should not be named as such.

Loss or gain of whole chromosomes or chromosome sets. During cell division, something occasionally goes wrong with partitioning of chromosomes to daughter cells. Each should receive the same number (after doubling of the chromosomes) as the parent cell had originally. A single chromosome might end up in the wrong cell, leading to aneuploidy and often low fertility. Occasionally, all chromosomes migrate to a single cell, leading to a doubling of the chromosomes in a single cell. This cell may give rise to a whole layer with a double number of chromosomes, known as a ploidy chimera. Several of these have been found in *Hosta* (Zonneveld and van Iren 2000) and *Sanseveria*. It is peculiar that, at least in *Hosta*, the change in ploidy in one of the layers always coincides with a change in leaf color. All ten or so cases of ploidy chimeras in *Hosta* are of this type. *Sanseveria trifasciata* 'Laurentii' has a central green diploid band, but the yellow margin is tetraploid.

How to Discriminate between Different Types of Variegation

Leaves can have different variegation patterns. If we confine ourselves to yellow mutations we can find the yellow color as a margin, a center, spots, streaks, veins, leaf tips, leaf bases, or entire leaves. Yellow spots, for instance, can be due to a virus as in *Aucuba*, due to a mutation as in *Aspidistra*, or be a natural variegation as in *Dracaena surculosa*. Only experiments, especially crossings, can prove what we have.

Environmentally induced variegation can usually be traced by transplanting the green and the seemingly variegated plant to identical locales; assuming the environmental deficiencies are rectified, the variegation will disappear. To exclude the possibility that variegation is due to a virus, graft a green scion on a variegated stock. If the stock has a virus, it often will be transmitted to the green scion. Natural and true/chimeral variegation can be differentiated because the latter often gives rise to yellow or green branches.

Seedlings can also be reared to differentiate between natural and true/chimeral variegation. Natural variegation is inherited as 100 percent true, and it is usually found as such in all wild members of that species. Plants with a chimeral variegation, however, cannot be grown from seed but must be vegetatively propagated. If sown, one usually gets only green or only yellow/white offspring from plants with a chimeral variegation. The exceptions are plants with irregular yellow or white streaks, which can give a fair number of streaked offspring that in time will result in stable periclinal chimeras.

To find out whether streaked variegation or entirely yellow leaves are inherited only from the seed parent or from the pollen parent also, one has to perform reciprocal crosses. If the variegation is cytoplasmically inherited, only a streaked maternal parent will produce streaked offspring and the pollen parent is irrelevant. However, if the variegation is inherited via nuclear genes, either a seed or pollen parent could produce streaked offspring.

APPENDIX B
Variegated Woody Plants by Family

In the text, I only occasionally mention which family the plants belong to. These are important facts, however, especially when looking at relationships between plants. Therefore, I present a list of all families and their genera. When writing this book I mainly used the *List of Names of Woody Plants* (Hoffman et al. 2000) for the correct naming of genera, species, hybrids, and cultivars as well as the *International Code of Nomenclature for Cultivated Plants* (1995). For the classification by family, however, I used the *Annals of the Missouri Botanical Garden*. In 1998 Bremer et al. published a widely accepted ordinal classification in the journal. Major differences with the traditional classification are that Aceraceae and Hippocastanaceae are included in the Sapindaceae and that the large but diverse Caprifoliaceae are split into several smaller families.

ACERACEAE, see SAPINDACEAE

ACTINIDIACEAE
Actinidia

ADOXACEAE
Sambucus
Viburnum

AGAVACEAE
Yucca

APOCYNACEAE
Trachelospermum
Vinca

AQUIFOLIACEAE
Ilex

ARALIACEAE
Aralia
Eleutherococcus
×Fatshedera
Fatsia
Hedera
Pseudopanax

ASTERACEAE
Olearia

AUCUBACEAE
Aucuba

BERBERIDACEAE
Berberis
Mahonia

BETULACEAE
Carpinus

BIGNONIACEAE
Catalpa

BUDDLEJACEAE
Buddleja

BUXACEAE
Buxus
Pachysandra

CAPRIFOLIACEAE (see also ADOXACEAE, DIERVILLACEAE, and LINNAEACEAE)
Lonicera
Symphoricarpos

CELASTRACEAE
Euonymus

CISTACEAE
Cistus

CLETHRACEAE
Clethra

CLUSIACEAE
Hypericum

CORNACEAE (see also AUCUBACEAE and GRISELINIACEAE)
Cornus

CUNONIACEAE
Weinmannia

CUPRESSACEAE
Calocedrus
Chamaecyparis
Cupressus
×*Cuprocyparis*
Juniperus
Microbiota
Thuja
Thujopsis
Xanthocyparis

DIERVILLACEAE
Weigela

ELAEAGNACEAE
Elaeagnus

ERICACEAE
Daboecia
Enkianthus
Leucothoe
Pieris
Rhododendron
Vaccinium

FABACEAE
Caragana
Cercis
Gymnocladus
Sophora
Wisteria

FAGACEAE
Castanea
Fagus
Quercus

FLACOURTIACEAE
Azara

GINKGOACEAE
Ginkgo

GRISELINIACEAE
Griselinia

GROSSULARIACEAE
Escallonia
Ribes

HAMAMELIDACEAE
Hamamelis
Liquidambar
Parrotia

HIPPOCASTANACEAE, see SAPINDACEAE

HYDRANGEACEAE
Deutzia
Hydrangea
Philadelphus
Schizophragma

LAMIACEAE
Caryopteris
Clerodendrum
Lavandula
Rosmarinus
Salvia

LARDIZABALACEAE
Akebia

LINNAEACEAE
Abelia

MAGNOLIACEAE
Liriodendron
Magnolia

MALVACEAE
Hibiscus
Hoheria
Lavatera
Tilia

MYRTACEAE
Lophomyrtus
Luma
Metrosideros
Myrtus
Ugni

OLEACEAE
Forsythia
Fraxinus
Jasminum
Ligustrum
Osmanthus
Syringa

ONAGRACEAE
Fuchsia

PINACEAE
Cedrus
Picea
Pinus

PITTOSPORACEAE
Pittosporum

PLATANACEAE
Platanus

PODOCARPACEAE
Podocarpus

RHAMNACEAE
Berchemia
Ceanothus
Rhamnus

ROSACEAE
Cotoneaster
Crataegus
Kerria
Malus
Photinia
Potentilla
Prunus
Pyracantha
Rosa
Rubus
Sorbus
Spiraea

RUBIACEAE
Coprosma

RUTACEAE
Citrus
Orixa
Ruta

SALICACEAE
Populus
Salix

SAPINDACEAE
Acer
Aesculus

SCHISANDRACEAE
Kadsura

SCROPHULARIACEAE
Hebe

SIMAROUBACEAE
Ailanthus

SOLANACEAE
Lycianthes
Solanum

STACHYURACEAE
Stachyurus

STYRACACEAE
Halesia

TAXACEAE
Taxus
Torreya

TAXODIACEAE
Cryptomeria
Metasequoia
Sciadopitys
Sequoia
Sequoiadendron

THEACEAE
Camellia
Cleyera

THYMELAEACEAE
Daphne

TILIACEAE, see MALVACEAE

ULMACEAE
Ulmus
Zelkova

VERBENACEAE, see LAMIACEAE

VITACEAE
Ampelopsis

WINTERACEAE
Pseudowintera
Tasmannia

APPENDIX C
Plant Lists

The plant lists in this appendix can be used to help you find the right variegated plant for the right place. All plants mentioned here refer only to plants described in this book. For example, when it states "*Magnolia* (all)" under "Variegated plants with white flowers," this means that all variegated magnolias described here are white flowering, not that all magnolias are white flowering.

Variegated Plants by Habit

Although the habit and height of a plant sometimes depends on the climate, these characteristics can be divided into major groups.

Large variegated trees

Large trees are usually vigorous growers and are only suitable in large gardens, parks, and as street trees. Of course, they make good trees in the landscape as well, but because their foliage is variegated, the effect is not very natural. All trees mentioned are deciduous.

Acer negundo (all)
Acer platanoides 'Drummondii'
Acer pseudoplatanus (all)
Ailanthus altissima 'Aucubaefolia'
Carpinus betulus 'Variegatus'
Castanea (all)
Fagus sylvatica 'Franken'
Fagus sylvatica 'Marmorata'
Fagus sylvatica 'Marmor Star'
Fagus sylvatica 'Oudenbosch'
Fagus sylvatica 'Rolf Marquardt'
Fagus sylvatica 'Striata'
Fagus sylvatica 'Viridivariegata'
Fraxinus (all)
Gymnocladus dioica 'Variegatus'
Liriodendron (all)
Platanus ×acerifolia 'Suttneri'
Populus candicans 'Aurora'
Quercus (all)

Small to medium-sized variegated trees

Vigorous to moderately vigorous trees that grow to about 7 m high. They are suitable for large as well as small gardens. Most are not vigorous enough to work well as street trees. However, they can be used as specimen trees in landscaping or public parks. All trees mentioned are deciduous.

Acer buergerianum (all)
Acer campestre (all)
Acer crataegifolium 'Veitchii'
Acer palmatum 'Ao Kanzashi'
Acer palmatum 'Asahi Zuru'
Acer palmatum 'Higasayama'
Acer palmatum 'Kagiri Nishiki'
Acer palmatum 'Kara Ori Nishiki'
Acer palmatum 'Pevé Multicolor'
Acer pectinatum 'Alice'
Acer platanoides 'Walderseei'
Acer rufinerve (all)
Aesculus (all)
Catalpa (all)
Cornus nuttallii 'Goldspot'
Crataegus (all)
Fagus sylvatica 'Albomarginata'

Fagus sylvatica 'Argenteomarmorata'
Fagus sylvatica 'Bicolor Sartini'
Fagus sylvatica 'Feuerglut'
Fagus sylvatica 'Feuermarmor'
Fagus sylvatica 'Luteovariegata'
Fagus sylvatica 'Purpurea Tricolor'
Fagus sylvatica 'Silberthaler'
Fagus sylvatica 'Silverwood'
Halesia (all)
Liquidambar (all)
Luma apiculata 'Glanleam Gold'
Magnolia (all)
Malus 'Dovar'
Salix cinerea (all)
Sophora japonica 'Variegata'
Sorbus (all)
Syringa vulgaris 'Aucubaefolia'
Tilia cordata 'Mixed Emotions'
Ulmus minor 'Argenteovariegata'
Ulmus minor 'Variegata'
Zelkova (all)

Large variegated shrubs

Most large shrubs are fast growing and reach about 5 m high. They are suitable for all except the smallest gardens and usually make excellent specimen plants. Because of their size, large variegated shrubs are less suitable for use in group plantings.

DECIDUOUS
Acer palmatum 'Aka Shigi Tatsu Sawa'
Acer palmatum 'Beni Shichi Henge'
Acer palmatum 'Butterfly'
Acer palmatum 'Kara Ori Nishiki'
Acer palmatum 'Karasugawa'
Acer palmatum 'Kasagiyama'
Acer palmatum 'Matsugae'
Acer palmatum 'Nishiki Gasane'
Acer palmatum 'Okukuji Nishiki'
Acer palmatum 'Rugose Select'
Acer palmatum 'Shojo-no-mai'
Acer palmatum 'Tsuma Gaki'
Acer palmatum 'Uki Gumo'
Acer pictum 'Hoshi Yadori'
Acer rubescens (all)
Aralia (all)
Cercis canadensis 'Silver Cloud'
Clerodendron trichotomum 'Carnival'
Cornus controversa 'Variegata'
Cornus florida (all)
Cornus kousa (all)
Cornus mas (all)
Disanthus cercidifolius 'Ena Nishiki'
Lavatera arborea 'Variegata'
Parrotia persica 'Lamplighter'
Ribes (all)
Sambucus nigra (all)
Ulmus minor 'Silvery Gem'
Ulmus parvifolia 'Frosty'

EVERGREEN
Ceanothus griseus 'Silver Surprise'
Ceanothus 'Pershore Zanzibar' ZANZIBAR™
Cornus capitata 'Ragdoll'
Elaeagnus ×ebbingei (all)
Griselinia (all)
Hoheria populnea 'Alba Variegata'
Ilex ×altaclerensis (all)
Ilex aquifolium 'Angustimarginata Aurea'
Ilex aquifolium 'Argentea Marginata'
Ilex aquifolium 'Argentea Marginata Pendula'
Ilex aquifolium 'Aurea Marginata Pendula'
Ilex aquifolium 'Aurifodina'
Ilex aquifolium 'Crispa Aureo Picta'
Ilex aquifolium 'Elegantissima'
Ilex aquifolium 'Golden Milkboy'
Ilex aquifolium 'Golden Milkmaid'
Ilex aquifolium 'Golden Queen'
Ilex aquifolium 'Golden van Tol'
Ilex aquifolium 'Gold Flash'
Ilex aquifolium 'Handsworth New Silver'
Ilex aquifolium 'Laurifolia Aurea'
Ilex aquifolium 'Lurida Variegata'
Ilex aquifolium 'Madame Briot'
Ilex aquifolium 'Pyramidalis Aurea Marginata'
Ilex aquifolium 'Rubricaulis Aurea'
Ilex aquifolium 'Scotica Aureopicta'
Ilex aquifolium 'Silver Milkboy'
Ilex aquifolium 'Silver Milkmaid'
Ilex aquifolium 'Silver Queen'
Ilex aquifolium 'Silver van Tol'
Ilex aquifolium 'Watereriana'
Ilex aquifolium 'Whitesail'
Ligustrum japonicum (all)
Ligustrum lucidum (all)
Pittosporum 'Garnettii'
Pittosporum ralphii 'Variegatum'
Pittosporum tenuifolium 'Sterling Gold'
Pittosporum tenuifolium 'Sterling Mist'

Small to medium-sized variegated shrubs

Moderately to slow-growing shrubs that suit every garden, no matter the size. The largest shrubs in this group will eventually attain a height of 3 m, but many stay considerably smaller. Most *Berberis thunbergii* cultivars, for instance, will not grow higher than 1 m. The smallest shrubs, such as *Thymus*, are also suitable for rock gardens.

DECIDUOUS
Abelia (all)
Acer palmatum 'Goshiki Shidare'
Acer palmatum 'Kiyo Hime'
Acer palmatum 'Pink Ballerina'
Acer palmatum 'Toyama Nishiki'
Acer pictum 'Usu Gumo'
Berberis ×ottawensis 'Silver Miles'
Berberis thunbergii 'Atropurpurea'
Berberis thunbergii 'Atropurpurea Nana'
Berberis thunbergii 'Coronita'
Berberis thunbergii 'Golden Ring'
Berberis thunbergii 'Green Carpet'
Berberis thunbergii 'Harlequin'
Berberis thunbergii 'Kelleriis'
Berberis thunbergii 'Pink Attraction'
Berberis thunbergii 'Pink Queen'
Berberis thunbergii 'Rose Glow'
Berberis thunbergii 'Rosetta'
Berberis thunbergii 'Silver Beauty'
Berberis thunbergii 'Silver Bells'
Buddleja (all)
Caragana arborescens 'Anny's Golden Cascade'
Clerodendron bungei 'Pink Diamond'
Clethra alnifolia 'Creel's Calico'
Cornus alba (all)
Cornus alternifolia 'Variegata'
Cornus stolonifera (all)
Daphne ×burkwoodii (all)
Deutzia crenata 'Summer Snow'
Eleutherococcus (all)
Enkianthus campanulatus 'Tokyo Masquerade'

Euonymus europaeus 'Aucubifolius'
Euonymus hamiltonianus 'Rainbow'
Euonymus hamiltonianus 'Snow'
Euonymus phellomanus 'Silver Surprise'
Forsythia (all)
Fuchsia (all)
Hamamelis (all)
Hibiscus (all)
Hydrangea (all)
Hypericum (all)
Kerria (all)
Ligustrum vulgare 'Aureovariegatum'
Ligustrum tschonoskii 'Glimmer'
Lonicera canadensis 'Marble King'
Lycianthes rantonnetii 'Variegatum'
Orixa japonica 'Variegata'
Philadelphus (all)
Potentilla (all)
Prunus ceracifera 'Hessei'
Pyracantha (all)
Rhamnus frangula 'De Wildert'
Rosa (all)
Rubus microphyllus 'Variegatus'
Salix integra (all)
Salvia officinalis (all)
Spiraea (all)
Stachyurus (all)
Symphoricarpos (all)
Syringa emodi 'Aureovariegata'
Ulmus parvifolia 'Geisha'
Viburnum ×*carlcephalum* 'Van der Maat'
Viburnum lantana 'Variegatum'
Viburnum opulus 'Kaleidoscope'
Weigela (all)

EVERGREEN
Aucuba (all)
Azara microphylla 'Variegata'
Berberis stenophylla 'Pink Pearl'
Buxus (all)
Camellia ×*williamsii* 'Golden Spangles'
Ceanothus griseus 'Silver Surprise'
Ceanothus 'Perado' EL DORADO™
Ceanothus 'Pershore Zanzibar' ZANZIBAR™
Cistus (all)
Citrus (all)
Cleyera (all)
Coprosma (all)
Cotoneaster (all)
Daboecia cantabrica 'Rainbow'
Daphne cneorum 'Variegatum'
Daphne odora 'Aureomarginata'
Daphne odora 'Geisha Girl'
Daphne odora 'Variegata
Elaeagnus pungens (all)
Escallonia (all)
Euonymus fortunei (all)
Euonymus japonicus (all)
×*Fatshedera* (all)
Fatsia japonica 'Variegata'
Hebe (all)
Hedera helix 'Golden Wedding'
Hedera helix 'Ice Cream'
Ilex aquifolium 'Ferox Argentea'
Ilex aquifolium 'Ferox Aurea'
Ilex aquifolium 'Golden Hedgehog'
Ilex aquifolium 'Ingramii'
Ilex aquifolium 'Maderensis Variegata'
Ilex aquifolium 'Myrtifolia Aurea Maculata'
Ilex aquifolium 'Myrtifolia Aurea Marginata'
Ilex aquifolium 'Ovata Aurea'
Ilex cornuta 'O. Spring'
Ilex crenata (all)
Ilex ×*meserveae* 'Golden Prince'
Lavandula ×*intermedia* 'Burgoldeen'
Leucothoe walteri 'Rainbow'
Ligustrum ovalifolium (all)
Lonicera nitida (all)
Lophomyrtus (all)
Mahonia aquifolium 'Versicolor'
Metrosideros (all)
Myrtus communis 'Variegata'
Olearia (all)
Osmanthus (all)
Pachysandra (all)
Photinia (all)
Pieris (all)
Pittosporum crassifolium 'Variegatum'
Pittosporum eugenioides 'Variegatum'
Pittosporum heterophyllum 'La Blanca'
Pittosporum 'Mystery'
Pittosporum tenuifolium 'Elizabeth'
Pittosporum tenuifolium 'Gold Star'
Pittosporum tenuifolium 'Irene Paterson'
Pittosporum tenuifolium 'Marjorie Channon'
Pittosporum tenuifolium 'Silver Queen'
Pittosporum tenuifolium 'Variegatum'
Pittosporum tobira 'Variegatum'
Prunus laurocerasus (all)
Prunus lusitanica 'Variegata'
Pseudopanax lessonii 'Gold Splash'
Pseudowintera colorata
Rhododendron (Japanese azalea; all)
Rosmarinus (all)
Ruta graveolens 'Variegatus'
Tasmannia aromatica 'Suzette'
Thymus (all)
Ugni molinae 'Flambeau'
Vaccinium vitis-idaea 'Dolinda'
Viburnum rhytidophyllum 'Variegatum'
Viburnum tinus
Vinca (all)
Weinmannia racemosa 'Harlequin'
Yucca (all)

Variegated shrubs for groundcover

Variegated groundcover shrubs can be very useful in the garden. Because they are capable of covering the soil, fewer weeds will have a chance to grow and sow. Furthermore, they have an unexpected ornamental value, as the foliage is often brighter than the foliage of their green counterparts. Some plants, like *Euonymus fortunei* and *Hedera helix*, will climb on any obstacle they encounter. If this is not wanted, the climbing branches must be removed. All groundcover shrubs mentioned are evergreen, except *Berberis thunbergii* 'Silver Carpet'.

Berberis thunbergii 'Silver Carpet'
Ceanothus griseus 'Diamond Heights'
Coprosma ×*kirkii* 'Kirkii Variegata'
Coprosma 'Kiwi Gold'
Coprosma 'Kiwi Silver'
Cotoneaster (all)
Euonymus fortunei (all)
Hedera (all except *Hedera helix* 'Golden Wedding' and 'Ice Cream')
Leucothoe walteri (all)

Pachysandra (all)
Rhododendron (Japanese azalea)
Thymus 'Doone Valley'
Thymus praecox 'Goldstream'
Vaccinium vitis-idaea 'Dolinda'
Vinca (all)

Climbers

As with the groundcovers, the variegated climbers can also add something extra to a garden. Some are very common, such as *Ampelopsis glandulosa* 'Elegans' and *Hedera*, others, such as *Akebia quinata* 'Variegata' and *Trachelospermum*, are less common. There is a variegated climber for every wall or fence.

DECIDUOUS
Actinidia kolomikta
Actinidia pilosula
Akebia quinata 'Variegata'
Ampelopsis glandulosa 'Elegans'
Berchemia scandens 'Variegata'
Jasminum (all)
Lonicera ×*italica* 'Sherlite'
Rubus fruticosus 'Variegatus'
Schizophragma hydrangeoides 'Moonlight'
Solanum dulcamara 'Variegatum'
Wisteria floribunda 'Nishiki'

EVERGREEN
Hedera (all except *Hedera helix* 'Golden Wedding' and 'Ice Cream')
Kadsura japonica 'Fukurin'
Lonicera japonica (all)
Trachelospermum (all)

Variegated conifers by foliage texture

Conifers can roughly be divided into three groups. The first group is conifers with needles. The needles are placed solitary (*Picea*) or in bundles (*Cedrus*, *Pinus*), called fascicles. The second group consists of conifers with scaly foliage. The scales are usually quite small and placed on each other like roofing tiles. In some genera the scales spread a nice fragrance when crushed, of which *Thuja* is the best example. The third group simply consists of two taxa, *Ginkgo biloba* and *Metasequoia glyptostroboides*. *Ginkgo* is actually not a conifer but a gymnosperm. However, *Gingko* is usually placed with the conifers, its closest allies. *Ginkgo biloba* does not have needles or scales; it has leaves. Although most conifers are evergreen, some are deciduous. Only a handful of the deciduous conifers have variegated foliage.

VARIEGATED CONIFERS WITH NEEDLES
Cedrus
Metasequoia
Picea
Pinus
Podocarpus
Sciadopitys
Sequoia
Taxus
Torreya

VARIEGATED CONIFERS WITH SCALES
Calocedrus
Chamaecyparis
Cryptomeria
×*Cupressocyparis*
Cupressus
Juniperus
Microbiota decussata 'Sinclair'
Sequoiadendron
Thuja
Thujopsis

DECIDUOUS VARIEGATED CONIFERS
Ginkgo
Metasequoia

Additional Features of Variegated Plants

When choosing variegated plants more features than height or deciduousness are important. In the following lists, other features of variegated plants are highlighted.

Variegated plants with spines or thorns

Two types of prickles exist: spines and thorns. The spines grow more or less randomly on a branch or leaf. Good examples of spiny plants are *Ilex*, *Rosa*, and *Rubus*. In contrast, a thorn grows in a place where a branch, bud, or leaf is normally expected. Fine examples of thorny plants are *Berberis* and *Pyracantha*. Prickly plants can be used in so-called defensive plantings. When the owner of a garden does not want people to go through the garden, these prickly plants can be used to keep them out. Apart from their prickly habit, most of these have other ornamental values as well. At least they are good foliage plants.

DECIDUOUS
Aralia
Berberis ×*ottawensis* 'Silver Miles'
Berberis thunbergii (all)
Crataegus
Eleutherococcus
Prunus cerasifera 'Hessei'
Pyracantha
Rosa
Rubus

EVERGREEN
Berberis stenophylla 'Pink Pearl'
Citrus
Elaeagnus pungens
Ilex ×*altaclerensis*
Ilex aquifolium
Ilex cornuta
Ilex ×*meserveae*

Variegated flowering plants

Only plants with conspicuous flowers are mentioned in the following lists. Plants with inconspicuous flowers, such as *Ilex aquifolium*, are not mentioned. Although variegated foliage is usually the main feature of these plants, some have highly ornamental and very attractive flowers. In many cases, these go very well with the foliage. Of course, this is always a matter of personal taste.

WHITE FLOWERS, DECIDUOUS

Actinidia kolomikta
Aesculus hippocastanum 'Luteovariegata'
Berchemia scandens 'Variegata'
Clerodendron trichotomum 'Carnival'
Clethra alnifolia 'Creel's Calico'
Cornus florida florida 'Daybreak' CHEROKEE DAYBREAK™
Cornus florida 'First Lady'
Cornus florida 'George Henry Ford'
Cornus florida 'Golden Nugget'
Cornus florida 'Rainbow'
Cornus florida 'Welchii'
Cornus kousa (all)
Cornus nuttallii 'Goldspot'
Deutzia crenata 'Summer Snow'
Halesia (all)
Jasminum (all)
Kerria japonica 'White Cloud'
Ligustrum ovalifolium (all)
Ligustrum tschonoskii 'Glimmer'
Ligustrum vulgare (all)
Malus 'Dovar'
Philadelphus (all)
Pyracantha (all)
Rosa wichuraiana 'Variegata'
Spiraea (all)
Viburnum ×*carlcephalum* 'Van der Maat'
Viburnum lantana 'Variegatum'
Viburnum opulus 'Kaleidoscope'

WHITE FLOWERS, EVERGREEN

Citrus (all)
Hebe 'Silver Dollar'
Hoheria populnea 'Alba Variegata'
Leucothoe walteri
Ligustrum japonicum (all)
Ligustrum lucidum (all)
Ligustrum sinense 'Variegatum'
Lonicera japonica 'Aureoreticulata'
Lonicera japonica 'Mint Crisp'
Magnolia (all)
Olearia arborescens 'Variegata'
Pieris (all)
Pittosporum heterophyllum 'La Blanca'
Trachelospermum (all)
Viburnum rhytidophyllum 'Variegatum'
Viburnum tinus (all)
Vinca minor 'Alba Variegata'
Yucca (all)

PINK OR PINKISH FLOWERS, DECIDUOUS

Actinidia pilosula
Akebia quinata 'Variegata'
Cercis canadensis 'Silver Cloud'
Clerodendron bungei 'Pink Diamond'
Cornus florida 'Junior Miss Variegated'
Cornus florida 'Pink Flame'
Cornus florida 'Sunset' CHEROKEE SUNSET™
Daphne ×*burkwoodii* (all)
Fuchsia magellanica 'Sharpitor'
Hydrangea macrophylla (all)
Lonicera ×*italica* 'Sherlite'
Prunus cerasifera 'Hessei'
Rosa 'Verschuren'
Syringa (all)
Weigela 'Courtatom' COULEUR D'AUTOMNE™
Weigela florida 'Caricature'
Weigela florida 'Nana Variegata'
Weigela florida 'Sunny Princess'
Weigela florida 'Suzanne'
Weigela florida 'Variegata'
Weigela 'Looymansii Variegata'

PINK OR PINKISH FLOWERS, EVERGREEN

Cistus (all)
Daphne cneorum 'Variegatum'
Daphne odora (all)
Escallonia (all)
Hebe 'Goldrush'
Hebe 'Lady Ann'
Hebe 'Orphan Annie'
Lonicera japonica 'Maskerade'
Rhododendron 'Blattgold'
Rhododendron 'Goldflimmer'
Rhododendron 'Silver Sword' (Japanese azalea)
Rhododendron 'Salmon's Leap' (Japanese azalea)
Rhododendron 'Silver Queen' (Japanese azalea)
Thymus (all)

RED FLOWERS, DECIDUOUS

Aesculus ×*carnea* 'Aureomarginata'
Fuchsia 'John Ridding' FIRECRACKER™
Rosa 'Cocty' CURIOSITY™
Weigela 'Brigela' FRENCH LACE™
Weigela 'Olympiade'

RED FLOWERS, EVERGREEN

Metrosideros (all)
Rhododendron 'Hot Shot Variegated' (Japanese azalea)

PURPLE FLOWERS, DECIDUOUS

Buddleja davidii (all)
Fuchsia magellanica 'Variegata'
Fuchsia magellanica 'Versicolor'
Fuchsia 'Tom West'
Hibiscus (all)
Lavatera arborea 'Variegata'
Lycianthes rantonnetii 'Variegatum'
Wisteria floribunda 'Nishiki'

PURPLE FLOWERS, EVERGREEN

Daboecia cantabrica 'Rainbow'
Hebe ×*andersonii* (all)
Hebe ×*franciscana* 'Variegata'
Hebe 'Lopen'
Rhododendron 'Silver Streak' (Japanese azalea)
Rhododendron ponticum 'Variegatum'
Rhododendron 'President Roosevelt'

BLUE FLOWERS, DECIDUOUS

Lavandula ×*intermedia* 'Burgoldeen'
Salvia (all)
Solanum dulcamara 'Variegatum'

BLUE FLOWERS, EVERGREEN

Ceanothus (all)
Rosmarinus (all)
Vinca major 'Maculata'
Vinca major 'Reticulata'
Vinca major 'Surrey Marble'
Vinca major 'Variegata'
Vinca major 'Wojo's Gem'
Vinca minor 'Argenteomarginata'
Vinca minor 'Argenteovariegata'
Vinca minor 'Aureovariegata'

Vinca minor 'Illumination'
Vinca minor 'Sebastian'
Vinca minor 'Sterling Silver'

YELLOW FLOWERS, DECIDUOUS
Cornus mas (all)
Forsythia (all)
Hamamelis (all)
Hypericum (all)
Kerria japonica 'Aureovariegata'
Liriodendron (all)
Potentilla fruticosa 'Chilo'
Stachyurus (all)

YELLOW FLOWERS, EVERGREEN
Pittosporum eugenioides 'Variegatum'
Ruta graveolens 'Variegata'

Variegated plants with attractive fruits

The presence of attractive fruits can add much to the ornamental value of any shrub. Perhaps this goes even more for variegated plants. Usually red or black fruits work very well against white or yellow variegated foliage.

RED TO ORANGE-RED FRUITS
Aucuba (female cultivars only)
Cornus florida (all)
Cornus kousa (all)
Cornus mas (all)
Cotoneaster (all)
Crataegus (all)
Ilex ×*altaclerensis* (all)
Ilex aquifolium 'Argentea Marginata'
Ilex aquifolium 'Argentea Marginata Pendula'
Ilex aquifolium 'Aurea Marginata Pendula'
Ilex aquifolium 'Aurifodina'
Ilex aquifolium 'Golden Milkmaid'
Ilex aquifolium 'Golden van Tol'
Ilex aquifolium 'Gold Flash'
Ilex aquifolium 'Handsworth New Silver'
Ilex aquifolium 'Madame Briot'
Ilex aquifolium 'Pyramidalis Aurea Marginata'
Ilex aquifolium 'Rubricaulis Aurea'
Ilex aquifolium 'Silver Milkmaid'
Ilex aquifolium 'Silver van Tol'
Ilex ×*meserveae*
Photinia (all)
Pyracantha (all)
Solanum dulcamara 'Variegatum'
Taxus (all)
Vaccinium vitis-idaea 'Dolinda'

BLACK FRUITS
Berchemia scandens 'Variegata'
Ligustrum (all)
Rhamnus frangula 'De Wildert'
Rubus (all)
Sambucus nigra 'Aureomarginata'
Sambucus nigra 'Marginata'
Viburnum (all)

BLUE FRUITS
Clerodendron trichotomum 'Carnival'

GREENISH TO YELLOWISH FRUITS
Citrus (all)

APPENDIX D

Hardiness Zone Temperature Ranges

Average annual minimum temperature for each hardiness zone

HARDINESS ZONE	DEGREES FARENHEIT	DEGREES CENTIGRADE
1	less than −50	less than −45.5
2	−50 to −40	−45.5 to −40.1
3	−40 to −30	−40.0 to −34.5
4	−30 to −20	−34.4 to −28.9
5	−20 to −10	−28.8 to −23.4
6	−10 to 0	−23.3 to −17.8
7	0 to 10	−17.7 to −12.3
8	10 to 20	−12.2 to −6.7
9	20 to 30	−6.6 to −1.2
10	30 to 40	−1.1 to 4.4
11	more than 40	more than 4.4

APPENDIX E

Conversion Charts

CENTIMETERS	INCHES
0.2	0.08
0.3	0.13
0.4	0.16
0.5	0.20
0.6	0.25
0.8	0.31
0.9	0.35
1.0	0.40
1.25	0.49
2.5	1.0
3	1.2
4	1.6
5	2.0
6	2.3
7	2.7
8	3.1
9	3.5
10	3.9

METERS	FEET
0.2	0.7
0.5	1.6
0.75	2.5
1	3.3
2	6.6
3	9.8
4	13.1
5	16.4
6	19.7
7	23.0
8	26.3
9	29.5
10	32.8
100	328

APPENDIX F
Further Reading

Allan, H. H. 1961. *Flora of New Zealand*. Vol. 1, *Indigenous Tracheophyta*. Reprint. Wellington: P. D. Hasselberg, 1982.

Bagust, Harold. 1996. *The Gardener's Dictionary of Horticultural Terms*. London: Cassell Publishers Ltd.

Batdorf, L. R. 1995. *Boxwood Handbook*. Boyce, Virginia: The American Boxwood Society.

Bean, W. J. 1996. *Trees and Shrubs Hardy in the British Isles*. 4 vols. and supplement. London: John Murray.

Boom, B. K. 1956. *Jaarboek 20, 1954/1955*. The Netherlands: Nederlandse Dendrologische Vereniging.

Boom, B. K. 1982. *Nederlandse Dendrologie*. 12th ed. Wageningen: H. Veenman & Zonen.

Boom, B. K. 2000. *Nederlandse Dendrologie*. 13th rev. ed. Ed. I. J. De Koning et al. Wageningen: H. Veenman & Zonen.

Bree, I. R. G. 1998. *Rapport 49: Cultuur—en Gebruikswaardeonderzoek Hydrangea macrophylla en Hydrangea serrata*. Boskoop: Research Station for Nursery Stock.

Bremer, Kåre, Mark W. Chase, and Peter F. Stevens. 1998. An ordinal classification for the families of flowering plants. *Ann. Missouri Bot. Gard.* 85 (4): 531–553.

Brenzel, Kathleen N., ed. 1997. *Sunset Western Garden Book*. Menlo Park, California: Sunset Publishing.

Brickell, C., ed. 1996. *The RHS A–Z Encyclopedia of Garden Plants*. London: Doring Kindersley Ltd.

Callaway, Dorothy J. 1994. *The World of Magnolias*. Portland, Oregon: Timber Press.

Chalk, Douglas. 1988. *Hebes and Parahebes*. Portland, Oregon: Timber Press.

Conder, Susan, and Andrew Lawson. 1994. *Variegated Plants*. Portland, Oregon: Timber Press.

Corriveau, J. L., and A. W. Coleman. 1988. Rapid screening method to detect potential biparental inheritance of plastid DNA and results for more than 2000 angiosperm species. *Amer. J. Bot.* 75 (10): 1443–1458.

de Jong, P. C., and D. Benoit. 1998. *Aesculus*–paardekastanje. *Dendroflora* 34/1997: 3–23.

de Jong, P. C., and L. K. J. Ilsink. 1996. *Cornus*–kornoelje. *Dendroflora* 32/1995: 24–57.

den Ouden, P., and B. K. Boom. 1965. *Manual of Cultivated Conifers*. The Hague: Martinus Nijhoff.

Dirr, Michael A. 1998. *Manual of Woody Landscape Plants*. Champaign, Illinois: Stipes Publishing.

Fearnley-Whittingstall, Jane. 1992. *Ivies*. New York: Random House.

Fiala, John L. 1988. *Lilacs: The Genus Syringa*. Portland, Oregon: Timber Press.

Fortgens, I. G. 1992. *Deutzia*–keuringsrapport. *Dendroflora* 28/1991: 7–26.

Fortgens, I. G. 1993. *Thymus*–sortiments en gebruikswaardeonderzoek. *Dendroflora* 29/1992: 19–33.

Galle, Fred C. 1997. *Hollies: The Genus Ilex*. Portland, Oregon: Timber Press.

Griffith, Mark. 1994. *Index of Garden Plants*. London: Macmillan.

Heieck, Ingobert. 1994. *Klimop*. Bloemendaal: J. H. Gottmer.

Heywood, V. H., ed. 1979. *Flowering Plants of the World*. Oxford, U.K.: Oxford University Press.

Hillier Nurseries Ltd. 1994. *The Hillier Manual of Trees and Shrubs*. 6th ed. Newton Abbot, U.K.: David & Charles.

Hillier Nurseries Ltd. 2002. *The Hillier Manual of Trees and Shrubs*. 6th updated ed. Newton Abbot, U.K.: David & Charles.

Hirose, Y., and M. Yokoi. 1998. *Variegated Plants in Color*. Iwakuni, Japan: Varie Nine Ltd.

Hirose, Y., and M. Yokoi. 2001. *Variegated Plants in Color*. Vol. 2. Iwakuni, Japan: Varie Nine Ltd.

Hoffman, I. M. H. A., and M. B. M. Ravesloot. 1998. *Winterhardheid van Boomkwekerijgewassen*. Boskoop: Boomteeltpraktijkonderzoek.

Hoffman, I. M. H. A., H. J. van de Laar, P. C. de Jong, eds. 2000. *List of Names of Woody Plants*. Boskoop: Applied Research for Nursery Stock.

Houtman, R. T. 1997. *Stachyurus*–staartaar. *Dendroflora* 33/1996: 129–138.

Houtman, R. T. 1999. *Viburnum*–keuringsrapport. *Dendroflora* 35/1998: 96–131.

Hutchins, Graham. 1997. *Hebes Here and There*. Reading, U.K.: Hutchins & Davies.

Kortmann, J. P. 2000. *Pinus mugo*–keuringsrapport. *Dendroflora* 36/1999: 76–91.

Krüssmann, G. 1984. *Manual of Cultivated Broad-leaved Trees and Shrubs*. 3 vols. Beaverton, Oregon: Timber Press.

Krüssmann, G. 1985. *Manual of Cultivated Conifers*. Beaverton, Oregon: Timber Press.

Laros, A. J. 2001. De collectie Abelia. *Arbor Vitae* 11 (4): 12–21.

Lewis, John. 1987. *The International Conifer Register*. Part 1, *Abies to Austrotaxus*. London: The Royal Horticultural Society.

Lewis, John. 1989. *The International Conifer Register*. Part 2, *Belis to Pherosphaera*. London: The Royal Horticultural Society.

Lewis, John. 1992. *The International Conifer Register*. Part 3, *The Cypresses*. London: The Royal Horticultural Society.

Mabberley, D. J. 1993. *The Plant-Book: A Portable Dictionary of the Higher Plants*. Cambridge, U.K.: Cambridge University Press.

Mallet, Corinne, Robert Mallet, and Harry van Trier. 1995. *Hortensien*. Transl. Rudolf Dirr. Stuttgart: Verlag Eugen Ulmer.

Marcotrigiano, M. 1997. Chimeras and variegation: Patterns of deceit. *HortScience* 32: 773–784.

Mesterházy, Zsolt. 1995. *A fenyök kincsestára (Conifer Treasury of the World)*. Budapest: National Institute for Agricultural Quality Control.

Metcalf, L. J. 1987. *The Cultivation of New Zealand Trees and Shrubs*. Auckland: Reed Methuen Publishers Ltd.

Metcalf, L. J. 2000. *The Cultivation of New Zealand Trees and Shrubs*. Auckland: Reed Methuen Publishers Ltd.

Nelson, Charles A. 2000. *A Heritage of Beauty: The Garden Plants of Ireland*. Dublin: The Irish Garden Plant Society

Palmer, S. J. 1994. *Palmer's Manual of Trees, Shrubs and Climbers*. Runaway Bay, Australia: Lancewood Publishing.

Pohlheim, F. 1971. Untersuchungen zur Sprossvariation der Cupressaceae. 1. Nachweis immerspaltenden Periclinal Chimeren. *Flora* 160: 264–293.

Rehder, A. 1927. *Manual of Cultivated Trees and Shrubs*. New York: Macmillan.

Rehder, A. 1940. *Manual of Cultivated Trees and Shrubs*. 2d ed. New York: Macmillan.

Rose, Peter Q. 1996. *The Gardener's Guide to Growing Ivies*. Portland, Oregon: Timber Press.

Salmon, J. T. 1996. *The Native Trees of New Zealand*. Auckland: Reed Books.

Santamour, F. S., Jr., and A. J. McArdle. 1983. Checklist of cultivars of European ash (*Fraxinus*) species. *Journal of Arboriculture* 9(10): 21–32.

Satina, S., A. F. Blakeslee, and A. G. Avery. 1940.

Demonstration of three germlayers in the shoot apex of *Datura* by means of induced polyploidy in periclinal chimeras. *Am. J. Bot.* 27: 895–905.

Saunders, Richard M. K. 1998. Monograph of *Kadsura* (Schisandraceae). *Systematic Botany Monographs*, Vol. 54. Ann Arbor, Michigan: The American Society of Plant Taxonomists.

Savige, Thomas J. 1993. *International Camellia Register*. Vol. 1. Sydney: The International Camellia Society.

Schaepman, Henri K. E. 1975. *Preliminary Checklist of Cultivated Hedera*. Part I, *Juvenile Varieties and Cultivars of Hedera helix*. Mt. Vernon, Virginia: The American Ivy Society.

Schneider, C. K. 1906–1912. *Illustriertes Handbuch der Laubholzkunde*. 2 vols. Jena: Verlag von Gustav Fischer.

Steward, R. N., and H. Dermen. 1979. Ontogeny in monocotyledons as revealed by studies of the developmental anatomy of periclinal chloroplast chimeras *Amer. J. Bot.* 66: 47–58.

Taylor, J. 1987. *Climbing Plants*. London: The Royal Botanic Gardens, Kew.

Thomas, Graham Stuart. 1992. *Ornamental Shrubs, Climbers and Bamboos*. London: John Murray Ltd.

Tilney-Basset, R. A. E. 1963. The structure of periclinal chimeras. *Heredity* 18: 265–294.

Trehane, P., ed. 1995. *International Code of Nomenclature for Cultivated Plants*. Wimborne, Dorset, U.K.: Quarterjack Publishing.

Tromp, J. 1986. *Boskoops Koninklijke, 1861–1986*. Boskoop: Koninklijke Vereniging voor Boskoopse Culturen.

van de Laar, H. J. 1972. *Berberis*–keuringsrapport. *Dendroflora* 9/1972: 9–37.

van der Meijden, R. 1996. *Heukels' Flora van Nederland*. Groningen: Wolters-Noordhoff.

van Gelderen, C. J., and D. M. van Gelderen. 1999. *Maples for Gardens*. Portland, Oregon: Timber Press.

van Gelderen, D. M. 1989. *Ilex aquifolium* en *Ilex ?altaclerensis*. *Dendroflora* 25/1988: 7–34.

van Gelderen, D. M., and J. R. P. van Hoey Smith. 1992. *Rhododendron Atlas*. Portland, Oregon: Timber Press.

van Gelderen, D. M., and J. R. P. van Hoey Smith. 1996. *Conifers: The Illustrated Encyclopedia*. 2 vols. Portland, Oregon: Timber Press.

van Gelderen, D. M., P. C. de Jong, and H. J. Oterdoom. 1994. *Maples of the World*. Portland, Oregon: Timber Press.

van Hoey Smith, J. R. P. 2001. *Arboretum Trompenburg, Bomenrijk in Rotterdam*. Rotterdam: Stichting Bevordering van Volkskracht.

Vaughn, K. C., K. G. Wilson, and K. D. Stewart. 1978. Light-harvesting pigment-protein complex deficiency in *Hosta* (Liliaceae). *Planta* 143: 275–278.

Vertrees, J. D. 2001. *Japanese Maples*. 3rd ed. Ed. Peter Gregory. Portland, Oregon: Timber Press.

Welch, H. J. 1966. *Dwarf Conifers: A Complete Guide*. London: Faber and Faber.

Welch, Humphrey, and Gordon Haddow. 1993. *The World Checklist of Conifers*. Bromyard: Landsman's Bookshop for World Conifer Data Pool.

Winkler, H. 1907. Uber Propfbastarde und Planzliche Chimaren. *Ber. Deutsche Bot. Ges.* 25: 568–576.

Yinger, B. R., and C. R. Hahn. 1983. Cultivars of Japanese plants at Brookside Gardens. *Arnoldia* 43(4): 3–19.

Zonneveld, B. J. M., and F. van Iren. 2000. Flow cytometric analysis of DNA content reveals ploidy chimera in *Hosta*. *Euphytica* 111: 105–110.

Index

Pages with color plates are indicated in bold type.